The *Journal*:

60 years of people, prose, and publication

by JSP Cummins

A special thank you goes out to Sara Gwendolyn Ross and Omar Soliman for their telephone interviews of alumni as well as editorial work on prior drafts. Especially to Ms. Ross, who made it through the entirety of the original draft and gave brilliant guidance on my somewhat rough citations (however rough they may still be)!

I also want to thank the team at the McGill University archives; Professor Ian Pilarczyk of Boston University for allowing me to use portions of his pivotal history book; the Quid Novi of McGill University for their permissions; Maryvon Côté of the Nahum Gelber Law Library; Alex Sauveplane; Katie Webber, Anna Piekarzewski, and Ilana Ludwin for the transcription of telephone interviews; Nicole for adding her beautiful wisdom to the front of this work; and all those who interviewed for the book, without whose words little of this would have been possible.

When members of the past quarter century of the *Journal* were asked about their best memories or the most important parts of their experience there was an overwhelming consensus among many: Nicole Leger. During the 60th Anniversary of the *Journal* she will have been with the MLJ for twenty-seven years. Here is just some of what the *Journal* alumni had to say:

"I remember countless hardware meltdowns tempered by the good nature, patience and expertise of Nicole Leger in what was then the early years of a brave new world."

- Marc Lemieux, Editor-in-Chief of Volume Thirty-Two

"The only way of knowing what had gone on with the Boards before us was to ask Nicole … [After two and a half years] she was already indispensable to us. We thought she was great."

- David Lametti, Executive Editor of Volume Thirty-Four

"[T]he *Journal*'s Person Friday"

- Jodi Lackman, Editor-in-Chief of Volume Forty

"I would … be remiss not to mention the great memories of working with Nicole."

- Martin Valasek, Editor-in-Chief of Volume Forty-Two

"Ultimately, she held it all together. Her stable and reliable presence was invaluable to everyone, and her experience with prior volumes enabled a transmission of knowledge from year to year."

- Rachel Parsons, Executive Editor of Volume Forty-Eight

"It wasn't until you worked with her that you realized how crucial what she did was. While the students passed through year after year, she was a constant."

- Reagan Morris, Executive Editor of Volume Forty-Nine

"She is an angel with corporate memory and patience beyond what I could ever hope to muster."

- Maegen Hough, Managing Editor of Volume Fifty-Two

One of Three Most Significant Memories: "Swapping gym tips with Nicole."

- Dorian Needham, senior editor of Volume Fifty-Four

"Our institutional memory … lived in Nicole."

- Eytan Bensoussan, Managing Editor of Volume Fifty-Four

"She really understands how an EIC's mind works and develops through the year and it was nice to have a "kindred spirit" in the office. It is rare to meet people that are just so selfless and commited to what they're doing; so kind and full of patience; generous and self-sacrificing. And that's Nicole."

- Sara Ross, Editor-in-Chief of Volume Fifty-Six

The *Journal*:

60 years of people, prose, and publication

Contents

Foreword

By Nicole Leger

When I was asked to write something for the 60th anniversary book of the *McGill Law Journal*, I admit to feeling some conflicting emotions. Although it was a great honour, I was also intimidated by the task and, to be quite honest, a little bit embarrassed about admitting to the world that I've been working at the *Journal* for 25 years. It's not that I'm ashamed of the work I do. On the contrary, I'm very grateful to have had a job that doesn't require me to punch a time clock, that has given me enough time to explore some of my other interests, that has allowed me to wear jeans to the office, and that has given me the feeling of being part of a team and working towards a common goal. I do think, however, that I fell into the trap of worrying too much about what other people would think of me. People whom I'd worked with many years ago were now partners at law firms, professors, and great successes in their field. Although my job description has changed quite a bit over the years, here I was still toiling away at the *Journal*. As I started the process of writing this introduction, which so many people will be reading, I realized the irony of the situation. I would be putting down on paper, all the things that I'd always felt embarrassed about and wanted to hide.

I wish I could say that I first applied for the job at the *Journal* because I had a hankering to learn about the law. I wish I could say that I realized I'd missed my calling by not attending law school, and how I knew this would be the opportunity to finally realize my dream of becoming a lawyer. That would be far from the truth, however. The real story is that my dad had been putting some pressure on me to go out and get a summer job. I don't even remember how, but I came across the name of the *McGill Law Journal* in the phone book (no internet searches in those days), and decided to give them a call. I had absolutely no idea what the *Journal* was but figured it would be great to work at McGill since I was still in the process of finishing my degree in Communications. I called the office, knowing there would not be any opportunity to work there, but thinking I could add it to the list of places I'd contacted. This would be the list I'd present to my dad, to prove to him how hard I'd been pounding the pavement. Well imagine my surprise when they told me their typist had just left and they were looking for a replacement.

At that time, the office of the *Journal* was located in the basement of Old Chancellor Day Hall. It was ridiculously small. I didn't realize how many people worked at the *Journal* because I'd usually see the same 3 or 4 people each time I was in the office. In those days I was painfully shy and 3 or 4 people were more than enough for me. Everyone was so nice but I definitely felt like a fish out of water.

Before I started working at the *Journal* I had some embarrassingly stereotypical ideas about law students and how they must be. I pictured them as snobs and was sure I was about to enter an environment that would make me feel intellectually challenged (or, in my own words, dumb as a doornail). My friends asked me why I wanted the job. I didn't know what to tell them. Why did it really matter anyway? I'd be there for 6 months, perhaps a year, certainly no longer than that. My ideas about law students, and my projection as to how long I would be working at the *Journal*, couldn't have been further from the truth. I truly believe it's the people I've met who have played an integral role in keeping me around for all these years.

Every year I manage to convince myself that no one in the office really knows how long I've been at the *Journal*. Although my name is clearly displayed on the masthead of Volume 32, I continue to fool myself into thinking that nobody would take the time to look back through those ancient issues. Then, usually once or twice a year, I will hear someone in the office talking about the hours they spent looking through old volumes, and all the interesting tidbits of information they'd found. Usually it would be a newcomer, someone recently chosen for the junior board, who wanted to know everything there was to know about the *Journal*. Without even the slightest hint of sarcasm, they would ask me, "Hey, I noticed your name on the Volume 32 masthead. Have you really been here that long?" That would be the moment I would get a queasy feeling in my stomach and wonder why oh why we still keep all those back issues lying around the office.

In the early days, when I first started working at the *Journal*, my duties were limited to typing in editorial changes that different editors had made to the articles they were working on. If memory serves me, I even had to type the occasional article from scratch as some authors submitted paper copies that they had typed (with an actual typewriter). Most of the articles were submitted on a floppy disk (I am throwing all caution to the wind now and totally dating myself). I often wonder how the *Journal* could possibly have existed in the days before computers. I have a recurring comical image in my mind of an editor noticing a typographical error on the last page of a sixty page article. Did the article then have to be completely retyped? Did someone order extra liquid paper? Oh how times have changed!

A year or two after I started at the *Journal*, the office moved from the basement of Old Chancellor Day Hall to the second floor of New Chancellor Day Hall. We finally had a bit more office space but only later, when we moved across the street to the basement of 3661 Peel Street, did we really enjoy a surplus of space. At that time I had my own office with an actual door. Connected to my office was another room where three or four people could work, and down the hall was the executive office where the four Executive Board members (four in those days although we now have five) would do their work. Within the executive office was another small room where the Editor-in-Chief worked. That office did not have a door. I remember finding it quite amusing that I had such a great, quiet work space while the poor Editor-in-Chief had an office without a door, making it almost impossible to work without interruption for any length of time.

Ultimately, however, the joke was on me. I ended up losing my office when the *Journal of Sustainable Development Law and Policy* (JSDLP) was created and moved into 3661 Peel. At that time, much like today, there was a shortage of space available at McGill and this time it was I who got caught in the crunch. It was a difficult transition at the beginning, but I soon discovered that it was fun to work in the same space as all the editors and feel the tension and excitement whenever a production deadline would approach. I also enjoyed meeting the people at the JSDLP and hearing the excitement at their end of the building as their first issue was set to be published. I really enjoyed helping them out in any way I could and they were kind enough to invite me to their official launch party after their first issue was printed. I still remember being given a beautiful bouquet of flowers to thank me for that help, even though it was very minimal.

While at 3661 Peel, we also had a boardroom available for meetings, and a big kitchen where people would make coffee, bring their home-made lunches, and hang out when they were in between classes. I really liked the environment, particularly the fact that the work space looked more like a home than an office. It may not have been a fancy environment, and there were more than a few bugs crawling along the floor, but I still remember coming in on snowy days in the winter, leaving my boots at the door, putting on a pair of slippers, and smelling fresh coffee that an over-worked editor had already brewed. I also remember having chair races in the long corridor of 3661 Peel. All the office chairs had wheels, and I still have visions of myself flying down the hall at break-neck speed, an editor pushing my chair, while a third person (usually another editor desperately trying to escape their work) waited at the other end of the hall to confirm my finish time. It sure beat working in an industrial park and having to run out on my 15 minute break to see what was available at the canteen.

I also remember spending some very difficult periods of my life in that office. In 2001, my closest friend in the world became ill with cancer. I remember running to the Royal Victoria Hospital before work, after work, and sometimes in the middle of the day. It was one of the saddest periods in my life and at that time the *Journal* became a refuge for me. There was a great comfort in hearing people laugh, hearing them talk about their classes, and worry about the stress of an upcoming exam. My friend passed away a few months after her diagnosis, and I remember a co-worker leaving a plant on my desk with a beautiful note. I also remember the Editor-in-Chief at the time, Robert Leckey, being incredibly kind and supportive. He wrote me a card which meant a great deal to me and which I still have tucked away in a box in my home.

I have many funny memories of my time at the *Journal*. Several years ago, I entered the office to find two editors engaged in a heated debate. I asked them what was going on and one of them came towards me, waving a single printed page in the air. To me it looked like a regular page of printed text. I hadn't noticed, however, that there were two ellipses on that page. They both looked at me and asked me if I felt that one of the ellipses was spaced differently than the other one. I believe they had a ruler to resolve this conflict. My first thought was that they were playing a prank on me. I started to laugh, but when I saw their reactions to my laughter, I realized this was no joke. It would be quite horrible for our readers to notice this kind of inconsistency and I soon learned that these things should not be taken lightly. I've since learned my lesson. I've also come to realize that there are certain things I can always count on when I enter the *Journal* office. It doesn't matter who the current board members are, or what the personality types are.

Here are some of my observations: managers and editors are totally different breeds. This is evident at recruitment time. When job interviews roll around, managers tend to look euphoric in their fancy attire, ready to wow everyone at the twelve cocktails they will be attending that night. Editors, on the other hand, often go through an internal crisis during recruitment time. Is corporate law really for them? Is this really the environment they want to spend the rest of their lives working in? The only thing that stops them from being able to ponder the question more deeply, is the whistling sound coming from the other side of the room while some manager gives their shoes a final polish before heading off to their first cocktail of the evening.

There is a period of transition every year, usually towards the end of October or early November, though it can also occur earlier in the year. Before that time, there is a jovial mood around the office. Everyone is excited about the challenges that lie ahead and are elated at the prospect of contributing to the production of respected legal scholarship. They will make schedules, specifying when they will be in the office, and perhaps even create a chart indicating how the work station could be shared when they are not there. What a shame that office space is so limited! It would be wonderful if everyone could work together all the time in one big office.

Then, and it always seems to happen overnight, panic sets in. From one day to the next, there is a drastic shift in the mood of the office. People's facial expressions suddenly change. That look of excitement and elation suddenly turns into one of stress and horror. This is the point when someone has foolishly started to look at the calendar, and has noticed there aren't many weeks left until exams start. Another person might comment that they haven't yet removed their textbooks from the plastic wrap they originally came in. Instead of laughter and conversation, there is an unsettling quiet in the air. Though people are still physically present, there seems to be a slightly dazed look on many of their faces. A few days later, the problem with a shortage of office space is quickly resolved, as people stop coming to the office entirely.[11]

I have also noticed a few differences based on whether the executive members are mostly male or mostly female. If an executive board is predominantly female, I can look forward to Halloween candy on my desk in October (my favourites are "rockets"), chocolate hearts on my desk on Valentine's day (dark chocolate is always the best), regular e-mails informing us when it's someone's birthday, home-made cookies to celebrate those birthdays, and perhaps a monthly get-together where we flip open the office supplies catalogue and look lovingly at all the different colors of post-it notes that are available. If the board is predominantly male, however, expect completely blank facial expressions if any of the above suggestions are made, and perhaps a gasp of horror at the mere thought of having to surround someone's desk while singing a chorus of "Happy Birthday". I can also say, with conviction, that no predominantly-male executive board has ever color-coordinated their outfits in advance of the annual *Law Journal* photo, or had a pre-photo dress rehearsal to decide in which direction they would cross their legs. Even the selection process of the photo differs greatly, based on the gender of the board. If there are more women on the board it can take several weeks to make the selection. If the board is

1 [1] There is absolutely no purpose for this footnote but I wanted to take the opportunity to feel like a true scholar.

predominantly male, however, I'll usually be told to pick whichever one I think looks good.

Speaking of the annual *Law Journal* photo, it's always been rather traditional in nature. The setting for the photo is always the common room of Old Chancellor Day Hall and, for many years, everyone would show up wearing their dark suits and serious expressions. A few years back, however, one of the boards decided to jazz up the photo just a bit. After the traditional serious photo had been shot, they put on their silliest expressions, waved their hands in the air, and threw caution to the wind. When it came time to select the photo that would adorn the *Journal* wall, they selected the funny photo. Some people were fine with the decision while others seemed slightly perturbed. How could *Journal* tradition be disrespected in such a serious way?

Since every board always has its mix of personality types, it would be impossible to please all of the people all of the time. After that first photo appeared, however, it became a new tradition to ask our photographer to take at least one crazy shot. Though that photo didn't always go on the wall, it was still fun to see the competitive nature of each board come out when they tried to come up with an idea that was even funnier than the previous year. Even more amusing was seeing a relatively shy person forced to wave a spatula in the air (sometimes props were included) while donning a crazy expression on their face. I may not be a law student, but I had the intelligence many years ago to stop appearing in the photos. There were many reasons for my decision. It might have been utter fear, after having seen photos from years ago where people were wearing checkerboard pants, or perhaps a nice pair of wooden clogs. Did I really need to have my fashion crimes permanently bolted onto the *Journal* walls for years to come? I also didn't need to have a visual record of my aging process, displayed on the wall for everyone to see. Vanity is an ugly thing.

Another thing I've observed during my time at the *Journal* is that, at some point during the year there will be a heated debate between the Managing Editor and the Editor-in-Chief about what kind of food should be provided for a late-night, work-related meeting. The Managing Editor will remind the EIC that we are almost bankrupt. Perhaps some bread and water could be provided but that's it. The Editor-in-Chief, however, or sometimes just a plain regular editor, will go online and check if that new Thai place delivers and how much it would cost to place 25 orders.

Also, at some point in the year, I will find myself having a conversation with someone who has a grade point average of 4.0, who has secured a clerkship at the Supreme Court, who has five law firms offering them articling positions, and who fills up their spare time by going to medical school. That person will confess, in hushed tones, that they feel like an under-achiever.

Over the years I've gathered a lot of knowledge that is completely useless in the outside world. While I do know the difference between a straight quotation mark and a curly quotation mark, and I certainly know the difference between an en-dash and an em-dash, does this knowledge really serve me in any way once I leave the cozy confines of the *Journal*? While I've often heard debates as to why the em-dash is the chosen dash of the *McGill Law Journal* (I remember a former editor telling me that the "em-dash" was sexier, but surely there must have been another reason), I would receive only blank stares if I were to bring this up in a dinner conversation with my friends.

One of the greatest gifts that my time at the *Journal* has given me, is that it has helped me overcome my shyness. I think most people who have traditional jobs would find it challenging to work with an entirely new group of people every year. There are certainly negative things about it. I've become close to many of the people I've worked with and it's always difficult to know that they will be moving on. The first of May tends to be a struggle for me. That's the day I walk into the office and find an entirely new group of people. New personalities to get used to, and people I've developed a bond with no longer there. On the positive side though, I think it's this exact situation that's helped me grow as a person. There always comes a moment when I realize how much I like the new group of people I'm working with, even if I continue to miss some of the people who have left. I now see how lucky I am to have met so many new people every year, and to have had the opportunity to develop lasting friendships. What a great gift that has been.

Every year tends to be different. It usually takes me a bit of time to figure out how the mood in the office will be in a given year. Some years the mood can be zany. One former EIC would often greet me by pulling the lever in the back of my chair so I would sink to the floor. It was always in good fun, however, and I couldn't help but laugh every time I didn't seem him coming and suddenly felt myself plunging to the ground. In other years, there has been a much more serious tone in the office. That's not a bad thing at all, but it definitely takes a bit of time to adjust. Often the people who seem the most serious at the beginning are the ones who turn out to be the funniest. I've learned not to judge a book by its cover. I've developed lasting friendships with people who intimidated me when I first met them.

Over the years I've had the opportunity to attend a wedding between executive board members, to work late into the evening with an Editor-in-Chief who was eight and a half months pregnant and looked like she could go into labour at any moment, and to have a janitor run to his car so he could come back and show me the high quality undershirts he had just bought for himself. I had a severe panic attack when I mistakenly thought I had deleted an entire issue off the server right before our production deadline and I've taken taxis back home at three o'clock in the morning when something that was supposed to take three hours to complete ended up taking 10 hours to complete (everyone who has worked at the *Journal* soon realizes that *Journal* hours are not the same as those in the outside world).

As I mentioned a little earlier, my responsibilities have changed a good deal over the years. Early on, we never did layout in-house. We would always send the work to another company who would do it for us. A few years after I started at the *Journal*, however, a decision was made to take care of the layout ourselves. Fred Purkey, who was Managing Editor at the time, designed a template and trained me so that I would be able to take on this responsibility. We also changed our accounting system soon after that. I was trained on the new system and took over the responsibility of handling our subscription database. I also developed contacts with our printing company and distribution companies, and became more involved in the production aspect of the *Journal*. I like the variety and it's helped make things a bit more interesting.

One of the biggest changes happened a few years ago when we left 3661 Peel Street and headed back to New Chancellor Day Hall. This time, however, we were in brand new offices that had just been built for us on the third floor. The transition was a bit difficult for me. Though everyone was happy to be in a great new (and more professional-looking) space, though I had a beautiful view of Dr. Penfield avenue from my desk, and though there was not a bug to be seen crawling along the floor, I found the new environment a little hard to get used to. I liked the casual feeling of the old office and missed it quite a bit. I remember dragging a battered supply cabinet from the old office to the new one, with the help of a few co-workers. It didn't particularly fit our new décor, but it felt good to have that little piece of the past in the new space. I've now totally adjusted to the new office and am enjoying the great view that I have from my desk, but I'll always have a soft spot in my heart for that battered space at 3661 Peel.

I may joke about the eccentricities of *Journal* people and the amount of stress that can arise as the result of an accidentally italicized comma, but I am definitely not immune to these quirks. It's no longer possible for me to read a book for pleasure. My eye is always on the lookout for a typographical error. I might even do a casual check to see if the beginning of a new chapter is on the same page that's indicated in the table of contents, and I might triple check the birthday cards I write to my friends, making sure there are no problems with the grammar. Even the casual e-mail to a co-worker needs to be re-read several times. It's just a fact of life when your co-workers are all editors. Talk about pressure.

It doesn't matter how long I've been at the *Journal*. I still continue to be amazed at the amount of work that is required to publish a single issue. I have a great deal of respect for everyone I've worked with over the years. The ability to balance a full load of classes, to apply for articling positions and clerkships, and to still work tirelessly on the publication of the *Journal*, is truly extraordinary. I realize now, after having written this short piece, that rather than feeling shy or embarrassed about having been at the *Journal* for 25 years, I should feel proud to have played a small part in the history of the *McGill Law Journal*, and to have had the opportunity to contribute to this 60th Anniversary book. I truly appreciate the fact that I've been given the opportunity. As the *Journal* enters the Twitter and Facebook era this year, I look forward to all the changes that lie ahead.

Chapter One:

It All Started with a Single Conversation …

"A serious situation is developing in Quebec":[2] these were the first words to appear on page one, issue one, volume one of the *McGill Law Journal* (MLJ). They were written by Gerald Eric Le Dain, who was finishing his graduate studies and preparing to begin as a Sessional Lecturer at McGill University's Faculty of Law. Le Dain would become better known fifteen years later as the Dean of Law at Osgoode Hall, and thirty-two years later as Mr. Justice Gerald Le Dain of the Supreme Court of Canada—a judgeship he would hold from 1984 to 1988. His inaugural article on the state of the judiciary in Quebec wrote of a "long and cherished tradition … being swept away"[3] within a rapidly changing legal environment.

Thus began the story of a small academic journal that would one day become one of the most important in the world. Like the author of its very first article, the MLJ would ascend the ranks of the legal community in order to make thorough and important contributions to the field which it serves. But now, sixty years from that epic beginning, the MLJ is experiencing a sweeping away of its own long and cherished tradition. The first page of the first article in MLJ history stands as a somewhat eerie parallel to the history of the institution it launched. The appearance of the MLJ was an important event in the legal evolution of the Province of Quebec; and today, after six decades, the history of the *Journal* institution has almost ebbed away entirely.

No official history has ever been written about the *Journal*, and the few times recollections of the first days of the *Journal* have been printed in the publication's pages, the information has been somewhat incomplete. Thus on the occasion of the MLJ's sixtieth anniversary, which will occur at the start of volume fifty-eight in the autumn of 2012, this project is being undertaken to preserve that history. It is the first of its kind—never before has a history book been produced on the subject of a Canadian law journal, or even on the subject of Canadian law journals in general.

In 1952, the MLJ became the third student law review to be founded in Canada, the first being the *University of New Brunswick Law Journal* (UNBLJ), established in 1947.[4] Though the *University of Toronto Faculty of Law Review* (UTFLR) was founded in 1942, five years before the UNBLJ, it started out as a student newspaper and did not transform into a law journal until after the founding of the UNBLJ. This is also true of the *University of British Columbia Law Review*, which, though it would not officially form until 1959, had existed in an early incarnation (comprised merely of student essays) under the name *UBC Legal Notes* as early as 1949.[5]

It was in 1951 that the UTFLR changed from its student newspaper format into an actual magazine/journal. The 1949-50 UTFLR newspaper was only sixteen pages long.[6] The 1951 volume was the first to be dedicated to academic articles, though only one article was not produced by a student:[7] its full length was forty-four pages (thirty-seven pages of which were articles).[8] In the preface to the volume, their Editor-in-Chief Gordon Landeg wrote, "These are but first steps. Yet it is our feeling that in some small way they reflect the changing character of the school. Possessing only limited experience, we are quick to recognize our shortcomings, but make no apologies for our effort. In subsequent years we hope and expect to be overshadowed."[9] This was the year before the founding of the MLJ—the first two issues of which would be four times longer than the UTFLR volume of the previous year, and longer than the 1951, 1952, and 1953 volumes of the UTFLR combined.[10]

The *Alberta Law Review* (ALR) was the fourth

2 Gerald E LeDain, "The Twilight of Judicial Control in the Province of Quebec?" (1952) 1:1 *McGill LJ* 1 at 1.

3 *Ibid.*

4 Omar Ha-Redeye "The Birth of a Student Law Review" *Slaw* (27 February 27, 2011), online: < http://www.slaw.ca >

5 *University of British Columbia Law Review* "About the UBC Law Review" *UBCLR* (March 12, 2013), online: < http://faculty.law.ubc.ca/LawReview/ >

6 *University of Toronto Faculty of Law Review*, "Introduction" (1949-50) 8:1 *UTFLR* 1 at ff.

7 JC McRuer, "Law Enforcement" (1951) 9:1 *UTFLR* 2.

8 *University of Toronto Faculty of Law Review*, "Introduction" (1951) 9:1-2 *UTFLR* 1 at ff.

9 Gordon Landeg, "Foreword" (1951) 9:1 *UTFLR* 1 at 1.

10 *UTFLR* 51, *supra* note 7; *University of Toronto Faculty of Law Review*, "Introduction" (1952) 10:1-2 *UTFLR* 1 at ff; *University of Toronto Faculty of Law Review*, "Introduction" (1953) 11:1-2 *UTFLR* 1 at ff.

student law journal to begin publishing in Canada, producing its first issue in 1955 as the MLJ was completing its first volume. The ALR, in fact, would take twice as long to produce its first volume as did the MLJ, as the first volume of the ALR was published over the course of six years, between 1955 and 1961. For several decades nearly all law journals in Canada were run by students. Many other journals from this era, however, such as the *Osgoode Hall Law Journal* (OHLJ) (est. 1958), *Manitoba Law Journal* (MLJ) (est. 1961), and the *Saskatchewan Law Review* (SLR) (first published as the *Saskatchewan Bar Review* in 1936 and edited by members of the bar, not students),[11] have all witnessed some form of faculty takeover since or were complemented by faculty or professional involvement from the very beginning.

In contrast, the MLJ remains to this day the only general practice law journal to be entirely student-run both at McGill University and in the Province of Quebec. But even as the number of specialist law journals in the country grows, the MLJ is still part of a very small club: only two purely student-run law journals in the country publish four issues each year (the ALR being the other one as the OHLJ, while largely student-run, has had a Faculty Editor-in-Chief since 1984).[12]

Over the publication period of its first volume, the MLJ had three separate Editors-in-Chief: Jacques-Yvan Morin (Editor-in-Chief from 1952-53; issue one), Fred Kaufman (Editor-in-Chief from 1953-54; issues two and three), and William H. Reynolds (Editor-in-Chief from 1954-55; issue four). In future years, Jacques-Yvan Morin would become the leader of the Official Opposition for the Parti Québécois (PQ) in the National Assembly of Quebec, until 1976 when the party won its first majority; in addition, he would write the draft constitution for the PQ, used as the basis of what the PQ intended for the future of the Province of Quebec. Afterwards he served as the Deputy Premier of Quebec until 1984 in support of Parti Québécois founder and Premier René Lévesque. Fred Kaufman, in later years, was appointed a Judge of the Quebec Court of Appeal in 1973 and served as acting Chief Justice of the court from 1990 to 1991. He also taught as a professor at McGill in three different faculties—Law, Medicine, and Management.

On the occasion of the MLJ's fortieth volume, Jacques-Yvan Morin—at the time a *professeur titulaire* at the Université de Montréal Faculty of Law—wrote a short piece on his experience founding the MLJ. According to Morin, the idea of founding a student-run journal at McGill Law had been around for several years, but it appeared to be too costly a project to pull off.[13] There was also nearly no encouragement from the Faculty.[14]

In order to add some shading to this early history, Morin provided a short statement recalling the rest of that period for the purposes of this book. He recalled that:

> The idea of a law review surfaced in a conversation with Gerald Le Dain, who had just finished an essay on judicial control in Quebec. I read it, and the next day I asked him if he had thought of publishing it. He said "not really", because the bar reviews seldom had any place for student articles. We agreed that it would be a plus for the Faculty to have a Review in order to publish student papers.[15]

That conversation—the seed from which the *Journal* was born—occurred some time in the spring of 1952, during the scholastic year before the official founding of the *Journal*. It was a conversation between two future iconoclasts; two men who would go on to help change the face of Canada, and their talk that day represents perhaps the very first nation-altering moments of their illustrious careers. The impact of the *Journal*, its *Guide* (the *Canadian Guide to Uniform Legal Citation*), and the many other achievements that came out of this one conversation would be difficult to understate. Morin continued, recalling that

> We thought [about] the *Yale Law Journal*, for instance, and the fact that the Université de Montréal had the *Revue Thémis*; why not McGill? For a few months I talked about this idea with other students—Raymond LaChapelle, Fred Kaufman, Jim Ross, and many others were consulted. We also needed Faculty support, both intellectual and financial, but they were hesitant with the exception of Frank Scott, who encouraged us to pursue it.
>
> We asked ourselves why we should undertake such a task. I had published a college review and it had turned out to

11 *University of Saskatchewan Law Review*. "Saskatchewan Law Review History" *SLR* (March 12, 2013) , online: < http://www.usask.ca/law/current_students/sask_law_review/history.php >

12 "*Osgoode Hall Law Journal,* "History" *OHLJ* (May 16, 2012), online: < http://www.ohlj.ca/english/history.htm >

13 Jacques-Yvan Morin, "Avant-propos : Ce que toute jeune revue doit savoir" (1995) 40:4 *McGill LJ* 819 at 819.

14 *Ibid.*

15 Interview of Jacques-Yvan Morin by James Cummins (27 October, 2011).

be quite an effort. This was before the digital era—typewriting and proof reading were very time consuming. We had a few informal meetings and the consensus emerged that we needed a critical forum for students to debate current issues, and emerging legal and social problems: "Why shouldn't our law school have its review, to provide analysis of court decisions and doctrine?" A journal could provide an opportunity to further student research and scholarship; it would provide a forum more topical, more critical, if not more pungent than the usual textbook.

> Finally, it was decided to give it a try, and I was encouraged to find articles and comments. Within three weeks I had enough material to publish volume one, number one. The Faculty decided to support us financially and we found a competent printer: and the *McGill Law Journal* was born.[16]

Putting this in a global context, just one month before Morin put his new, determined institution to work, a then little-known author named Jack Kerouac wrote a letter to an also then little-known poet name Carl Solomon, reminding his friend that,

> Hemingway says that before 1927 all his stories were returned by editors "with notes of rejection that would never call them stories, but always anecdotes, sketches, contes." Thus only a few years ago even Hemingway with all his clarity was considered unprintable. What happened in the few years since? "Ulysses" which was considered difficult reading is now hailed as a classic and everyone understands it … By the same token, and in its time, I believe "On the Road" because its new vision roughs against the grain of established ideas is going to be considered unprintable for awhile to come.[17]

The world was aflutter with approaching innovation and literary excellence that only a "few years" before, as Kerouac labels it, could never have seen the light of day. In Quebec, one of the leaders of this monumental shift was Morin and his *Journal*.

He and his colleagues saw that there was a gap in periodicals carrying legal issues and ideas relevant to Montreal and the legal microclimate of Quebec.[18] A solution to this called for what Morin described as a "*lieu de recontre permanent*";[19] a "permanent meeting place" for Quebec legal thought. The feeling Morin described in those early days was that "*décidément, il nous fallait cette revue!*";[20] that Quebec was in true need of their new journal.

The general climate for legal periodicals in 1952 was not welcoming regardless of whether or not they were run by students, academics, or professionals. As a very clear example of this, Gordon Bale writes that,

> In 1950, in *Reference Re the Wartime Leasehold Regulation*, Maurice Wright, counsel for the Canadian Congress of Labour, sought to file documentary evidence indicating that there was a continuing emergency in regard to rental accommodation. Wright submitted that the material in his factum about the housing shortage was "proven facts," and that in previous constitutional references the court had undertaken an investigation into questions of "fact". In support of this argument, Wright tried to cite and read excerpts from Vincent C. MacDonald's article, "Constitutional Interpretation and Extrinsic Evidence." However, Rinfret C.J. stopped him, and remarked that "the *Canadian Bar Review* is not an authority in this Court."[21]

Regardless of the academic climate in Canada's highest court, two years after that moment Morin was doing everything he could to ensure the MLJ got off to the right start. Surprisingly, the most encouraging figure in the legal community was one G.V.V. Nicholls—sitting Editor-in-Chief of the very *Canadian Bar Review* dismissed by Chief Justice Rinfret. Morin was certain before meeting with Nicholls that Nicholls may not be too keen on seeing an upshot in competition—especially in light of its own struggles for legitimacy—but Nicholls was, instead, very interested in helping the young MLJ up on its feet.[22]

16 *Ibid.*

17 Letter from Jack Kerouac to Carl Solomon (5 August, 1952) in Jack Kerouac, *Selected Letters* (New York: Penguin Books, 1995) at 376.

18 Morin 95, *supra* note 12.

19 *Ibid.*

20 *Ibid.*

21 Gordon Bale, "W.R. Lederman and the Citation of Legal Periodicals by the Supreme Court of Canada" (1993) 36:1 *Queen's LJ* 36 at 49-50.

22 Morin 95, *supra* note 12 at 820.

Morin went back to Nicholls several more times for advice on many different aspects of how to create, edit, and produce the first issue of the MLJ, and especially for what Morin called the "black beast" of a journal's editorial team: footnotes.[23] It is of some note that Nicholls would be replaced as Editor-in-Chief by Professor Jean-Gabriel Castel in 1957, as Castel would serve as both Editor-in-Chief of the *Canadian Bar Review* and as Faculty Advisor to the *McGill Law Journal* from 1957 to 1959. Castel was actually the first Faculty Advisor of the MLJ to appear on the masthead, and appeared from the fourth issue of volume one through to volume five. As one editor during his tenure remembered, "He was a very young professor at the time. And he endured a lot of hardship from the students ... we weren't any rowdier than you and your classmates may have been, but we were fairly, fairly rowdy. And Castel did not have much authority because he wasn't much older than we were."[24]

Morin writes in his article for volume forty that Le Dain's article was an ideal piece to start a new journal.[25] The theory of Morin and his colleagues—that a *rendez-vous* point for the blossoming ideas of the legal community of Quebec was much needed—was proven right almost immediately after this. The McGill Institute of Air Law,[26] also in its infancy after opening its doors in 1951, came to Morin to let him know that they were looking for some place to publish their new, cutting-edge research. The head of the Institute, John C. Cooper, would be the second author to be published by the MLJ.[27] Cooper had been Vice-President of Pan American Airways and Vice-President of the Havana Conference where the articles of association were adopted that created the International Air Transport Association.[28] Following meetings between Morin and Cooper, the constitution of the MLJ would declare that part of its mandate would be to publish articles on International Air Law in addition to articles on the law of the Province of Quebec.[29]

The first editorial board of the MLJ published the first issue of the *Journal* within the calendar year of 1952—within the first semester of their tenure, a triumph that many of the next fifty-eight editorial boards would know the difficulty of. There are some pressures, however, that current boards no longer endure. Morin writes that the printing of that first issue only happened through a process of significant arm-twisting, with students pushing law firms to commit to ad-buys. In contrast, today's *Journal* has been financially stable, especially since the advent of the *Canadian Guide to Uniform Legal Citation* (also known today as the "*McGill Guide*").

Of course, the *McGill Guide* has provided students at the *McGill Law Journal* with much more than financial stability. Morin shared another trial from the march to publication for their first issue. John C. Cooper submitted a manuscript that did not have the same footnote formatting as the articles of Le Dain and the article by John Fenston and Hamilton De Saussure—the third and final article published within the MLJ's first issue (Fenston and De Saussure were also members of the Institute of International Air Law).[30] Naturally, and no doubt after some advice from Mr. Nicholls, Morin ensured that Cooper's footnotes were standardized to fit the style of the rest of their first issue.

What ensued is something only the power of the *McGill Guide* could have prevented. Cooper was incensed. He stormed the MLJ offices and tore a strip off Morin. He insisted that his own personal style of citations was critical to his work and that all of the footnotes must be returned to Cooper's original style.[31] Morin acquiesced, reversing his editorial changes, but he had already set in motion in that first editorial attempt something that would revolutionize the history of Canadian legal periodicals—a unique McGill-style citation system for legal scholarship, and one that would eventually become adopted nationally by the Canadian legal community. Nonetheless the cost of changing the article *after* it had been sent to print in 1952 was not something the *Journal* could afford. Its initial financing had not left much room for this kind of demand—the changes to Cooper's article cost hundreds of dollars.[32] According the Bank of Canada, $100 in 1952 would be

23 *Ibid.* In the original French, Morin referred to footnotes as "*la bête noire des directeurs des revues*".

24 Interview of Yves Fortier by Omar Soliman (11 January, 2011).

25 *Ibid.*

26 The Institute would change its name to the Institute of Air and Space Law in 1957. See: Louis Grossman, "History of the Institute" in *Institute of Air and Space Law/Institut de droit aérien et spatial: 50 years* (17 October, 2011), online: < http://www.mcgill.ca/files/iasl/book-commemorative.pdf > at 2.

27 John C Cooper, "Roman Law and the Maxim Cujus Est Solum in International Air Law" (1952) 1:1 *McGill LJ* 23.

28 Ian C Pilarczyk *"A Noble Roster": One Hundred And Fifty Years of Law at McGill* (Montreal: McGill University Faculty of Law, 1999) at 37.

29 See Appendix E, Page 1.

30 John Fenston & Hamilton De Saussure, "Conflict in the Competence and Jurisdiction of Courts of Different States to Deal with Crimes Committed on Board Aircraft and the Persons Involved Therein" (1952) 1:1 *McGill LJ* 66.

31 Morin 95, *supra* note 12.

32 *Ibid.*

equal to $853.19 in 2011.[33] The equivalent thousands of dollars would be enough to put a new venture of this kind out of business even today. The first issues of the *Journal* sold for $2.25 a piece.[34]

Morin printed the first issue of the *McGill Law Journal* without knowing how this bill was going to be paid; nothing was going to stop this small enterprise from getting off the ground. After a tussle with the Dean—W.C.J. Meredith—and a request for personal help from the Faculty Advisor, somehow, someway, the bill got paid. Supporters of the *Journal* at the Faculty began to grow. Roderick A. MacDonald, the FR Scott Professor of Constitutional and Public Law at McGill and President of the Royal Society of Canada, wrote that Maxwell Cohen, newly minted with a full professorship in 1952,[35] was enthusiastic about the establishment of the *McGill Law Journal* rather early on.[36] Morin writes that FR Scott—the *Journal*'s original ally at the Faculty as well as future co-founder of the New Democrat Party in Canada and long-time McGill Professor of Law—raved about the quality of the first issue.[37] And that first issue began with the following foreword:

> For a good many years now the students of the Faculty of Law of McGill University have felt the need for a legal periodical of their own, edited by students and, largely, contributed to by students. This first number of the *McGill Law Journal* is the result of much discussion and consultation among students and faculty.
>
> The *Journal*, its editors hope, will find a place in the lives of both student and advocate. To the latter, it will provide a means of voicing his opinions about the law. To the former, it will be a challenge to integrate himself into the legal process by contributing some original research and, at the same time, an opportunity to develop his legal mind.
>
> There is one specific aspect about McGill's Faculty of Law which is too frequently forgotten: it is the only law school in Canada where the Civil Law is taught in an English-speaking atmosphere. The fact that Quebec stands at the confluence of two great systems of Private Law makes McGill's potential contribution to a better mutual understanding unique. We feel that a great opportunity, in fact a challenge, lies before us. The time has arrived for us to meet this challenge and to this purpose we dedicate our efforts.[38]

The statement was truer than Morin knew. Though graduating at the end of the year, he would continue on as an "Advisory Editor" as the first volume of the MLJ moved on to issue two.

Jerome C. Smyth, editor for volume one, issue one, and then Managing Editor for issues two and three wrote further of the environment that existed at McGill Law during these early years:

> In September of 1951 ... a motley crew of some 100 individuals, coming from various points of the compass ... strode, walked, plodded or trudged up Peel Street to Chancellor Day Hall to begin their work as first year law students. There was a good deal more conformity to perceived or real standards in those days. Most of us wore a suit or, at worst, a blazer or sports jacket, and shirt and tie. Many even wore hats of the fedora brand. Although most of us came from different circumstances, I think we generally encountered a good deal more discipline in our growing and college years; certainly we shared this aspect of our previous years and we also shared the initial belief that this was a serious business, to be taken seriously by serious young people.[39]

Over time, however, the student body began to look for other items to focus themselves on outside of class and note-taking. Smyth wrote that,

> Moving pictures were not open in the morning, nor were the taverns. There were no malls to hang about; no video game establishments. What came to the rescue? The Common Room and another

33 "Inflation Calculator" (17 October, 2011) *Bank of Canada* online: < http://www.bankofcanada.ca/rates/related/inflation-calculator/ >

34 "Introduction" (1952) 1:1 *McGill LJ* ii.

35 Pilarczyk, *supra* note 27 at 36.

36 Roderick A MacDonald, "Cohen and McGill's National Law Programme" in *Law, Policy, and International Justice: Essays in Honour of Maxwell Cohen* (Montreal: McGill-Queen's University Press, 1993) at 411.

37 Morin 95, *supra* note 12.

38 Jacques-Yvan Morin, "Foreword" (1952) 1:1 *McGill LJ* i at i.

39 Pilarczyk, *supra* note 27 at 126.

> very simple device, a deck of playing cards. And so was born the in-Faculty blackjack competition.[40]

It can be difficult to picture these men and women, many of whom are now pillars of society, as a step above children. These were young people, they were students. Some were married and had families, but many of them were still breaking out of their adolescence. But, as Arthur C. Clarke wrote in his novel about the root of mankind's innovative nature in *Childhood's End*—incidentally published on August 24, 1953,[41] mere days before the official tenure of volume one, issue two—"among all the distractions and diversions of a [place] which now seemed well on the way to becoming one vast playground, there were some who still found time to repeat an ancient and never-answered question: *'Where do we go from here?'*."[42]

As for a further historical context: the *Journal* first began its march to publishing issue one in the same month that television first came to Canada, both happenings occurring in the same city—Montreal. In November of that semester, the Slánský show trials were held by the Soviet Union in Czechoslovakia. The word "smog" was coined for the first time in December. The electronic age, the concept of modern human rights, and global environmental concern were all just beginning to take form—all subjects of future scholarship that would find a steady and cutting-edge forum in the MLJ as the years progressed.

Beyond the first three authors, the volume also contained articles by Dean W.C.J. Meredith,[43] future namesake of the Meredith Memorial Lectures given at McGill Law; and Maxwell Cohen,[44] who would develop the National Programme at McGill Law during his future deanship. Alongside Morin and Kaufman, those first editorial boards included issues one and two's Case and Comment Editor John L. Bishop, who went on to sit on the Quebec Superior Court; issue one's Book Review Editor Natalie Fochs Isaacs, the only female member of the first issue of the *Journal*, and now marquee partner of Yarosky, Daviault & Isaacs; graduate student Sheila F. Macbrayne, who was the International Air Law editor for issue four and founded the Institute of Air and Space Law Association that same year; and issue one editor Perry Meyers, issue one editor Melvin L. Rothman, and issue four's Articles Editor Gerald Cooper, all of whom served on the Quebec Court of Appeal.

Jean-Gabriel Castel, the first ever Faculty Advisor to the MLJ, would start in 1954—serving in the position for the fourth issue of the *Journal* and remaining as Faculty Advisor until volume five. He replaced Jacques-Yvan Morin, who was not of the Faculty but had served as their independent advisor for the issues of the previous year (issues two and three). Castel had just started at the Faculty and was brought into the *Journal* project his "colleague Gerry Le Dain ... there were only about five to seven members of the Faculty at the time. Since I had written and published some comments in American and French legal periodicals they felt that I should take an interest in [the] starting [of the] *McGill Law Journal*".[45]

Castel had come to McGill as a law professor immediately after his degree at the University of Michigan, due to his previous degrees in the civil law, which he had received in Paris. He had been accepted by a number of American law schools after taking the LSAT test at the American Embassy in Paris. He decided to go to Michigan where he received a more substantial scholarship; after the Second World War there was not much money to go around sending students from Europe to school in the US. But as a Fulbright Scholar, he was able to cross the ocean and find his way into the world of North-American law.[46] He would later attend Harvard for graduate school.

Castel continued to recall his time with the *Journal* stating that,

> It wasn't easy at the time because there wasn't yet a tradition of people writing for legal periodicals. The most difficult thing was to find proper articles. We even published some of mine there to fill the pages ... and then I was appointed to the *Canadian Bar Review* in 1957 ... At the time, if I recall, the *Journal* was not bilingual ... the *Canadian Bar Review* was also purely English, and I transformed [it] into a bilingual review. It was natural at McGill to have both English and French, civil law and common law, although there was only one degree at the time—it was just a civil law degree. It was only later

40 *Ibid.*

41 Arthur C Clarke, *Childhood's End* (New York: Del Ray Books, 1990) at iii.

42 *Ibid* at 105.

43 WCJ Meredith, "Interpretation of Verdicts in Civil Jury Cases" (1953) 1:2 *McGill LJ* 99.

44 Maxwell Cohen, "The United States and the United Nations Secretariat: A Preliminary Appraisal" (1953) 1:3 *McGill LJ* 169.

45 Interview of Jean-Gabriel Castel by James Cummins (18 November, 2011).

46 *Ibid.*

> on, after Professor Cohen had become the Dean, that it became bilingual and bijuridical with the two degrees ... They were happy to get some young member of the Faculty to take care of [the *Journal*] so that they wouldn't have to be bothered with it. [We] got the support of the Faculty, though I can't remember whether that was for the first issues ... there weren't too many Faculty members ... I was the one who was pushing for it, because I always liked—if you look at my career I've written many books and hundreds of articles—legal scholarship; it's something that I enjoy ...
>
> I was the graduate of two American law schools with a strong tradition of legal writing and legal periodicals, so I thought there should be one at McGill too.[47]

John E.C. Brierley, Executive Editor of volume five and Faculty Advisor to the *Journal* from volume eleven to fourteen, wrote in the preface to the twenty-fifth anniversary issue of the MLJ that, "There was no fanfare or ringing preface when the first number of the first volume appeared in the autumn of 1952, and editors in the years since have shown similar restraint. They have wisely concentrated their efforts upon producing one of the substantively more interesting and attractively printed reviews published in Canada."[48] Then Dean of the Faculty of Law at McGill, Brierley alerts us to a trend that has lasted throughout the decades at the MLJ: that the people who work there, more often than not, put aside their egos and all other commitments to produce as fine a volume of the *McGill Law Journal* as they can muster, and most times this effort comes with little hoopla.

In concurrence with Brierley, the Honourable John H. Gomery stated in the 2006 *McGill Law Journal* Annual Lecture that in 1955 the "*Journal* was at that time a newborn publication and it was, I think it is fair to say, much less prestigious than it is today."[49] Gomery served as Advertising Editor for volume two, and true to the spirit of Brierley's words, stated in his lecture that, "My participation in the success of the publication was limited to selling advertising space to Montreal law firms. I made no contribution to its editorial content but I sold quite a lot of advertising space."[50] As we know from Morin's history of the first issue of the MLJ, that advertising space was as critical to the *Journal*'s existence as anything the other editors may have been doing, despite his MLJ-style modesty.

The hesitancy of the Montreal legal community to full-on support the *Journal* was still there in volume two, as Gomery stated in a later interview that, while soliciting advertisements and business cards for the MLJ, he "found that the law firms were not very receptive; we had to insist."[51] Gomery was also asked about the contrast between what he and others had envisioned for the *Journal*'s future and what the MLJ had become by the time he gave the 2006 Lecture. He replied simply that "the *Journal* has developed ... far beyond our expectations".[52]

Gomery stated that the original editors of the MLJ "started with high hopes, and limited resources."[53] Those hopes followed a tradition of McGill law students who were very interested in writing while pursuing their law degrees. On November 21, 1926, future McGill Law graduate John P Humphrey (who would become the author of the first draft of the *Universal Declaration of Human Rights* and a professor at McGill Law) wrote his sister the following letter referring to the campus publication and literary group he worked for at the time:

> I've had some interesting discussions this last week. I had the idea that the "Lit" should publish a quarterly, something like the Dalhousie Review, and brought it up at an executive meeting. Then I started to look into details more carefully. Yesterday afternoon, after the Varsity-McGill football game, I had tea at a chap's apartment and met the editor of the McGill News. They are planning to change the character of the News from a mere graduate information bureau to a regular quarterly. Well we had a very interesting discussion. Frank Scott, at whose apartment I was, is editor of "Fortnightly"[54] so you see what little I

47 *Ibid.*

48 John EC Brierley, "Preface to the Twenty-fifth Anniversary Volume" (1979) 25:1 *McGill LJ* 1 at 1.

49 John H Gomery, "The Pros and Cons of Commissions of Inquiry" (2006) 51:4 *McGill LJ* 784 at 784.

50 *Ibid.*

51 Interview of John H Gomery by James Cummins (11 October, 2011). Interview was conducted via a handwritten response sent by fax on this date.

52 *Ibid.*

53 *Ibid.*

54 "The *McGill Fortnightly Review* began life as a literary supplement to the *McGill Daily* in 1924. It was published independently from 1925-1927, but did not survive the graduation of its two leading lights, A.J.M. Smith

> knew about magazines wouldn't have much effect in such company, but I made up for it in enthusiasm. The outcome was that the "Lit" will not publish a quarterly this year, but will cooperate with this other attempt. It is quite exciting to have a part, even if it's a small one, in the creation of a new magazine. I'll send you the first copy.[55]

During this fateful meeting, FR Scott was in his final year of law school,[56] though he was still present enough at the Faculty to beat John P Humphrey out for a trip to England with their debate club, after which Humphrey wrote, "Well, the opportunity is gone forever. The future may hide bright things for me, and perhaps it may not, but it's certain that I shall never be part of the first McGill debating team to visit Oxford, Cambridge, etc."[57]

Here we find future luminaries of McGill Law throwing themselves into writing; it is not surprising that those students that Humphrey and Scott would one day teach would follow in the footsteps of their ancestral peers. It is of additional interest to note that Humphrey had been able to attend law school to begin with through the efforts of Professor Stephen Leacock,[58] both one of the greatest Canadian writers of the early 20th Century and one of history's greatest humorists. Though these students were as unsure about their future as those that would come after them, as Humphrey wrote at the beginning of his third year of studies:

> I feel that I am the world's greatest dreamer set by some cruel joke of fate in the most practical of environments. I sometimes wonder if it wouldn't be better for my happiness and usefulness if I gave up my great ambitions and would be content to play a smaller role. Perhaps I could achieve something tangible then, however small. I have enough sense to realize that I can't step out of McGill and by the aid of a few clever words or acts change Montreal into Utopia. Success, if it comes, will be slow and after many setbacks, but will it come? I think you know me well enough to know that for me success isn't measured in motor cars or country estates, or even in fame. When I die I want men to say "the world is a better place to live in because that man lived" and unless men are willing to say that about me then my life has been a failure. These are not just words although it may look that way on paper. It is my very religion. To me immortality is to live on in the contributions that one makes to humanity.[59]

As the founding Editor-in-Chief of the *Harvard Law Review* John Jay McKelvey said in a 1937 speech in remembrance of his *Review*'s fiftieth anniversary, "It is clear that there has been no marked change in the law school review in its character, purpose and usefulness during the half century of its progress ... It has reached a maturity which has brought self-confidence, a clear conception of its field, and a sureness of purpose and performance."[60] On its sixtieth anniversary, it appears that the *McGill Law Journal* has done the same thing in Canada—set the standard for what a law review should be like. But this is something that we will get into later on. For now, it is important to see what kind of student law review culture the first few volumes of the MLJ grew up within. There were very few contemporaries within Canada, so to understand the history of law reviews before the MLJ one must look to law reviews and journals outside of its borders.

The first legal periodical in independent North America was the *American Law Journal and Miscellaneous Repertory*,[61] published in the June of 1808 in Baltimore, Maryland. This first journal was furnished with a preface from its editors that read,

> In almost every department of science its professors have established periodical journals to aid them in the prosecution of their various inquiries; but until very recently, the Bar has been entirely without this assistance.
>
> In the year 1803, a Law Journal was commenced in London by John Morgan and Thomas Walter Williams, Esqurs. which has been found of eminent utility, not only to the profssion, but to the community at large. The frequent

and F.R. Scott." in Alan J Hobbins, ""Dear Rufus ...": A Law Student's Life at McGill in the Roaring Twenties from the Letters of John P Humphrey " (1999) 44:3 *McGill LJ* 753 at 760.

55 *Ibid* at 759-60.

56 *Ibid* at 760.

57 *Ibid* at 762.

58 *Ibid* at 757.

59 *Ibid* at 775.

60 John J McKelvey, "The Law Review 1887-1937" (1937) 50:6 *Harv L Rev* 868 at 872.

61 Michael I Swygert & Jon W Bruce, "The Historical Origins, Founding, and Early Development of Student-Edited Law Reviews" (1985) 36:5 *Hastings LJ* 739 at 751.

> recurrence of publication enabled the editors to give the earliest intelligence of new and important decidions on points in which the commercial world was deeply interested; while *the immunities of invisibility* offered a fair opportunity to professional gentlemen, to prosecute their researches by anonymous communications…
>
> If a Law Journal has been found to be so useful and necessary in Great Britain, where notoriety and uniformity may be established by an appeal to one supreme tribunal, how important would such a publication be, in our country, governed as it is by various and conflicting laws and different states, which are yet so intimately connected by commercial and political relations?[62]

The 1803 periodical in London referred to in this preface was the first periodical of its kind ever created, five years before the *American Law Journal* was published, according to most scholars.[63] However the history of *The Law Journal* goes back at least five more years, when its chief editor Thomas Walter Williams was editor of the first volume of a publication called *An abridgment of cases argued and determined in the courts of law: during the reign of his present majesty, King George the Third*, published in 1798. This earlier work was prefaced by the editor as follows:

> The following Abridgment of the Judicial Deci[s]ions of the Courts of Law in We[s]tmin[s]ter Hall was undertaken at the in[s]tance of [s]ome profe[ss]ional friends, and under an idea that a work of this nature is much wanted in the law-library to facilitate re[s]earch. It commences with, and includes, the adjudications of the pre[s]ent reign; and forms a conci[s]e, but at the [s]ame time clear and intelligible, Dige[s]t of the principle matters contained in Sire James Burrow's and other [s]ub[s]equent reporters, arranged under proper titles … In this compilation, the Editor has only con[s]ulted books of unexceptionable repute …
>
> This is the general plan of the undertaking; and the final end of the Editor's de[s]ign has been to relieve gentlemen from the irk[s]ome ta[s]k of referring to a variety of books; by concentrating, in one work, the [s]ub[s]tance of the Deci[s]ions in the Courts of Law during the pre[s]ent reign, with correct references to the reporters in which they are to be found.[64]

Williams began his law reporting career in 1787 at the age of 24, when he prefaced his first law reporter/compendium writing about the "progre[ss]ive refinement and variation of [s]ucceding ages" when it came to reporting on and thinking about the law.[65] At that time Williams was at the age many, if not most, editors begin their two-year tenure with the law reviews of their chosen universities. Over his canon we can see the spirit of a true law journal peeking through, in a way that presages Williams' 1803 project—history's first law journal.

The first student law review was the *Albany School Law Journal*, first published in 1875,[66] followed by the *Columbia Jurist* out of Columbia University in 1885.[67] The *Harvard Law Review* was partially inspired by a copy of the *Jurist*, which had fallen into the lap of McKelvey and his colleagues, who then founded the *Review* in 1887.[68] By this time both the Albany and Columbia student journals had folded, and the *Harvard Law Review* was the only student-run law journal in North America. Interestingly enough, the first student editors of the *Review* invited the Faculty members of Harvard Law to take an active role in the administration of their journal. It was an offer the professors declined.[69] If we are to include publications that were once run by professionals and are now run by students, the oldest law review of that kind is the *University of Pennsylvania Law Review*, which began its life in 1852 under the

62 John Elihu Hall, "Preface" (1808) 1:1 *The American Law Journal and Miscellaneous Repertory* i at v-vi.

63 Charles Warren, *History of the Harvard Law School and of Early Legal Conditions in America* (New York: The Law Book Exchange, 1999) at 213.

64 Thomas Walter Williams, "To the Gentlemen of the Law" (1798) 1:1 *An abridgment of cases argued and determined in the courts of law: during the reign of his present majesty, King George the Third* i at vi-viii.

65 Thomas Walter Williams, *A compendious digest of the statute law, comprising the substance and effect of all the public acts of Parliament in force, from Magna Charta in the ninth year of King Henry III. to the twenty-seventh year of His present Majesty King George III. Inclusive* (London: G. Kearsley, 1787) at v.

66 Swygert & Bruce, *supra* note 60 at 764.

67 Swygert & Bruce, *supra* note 60 at 766-8.

68 Swygert & Bruce, *supra* note 60 at 768.

69 Swygert & Bruce, *supra* note 60 at 771.

name the *American Law Register*. However its editorial board was not assumed by law students until 1896, when its editor William Draper Lewis became Dean of the law school at the University of Pennsylvania, and arranged for the *Register* to be published by the faculty of law and its student body. In 1908 it changed its name to the *University of Pennsylvania Law Review and American Law Register*, and in 1945 it dropped the second part of that name in response to a new postal regulation.[70]

The first true student law review, the *Harvard Law Review*, went out of its way to help out new competitors and spread its model across the US during the late nineteenth century and early twentieth. Returning the favour to Columbia specifically, when the *Columbia Law Review* (Columbia's third and final attempt at launching a law review) was finally ready to start publishing in 1901, Harvard student editors provided a large amount of advice. As Michael Swygert and Jon Bruce wrote in an article about the early history of law journals in the US, in order to get things off the ground at Columbia,

> [Columbia Law's] Dean William Keener ... demanded that "the new periodical follow closely the pattern of the *Harvard Law Review*." The student editors of the *Columbia Law Review* adhered to Dean Keener's wishes and sought advice from their counterparts at Harvard. The first issue of the *Columbia Law Review*, published in 1901, carried an editorial that contained the following statement: "In particular, we wish to thank the editors, past and present, of the *Harvard Law Review*, not only for setting before us a standard to which we some day hope to attain, but also for their kindly suggestions."[71]

The *McGill Law Journal* was similarly aided by letters of support and advice from the *Harvard Law Review*, as well as *Yale Law Review* in its first years—advice that was added by the first editorial board as an appendix to the original MLJ constitution.[72]

In McKelvey's speech, he stated further that "[t]he centers of legal thought ... are found in the law schools which today alone of all agencies, untrammeled and unconfined, pursue the broad principles of truth and justice, as they may be applied to the building of a better civilization."[73]

Part of how law reviews are able to help in this endeavour is the constant infusion of new blood into their institutions. As Robert Weisberg, who was both a former editor of the *Stanford Law Review* and current member of the Stanford Faculty of Law, wrote of law reviews:

> [T]he wheel regularly gets reinvented. Indeed, a key feature of any law review is its lack of coherent history. When invited to chat with law students about times past at the *Stanford Law Review*, I have few common allusions from which to draw. Though there are characters who are legendary in my own mind, because I knew them at interesting times, no subsequent law review staff has any reason to have heard of these people.[74]

Nonetheless, law reviews in the US were able to find growing acceptance as a legitimate—and sometimes even favoured—source of legal scholarship over the first half of the twentieth century.

For example, between 1924 and 1930, only fifteen opinions by the United States Supreme Court cited legal periodicals—citing to a total of twenty-six periodicals. Yet by 1942, it was not uncommon for the US Supreme Court to cite more than one hundred periodicals in one year in their opinions. In 1945, nearly one third of all US Supreme Court opinions cited periodicals (32.8%).[75] Of these periodicals, the *Harvard Law Review* was cited more than twice as often as its next competitor between 1924 and 1956, the year volume two of the MLJ was being produced.[76]

In Canada around this time, the practitioner-run law journal *Canadian Bar Review* (CBR) began publishing in January of 1923. The idea for the CBR first arose in 1921 at a meeting of Canadian Bar Association (CBA), when members of the bar began to ask why the association did not have its own publication. In March of 1922 at a meeting in Montreal, a committee was launched to determine the viability and needs of such a project. At the 1922 annual general meeting of the CBA, the findings of the committee were presented by George F. Henderson, K.C., and the project moved to the next step. A new committee was assembled in order

70 Joseph P Flanagan, "Preface" (1951) 100:1 *U Pa L Rev* 69 at 69.

71 Swygert & Bruce, *supra* note 60 at 783.

72 See Appendix E.

73 McKelvey, *supra* note 59 at 877.

74 Robert Weisberg, "Some Ways To Think About Law Reviews" (1995) 47:6 *Stan L Rev* 1147 at 1150.

75 Chester A Newland, "Legal Periodicals and the United States Supreme Court" (1959) 3:1 *Midwest Journal of Political Science* at 60.

76 *Ibid* at 64.

to confer with the *Canada Law Journal*, the *Canadian Law Times*, and other Canadian publishers about how to start publishing the periodical. The result was the merger of the *Canada Law Journal* and *Canadian Law Times* (the only two legal magazines in Canada at that point in time) within the *Canadian Bar Review* from that point forward.[77] The rise of the CBR was the product of a major reconfiguration of the legal publishing field in Canada.

According to the President of the Canadian Bar Association, Lieutenant-Governor of Manitoba James Albert Manning Aikins,[78] the *Canada Law Journal*'s long time publisher Henry O'Brien stated during the negotiations to merge the periodicals that his journal was "not started as a commercial venture but had been a labour of love and not for profit."[79] O'Brien himself wrote in the first issue of the *Canadian Bar review* that,

> In throwing our mantle to our successors, the editors of the Canada Law Journal do so with bright hopes and best wishes for the usefulness and consequent success of the new journal. As we have for over half a century endeavoured to help our brothers along the legal highway with, we believe, some measure of success, so we venture to predict that the CANADIAN BAR REVIEW will, in the future, be even more helpful.
>
> This really ought to be the case, for ours was largely pioneer work, "blazing a trail," bumping over "corduroy roads" and make-shift bridges, looking ahead with initiative peerings into the distant landscape of legal scenery. The name of our successor is somewhat suggestive in this respect; for a "Review" not only considers the present, but also takes cognizance of the past, and can calmly contemplate what the future may have in store for its country through the agency of a profession which largely moulds its future.[80]

The *Canada Law Journal* began its existence as the *Lower Canada Law Journal*, first publishing in 1865, two years before Confederation, and first edited by lawyer James Kirby. The journal was published by the Dawson Brothers publishing company of Montreal.[81] The introduction to their first issue reads almost no differently than the first lines of a new legal periodical would in 2012, as the editor compared the new publication to the even older Canadian legal publication the *Lower Canada Jurist* with deference to the *Jurist*'s history and place in the Canadian legal field. The editor wrote, however, in that July 1865 issue that,

> We trust to see the LAW JOURNAL become a medium in the pages of which members of the bar and others can communicate their opinions, and advocate such improvements and amendments in the law as they may desire to see carried out. It is unnecessary to say that no personal reflections, or remarks passing the bounds of fair criticism, will find a place in these columns. Though the JOURNAL is not designed for a Reporter, we propose to publish concise reports of the proceedings and decisions of our courts, paying particular attention to the courts of Review and Appeal. Interesting points arising in the course of criminal trials, and all important criminal cases, so far as they can be procured, will be noted and commented upon. New books issuing from the Provincial and British Press, will be reviewed and criticized. Correspondence, legal appointments, calls to the bar, and compilations, will also find a place. The remainder of each number will be devoted to interesting matter selected from English and American periodicals…
>
> [O]ur beginning has equalled the most sanguine expectations, and given a fair promise of continued vitality and progress.[82]

While the beginnings of this periodical may remind one of modern start-ups, the content within is a far cry from what we would expect to appear in contemporary scholarly publications. Take for example the article "A Daring Forgery" in the *Lower Canada Law Journal*'s first issue, which tells the story of "an extraordinary instance of daring and successful crime";[83] or the series of articles entitled "Remarkable Trials in Lower Canada" that appeared over its first volume, including the "Case of Dr. Sabourin"[84] or "The St. Jerome Murder of 1858", which

77 James Albert Manning Aikins, "Foreword By The President" (1923) 1:1 *Can Bar Rev* 1 at 1-2.

78 JM Bumsted, *Dictionary of Manitoba Biography* (Ebook: University of Manitoba Press, 1999) at 4.

79 Aikins, *supra* note 76 at 2.

80 Henry O'Brien, "The Canadian Law Journal's Greeting to the Canadian Bar Review" (1923) 1:1 *Can Bar Rev* 4 at 4.

81 "Cover page" (1866) 1:1, *LCLJ* i.

82 "Proem" (1865) 1:1 *LCLJ* 8 at 9.

83 "A Daring Forgery" (1865) 1:1 *LCLJ* 14.

84 "Remarkable Trials of Lower Canada: No. 1 Case of Dr.

begins with the following: "The village of St. Jerome, on the night of the 18th January, 1858, was the scene of a most atrocious and dastardly murder."[85] The titles and style of writing appear more akin to what you would find in a comic book or radio drama than a scholarly publication.

The *Lower Canada Law Journal* was, as previously mentioned, preceeded by the *Lower Canada Jurist*, which began publishing in 1857, also in Montreal. It may in a sense be considered the first McGill Law-affiliated periodical, as on the editorial board of the *Jurist* sat, among others, Professors of Law P.R. Lafrenaye, R. Laflamme, and F.W. Torrance, each of the McGill College, as well as the Dean of the McGill school of law and future Prime Minister of Canada, John Abbott.[86] The editors of the *Jurist* wrote in preface to their own first issue that,

> It has been well observed by high authority, that the reports of judicial decisions contain the most certain evidence, and the most authoritative and precise application of the rules of the common law ... Such, then, being the importance of law reports in all civilized countries, they have a special value in Lower Canada, which derives its jurisprudence as well from France as from England, and in which the not infrequent conflict between opposite systems of law, renders it indispensable for the fixing of the jurisprudence that a faithful record of the decisions of the Courts and the reasoning of the Judges should be preserved and published in the country.
>
> Prior to 1850, nothing had been done by the Legislature to secure so great a boon. Althought Upper Canada had had periodical reports of the decisions of her tribunals for nearly twenty years before, and although almost every State of the American Union had had for many years its official reporter of such decisions, yet in Lower Canada we could not in 1850 name more than four volumes, moderate in size recording decisions of the Courts.[87]

Frustruated with official legislative efforts to produce a reliably published reporter of Lower Canada court decisions, in 1854 advocate Thomas Kennedy Ramsay came up with the idea of producing a reporter on his own published under the name *The Law Reporter – Journal de Jurisprudence*, a bilingual publication (some articles in French, some in English)[88] he published himself and edited with L.S. Morin.[89] The publication lasted only a year, however, in 1856 he developed the idea for the *Jurist*, bringing together a team of thirteen editors that included the four McGill professors of law.[90] The *Jurist* acted as both a court reporter and a vehicle for publishing legal essays on the issues of the day.[91]

In the preface to their first issue the editors wrote further that,

> The Editors in this publication ventured upon an experiment, of the success of which they could not be certain, owing to the comparatively small number of individuals who feel an interest in the jurisprudence of the country, so far as to purchase the reports ... A great debt of commendation is also due to the enterprising publisher, Mr. John Lovell, who of his own accord has mostly liberally exonerated the Editors from any personal liability consequent upon the undertaking, and has declared himself satisfied to look for compensation to the subscriptions and to the sale of the volumes published.[92]

The first essay published by the *Jurist* would be on the administration of justice in Canada while it was under the jurisdiction of France, written by the former Attorney General for the Province of Quebec Francis Maseres.[93] Right from the start, legal publishing in Province of Quebec has been polyjurisdictional.

The other legal periodical to merge with the *Canadian Bar Review* and the *Canada Law Journal*, was the *Canadian Law Times*, which began publishing

Sabourin" (1865) 1:1 *LCLJ* 12.

85 "Remarkable Trials of Lower Canada: No. 2 The St. Jerome Murder of 1858" (1865) 1:2 *LCLJ* 44.

86 "Cover page" (1857) 1:1 *LC Jurist* i.

87 Editorial Board, "Preface to the First Volume" (1857) 1:1 *LC Jurist* i at v-vi.

88 (1854) 1:1 *The Law Reporter – Journal de Jurisprudence* 1 at 1-8.

89 "Cover page" (1854) 1:1 *The Law Reporter – Journal de Jurisprudence* i.

90 Ed board *LC Jurist*, *supra* note 86 at vii-viii; "Ramsay, Thomas Kennedy" *Dictionary of Canadian Biography Online*, University of Toronto (2000), online: < http://www.biographi.ca/EN/EN/009004-119.01-e.php?id_nbr=5785 >

91 *Ibid* at viii.

92 *Ibid*.

93 Francis Maseres, "A View of the Civil Government and Administration of Justice in the Province of Canada While it was Subject to the Crown of France" (1857) 1:1 *LC Jurist* Essay Section 1 1 at 1.

in 1881 under the editor Edward Douglas Armour in conjunction with Osgoode Hall.[94] However, this publication was not a law review at its start, but rather began its publishing history as a magazine reporting on the law in Canada.[95] Its first issue spoke of subjects not uncommon to the legal mind of 2012, including abortion,[96] issues surrounding the practices of banks and lenders when it comes to the housing market,[97] and issues of determining national allegiances in the face of multiple factors such as heritage and where one was born.[98]

Before the *Jurist*, law reporting in Lower Canada had only been done on five separate occasions, the first of which was published in 1811 by George Pyke[99] under the title *Pyke's Reports of cases argued and determined in the Court of King's Bench for the district of Quebec in the Province of Lower Canada: in Hilary term, in the fiftieth year of the reign of George III.*[100] Another attempt was made in 1834 by George Okill Stuart, and then again with the French publication *Revue de législation et de jurisprudence*, which was published annually from 1845-48,[101] first edited by M.M. Louis, O. Le Tourneux, S. Lelièvre, and F. Réal Angers.[102] Of course, law reporting is not the same thing as scholarly publishing, however the editors and authors of these volumes did add their expertise to explaining and recording the courts' decisions and their original contexts within the bounds of the reporters. Again, as we saw with examples like Thomas Walter Williams of *The Law Journal* in London, or the origin of the *University of Pennsylvania Law Review*, in many ways law journals as a class of publications grew from the seed of nineteenth-century law reporters.

While French law was as a large an influence on the law in Quebec as English law was on the common law of Canada, tracing the history of legal publishing in France back to the same point is a more difficult task. As Carla Hesse writes, "despite the theoretical assertions of literary critics and legal theorists, we know surprisingly little about the history of authorship and publishing during the period of the French Revolution, the particular moment in which the modern notion of the author crystallized into a legal identity in France."[103] We do know that in the same year as the *American Law Journal* began publishing, 1808, the *Bibliothèque (ou Journal) du Barreau et des Écoles de Droit* began publishing in France.[104] The goal of the publication was to give opinions on the laws of the French Empire and the legal ongoings of the day.[105] By the middle of the nineteenth century, there appear to be a healthy amount of law journals and reviews publishing in France on the subject of French and foreign law.[106] However these journals took a very different path than their American and Canadian counterparts, as almost no law reviews in France (or England for that matter) became student-run. Therefore the link between Canadian student-run law journals, and French and British legal publishing, is less substantial than the link between American and Canadian journals.

In Upper Canada, the *Upper Canada Law Journal* began publishing in 1855, in the year before the founding of the *Lower Canada Jurist*.[107] Its first editor was James Patton, and the periodical was published in Toronto.[108] In the *Upper Canada Law Journal* we find the first true space for law students, in a small column they labelled "The Student's Portfolio". In introduction of the student space in the periodical's first issue was written,

> For our young friends a space has been reserved, and we trust that the gleanings which will be presented to them, *monthly*, may prove interesting and interactive. The extracts given will be necessarily brief, but may serve to encourage reflection, (as well as invite to solid and extended reading) among those of our Student friends who

94 "Cover page" (1881) 1:1 *Canadian LT* i.

95 "Introductory" (1881) 1:1 *Canadian LT* iv.

96 "Abortion: Adminstering 'Noxious Thing'" (1881) 1:1 *Canadian LT* 30.

97 "Does a Power to Sell Imply a Power to Mortgage" (1881) 1:1 *Canadian LT* 21.

98 "The Law of Allegiance in Canada" (1881) 1:1 *Canadian LT* 1.

99 Brian J Young, *The Politics of Codification: The Lower Canadian Civil Code of 1866* (Montreal: McGill-Queen's University Press, 1994) at 232.

100 George Pyke, *Pyke's Reports of cases argued and determined in the Court of King's Bench for the district of Quebec in the Province of Lower Canada: in Hilary term, in the fiftieth year of the reign of George III*, (Montreal: George Pyke, 1811) 1 at ff.

101 Young, *supra* note 98. It should be noted that the start date in Young's text for the periodical is incorrect, as the date on the front page of the first issue is October 1845, see (1854) 1:1 *R de L* 1.

102 "Cover page" (1854) 1:1 *R de L* i.

103 Carla Hesse, "Enlightenment Epistemology and the Law of Authorship in Revolutionary France, 1777-1793" in *Law and the Order of Culture* (Los Angeles: University of California Press, 1991) at 110.

104 "Cover page" (1808) 1:1 *Bibliothèque (ou Journal) du Barreau et des Écoles de Droit* i.

105 "Plan de L'Ouvrage" (1808) 1:1 *Bibliothèque (ou Journal) du Barreau et des Écoles de Droit* iii.

106 "Relevé des ouvrages relatifs à la science du droit qui ont paru en France en 1841" (1842) 5:1 *Revue des Revues de Droit Publiées a l'étranger* 287.

107 "Cover page" (1855) 1:1 *UCLJ* i.

108 "Our Prospectus" (1855) 1:1 *UCLJ* 1.

> desire not to *pick up* the law as a trade, but to study it as a professor—to qualify themselves for that dignified calling, "which has, amongst things temporal, no superior or equal."[109]

In the first issue the space was not yet afforded to excerpts from pieces written by students, but instead pieces written for students. The section was no longer included as of the fourth volume.[110] The *Upper Canada Law Journal* was preceeded in terms of court reporters by the *Upper Canada Law Reports*, which began publishing in 1841 and was edited John Hillyard Cameron until 1846,[111] who Christopher Moore writes, "put the reports on sound professional and commercial footing for the first time."[112]

Returning to the time frame of the founding of the *Canadian Bar Review*, several other legal periodicals would be founded in the years afterwards, run by either practitioners or academics. The *Alberta Law Quarterly* was founded in 1934 by Professor Malcolm MacIntyre, but dissolved in 1944.[113] In 1936, as was previously mentioned, the *Saskatchewan Bar Review* was founded—though it would eventually morph into the *Saskatchewan Law Journal.*

Meanwhile at McGill, as Stanley Frost (former Vice-Principal of Administration & Professional Affairs of McGill University) and the future Governor General of Canada David L. Johnston (at that time the Principal of McGill University) wrote in a 1981 article about the half century before the MLJ was founded, "It should be recalled that the McGill Law Faculty was in a position shared by very few institutions in the world. Because it was situated in the province of Quebec, it was teaching civil law, a legal system derived from French jurisprudence and based on Roman law, but it was doing so in English."[114] By 1920, Dean Robert Warden Lee had established the first predecessor of McGill's current national law programme by having McGill establish a program that offered both common law and civil law degrees.[115] This program only lasted four years, but it set up a culture that would allow Dean Maxwell Cohen to bring the idea back permanently in 1968.

Interestingly, the importance of bijuridical law was important to McGill University long before the founding of its Faculty of Law. Frost explains, in a different article, that "in the 1820's … the Desrivières family contested James McGill's bequest of land and endowment for the establishing of McGill College" and that the Desrivières family sought "support for [their] case in French jurisprudence. However, it was determined that the issues should be judged with respect to English law, not French, and finally the … suits … were decided in favour of the McGill College trustees, by the Privy Council in England."[116] The ability to move between legal systems smoothly is as integral to McGill University as James McGill himself.

Some of the reasons why there was no journal at McGill before 1952 cannot be understood without looking at the reality of the McGill Law programme in the decades before it. In 1926, the year in which the previously cited letter by Humphrey to his sister about FR Scott and writing at McGill was sent, McGill Law was not yet a full-time place of study. In fact, Johnston and Frost indicate that it was only in 1927 that the Law Faculty of McGill required students to come to school for their entire days. Up until this point, classes were "given between 8:30 and 9:30 a.m., and 4:00 and 6:30 p.m. - obviously because most law students spent the day in legal offices."[117]

Even the professors did not give much time to the Faculty of Law. Frost wrote, as an example of the kinds of professors teaching at McGill Law during the late nineteenth century, that "Dean John Abbott (who was to succeed John A. MacDonald as Prime Minister of Canada) obviously brought great prestige to the McGill law school, but he cannot have had much time for his students and deanship."[118]

Looking at it with a knowledge of the history that Johnston and Frost wrote up as a part of the History of McGill Project, of which Frost was the director from 1975 to 2003, many of the elements that formed the culture of the *McGill Law Journal* were not yet in existence until former McGill Law student John Humphrey returned to the university to teach in 1936. Johnston and Frost write that,

> Recognizing that the average law

109 Emphasis not added. "The Student Portfolio" (1855) 1:1 *UCLJ* 20 at 20.

110 *UCLJ*, (1858) 4:1 *UCLJ* 1 at ff.

111 Hereward Senior, "John Hillyard Cameron (1817-1876): Canadian Scot and Orange Grand Master" (1982) 12:1, *International Review of Scottish Studies*, 115 at 117.

112 Christopher Moore, *The Law Society of Upper Canada and Ontario's Lawyers, 1797-1997* (Toronto: University of Toronto Press, 1997) at 105.

113 "History of the Alberta Law Review" *ALR* (13 May, 2012), online: < http://www.albertalawreview.com/index.php/alr/pages/view/history >

114 David L Johnston & Stanley Frost, "Law at McGill: Past, Present and Future" (1981) 27:1 *McGill LJ* 31 at 34.

115 *Ibid* at 35.

116 Frost, Stanley, "Early Days of Law Teaching at McGill" (1984) 9:1, *Dalhousie LJ* 150 at 151.

117 Johnston & Frost, *supra* note 113 at 37.

118 Frost, *supra* note 115 at 157.

> student would find the subject of little practical advantage, Humphrey sought to teach international law as an exercise in legal science, thus requiring even the most practice-oriented student to consider the further implications of his profession at least once during the course of his legal education.[119]

That the *McGill Law Journal* was born into a Faculty of Law where a former writing enthusiast—who would go on to write one of the world's great legal masterpieces[120]—would bring to life an interest in international law long before it was the important field it is today, is something that very much allowed the MLJ to become a unique institution.

It should be remembered that this was a time before the United Nations—Humphrey would depart from McGill Law to the United Nations in 1944. During these eight years he spent at McGill, it is difficult to imagine the lack of focus the world placed on international law, which is now one of the most important subjects written on the *McGill Law Journal*; as it has been since the MLJ's inception (two of the articles in the MLJ's first issue were written about international law). As the 2011 *McGill Law Journal* Annual Lecturer Carlos Fuentes—considered to be one of the most important novelists of the last century, who himself studied international law at the graduate school level in Geneva during the 1950s—said of one of his great mentors, Professor Paul Guggenheim, "[H]e realized the rudimentary character of international law—how rudimentary international law truly was—and the consequent recourse to illicit measures because, precisely, of that rudimentary character; and the need to go forward in perfecting international rights and duties."[121] The same can no doubt be said of Professor Humphrey.

Another consideration taken from the history of Johnston and Frost is that the McGill Law student body would not have been large enough to maintain a consistent editorial staff. They report that the "growth of the student body has also been a major factor" in the overall success of many things at the Faculty, as it went from "approximately fifty students in 1940, to one hundred and eight in 1950, to two hundred and thirty in 1960, to two hundred and seventy in 1970 and to over five hundred in 1980".[122] Considering that over thirty-five editors and managers are employed by the *Journal* today, it is no wonder that there was not enough man power to put together a legal periodical much before the advent of the MLJ. It becomes more and more understandable as to why a student run law journal was only effected at McGill a full 104 years after the founding of the Faculty—McGill being the oldest law school in Canada.[123]

As Roderick A. MacDonald wrote of the university environment where the *McGill Law Journal* was born, "The university of the time was one of the few places where dissent from orthodoxy was possible. But even in its sacred precincts there were costs to truth telling."[124] Perhaps the purest form of truth-telling occurs through law journals. With its constant turnover of staff, what comes out in the pages of a law journal is difficult to pin to any one person or group of persons. This allows a precociousness and freedom in how law journal editors are able to address the contemporary legal scholarship around them. It allows journal editors to be free from conventions and helps to push the edge of legal scholarship forward. This aspect of law journals and reviews is unique among fields of study. As JC Oleson, a former law review editor turned academic, wrote, "The student-run law review is a puzzling phenomenon. To the legal outsider, the practice of allowing second- and third-year law students to select and edit the research of established scholars seems preposterous."[125]

This preposterousness is highlighted in an excellent anecdote provided by Professor Jean Leclair in his keynote address to the first "national conference of student law journal editors"[126] held by the *Queen's Law Journal*, delivered on March 4, 2005 (though Queen's had been holding regional law review conferences as far back as the 1980s).[127] Leclair began by quoting a letter

119 Johnston & Frost, *supra* note 113 at 38.

120 In describing the *Declaration* in this manner, a caveat should be observed coming from the words of Humphrey himself, as he stated in the inaugural John P Humphrey Lectureship on Human Rights on 16 November, 1988 that, "The fact is … that the *Declaration* had no father in the sense that Thomas Jefferson was the father of the American *Declaration of Independence*. One of the reasons for the *Declaration's* great authority is indeed its very anonymity." John P Humphrey, "The Dean Who Never Was" (1989) 34:2 *McGill LJ* 191 at 197.

121 Carlos Fuentes, "McGill Law Journal Annual Lecture Series" (2011) 56:4 *McGill LJ* 1189 at 1196.

122 Johnston & Frost, *supra* note 113 at 42.

123 *Ibid* at 44.

124 Roderick A MacDonald, "FR Scott's Constitution (Inaugural Lecture) 27" (1996) 42:1 *McGill LJ* 11 at 27.

125 James C Oleson, "You Make Me (*Sic*): Confessions of a Sadistic Law Review Editor" (2004) 37:4 *UC Davis L Rev* 1135 at 1136.

126 In 2010 Queen's University held the second conference, and changed the name of the event to the National Law Journal Conference.

127 "The *McGill Law Journal* Alumni Newsletter" MLJ

written to an American professor regarding the student editors at the *Harvard Law Review*. The letter stated that:

> Meanwhile a spot of trouble! The L. Rev. boys ha[ve] *mutilated* my article by making major excisions of what they think is irrelevant or fanciful. They have made a ghastly mess of it and of the references to Bentham and I have written to say they must not publish it under my name with these cuts which often destroy the precise nuance. I took great care and much time over what they have coolly cut out.
>
> Could you induce them to be sensible? Such an interference with an author's draft is unthinkable here and I am astonished that so gross an insensitive a thing should be possible at Harvard ...
>
> So sorry but it is important to me to get precisely what I said printed. Best of wishes.[128]

Leclair then read aloud the response from the American scholar:

> After receiving your letter I went over to the Review and found the President busily engaged in restoring your article to its original form. I am sorry for what they did, though I have to confess that this sort of thing comes close to being standard practice with articles written by American authors. Being near at hand I could save my baby from mayhem. Had I dreamed they would take such liberties with your text, I would have stood over them.[129]

Leclair then explained that "the pieces of scholarship these two men were referring to were H.L.A. Hart's 'Positivism and Separation of the Law and Morals' and Lon Luvois Fuller's 'Positivism and Fidelity to Law: A Reply to Professor Hart,' both of which appeared in the 1958 issue of the *Harvard Law Review*. That such masterpieces could be altered by third-year law students is mind boggling."[130] Though Hart and Fuller were on different sides of a grand historical debate, only together could they combat the all-powerful stroke of a law review editor's pen.

Two years before this exchange, the *McGill Law Journal* published a short memoir from Chief Justice Thibeudeaud Rinfret of the Supreme Court of Canada (a graduate of McGill Law, class of 1900), about his thirty years on the Court.[131] The article appeared on the first page of only *volume three*—that the institution of the *McGill Law Journal* could so quickly become such a substantial venue for scholarship and legal history, and have similar items of historical importance handed to it, is astounding. However, it is in line with how the *Journal* itself began. Unlike the history of the *University of Toronto Faculty of Law Review*, the MLJ's predecessor in Canada, things moved very quickly at the MLJ.

As Fred Kaufman, the second Editor-in-Chief of the *McGill Law Journal*'s first volume, described it all in an October 2011 interview:

> I was in my first year and Jacques-Yvan [Morin] came to me and said, "Look, I plan to spearhead the establishment of a McGill law journal, and it will be edited primarily by students" because there were some law journals ... that were published by the faculty, some by the students, some are a mix, and his idea was to have it primarily a student publication. The reason he came to me was that I had newspaper experience. I spent seven years before I went to law school on the now defunct *Montreal Star*, so I knew something about publishing and I knew something about editing. He had heard about that and asked me, "Are you prepared to help me with this?"
>
> I was quite enthusiastic about it, and that was the beginning. He worked extremely hard to get his goal; he had to deal with the Faculty. There were some misgivings whether the students could do it and if it was a good idea, which were perhaps reasonable precautions. The Faculty wanted to be sure—the Dean wanted to be sure—that it in fact could be

Editorial Board (1986) 2.

128 Nicola Lacey, *A Life of H.L.A. Hart: The Nightmare and the Noble Dream* (New York: Oxford University Press, 2004) at 200, cited in, Jean Leclair, "A Review of Law Reviews: Comments of a Contented Victim" (2005) 31:1 *Queen's LJ* 385 at 387. Leclair, in turn, gave thanks in his footnote to Justice Yves-Marie Morissette (Faculty Advisor for the *McGill Law Journal* from Volume 26 through Volume 31) for pointing him to the anecdote in the first place. From Lacey to Morissette to Leclair to this book, we see a passing of knowledge truly representative of Morin's envisioned "permanent meeting place".

129 Lacey, *supra* note 127 at 200; Leclair, *supra* note 127 at 388.

130 Leclair, *supra* note 127 at 388.

131 Thibeudeaud Rinfret, "Reminiscences from the Supreme Court of Canada" (1956) 3:1 *McGill LJ* 1.

done …

What we had to do was get the idea, find out from printing houses how this could be done, what it would cost, how long it would take, what format it should take; and both of us were running around speaking to both Faculty and students to see who was prepared to write. Everybody said, 'Yes, we'll be happy to do it, when do you need it?' and we said, "We'd like to have it in a couple of months, something like that, if it would be possible," but it did produce the usual problems of publication. But we got it going …

We took a collection of law journals from across the country and the US, and [said], "What do we want in here? We want articles, we want book reviews, we want case reviews," and then of course we also needed some advertising, as the Faculty said, "Who's going to pay for all of this?'"

We had about three or four pages of professional cards [for our first issue], law firms were pretty good about helping out. Interesting to note, as I look at them now, on the first page of the ads there's an ad by Stikeman Elliot—and if I count the number of lawyers, they had five lawyers.[132] Today Stikeman Elliot is across the country and the world practically … So you see the early beginnings of some law firms as well as the *Law Journal*. There are some others: [a firm] now known as the Ogilvy Renault firm—lately know as Norton Rose.[133] They didn't give their number of lawyers, but they were known as "the factory" at the time, because they had eighteen lawyers, that's my recollection…

The book reviews were all written by students: Morin wrote one, I wrote one, Gerry McCarthy—who became a judge with the Court of Appeal—he wrote one, and John Bishop wrote one… [Morin] was a good academic, before he became a politician he was a *very* good academic, and with my editing experience, we were very fussy about accurate footnotes—to have the citations to conform to acceptable standards. The editing was difficult, because the people that were writing for us (except for Gerry Le Dain, perhaps, who had experience) had no idea how to footnote things; they had very little idea as to how to give proper references, so we work hard on that.

Then Morin left, he graduated, so I kept it going for the next two or three years … there were about fifteen students involved, a couple of freshmen—say about twenty students were involved, so it was a joint effort. The Faculty took about two or three years to warm up to the project—to really embrace it—and once we had put out three or four volumes it became easier to convince people to write for the *Law Journal*, because academics—publications are important to them—they always wanted to know, "Well what's your circulation? Who's going to read it? Is it worth my while to spend time on this …

We made it quite clear to anybody who asked to join the Editorial Board that it was sort of by invitation only. What I mean by invitation: we let it be known that anybody who would like to be active should let us know, [but] we didn't necessarily accept them because we wanted serious people. We made them realize that this was a time consuming job … It did take up a lot of time, but it was thoroughly enjoyable, and certainly to be on the Editorial Board became full of meaning … My wife was at McGill about twenty or twenty-five years ago and she was on the Editorial Board, and she was very proud of that, because students that were invited to join in later years, when it became an established institution, [had] a very nice thing to have on your cv…

[Morin] felt that an old and well established law school like McGill should have a law journal. And I think he was absolutely right. But nobody before him had taken the time to do it, or taken sufficient interest, and he was the one who brought it to fruition. It was entirely his idea. I was just lucky that he came to me, because he found out about my publishing experience … I was certainly the first person that was active with him, and many

132 Stikeman Elliot was indeed founded in 1952 as a tax law boutique in Montreal.

133 Ogilvy Renault was incorporated into the global law firm Norton Rose in 2011.

> nights it was just the two of us saying, "What can we do, where can we go with this?" ... Our hope was always that there would be a volume per year.

Kaufman says that he met with Morin in Fall 1952, when Kaufman had first started as a law student at McGill. Remarkably, the first issue of the MLJ was put out before the end of that year. As Kaufman stated,

> It was a relatively short period ... we had to run around and sign printers, to get quotations, and the matters of printing: of course we had to find the right kind of type, and there are hundreds of type faces; then you have to learn about the sizing, you have to print the pages in multiples of four, because the pages are cut that way—and you don't want to end up with a couple of empty pages, as that would look funny; that kind of thing. We spent night after night—I should say evening after evening, that would be more accurate—in deciding whether this should be on the left hand side of the page or the right hand side of the page, because basically all that was left to us ... When you're beginning then you have some very keen people, but they don't always work out ... understandably they've got exams coming up. [They might say], "I'd love to do it, but I can't do it for six weeks" ... well, we haven't got six weeks.
>
> You run up against that, but being in a volunteer organization, you've got to be very nice to people, because they are putting in a lot of time. They mean well and they do well.[134]

Kaufman was writing for the *Montreal Star* for seven years before he came to law school. He also had a part-time job during law school working as the Montreal correspondent for the *New York Times*, on top of working for *Life* magazine, *Sports Illustrated*, and *Saturday Night*.[135] During the interview, Kaufman made it extremely clear that the *Journal* could not have come out without the firm dedication and contributions of the entire team. He was, in fact, still in contact with many of the people he worked with on that first volume, and detailed the careers of the people he remembered as he reviewed the masthead. There were colleagues who later became judges, very successful lawyers, and academics. As Kaufman said, "They were all good students."[136] In spite of this, when asked if Kaufman and his colleagues were very sure that their new venture would be successful and endure as a lasting legal institution, he replied, "No. No, we were hoping, we were quite prepared to make the effort, put in whatever time it might take, but, well, we had no guarantees."[137]

It is difficult to get the perfect picture of the *Journal* at its beginning point, for as Kaufman says, "It was sixty years ago, and to be in law school—to be involved—you had to be at least twenty-three/twenty-four in those days: that was before CEGEPs."[138] As of the time of researching and writing this book, every editor of the original *McGill Law Journal* is at the very least in their eighties—which is what makes the timing of the project all the more critical.

Words from those no longer with us add context to the situation. Stories that are as prevalent today as they were when they occurred have been or almost been lost. For example, John Brierley, Executive Editor of volume five as well as future Dean of the Faculty of Law at McGill, remembered two years before his death that,

> In those days [the *Journal*] was located in a cupboard on the fourth floor of Old Chancellor Day Hall, with a slanting roof. The then-Dean, W.C.J. Meredith, a very fierce person, submitted an article on an aspect of procedure that had just been reformed, Article 286(a) of the *Code of Civil Procedure*. As law journal editors are wont to do, we made changes. He was a very choleric individual, and when he received the proofs he hit the roof. The Editor-in-Chief was conveniently away, so I was summoned to the Dean's office and was dressed down in a way I'll never forget—he was practically apoplectic.[139]

Over the years, however, Brierley must have come around to Meredith's point of view, as McGill Law Professor Richard Janda reported that, during Brierley's later McGill Law deanship, "Once, confronting the editor of the student newspaper over an editorial he found beyond the pale, he said in his slow, deliberate way, 'You know I wouldn't hesitate to sue.'"[140]

134 Interview of Fred Kaufman by James Cummins (18 October, 2011).

135 Fred Kaufman, *Searching for Justice: An Autobiography* (Toronto: University of Toronto Press, 2005) at 84.

136 *Ibid.*

137 *Ibid.*

138 *Ibid.*

139 Pilarczyk, *supra* note 27 at 127.

140 Richard Janda, "In Memoriam: John E.C. Brierley" *McGill Faculty of Law Newsletter 2002/2003* (2002), online: < http://www.mcgill.ca/files/law/newsletter-2002.pdf >

Dear Professor Lucceius,

I saw that your history of the Italian and Civil Wars was now all but finished, and because also you told me that you were already embarking upon the remaining portions of your work, I determined not to lose my chance for the want of suggesting to you to consider whether you preferred to weave your account… into the main context of your history, or whether, as many Greek writers have done—Callisthenes, the Phocian War; Timeus, the war of Pyrrhus; Polybius, that of Numantia; all of whom separated the wars I have named from their main narratives—you would, like them, separate the civil conspiracy from public and external wars.

For my part, I do not see that it matters much to my reputation, but it does somewhat concern my impatience, that you should not wait till you come to the proper place, but should at once anticipate the discussion of that question as a whole and the history of that epoch. And at the same time, if your whole thoughts are engaged on one incident and one person, I can see in imagination how much fuller your material will be, and how much more elaborately worked out.

I am quite aware, however, what little modesty I display, first, in imposing on you so heavy a burden (for your engagements may well prevent your compliance with my request), and in the second place, in asking you to shew me off to advantage. What if those transactions are not in your judgment so very deserving of commendation? Yet, after all, a man who has once passed the border-line of modesty had better put a bold face on it and be frankly impudent.

And so I again and again ask you outright, both to praise those actions of mine in warmer terms than you perhaps feel, and in that respect to neglect the laws of history. I ask you, too, in regard to the personal predilection, on which you wrote in a certain introductory chapter in the most gratifying and explicit terms—and by which you shew that you were as incapable of being diverted as Xenophon's Hercules by Pleasure—not to go against it, but to yield to your affection for me a little more than truth shall justify. But if I can induce you to undertake this, you will have, I am persuaded, matter worthy of your genius and your wealth of language.

All the Best,

Marcus Tillius Cicero
Editor (self-appointed), Historical Works of the Roman Empire

Figure 1: Letter from Cicero to Lucceius reformatted as MLJ Letter of Justification.

As Yves Fortier, Advertising Editor for volume four, also wrote of these early times:

> [T]he *McGill Law Journal* was very much in its infancy at the time. It was a very ambitious program on the part of any student to be associated with this; this was a new journal … I mean it started in '52; I find that difficult to believe. You know, if you were going to be an important jock at the Law Faculty, you know, you aspired to participate as a member of the editorial team of the *Journal* … we were, my colleagues and I, associated with the commencement of the *Journal* and we were very proud of it.[141]

Fortier would later in life become Chairman of the law firm Ogilvy Renault, and continue on as Chairman Emeritus of Norton Rose OR. He also served as Canada's Ambassador to the United Nations from 1988 to 1992, and was President of the United Nations Security Council in 1989 as well as Vice-President of the 45th United Nations Assembly in 1990. Afterwards, he would become the Chairman of the Hudson's Bay Company, North America's oldest corporation, and is most recently the namesake of the L. Yves Fortier Chair in International Arbitration and International Commercial Law at the McGill Faculty of Law.

Fortier said of those early days that "because the class was so small, you know, we spent a lot of time together … studying, working on the *Journal*, playing – hah! It was almost incestuous, the relationship between all of us, in the law school in those days,"[142] while discussing friends like Editor-in-Chief Raymond Barakett (of the future Monette-Barakett law firm); Articles Editor Yoine Goldstein (future member of the Senate of Canada); and Comments Editor Jean-Louis Baudouin (future Justice for the Court of Appeal of Quebec and namesake of the *Chaire Jean-Louis Baudouin en droit civil* at the Université de Montréal's Faculty of Law).

Baudouin recalled of the *Journal* of the time that,

> One has to

141 Fortier interview, *supra* note 23.

142 *Ibid.*

> realize that at that time the *McGill Law Journal* was a very small law review ... we had, at that time, to try to get enough subscriptions to the review to make it live. I distinctly remember that we used to knock on the doors of every single law office in Montreal and ask them for a subscription to the law review—with mixed results I must say. At that time, first, the number of lawyers was very limited, probably around three [to] four thousand in Montreal and doctrine was not something very popular with practising lawyers.[143]

The entire *Journal* was involved in more than just editing—everybody had to pitch in. Baudouin recalls further that: "I remember that I had a distinct advantage because my father was a law professor. Every time I'd walk into the law offices, they would say 'Are you the son of Louis Baudouin?' and I would say 'Yes', and we would get a subscription."[144]

Baudouin also recalled how case comments—now a staple of law journals across the country—were perceived at the time. He stated that,

> The second thing that I remember very distinctly is that case comments were viewed by the judges with high suspicion. I wrote a review on the issue of whether or not in a contract of sale you could have an action *quanti minoris* instead of having to annul the whole contract.[145] I criticized but with all respect, et cetera, a decision of the Court of Appeal, and my father—who was a law professor at McGill at that time—got, from the Chief Justice, a phone call saying "your son should be very careful and *not...*" It was taken very badly by the judiciary.[146]

Of course, Baudouin would go on to become a high-ranking judge himself. His comments are reminiscent of those of John Jay McKelvey about the founding years of the *Harvard Law Review*.

Largely though, Yves Fortier stated that things today were not likely all that different today his time on the *Journal*. As much as things change over time, they really can stay the same. As evidence of this, I point to a letter written over two thousand years ago by perhaps the very first great legal philosopher to stand the test of time: Cicero. He was Roman political theorist and champion of democracy long before the word came into use, but above all he was a scholar. And, as all scholars are apt to do every once in a while, he did on occasion come to desire for a fellow scholar to edit his work.

I have here taken the liberty of taking one of his letters to one such character and placing it in the contemporary template of the so-called "letter of justification" that has been sent to authors alongside their edited text for most of the *Journal*'s modern history, allowing the author to know what has been changed and why. The resulting combination can be seen on the accompanying page.[147]

Structured like a letter between an editor and their author, it appears that the methodology behind imploring upon an author to alter their piece has not changed much in over two thousand years. *Journal* editors, in general, tend to connect themselves to the articles under their care, and take great pride in their final form. The terms "my article" or "author crush" are not uncommon when hearing editor's discussing the piece they have been tasked to bring out the best of. Although Cicero was perhaps more forward than an editor would be in the final sentence of the full form of his letter, as he writes, "Meanwhile, do not relax your efforts, and thoroughly polish what you have already on the stocks, and ... continue to love me."[148]

At the end of the day, the article leaves the hands of the editor, and it is no longer theirs. The blood, sweat, and tears that went into bringing the piece into form are often quickly forgotten (though sometimes not so quickly) as the next assignment rolls in. And the next one after that; and the next one after that. Thus many of those who have not set foot into a MLJ office in nearly sixty years still have some editorial acts forever burnt into their memories.

143 Interview of Jean-Louis Baudouin by James Cummins (24 November, 2011).

144 *Ibid.*

145 Jean-Louis Baudouin, "Foley v. Marcoux" Case Comment (1985) 4:2 *McGill LJ* 289.

146 Baudouin interview, *supra* note 142.

147 Marcus Tillius Cicero, "Letter X" in *Letters of Cicero Guteburg.org*, online: < http://www.gutenberg.org/cache/epub/2812/pg2812.html > Salutations and signature added by author.

148 *Ibid.*

Chapter Two:

Developing the Shoulders of Giants

The first several volumes of the *McGill Law Journal* were fairly modest in terms of size. The first volume took between 1952 and 1955 to complete four issues. As announced in the final issue of volume one, "Commencing with the second volume, the Journal will be published semi-annually, each volume to contain two numbers."[149] This would remain the norm for both the third and fourth volumes. Volume five, however, saw a return of the MLJ to a four issue per volume journal.

This does not mean that volumes two through four were without great highlights. The first issue of volume three opened with one of the most important historical pieces ever published by the MLJ. Thibeudeaud Rinfret, at that time Chief Justice of the Supreme Court of Canada, had been serving as a Justice on the Supreme Court for thirty years (1924-54): the second longest term a Supreme Court Justice ever held in Canada.[150] His tenure as Chief Justice lasted 10 years and 165 days (1944-54). Chief Justice Beverley McLachlin only overtook Rinfret as the longest serving Chief Justice since his tenure in May of 2011. And Chief Justice Rinfret chose the MLJ as the platform for remembering his term in office over four pages he called "Reminiscences from the Supreme Court of Canada", the first article of volume three. Given the content of his words and the future place of the MLJ in global legal scholarship, there could not have been a better place.

Rinfret reminisced that,

> On a not too remote visit to Australia, where I attended a congress which brought together Jurists representing all countries of the British Commonwealth, I was asked continually how the Supreme Court of Canada could succeed in having to hear and decide appeals now under the Common Law and then under the Civil Law - to which should be added what they supposed to be a further difficulty that, while most of the appeals were, of course, argued in the English language, some of them were presented in the French language and, in those cases, the greater part of the Record and the Factums was in the French language. I kept on trying to convince them that this offered no handicap. In such a task I was helped by the Chief Justice of South Africa, where a similar situation occurs, except that there the French language is replaced by the Dutch language, and the French Civil law by the Roman Dutch law.[151]

Rinfret wrote further, stating that,

> The constant practice of delving into comparative law is apt to buttress one's knowledge of the fundamental principles of Justice as it has been envisaged throughout the ages by the wisdom of the different countries of the world. The solutions brought by them to the problems of human relationship illuminate and clarify the rules whereby it must be governed. And I say that advisedly.[152]

In 1956, McGill Law had not yet acquired its international reputation for comparative law, and the future Editor-in-Chief of the MLJ turned Dean of the Faculty of Law at McGill who would put the transsystemic program into place at McGill (Stephen Toope) was not yet born. But these words from Chief Justice Rinfret show that the truth behind the value of the teaching methodology of contemporary McGill goes back a long time. The very soul of what McGill Law and the MLJ has come to stand for can be found throughout Chief Justice Rinfret's piece. He wrote further that,

> I repeat that in exploring the relations between the two great races which go to make up our country we insist too much upon our so-called differences and we do not stop sufficiently to consider our similarities. It stands as an obstacle on

149 "Editorial Board" (1955) 1:4 *McGill LJ* 258.

150 The longest serving Supreme Court Justice in Canadian history was Lynman Poor Duff, who served for almost forty years between 1906 and 1944.

151 Rinfret, *supra* note 130.

152 *Ibid* at 2.

> the road leading to what is known among Canadians as the "bonne entente".
>
> Why persist in regarding "bonne entente" as meaning the assimilation of the two races? Even individuals forming part of the same race are not similar; they each have their own characteristics and peculiarities. At a time when the civilized nations of the world strive to achieve unity, it would be surprising indeed that the two races to which Providence has entrusted the task of forming together our Canada should find difficulty in living in harmony.
>
> If it be true that the fundamental principles of law are the same and that dissimilarities are found only in matters of form in order to reach the same results, could it not be said that a similar situation exists with regard to religion and to language. The essential principle of Religion is the worship of the Supreme Being. That is the substance of the matter. This worship is expressed in a different way. Yet, it is nevertheless religion with the same object: the worship of the same Supreme Being. The difference exists in the form of the Worship.
>
> And so may it be said of language. The words are only the means of communicating our thoughts, and again, in whatever language, it resumes itself into a question of form.
>
> I have used that expression elsewhere and I wish to repeat it again! We are all Canadians.[153]

It should be noted that Chief Justice Rinfret is the same Chief Justice that Gordon Bale reminds us stated plainly in 1950 that publications like the *Canadian Bar Review* were not an authority in the Supreme Court of Canada. To that end, this piece by Rinfret is the beginning of yet another story beyond that of the MLJ itself—that of the Supreme Court of Canada's eventual acceptance of legal periodicals as an important part in the formation of their opinions—a topic which will be covered in a future chapter. Rinfret also wrote a short piece advocating for a new *Civil Code* in Quebec,[154] which was published at the end of the final issue of the volume. In a sense, we see a symbolic "embrace" of the *Journal* by a man who once stood in the way of the MLJ's greatest supporter, with his articles bookending the beginning and end of the MLJ's 1956 volume.

Having future and present scholarly heavyweights publish not once but twice within a volume or series of volumes was not uncommon in the first years of the MLJ. Future Justice of the Supreme Court Gerald Le Dain published twice within volume one of the *Journal*. Le Dain's second article appeared in issue four, and covered (among other things) a comparative legal argument surrounding the transfer of property.[155] He also published on the subject of property law in volumes two[156] and four[157] respectively, as well as a book review in volume three,[158] by which time he had become an Associate Professor at the Faculty of Law.

Other esteemed authors included J.R. Mallory, a Professor of Political Science at McGill, who is the namesake of the J.R. Mallory Lecture in Canadian Studies given annually at the McGill Institute for the Study of Canada, an event that has hosted prestigious speakers on the McGill campus since 1995. Mallory was considered Canada's leading constitutional expert for many years, and in volume three wrote of the division of powers within provincial governments.[159]

Volume four saw several interesting pieces published. J.E.C. Brierley, who would go on to make a significant imprint on the legal community, had his first ever publication as a legal scholar in his second year of law school—publishing a case comment entitled "Saint-Pierre and Another v. McCarthy". In it the young student defended a ruling of the Court of Appeal[160] in addition to discussing what he called the "mysteries of art. 1053".[161] Jean-Gabriel Castel also contributed the first of his five articles that would appear in the MLJ over the coming decades.[162]

The volume also marked the scholastic year where Castel assumed the editorship of the *Canadian Bar Review*. He recalled of the time that,

153 *Ibid* at 4.

154 Thibeaudeaud Rinfret, "The Revision of the Civil Code" (1957) 3:2 *McGill LJ* at 228-29.

155 Gerald E LeDain, "The Transfer of Property and Risk in the Sale of Fungibles" (1954-55) 1:4 *McGill LJ* 251.

156 Gerald E LeDain, "Security upon Moveable Property in the Province of Quebec" (1956) 2:2 *McGill LJ* 77.

157 Gerald E LeDain, "The Real Estate Broker" (1958) 4:2 *McGill LJ* 219.

158 Gerald E LeDain, "Banking and Bills of Exchange by John Delatre Falconbride" Book Review (1956) 3:1 *McGill LJ* 113.

159 James R Mallory, "Cabinet Government in the Provinces of Canada" (1957) 3:2 *McGill LJ* 195.

160 JEC Brierley, "*Saint-Pierre and Another v. McCarthy*" (1958) 4:2 *McGill LJ* 298 at 301.

161 *Ibid* at 298.

162 Jean-Gabriel Castel, "Jurisdiction and Money Judgments Rendered Abroad. Anglo-American and French Practice Compared" (1958) 4:2 *McGill LJ* 152.

> It was judge [George S.] Challies of the Superior Court of Quebec, who was teaching at McGill at the time. We became friends and the Editor of the *Canadian Bar Review* was retiring, and they were looking for someone who was versed both the civil and the common law. In those days you'd have to go through the whole legal system, it was not like now where you can do it in four years ... They were looking for an academic, because there used to be an issue of the *Bar Review* every month ... but they had decided to reduce it to a quarterly. There wasn't enough money to have someone full-time because George Nicholls, who was a graduate from McGill—the Editor at that time—couldn't have survived on a quarterly. So they were looking for someone part-time ...
>
> But being Advisor to the *McGill Law Journal* was the first step to becoming Editor-in-Chief of the *Canadian Bar Review*.[163]

Professor René-H Mankiewicz, a man that the President of the United Nations Administrative Tribunal Arnold Kean said in 1982 "is widely esteemed as a grand old man of international civil aviation law",[164] contributed an article on criminal law in aviation.[165] Another article on criminal law was published by Professor of the McGill Faculty of Law and two-term Quebec MNA Joseph Cohen.[166] Professor Germain Brière, for whom the annual Germain Brière Day is now celebrated at the University of Ottawa Faculty of Law, wrote on the topic of nullifying marriage contracts.[167] Professor Edward McWhinney, the first Canadian ever elected to the *Institut de Droit International* in Geneva (he served as President of the Institute as well), contributed an article on the difference between English and British legal philosophy.[168]

Following up on the idea that a scholar like Brierley would see his first academic publication so early in life, an investigation of other scholars that published their first scholarly works in the case comments and book reviews of the early volumes of the *McGill Law Journal* reveals several other highlights. In volume one, we find case comments published by students Ronald St. John Macdonald[169] (esteemed scholar and the only non-European to sit on the European Court of Human Rights from 1980-98); volume one Articles Editor Gerald Cooper;[170] Fred Kaufman;[171] and volume one Case and Comment Editor John L. Bishop.[172]

In volume two, we find Managing Editor John Ciaccia[173] (long time MNA for the Quebec Liberal Party from 1973-98 and former Quebec Native Affairs Minister) and volume three Executive Editor Benjamin J. Greenberg[174] (who would go on to become a Justice of the Superior Court of Quebec). As mentioned before, John Gomery served as Advertising Editor for the volume. Volume three published the first works of volume four Comment Editor and future Justice Jean-Louis Baudouin,[175] and Editor-in-Chief of volume three Harold William Ashenmil[176] (future founder of the Kidney Foundation of Canada). Also serving on the volume three board was Comment Editor Mortimer M. Teitelbaum, future Justice of the Federal Court of Canada.

Volume four published the first works of volume four Comments Editor Claude-Armand Sheppard[177] (who was instrumental in the development of Canada's conception of official languages and the findings of the Royal Commission on Bilingualism

163 Castel interview, *supra* note 44.

164 Arnold Kean, "The Liability Regime of the International Air Carrier. By R. H. Mankiewicz" Book Review (1982) 31:3, *Int'l & Comp LQ* 591.

165 René-H Mankiewicz, "Le Droit Penal Et L'Aviation" (1957) 4:1 *McGill LJ* 13.

166 Joseph Cohen, "Common Law Rules of Evidence as Applied in Criminal Matters" (1958) 4:2 *McGill LJ* 144.

167 Germain Brière, "La Nullite Du Contrat De Mariage" (1958) 4:2 *McGill LJ* 204.

168 Edward McWhinney, "English Legal Philosophy and Canadian Legal Philosophy" (1958) 4:2 *McGill LJ* 213.

169 R St J MacDonald, "The Minquiers and Ecrehos Case" (1954-55) 1:4 *McGill LJ* 277.

170 Gerald Cooper, "Switzman v. Elbin" Case Comment (1954-55) 1:4 *McGill LJ* 281.

171 Fred Kaufman, "The Doctrine of Unjustified Enrichment in the Law of the Province of Quebec by Hon. George S. Challies" Book Review (1952) 1:1 *McGill LJ* at 90; Fred Kaufman, "The Saumur Case" (1953) 1:3 *McGill LJ* 223.

172 John Bishop, "*Canadian Constitutional Law* by Bora Laskin" Book Review (1952) 1:1 *McGill LJ* 95; John Bishop, "C.P.R. v. Kelly" Case Comment (1953) 1:3 *McGill LJ* 141.

173 John Ciaccia, "Perron v. School Trustess of the School Municipality of Rouyn" Case Comment (1955) 2:1 *McGill LJ* 42.

174 Benjamin J Greenberg, "Tremblay v. Bernier" Case Comment (1955) 2:1 *McGill LJ* 50.

175 Jean-Louis Baudouin,, "Dame Strasbourg v. Lavergne" Case Comment (1956) 3:1 *McGill LJ* 93.

176 Harold William Ashenmil, "Statutes of Quebec--Highlights of 1956" (1956) 3:1 *McGill LJ* 110.

177 Claude-Armand Sheppard, "Statutes of Quebec--Highlights of 1956" (1957) 4:1 *McGill LJ* 88; Claude-Armand Sheppard, "La Ville De Dorval v. Drouin" Case Comment (1958) 4:2 *McGill LJ* 301.

and Biculturalism);[178] Donald Johnston[179] (future Federal Minister of Justice, Attorney General of Canada, President of the Liberal Party of Canada, and Secretary-General of the United Nation's Organization for Economic Co-operation and Development); volume five Advertising Editor Clive V. Allen[180] (namesake of the Clive V. Allen Fellowship in International Business Law at McGill University); as well as volume four Editor-in-Chief Raymond Barakett[181] and volume four Advertising Editor Yves Fortier.[182] As Jean-Louis Baudouin recalled, "At that time we had very, very few candidates for publication, so accepted just anybody if they looked alright,"[183] though he noted that soon afterwards "the *Law Journal* became much more critical of the quality of the proposed contributions".[184]

By volume five more and more of the case comments and book reviews were being written by practitioners and academics. There had been others that had contributed to this section before, but these authors were far outnumbered by student submissions. Still, volume six Editor-in-Chief A. Derek Guthrie, future Justice of the Superior Court of Quebec and member of the MLJ Board of Advisors, found his first publication with a case comment in that issue.[185]

The focus turned to more established authors like Milton Handler—drafter of American legislation such as the *Federal Food, Drug and Cosmetic Act* of 1938, the *National Labor Relations Act*, and the *G.I. Bill of Rights*[186]—whose advice on competition, as one America's great regulators, was simple: "The rule of reason recognizes that some restraints, though foreclosing competition between the parties, strengthen the forces of competition in the market as a whole."[187] Finding the right balance within this idea is something that continues to mystify legislators to this day, as Handler wrote further of the movement he saw towards mass deregulation in the 1950s and 60s: "I perceive in this approach the demise of the small businessman in America."[188] It turns out, with the coming age of corporate conglomeration and big box stores, that in many ways Handler was right.

In 1959, the tail end of the volume, FR Scott would go on to win his seminal case—*Roncarelli v. Duplessis*—altering Canadian history forever. It would also greatly affect the MLJ and legal publishing at McGill. This volume was the last that Jean-Gabriel Castel would serve as Faculty Advisor to the *Journal*, leaving the Faculty to teach at Osgoode Hall the following year. Castel left for a few reasons. One big reason was that there were greater opportunities for advancement elsewhere—Osgoode Hall had offered him the position of full professor in advance of then-Osgoode Hall Dean Falconridge's retirement, a higher salary, and his own secretary. He had also left because he and Gerard Le Dain had proposed some changes to try and improve upon the McGill school program, yet their good friend Professor FR Scott had advised it would be difficult to have them approved due to the influence of some seniors colleagues. Castel's in-laws also lived in Toronto and wanted to be closer to their only child and grandchild.

But there was another reason interwoven into the rest of these optimistic portents of Castel's future. Following a conference with FR Scott and others about the *Roncarelli* case in the fall of 1959, Castel was assaulted and seriously injured at his farm in the Eastern Townships by allegedly two organizers of the Union Nationale. Upon reporting the assault, he received no help because "The Police of Granby pretended that the farm was within the jurisdiction of the police of Sherbrooke and the Police of Sherbrooke pretended that it was within the jurisdiction of the Police of Granby." Thinking on his feet, Castel dropped the complaint to the police.[189] The importance of Castel leaving under these conditions is significant—as with the *Canadian Bar Review* leaving McGill, the MLJ became was the sole generalist legal publication at one of the premier law schools in the country. With this the role of the MLJ at McGill expanded substantially.

The impact of the *Bar Review* leaving McGill

178 Claude-Armand Sheppard, *The Law of Languages in Canada*. (Ottawa: Studies of the Royal Commission on Bilingualism and Biculturalism, no.11 Information Canada, 1971) at 291; Michael Dorland & Maurice René Charland, *Law, Rhetoric and Irony in the Formation of Canadian Civil Culture* (Toronto: University of Toronto Press, 2002) at 77-79.

179 Donald Johnston & Marvin B Gameroff,, "Chabot v. Les Commissaires D'Ecoles De La Morandiere" Case Comment (1958) 4:2 *McGill LJ* 268.

180 Clive V Allen, "Prevost Et Dupont Construction Limited v. H. Bouthilier" Case Comment (1958) 4:2 *McGill LJ* 293.

181 Raymond Barakett & Sydney B Sederoff, "Statutes of Quebec--Highlights of 1957" (1958) 4:2 *McGill LJ* 305.

182 Yves Fortier, "Cases and Materials on Income Tax by John G. McDonald" Book Review (1958) 4:2 *McGill LJ* 310.

183 Baudouin interview, *supra* note 142.

184 *Ibid.*

185 A Derek Guthrie, "Rainville Automoblile LTD. v. Dame Primiano" Case Comment (1959) 5:2 *McGill LJ* 132.

186 Sylvia Nasar, "Milton Handler, 95, Is Dead; Antitrust Expert Wrote Laws" *The New York Times* (12 November, 1998), online: < http://www.nytimes.com/1998/11/12/business/milton-handler-95-is-dead-antitrust-expert-wrote-laws.html >

187 Milton Handler, "Varieties of Approach to the Problem of Competition" (1959) 5:4 *McGill LJ* 209 at 213.

188 *Ibid* at 216.

189 Castel interview, *supra* note 44.

cannot be overstated in terms of its historical relevance—as, if the *Review* had not left, it would have pitted the MLJ against a Faculty run journal during its nascent years. As an example of the alternative, at the University of Toronto the student-run *University of Toronto Faculty of Law Review* is forever in the shadow of the *University of Toronto Law Journal* (UTLJ), which is run by the Faculty. According to the UTLJ, today, "Out of comity with the University of Toronto Faculty of Law Review, which publishes exclusively student-written pieces, our policy is not to consider submissions by authors at the LLB/JD, articling/clerking or Masters level."[190] The UTFLR, whom the UTLJ is speaking of, in turn only publishes pieces written by authors that fall into those ignored categories. Here we see the kind of impact that a faculty run journal can have while on the same campus as a student-run journal: the delimiting of content, prestige, and the quality of possible submissions.

Castel would come back to work in Quebec afterwards on many occasions—even once a week for sixteen years to help draft the section of conflict of laws for the new *Civil Code of Quebec*—but he never returned full-time. He might have served as a visiting professor for many courses at McGill in later years, but, as he states himself, "When I left McGill I took the *Canadian Bar Review* with me."[191] If history had not turned this way, there is no telling if the MLJ would ever have become such a significant presence in Canada, sharing the same campus as the most important professional law journal in the country. At the time, neither journal was extremely important in the legal world (no law journal in Canada was), but that would soon change.

The following volume, volume six, saw publications by Albert Mayrand,[192] future Justice of the Court of Appeal of Quebec; Maxwell Cohen writing on the subject of public international law;[193] and Jacob S. Ziegel's article "Some Aspects of the Law of Contempt of Court in Canada, England and the United States".[194] Ziegel's article holds the distinction of being the first article published by a Canadian-based university-associated law journal (student-run or faculty-run) ever cited by the Supreme Court of Canada in its decisions, with its citation in the 1971 case *McKeown v. The Queen*.[195] It was cited once again in the 1987 case *R. v. Vermette*.[196] The reason for this late date and the rarity of such citations during this era will be discussed in a later chapter. Future luminaries that sat on the Editorial Board alongside future Justice A. Derek Guthrie included volume six Case Comments and Book Review Editor Roy L. Heenan, founder of Heenan Blaikie LLP.

Gerald Le Dain published once again in the following volume, alongside Justice Gerald Fateaux, who was serving on the Supreme Court of Canada at the time. Now entering its seventh volume, the MLJ had given itself a facelift. Alongside these changes, an editorial note was written describing these decisions:

> The extensive changes in the physical appearance and format of the Law Journal – ranging from the newly-designed cover and the improved paper quality to the introduction of regular correspondence and editorial sections – have doubtless come as a surprise to its readers. The Editorial Board of the Law Journal has introduced these changes in the hope of thereby creating a more interesting and readable legal periodical. We are aware, of course, that not all of the Journal's readers will find the innovations entirely to their liking, but we are confident that the over-all impression will be a favourable one, although we recognize that radical departures from tradition are not completely consistent with the accepted practices of the legal profession.[197]

It seems almost peculiar that there was a time when improving the quality of your product is something that needed to be apologized for. Though, knowing the

190 Email from the *University of Toronto Law Journal* to Sara Ross (16 December, 2011).

191 *Ibid.*

192 Albert Mayrand, "Brefs Commentaires Sur L'Interet Assurable Et La Responsabilite De L'Assureur" (1960) 6:2 *McGill LJ* 127.

193 Maxwell Cohen, "Some Bibliographical Problems of Public International Law" (1960) 6:4 *McGill LJ* 277.

194 Jacob S Ziegel, "Some Aspects of the Law of Contempt of Court in Canada, England and the United States", (1960) 6:4 *McGill LJ* 229.

195 This was discovered as the first such SCC citation through a full search through all SCC opinions from the advent of the first Canadian university law review, founded in 1942, through 10 November, 2011. An incomplete list had been assembled by volume fifty-two Managing Editor Meagan Hough in 2006, which was a helpful starting point during the scanning of all post-1942 Supreme Court decisions for law journal citations. The scanning involved the word searching of all individual SCC decisions, and was double-checked after the first count using a variety of methods to ensure its validity, including searches for additional keywords and a full website search of all decisions at < http://scc.lexum.org/en/ >. For a complete list of cited articles from the *McGill Law Journal* and the cases they were cited within, see Appendix A.

196 *Ibid.*

197 "Editorial Notes" (1960) 7:1 *McGill LJ* 1 at 1.

combative character many young editors had in the face of the whole of legal academia, the comments can be read as a bit backhanded. The "editorial note" in general was something innovated by volume seven. For each of their four issues, as well as the opening issue of volume eight, the editorial board included an introductory note that was at times fiercely political.

Accompanying the MLJ's explanation of its physical changes, the note also took the liberty of criticizing the Quebec government for "conspicuously fail[ing] to mention any contemplated action to hasten the long-awaited report of the Civil Code Revision Commission",[198] reminding the government that "the party that was victorious in last June's provincial elections advocated a revision of the Civil Code as part of its electoral platform."[199] The wording of the notice was surprisingly strong, even finishing with the following warning to the provincial government: "We are anxiously looking forward to the implementation of this promise."[200]

Things had changed in the nine years since the MLJ had been founded. Fred Kaufman, Editor-in-Chief of volume one for issues two and three, was labelled in the introduction as a volume seven author and "noted criminal lawyer".[201] The provocations of volume seven's editorial notes would continue throughout their volume. For issue two, the "editorial note" spent the first two full pages of the issue on a critique of how a lawyer's conservative political leanings could speed the conferring of the title "Queen's Counsel" upon them, even if they did not have as much experience as those of more liberal political leanings. The piece bordered on labelling the process as systemic political corruption, though did stop a few steps short of this.[202] Interestingly enough, the Editor-in-Chief at the time, Norman May, would go on to become a Queen's Counsel himself fifteen years later after serving as an Associate Professor at Osgoode Hall.

Other individuals that served alongside May included Case Comments and Book Reviews Editor Daniel Mettarlin, future namesake of the Daniel Mettarlin Memorial Scholarships awarded at McGill Law; and Articles Editor Harvey Yarosky, who would found Kaufman, Yarosky and Fish a few years later with fellow *Journal* alums Fred Kaufman and Morris Fish, who is discussed later in the chapter.

The third issue of volume seven started out with a somewhat biting editorial trashing the educational system at Harvard Law while building up the system at McGill as superior.[203] The fourth issue announced FR Scott as the new Dean, and then launched into a tirade against the then practice of the Quebec Bar of charging all law students in Quebec a fee on top of their tuition "in order that he be 'allowed' to study law."[204] He wrote that "[t]he payment of $152, however, may be meaningless, but it is anything but harmless to the generally impecunious law student who must struggle with very high law school fees and in many cases must support a family as well."[205] When asked about the editorial notes, Editor-in-Chief May could not recall who wrote them, but remembered well that, "we were constantly worried about receiving a sufficient number of acceptable contributions and welcomed them on virtually any relevant topic."[206]

As for those articles published within volume seven, they included an article from P.N. Thorsteinsson,[207] founder of Thorsteinssons LLP; from Professor Gérard Cornu,[208] future Dean of Law at the l'Université du Paris II Panthéon-Assas; and a round-table hosted by Maxwell Cohen based on the question "Are Quebec Arbitration Procedures Obsolete?".[209] Meanwhile, the tradition of the editorial note established in volume seven appears to have died out after the volume came to a close.

One more "editorial note" was recorded in the first issue of volume eight, but that was the last of them. The new editorial board appeared to have taken issue with the length of time the City of Montreal was taking in constructing its new courthouse—what would soon become a Montreal landmark, the Palais de Justice. The editorial sternly implored the City to finish the building by its intended opening date in 1965.[210] It, in the end, would be built, but it would not be completed until 1971: ten years after the editorial was published. As for actual articles published within volume eight, the Chief Justice of the Quebec Court of Appeal, the Honourable Lucien Tremblay, contributed an article on judicial discretion;[211] and another article by a future

198 *Ibid.*
199 *Ibid.*
200 *Ibid.*
201 *Ibid.*
202 "Editorial Notes" (1961) 7:2 *McGill LJ* 91-92.
203 "Editorial Notes" (1961) 7:3 *McGill LJ* 179-80.
204 "Editorial Notes" (1961) 7:4 *McGill LJ* 223-24.
205 *Ibid.*
206 Email exchange between Norman May and James Cummins (13 October, 2011).
207 Donald J Johnston & PN Thorsteinsson, "Some Aspects of Article 126" (1961) 7:2 *McGill LJ* 93.
208 Gérard Comu, "La maladie physique, élément de l'état des personnes" (1961) 7:4 *McGill LJ* 242.
209 "Are Quebec Arbitration Procedures Obsolete: A Panel Discussion" (1961) 7:4 *McGill LJ* 255.
210 "Editorial Notes" (1961) 8:1 *McGill LJ* 1 at 1-2.
211 Lucien Trembley, "Certains aspects de la discretion

Prime Minister that will be discussed over the course of the next few pages. The volume also included a piece by future Associate Chief Justice of the Superior Court of Quebec George S. Challies.[212]

Staff Photo by Mac Juster

Married "bachelors" — Arnold Isaacson and his wife, Sue Carol, both receive degrees at McGill today. Mr. Isaacson qualified for a bachelor of civil law degree, Mrs. Isaacson for a bachelor of arts. They were married last year.

Work Pays Dividends In Double Graduation

By MORRIS FISH

This is the second most important day in the lives of a charming young Montreal couple, Arnold and Sue Carol Isaacson.

August 27, 1961, the day they were married, still ranks ahead of today. But it's close. This morning they both received degrees at McGill's spring convocation.

Arnold, who this year held a major McGill scholarship, was awarded a bachelor of civil law degree. Sue Carol received a bachelor of arts.

Some university students can't even find enough time to study. They have a lot to learn from the Isaacsons.

Both held important extra-curricular positions on campus: this year Arnie was executive editor of the McGill Law Journal, a difficult and time-consuming job; while Sue Carol headed the Combined Charities campaign, a major student undertaking.

Because one of them had to find remunerative work, and because her curriculum seemed the more compatible with outside employment, Sue Carol held down two part-time jobs while running the charities campaign, studying her courses, and performing all the household duties incumbent upon a young married woman.

Arnie didn't just sit back and let his wife work — whenever necessary he helped his wife with domestic chores (though he insists he did little more than eat his wife's delicious meals), and won a scholarship which more than covered his tuition fees.

He also worked hard to entertain his classmates—by hosting delightfully stimulating parties, and by sheepishly slipping into every morning lecture at least 10 minutes late.

Arnie is now preparing to enter the notarial profession.

From *The Montreal Star*, May 30, 1962. (Courtesy of Arnold Isaacson)

judiciaire" (1962) 8:4 *McGill LJ* 239.

212 George S Challies, "Some Problems of Civil Procedure" (1961) 8:1 *McGill LJ* 3.

The Executive Editor for volume eight was Arnold Isaacson—future President of the Lord Reading Law Society (1999-2000)—who, when discussing his time on the *Journal* in an interview, said about joining the *Journal* that "I worked hard to get up to the Executive Editor level. I applied myself as best I could, and I did whatever I had to do, and I guess they appreciated that, and they made me Executive Editor. I didn't have the brains of an Alan Golden[213] and so maybe that's why they made me Editor, but I'm a hard worker."[214] Isaacson said that the atmosphere in his volume was "terrific"[215] and filled with "camaraderie".[216]

He remembered that "we had an office upstairs, and my job was to try to get contributors to the *Journal*, and I used to talk to professors all over the world, actually ... In fact it put me in very good stead later on in life, because I was the President of many organizations."[217] As for those academics closer to McGill, the relationship between the MLJ and the Faculty of Law had become very cordial. Professor Paul-A Crépeau served both as Faculty Advisor to the MLJ and as Isaacson's squash partner.[218] Isaacson served alongside several future luminaries, including Managing Editor W. David Angus (future Canadian Senator) and a second individual he discussed directly during his interview. Discussing what it was like in his class's social environment, he relayed that,

> I was one of the first ones to be married in the class; I married my childhood sweetheart who graduated with me. And so we had an apartment with no furniture, just hardwood floors and a bed, and all the class used to come up to my apartment with my wife, and we used to recite poetry on the floor. It was a

213 Editor-in-Chief for volume eight of the *McGill Law Journal*.

214 Interview of Arnold Isaacson by Omar Soliman (3 December, 2010).

215 *Ibid.*

216 *Ibid.*

217 *Ibid.*

218 *Ibid.*

> great class. It was a phenomenal class.[219]

Isaacson had some special words for one classmate and fellow editor in particular. The student was simultaneously going to law school and working for a newspaper, just as Fred Kaufman had done a decade earlier. Isaacson remembered that "he wrote an article, a full-page article in the *Montreal Star* about me and my wife, we graduated together. She had a BA and I had the B.C.L. And it was wonderful; he's a very good friend of mine."[220]

That student was Articles Editor for volume eight, Morris Fish, better known today as the Honourable Morris Fish, Justice of the Supreme Court of Canada. In a rare 2010 interview, while Fish was still sitting on the bench, he recalled his time on the *Journal*, and in particular a meeting he had with an author who was also destined for the top of the legal field in Canada:

> What I remember most was the special edition we did on fundamental liberties. I remember it particularly because this was around the time of the first *Bill of Rights* was coming, so it was in discussion, and we didn't at the time have the *Charter*, which as you know only came along twenty years later in 1982; and I remember it particularly because I associate it with two of the contributors. One was to become Prime Minister of Canada, Mr. Trudeau.
>
> He was then a professor and I remember going to visit with him on the veranda of his home in upper-Outremont to talk about civil liberties generally, so that was a highlight which he and I discussed forty or so years later at a conference in Cambridge—when I asked him whether he had anticipated the effect that the Canadian *Charter* would have on the legal and social fabric of Canada, whether he anticipated that in 1982 when it was adopted, and I said, "I know you've had a long and distinguished history and fighting for respect for human rights and fundamental freedoms."
>
> And he said, and that amazed me, "Well I remember you coming to see me." The other reason that I remember it so well is that another contributor was Tony Honoré and Professor Honoré was then visiting lecturer or visiting professor. He introduced me to writings of his colleague then, H.L.A. Hart, one of the great thinkers of our time and in 2007 I was the first Canadian invited to give the H.L.A. Hart memorial lecture at Oxford—and Tony Honoré attended, and we again reminisced about his contribution to the *McGill Law Journal*. So it provided me with an opportunity to meet two very different and both great contributors to the advancement of fundamental freedoms and political and social rights.[221]

Speaking further of Professor Honoré, Fish shared how different the experience of editors at the *McGill Law Journal* had become by that time when it came to addressing the shortcomings of their authors' work. Remembering that,

> Professor Honoré gave me a first draft that had very few footnotes. And so I went to see him with trepidation to say; here's this pipsqueak Articles Editor of the *Law Journal* who questioned the style and substance. And I said, "With the substance," I said, "it was wonderful, it's great, it's succinct, it's thoughtful, it's profound. Do you think it would be possible to add some references? Because I'm sure that readers will want to pursue some of the points that you've made." He said, "No problem," and the next day or two days later, came back with what you'll find in the *Journal*—all the footnotes. They were all there, but they were all in his head.[222]

The Trudeau that Justice Fish was talking about was, of course, Prime Minister Pierre Trudeau, who wrote an article entitled "Economic Rights". In it the future Prime Minister exposed the importance of including economic rights alongside civil rights within the law as it pertained to social justice.[223] Prime Minister Trudeau concluded his article by writing that

> if this society does not evolve an entirely new set of values, if it does not set itself urgently to producing those services which private enterprise is failing to produce, if it is not determined to plan its development for the good of all rather

219 *Ibid.*

220 *Ibid.*

221 Interview of Morris Fish by Sara Ross (23 November, 2010).

222 *Ibid.*

223 Pierre Elliot Trudeau, "Economic Rights" (1962) 8:2 *McGill LJ* at 121.

> than for the luxury of the few, and if every citizen fails to consider himself as the co-insurer of his fellow citizen against all socially-engineered economic calamities, it is vain to hope that Canada will ever really reach freedom from fear and freedom from want. Under such circumstances, any claim by lawyers that they have done their bit by upholding civil liberties will be dismissed as a hollow mockery.[224]

Morris Fish would, as has been previously discussed, go on to partner with Fred Kaufman and Harvey Yarosky—Articles Editor for volume seven—at the firm Kaufman, Yarosky and Fish, after the three lawyers split away from their previous partners around 1969. As Kaufman wrote in his autobiography,

> [I]t was a remarkable partnership. For one thing, we never got around to drafting a partnership agreement. Every major decision was made by consensus and I don't think we ever had an argument … As to the division of profits (or, God forbid, losses!), we sat down in my office on 5 January 1970, and each of us took a piece of paper. On it we wrote what we thought were the proper percentages, and when we disclosed the figures to each other, the high and the low were two per cent apart. We split the difference, wrote down the results, and initialled the paper. It was the only "contract" we ever had … We repeated the exercise once a year and never had a problem.[225]

This kind of altruistic attitude appeared to abound through the lives of Kaufman and Fish. Kaufman's own run-in with Professor Pierre Trudeau, for example, occurred on May 20, 1960 near the front doors of the Old Montreal courthouse—the year before the meeting on Trudeau's front porch between Fish and the future Prime Minister, and the MLJ's demand of the city to build the new Palais de Justice on time. In his book, Kaufman wrote that on that day,

> [W]e heard what sounded like an explosion, followed by loud voices and the sound of people running. We quickly realized that the noise had been a shot, and with our bodies cautiously protected behind a wall, we peeked around the corner. A man was lying on the ground, surrounded by officers and guards, flailing his arms and legs. As we approached, we saw that he was bleeding profusely from one leg.[226]

Five police officers forced the man down on the ground as a detective used his own shirt to try and make a tourniquet, weighing heavily on the suspect's chest.[227] Kaufman continues, recalling that "[a]t this precise moment in walked Pierre Trudeau … Trudeau quickly took in the scene and at once walked over to [the detective], tapped him on the shoulder, and asked what he was doing."[228] Trudeau then told them that "the injured man does not resist any longer. He can't save himself. Could you put less weight on his chest?".[229] For this Trudeau was arrested.

Kaufman had to act quickly—he found the closest high-ranking police officer he could to him and pled Trudeau's case; that it was purely a misunderstanding, and that both the police (needing to put on the tourniquet) and Trudeau (seeing a man being aggressively handled by the police) had cause to argue with one another. Kaufman relates that after this explanation, the officer "ordered Trudeau's immediate release."[230] Before that could be done, though, as Trudeau was threatening to sue the police that were abusing both he and the prisoner and the officers escorted him to the cells, the officers said outright: "Just try, you can be sure there will be perjury."[231] The incident stayed well within the memories of all involved. In 1973, when Kaufman would be called up to the bench, Trudeau called Kaufman himself and said, "Since you once got me out of jail, the least I can do is to tell you myself that you have just been appointed to the Court of Appeal."[232]

Kaufman here represented the kind of fighting spirit that had begun to take hold of Montreal in the 1960s, and the *Journal* was soon to follow. Volume nine would include editors such as Editor-in-Chief Mark M. Rosenstein, who would go on to be a founding partner in Lapointe Rosenstein LLP, and Managing Editor Alex Konigsberg, who was founding partner of the same firm. According to Rosenstein, Dean Maxwell Cohen would constantly confuse the two of them. Rosenstein recalled after Konigsberg's August 2010

224 *Ibid* at 125.

225 Kaufman 2005, *supra* note 134 at 236-37.

226 Kaufman 2005, *supra* note 134 at 118.

227 Kaufman 2005, *supra* note 134 at 118-19.

228 Kaufman 2005, *supra* note 134 at 119.

229 *Ibid.*

230 *Ibid.*

231 Kaufman 2005, *supra* note 134 at 120.

232 *Ibid.*

passing that,

> Eventually, I gave up trying to set the record straight and resigned myself to live with the confusion. In the years that followed our graduation, I would meet Professor Cohen from time to time at professional gatherings, McGill events or on the street, and he would invariably ask me "Konigsberg, how is your friend Rosenstein?" to which I would answer "he's fine, sir, he's fine". Professor Cohen would then say "Konigsberg, you know that fellow Rosenstein is a very bright, decent young man." To which I would answer "Yes, sir, indeed he is and indeed I know it." And, if the truth be told notwithstanding the mistaken identity, I was secretly pleased to be viewed as Alex's friend.[233]

Volume nine published articles by John W. Durnford,[234] future namesake of the McGill Law Students Association's (LSA) John W. Durnford Teaching Excellence Award and future Dean of McGill Law; Ivan L. Head,[235] future Special Advisor to Prime Minister Pierre Trudeau and Founding Director of the Liu Institute for Global Issues at the University of British Columbia; future Minister of Revenue for Quebec, Minister of Public Works and Supply for Quebec, and President of the International Maritime Arbitration Society William Tetley;[236] and future Major General and Judge Advocate General of the United States Air Force Walter D. Reed.

Reading the end of Reed's case comment brings to the foreground the slowly growing relationship between technology and the law that would become so prominent as the decades moved by. He wrote,

> It would seem to this writer that it would be no large step for the law to recognize that there can be invasion of one's property by unseen or unheard forces travelling freely through the air. Once such a recognition takes place, the door is clearly open to examine the magnitude of a such an invasion to determine if, under minimum standards of our modern society, a person has effectively been deprived of a right to the use and enjoyment of his property.
>
> The Court in this case was not required under existing precedent to take notice of an invasion of property by sound waves. However, it is respectfully submitted that the facts and the law would have permitted the Court to entertain a theory of effective and substantial deprivation of the use and enjoyment of property through a regular and frequent invasion by intense sound levels ... the principles of reasonableness and simple justice will eventually required recognition of the invasion of property not only by movement of a mass but also by forces from other types of energy such as sound pressure waves, radio frequencies, and radioactivity.[237]

The case Reed was analyzing the effects of Air Force jet emissions on private property, producing "an oily film"[238] over residents' homes, as well as accompanying "[n]oise, dust, vibration, smoke, powerful lights, and flights through airspace at low altitude."[239] Yet it is easy to see the powerful implications from this analysis—ranging from modern noise curfews to intellectual property to surveillance methods all starting to bubble up within society as it moved into the 1960s.

During this decade, the *Journal* was known to enable its platform for the cause of either protestations or political commentary. In volume ten, the board wrote something that can be seen as a note placing pressure on the new Dean Maxwell Cohen to listen to growing student concerns about the relationship between students and faculty. Upon his appointment they strongly advocated on behalf of the law student government,[240] writing:

> Dean Cohen's considerable talents will again tackle those problems that persist in all law schools - the curriculum, academic standards and teaching personnel. We hope he will also explore areas which have not been thoroughly analysed, or even casually examined in

233 Alan Hustak, "Alex Konigsberg" *The Subburban* (2010), online: < http://www.thesuburbannews.ca/content/en/4568 >

234 John W Durnford, "The Redhibitory Action and the Reasonable Diligence of Article 1530 C.C." (1963) 9:1 *McGill LJ* 16.

235 Ivan L Head, "Canadian Claims to Territorial Sovereignty in the Arctic Regions" (1963) 9:3 *McGill LJ* 200.

236 William Tetley, "Selected Problems of Maritime Law under the Hague Rules" (1963) 9:1 *McGill LJ* 53.

237 Walter D Reed, "William J. Batten and Katie M. Batten, his wife, v. United States of America" Case and Comment (1963) 9:3 *McGill LJ* 246 at 253.

238 *Ibid* at 247.

239 *Ibid* at 248.

240 "Dean Frank R. Scott Retires," Editorial, (1964) 10:4 *McGill LJ* 290 at 290.

> the past. In this regard a brief prepared by the Law Undergraduate Society should be of particular interest. Student-faculty relations, a program for first year students, the examination system, lecture presentation and many other areas of vital concern were the object of an intensive survey last Spring. We are confident this challenging student project will be seriously considered by the new Dean.[241]

Volume ten's board consisted of many future heavy-weights. Editor-in-Chief Joseph J. Oliver would become President of the Investment Dealers Association of Canada and the Minister of Natural Resources in the Canadian Parliament; Managing Editor Barry H. Shapiro went on to place his name on the firm Robinson Sheppard Shapiro; Articles Editor C.J. Michael Flavell went on to found the Ottawa law firm Flavell Kubrick; Advertising Editor Irwin Cotler went on to become the Minister of Justice and Attorney General of Canada; Coordinating Editor Jean Bélanger went on to become a Professor at McGill Law; and fellow Coordinating Editor Gordon L. Echenberg would endow the McGill Center of Human Rights and Legal Pluralism with the money used to create the Echenberg Family Conference on Human Rights—a global conference that has been held twice since 2007 at McGill.

Articles published by volume ten included contributions from Laurent E. Bélanger,[242] future Justice of the Quebec Court of Appeal; future Justice of the Supreme Court of British Columbia J.J. Gow[243] (to whom volume thirteen Contributing Editor and future award winning screenwriter Lionel Chetwynd accredits his final decision to not become a lawyer); and Wilhelm Wengler,[244] future Director of the Institute for International Comparative Law at the Freie Universitat Berlin. Book reviews were also contributed by the likes of Brunson MacChesney,[245] who was then President of the American Society of International Law.

The politically aggressive attitude of the 1960s had certainly infused itself into some of this decade's editorial boards. In volume eleven perhaps the most interesting—and most direct—of all political appeals was published at the start of an issue. The short piece was labelled as an "editorial", but it was not written by members of the MLJ board. Instead, it was a letter written by a group called the Committee for Neutral Schools. The piece railed against religious and language specifications within the public school system in Montreal (and Quebec in general) of 1965; looking for equality for all children within the Quebec school systems.[246] It is easy enough to simply flip past this relic from the past—the group never effected major change in the political arena of the time, though it did stand up for several Montreal families in need.[247] However, in the spirit of Kaufman and his careful reviewing of the fine print and back pages of the MLJ, we read that the President of the Committee for Neutral Schools—with his name signed to the published piece—is none other than Henry Morgentaler.[248]

Published two years before Morgentaler took up the cause of the woman's right to choose, a cause that would forever alter women's rights in Canada, he and the MLJ were taking up the cause of equality within Quebec's educational system. Long before Morgentaler's landmark Supreme Court of Canada decisions—*R. v. Morgentaler* [1988] and *R. v. Morgentaler* [1993]—the editors of the MLJ saw something in his causes worth fighting for.

Two of the other names on that letter's short list of authors were also destined for future success. The person who signed the article as legal advisor for the group was Richard Gottlieb, founder of the Montreal law firm Gottlieb and Associates, near the beginning of his career. The other individual was Professor C.G. Gifford.[249] Gifford was a long time New Democrat Party candidate in Montreal during the 1960s and a Professor of Social Work at McGill, as well as future Director of the Maritime School of Social Work at Dalhousie University. In addition, after his role as a squadron leader during the Bombing of Dresden massacre during the Second World War, he would also go on to found the Veterans Against Nuclear Arms—a key advocacy group for the end of nuclear proliferation, long before it was popular.[250]

---

241 *Ibid.*

242 Laurent E Bélanger, "Corps administratif—bref de prérogative" (1964) 10:3 *McGill LJ* 217.

243 Hamesh Gow, "A Comment on the Warranty in Sale against Latent Defects" (1964) 10:3 *McGill LJ* 243.

244 Wilhelm Wengler, "The Meaning of Neutrality in Peacetime" (1964) 10:4 *McGill LJ* 369.

245 Brunston MacChesney, "*Law and Politics in Space* by Maxwell Cohen" Book Review (1964) 10:3 *McGill LJ* 269.

246 H Morgentaler, C Eddis, B Robinson, C Dobson, G Discenza, R Gottlieb, CG Gifford & B Chadwick, "Editorial" (1965) 11:2 *McGill LJ* 97 at 97-98.

247 Roderick MacLeod & Mary Anne Poutanen, *A meeting of the people: school boards and Protestant communities in Quebec, 1801 - 1998* (Montreal: McGill-Queen's University Press) at 344.

248 Morgentaler, *supra* note 245.

249 *Ibid.*

250 Andrew Pakula & Mark Pancer, "Interview with a Peacemaker-Veteran" *Peace Magazine* (December 1985) at 17.

Volume eleven also featured the first of two contributions to the MLJ of future Chief Justice of the Supreme Court of Canada Bora Laskin. In a review of the *British North America Act*, the predecessor to Canada's modern Constitution, Laskin harshly points out sections of the *Act* that no longer held "constitutional force",[251] of which—according to the future Chief Justice—there were many. The article reads like a more complexly-written formatting of the late George Carlin's bit about there only really being two commandments.[252]

Other articles within the volume included contributions from former Dean of Law at Aderdeen University T.B. Smith;[253] Michael Milde,[254] future Director of the Institute of Air and Space Law at McGill; the future Justice of the Quebec Superior Court and volume twelve Articles Editor William Fraiberg's first academic publication;[255] a book review was contributed by future Professor of Law Emeritus at the University of Ottawa Paul-Yvan Marquis;[256] in addition, the volume featured the first ever academic legal publication from volume twelve Editor-in-Chief Stephen A. Scott;[257] and the first ever academic publication from volume twelve Case Comments and Book Review Editor Armand de Mestral,[258] future Jean Monnet Chair in the Law of International Economic Integration at McGill University. Armand de Mestral spoke briefly about his experience publishing, stating that, "I contributed a case comment on a case that involved Indian rights and migratory birds, both of which interested me at the time as a matter of international law and domestic Constitutional law."[259]

Returning to volume ten's editorial note: Morgentaler's words read very similarly to the contemporary philosophy of McGill Law itself. The Committee wrote that they wanted "schools which will prepare our children to live in a pluralist society, where they can sit together with children differing in religion, nationality, colour, and background, to learn mutual respect and trust in spite of all differences; where brotherhood, tolerance, and unity in diversity may become a living reality."[260] McGill Law was a very different place in the 1960s than it was today, however.

As Justice Morris Fish explained,

> McGill, generally and of the law school… was a very different place as you know. We were only about 45 students in our graduating class. We started out with 75 or so but at that time there was attrition. I gave two convocation speeches [since]. At one of them I mentioned you get 1200-1400 applicants, most of them first rate and only 150 or so are admitted. In my time, all you needed was 50% +1 and you were in but then about a third would fail. But then maybe those who were admitted, some never made it to the law school probably because they couldn't find it; this one little Chancellor Day Hall, set back, and people walking up and down Peel street for hours, maybe days [trying to find it], and then, deciding on a less challenging profession, and they became a dentist.[261]

Indeed, finding the Faculty of Law at McGill as a freshman can still be a daunting task today, even with its larger campus up at the tree line of Mont Royal. The *Journal* also appears in many ways to have evolved at that point to something similar to what you can see today. Fish stated further that,

> When I was a law student we did try to accomplish at least two things. One was to make a contribution to legal thinking for the benefit of academics and lawyers alike, and the other was to attempt on a more practical level to assist the limited number of practitioners; to give them access to some academic thinking and to provide it in an accessible, comprehensible format. And so I think that perhaps I'm being too kind to ourselves, but I do think that was in our minds then and now; I … see the contribution of the *McGill Law Journal* and others over time and what an impressive resource they provide for legal

251 Bora Laskin, "Amendment of the Constitution: Applying the Fulton-Favreau Formula" (1965) 11:1 *McGill LJ* 2 at 6-9.

252 George Carlin, *When Will Jesus Bring the Pork Chops?* (New York: Hyperion, 2004) 32-38.

253 TB Smith, "Public Interest and Safeguards for the Suspect" (1965) 11:1, *McGill LJ* 43.

254 Michael Milde, "Conflicts of Laws in the Law of the Air" (1965) 11:3, *McGill LJ* 220.

255 William Fraiberg, "Brazeau Transport Ltee v. Canadian Pacific *Railway*" Case and Comment in (1965) 11:4, *McGill LJ* 378.

256 Paul-Yvan Marquis, "Traité Théorique et Pratique de la Communauté de Biens by Roger Comtois" Book Review (1965) 11:4 *McGill LJ* 372.

257 Stephen A Scott, "Saumur v. the Attorney-General for Quebec" Case and Comment (1965) 11:1 *McGill LJ* 88.

258 ALC de Mestral, "Michael Sikyea v. Her Majesty the Queen" Case and Comment (1965) 11:2 *McGill LJ* 168.

259 Interview of Armand de Mestral by James Cummins (2 December, 2011).

260 Morgentaler, *supra* note 245.

261 Fish interview, *supra* note 220.

analysis—for decision-making too.[262]

Another Articles Editor from the 1960s was David O'Brien (volume eleven) who would go on to become Chairman of the Royal Bank of Canada and Chancellor of Concordia University in Montreal. In terms of his continuing relationship with McGill, in 2004 O'Brien granted a generous endowment to the McGill Center for Human Rights and Legal Pluralism, creating the O'Brien Fellowships for Human Rights and Legal Pluralism that bring graduate scholars from all over the world to study at McGill. O'Brien discussed one of the other tasks of the Articles Editor of the time beyond soliciting articles—deciding whether or not the articles received were publishable, as this was before law journals in Canada used peer reviews to determine publishability. In a 2010 interview he stated that the process of article selection went as follows:

> As I recall … I think in most cases I simply did it, unless there was a subject matter that—which was usually the case—I didn't feel really comfortable with; in which case I sought out another view and not necessarily another view from someone else working on the *Law Journal* … when articles were submitted, being a law student, you were not yet fully formed as a lawyer and then to be able to assess both the scholarship and the relevancy was a bit of a challenge … If I recall I consulted a fair amount as opposed to doing much original research.[263]

When asked what kinds of articles he thought was important to have in the *Journal* over time, he replied that, "I think it's important from time to time to have special issues on a given topic that cover it from various angles and I would encourage that some of it be of the broader nature, just as I have an interest in human rights; that it cover not just technical, legal issues but also broader societal issues."[264] Other members of the volume eleven editorial board included Co-ordinating Editor Joel I. Bell, who would become a founder of Petro-Canada and principal economic advisor to Prime Minister Pierre Trudeau.

Returning to O'Brien's theme, special issues have been a hallmark of the MLJ over the last sixty years. As the MLJ only returned to a four issue format in volume five, it is not surprising (in anything, perhaps, but the earliness of its occurrence) that the first special issue was edited by volume seven—the same volume that tried to implement the use of editorial notes as a platform for the social views of the editorial board. Issue three of the volume appeared in 1961, featuring articles by five scholars of substantial weight: Dean Maxwell Cohen; future Supreme Court Justice Gerald E. Le Dain; sitting Justice (at the time) and future Chief Justice of the Supreme Court of Canada Gérald Fauteux; A.L. Stein, who successfully argued the landmark *Roncarelli v. Duplessis* before Justice Fauteux and his fellow Supreme Court justices two years earlier alongside McGill luminary FR Scott; and Jean-Charles Bonenfant, namesake of the future Jean-Charles Bonenfant Foundation—which is chaired by the President of the National Assembly in Quebec to this day—and former Head Librarian of the Quebec Legislature.

The special issue was on "Legal Education". Cohen, who would set into motion all that McGill Law is today during his future tenure as Dean, wrote in his article of the era in which he would effect that change, stating that, "To a large extent … the civilian and common law points of view about scholarship and lawyership now seems to be moving closer together … Perhaps even more significant has been the considerable attention in the common law world within the past two generations to problems of legal theory and philosophy."[265] The poignancy of this comment in the context of what would become of McGill Law over the forty years following the publication of this article, is substantial. In this one excerpt we find the driving factor of more than four decades of legal education and scholarship, and the underlying educational philosophy of one of McGill's most influential scholars. This is the kind of value that O'Brien was speaking of when he touched on the idea of special issues.

Le Dain wrote in his article of the lifelong event that is legal education:

> The formation and cultivation of the lawyer—that is, his legal education—is a life-long process … The fact that at any particular stage a man must talk and act as if he knows what he is doing cannot conceal from him the awareness that he is still learning and growing. Some will tell you that it takes a certain minimum time, such as twenty-five years, to make a lawyer. In the absence of clients we may confess

262 *Ibid.*

263 Interview of David O'Brien by James Cummins (16 December, 2010).

264 *Ibid.*

265 Maxwell Cohen, "Lawyers and Learning: The Professional and Intellectual Traditions" (1961) 7:3 *McGill LJ 181* at 183.

> the hope that even this much time may prove sufficient.[266]

He also wrote that, "We must face the fact that we cannot reproduce in the classroom many of the conditions of professional life which test and strengthen the mental qualities that we seek to foster ... At best we can simulate or provide satisfactory substitutes for some of the conditions."[267] Over two pages in this one article, the future Justice managed to highlight two major problems that legal education faces, and of which law journals are part of the solution: the life long education of lawyers through reading journals, and the early education of the stresses and creativity required in practicing the law through the student-editing of law journals.

The Honourable Gérald Fauteux wrote about the interaction between law schools and the bar, something that the same volume he was publishing in had criticized in an editorial note to be published in the following issue. In a rare French contribution to the MLJ of the time, Justice Fauteux argued that it was time that the bar association was no longer purely in charge of educating lawyers past the end of law school.[268] This is, of course, something that would come to fruition over the years—as the Quebec Bar would begin accepting required educational hours from university-based events and courses as a part of their *formation continue* program. Fauteux argued for a combination of bar association and faculty of law attempts to keep lawyers informed past the end of their law degree.[269]

Stein wrote in his article that the most lacking aspect of legal education at the time was in the training of students for the

> every-day type of civil case which he will encounter most frequently during his first years ... Without such knowledge and the proper preparation, on that nervous, exciting morning when he enters into legal combat with a learned and usually much more experienced adversary, there is little hope for judgment in his client's favour ... Often at this point, the die is already cast.[270]

Again, we see here a contribution from a legendary litigator that may never have been passed on beyond the confines of his own firm if it was not for the idea of special issues. It is advice of the kind that Le Dain was talking about in his own article. Bonenfant's piece, which followed Stein's, exposed the virtues and importance of teaching Roman law.[271]

Stein's partner in arguing *Roncarelli v. Duplessis* may not have gone to McGill Law while there was a legal publication to enable his early interest in legal writing, but he was able to publish within the *Journal*'s first volumes on three different occasions. FR Scott's articles in volumes two, three, and six, ranged over the subject matter of tax law,[272] labour law,[273] and public law.[274] Two of these articles were published before the *Roncarelli* case, and one soon afterwards. Though being published in the MLJ was not likely as big of an event in his life as having the legendary Leonard Cohen add music to and sing Scott's poem "A Villanelle for Our Time". All articles were published before he was made Dean.

Scott did make substantial contributions to the MLJ as an author. Perhaps only he could take a tax law argument—as he did in volume two of the MLJ—and turn it into a case for greater Canadian dependence from the Crown. As he wrote,

> The dry bones of constitutional law are not the living flesh of Canadian politics. The problems involved in taxation agreements reach far beyond the ground covered in an analysis of legal rules... What is the nature of the B.N.A. Act? Is it a statute or a compact? ... If it is a compact, between whom was it made; between the four original provinces, between all the provinces and the Dominion, or simply, as the prevalent theory in Quebec seems to maintain, between races?[275]

In one sweeping section, he was able to touch on many things that would dominate the next fifty years of both Canadian history and the published pages of the MLJ: the right of Quebec to its own nation, the need for a new Canadian Constitution, and the balance of

266 Gerald E LeDain, "Theory and Practice of Legal Education" (1961) 7:3 *McGill LJ* 192 at 195.

267 *Ibid* at 196.

268 Gérald Fauteux, "Le Barreau et Les Facultes de Droit" (1961) 7:3 *McGill LJ* 203 at 204.

269 *Ibid* at 205.

270 AL Stein, "Practical Training for Trial of Civil Cases" (1961) 7:3 *McGill LJ* 207 at 209.

271 Jean-Charles Bonenfant, "L'Ensiegnement du Droit Romain" (1961) 7:3 *McGill LJ* 213 at 213-14.

272 FR Scott, "Constitutional Background of Taxation Agreements" (1955) 2:1 *McGill LJ* 1.

273 FR Scott, "Federal Jurisdiction over Labour Relations--A New Look" (1960) 6:3 *McGill LJ* 153.

274 FR Scott, "Areas of Conflict in the Field of Public Law and Policy" (1956) 3:1 *McGill LJ* 1.

275 FR Scott 1955, *supra* note 271 at 8-9.

powers between Ottawa and the provincial capitals from St. John's to Victoria. The man who wrote of Scott's early dabbling in the editorial life, John P Humphrey, also graced the pages of the MLJ as an author, though not until 1971.[276] Humphrey was, however, Faculty Advisor to the MLJ for volumes fifteen and sixteen (1969-70).

Pierre Trudeau's article was included in the second special issue the MLJ would assemble. In issue two of volume eight, it sat alongside four other articles making up the special issue focusing on civil rights. Perhaps no better synopsis for the reason behind this issue was that quoted from Trudeau's article earlier in this book. However, the *Journal* did admonish the limits of a special issue in that issue's introductory editorial note, writing that, "To do justice to the whole sphere of civil rights in a single issue of a journal, to present both sides of all the issues which may arise, is an editorial impossibility."[277]

Volume twelve would also include a special issue, led by Stephen A Scott, who would go on to become the Faculty Advisor for the MLJ three years after his tenure, serving in the position alongside Professor John P Humphrey, and publish two articles in the MLJ that were cited in Supreme Court of Canada decisions.[278] Other future luminaries on his board included Executive Editor Jean-Paul Hubert, Jr. (future Canadian Ambassador to Senegal, Belgium, Luxembourg, Argentina, Paraguay, Switzerland, and Lichtenstein), Circulation Editor Gerald Nemiroff (Professor Emeritus at Robson Hall), and Case Comment and Book Review Editor Armand de Mestral.

In an interview regarding his time on the *Journal*, Professor Stephen Scott outlined an inside look into his MLJ, which fell dead in the centre of the 1960s. Scott related that, "Now we look at this as very early years, but then—when you're that age—you look at a journal which is ten years old as a fairly old thing."[279] Asked how he became Editor-in-Chief, Scott replied that, "I was surprised at the meeting to find that my colleagues had elected me as Editor[-in-Chief] ... and I became so busy with *Journal* that I despaired of getting good grades in my third year—and I was totally amazed that I did and managed to get the medal."[280]

Scott continued, remembering that,

> We were a small group. We didn't have a lot of money. We did everything—so I tramped around town persuading lawyers to give us a cheque for a little box ad, we charged next to nothing for those. One of the lawyers was a bit of a tacky fellow ... he tried to kind of talk me into giving him a half a box for half of next to nothing ...
>
> I basically took a view as a tolerant editor. There's an article in there by a guy called Antaki[281] from Egypt, and he wanted all his paragraphs numbered, which was not our style at all. But if you look at it, the paragraphs are numbered, because I said we can be tolerant—I wasn't obsessed with imposing style ...
>
> We did everything. I would drive to pick up the boxes [of issues] ... then we would all put them in envelopes, and I would drive the stuff to the post office, which was downtown. It was all a somewhat primitively done cooperative group effort.[282]

Scott also recalled a specific story where,

> We got [Walter Gellhorn] who was a big guru on ombudsmen at Columbia, I got a piece from him on the Danish Ombudsman,[283] and he wanted a lot of off-prints—and off-prints would be expensive from our printer ... it was much cheaper to get full issues printed than off-prints. So I arrived at Columbia in my car, went up to his office, and dumped down this big box of entire issues in his office.[284]

Gellhorn was the Betts Professor of Law at Columbia University. Other authors of note within volume twelve included the first academic publication of Alan Lutfy,[285] junior board member and future Chief Justice of the Federal Court of Canada.

Next, Scott talked about the volume's special issue, which was on the search for a constitutional amendment process going on in Canada during those years. As he explained, the focus they placed on this issue blazed trails that otherwise may never have been

276 John P Humphrey, "Main Functions of the United Nations in the Year 2,000 A.D." (1971) 17:1 *McGill LJ* 219.

277 "Editorial Notes" (1962) 8:2 *McGill LJ* 75 at 75.

278 See Appendix A.

279 Interview of Stephen A Scott by James Cummins (9 November, 2011).

280 *Ibid.*

281 Kamil Antaki, "Garde de structure et garde de comportement" (1966) 12:1 *McGill LJ* 41 at ff.

282 Scott interview, *supra* note 278.

283 Walter Gellhorn, "The Ombudsman in Denmark" (1966) 12:1 *McGill LJ* 1 at ff.

284 Scott interview, *supra* note 278.

285 Alan Lutfy, "Creditor's Recourse for Deterioration of Immovable Security" (1966) 12:3 *McGill LJ* 327.

opened up during the later years of the process. He recalled that,

> It was delayed and delayed and delayed because people weren't doing stuff, and I was very determined to have a comprehensive set of interesting stuff. There's a piece by Guy Favreau[286] there which is in fact cited in the second patriation reference on conventions.[287] I was at a conference in Ottawa—those were his speaking notes from a constitutional law conference at the University of Toronto, and that was the *last copy*. We published that, otherwise it would have been lost forever, and it ends up being cited by the Supreme Court on his views as to whether or not the conventions required unanimity. So you just never know.

Guy Favreau had recently been the Attorney General and Minister of Justice for Canada, and had died only months before publication at the age of fifty, and as a newly appointed Justice of the Quebec Superior Court. He is also the namesake of the Guy-Favreau Complex in downtown Montreal.

In addition to articles, the issue also contained what is likely Scott's first genuine contribution to Canadian legal scholarship. At the start of the issue are thirty pages where, after his own thorough research, Scott pieced together the entire history of how the issue of finding a constitutional amendment formula arose and developed over the span of 1960 to 1967. From speeches given in the House of Commons to opinion columns in major Canadian newspapers, it tells the story of how Canada began to finally move towards its own Constitution. Scott recalled that,

> [Eugene A.] Forsey was supposed to give me a comprehensive introductory history, but he gave me a short piece...[288] and I was extremely frustrated because a wanted a *history* of the *events*. So I decided I would do that myself... I called it the "Editor's Diary"[289] and Bill Lederman, who was later Dean at Queen's and who was quite prominent in constitutional law all these years (I thought he was an old fussbudget frankly, but a scholar of prominence), said that it was a useful device ...
>
> What's interesting about that is that as people have pointed out through the years, that [the piece] is the best, easiest, and perhaps only way to find your way through the tangle of events through those years. For example, [the process] all got entangled into whether or not Quebec could reform the legislative council before having an amending formula which eliminated London. Because once London was eliminated, the legislative council could block any unilateral provincial amendments (changing the constitution of the province) and it could block any Federal amendment given the structure of the Fulton-Favreau formula ... A lot of people never quite understood what that was all about, but I have all the stuff in there about that.
>
> What's interesting about that too is that I could do that kind of thing because it was so recent; the course of events were so fresh in my mind as to what happened. I could go to newspapers and get history; I could go to the Canadian news archive... and I have a few things out of that, citing them. [For] legislative debates, I could look at the indexes. I knew basically what had happened and could construct that over those years. But that would be virtually impossible now for anybody who is not spending a couple of years doing that for a doctoral thesis, because you just wouldn't have known and you would have to go blindly. I could not myself do it now and I couldn't have done it ten years after I did do it.[290]

Volume twelve Case Comments and Book Review Editor Armand de Mestral also commented on the special issue, noting that,

> It was a time when Constitutional change was very, very much in the air. A lot of it focused on Constitutional amendment, so under Scott's leadership we held a conference ... It was one of the first in a long series of conferences and collections of papers either in journals or

286 Guy Favreau, "Constitutional Amendment in a Canadian Canada" (1966-67) 12:4 *McGill LJ* 384.

287 See Appendix A.

288 Eugene A Forsey, "Provincial Requests for Amendments to the B.N.A. Act" (1966-67) 12:4 *McGill LJ* 397.

289 Stephen A Scott, "Editor's Diary: The Search for an Amending Process 1960-67" (1966-67) 12:4 *McGill LJ* 337.

290 Scott interview, *supra* note 278.

> books that started dealing with what for a long time people called the "Constitutional crisis"—they still call it the Constitutional crisis, though it's gone away, seemingly... it certainly hasn't been rendered completely innocuous even today. It was a very big issue at the time, and remained so for at least another twenty or thirty years... The people who had come were the people who wrote papers—a mixture of legal scholars and political people.[291]

Of those people in the special issue were two separate Justices for the Supreme Court of Canada. Former Justice of the Supreme Court of Canada R.L. Kellock wrote, as Laskin did one volume prior, of the interpretation of the *B.N.A. Acts*. Kellock, at this point approximately ten years past his time with the SCC (Laskin wrote his words while still four years away from appointment), spends the piece writing back-and-forth to Scott. In the dialogue Scott implores former Justice Kellock to view the then-constitutional acts of Canada through what he sees as a "hopelessly paradoxical"[292] lens. Justice Kellock very kindly disagrees with the then-Editor-in-Chief, pointing out his different interpretation of the situation.[293] It is clear that Justice Kellock, unlike Laskin, had greater faith in the B.N.A. Acts that stood up until 1982. However, later articles by future Justices of the Supreme Court of Canada in the MLJ do appear to be more in line with the early pronunciations of Stephen Scott and Laskin—as will be seen over the course of this book.

The other Justice of the Supreme Court of Canada published in volume twelve was not yet appointed to the SCC and was then still a Professor of Law at the Université Laval: Justice Louis-Philippe Pigeon. The Justice's article fell within five pages of Kellock's piece in the volume. Pigeon discusses the use of the Fulton-Favreau formula to dissect the ability for Canada to amend its constitution at the time, in a method similar to how Laskin had done in his article published one year prior.[294] However, Pigeon offers a novel method of working around the ancient constitutional documents, and creating what would effectively be constitutional level changes indirectly rather than directly.[295]

After the end of Pigeon's article, Jacques-Yvan Morin was afforded a few pages of space himself in order to publish his response to Pigeon's words. The future leader of the Parti Quebecois and *Journal* founder argued vociferously with Pigeon over the ability for Quebec to be included in such discussions; insisting that the situation in Quebec was entirely different than the situation in other provinces.[296] It was almost as if, in this issue of the MLJ, the fight over the writing of a new Canadian constitution between Quebec and the rest of Canada was already being set fifteen years in advance.

Other authors within the special issue included future Federal Assistant Deputy Minister of Justice for Jean Chretien, B.L. Strayer;[297] William F. Ryan,[298] Dean of Law at the University of New Brunswick; Alexander Smith,[299] future namesake of The Smith Prize, given to the winner of the Laskin Moot; future Distinguished Professor Emeritus of Law at Robson Hall Dale Gibson;[300] Frank MacKinnon,[301] the Principal and Vice-Chancellor of Prince of Wales College in Prince Edward Island; future Downing Professor of the Laws of England Stanley Alexander de Smith;[302] and Geoffrey Marshall,[303] future Provost of Queen's College at Oxford University.

The final advice Scott culled from his experience as editor and future academic he summarized by saying, "You mustn't be parochial; you mustn't think you know better than everybody else; and you must have a sense of humour!"[304]

Fellow editors on Scott's staff included Managing Editor Charles E. Flam, who would become Managing Partner and Chief Executive Officer at Robinson

291 De Mestral interview, *supra* note 258.

292 RL Kellock and Stephen A Scott, "Correspondence with and Opinion of Hon. R. L. Kellock, Q.C. on Certain Questions of Interpretation" (1966-67) 12:4 *McGill LJ* 424 at 426.

293 *Ibid* at 424-30.

294 Louis-Philippe Pigeon, "Le Sens De La Formule Fulton-Favreau" (1966-67) 12:4 *McGill LJ* 403 at 403; Laskin 1965, *supra* note 250 at 2.

295 Pigeon *supra* note 293 at 416-17.

296 Jacques-Yvan Morin & Louis-Philippe Pigeon, "Un Extrait Du Debat Pigeon-Morin" (1966-67) 12:4 *McGill LJ* 420 at 421-22.

297 BL Strayer, "Saskatchewan and the Amendment of the Canadian Constitution" (1966-67) 12:4 *McGill LJ* 443.

298 William F Ryan, "The Fulton-Favreau Formula in New Brunswick" (1966-67) 12:4 *McGill LJ* 474.

299 Alexander Smith, "The Fulton-Favreau Formula in Alberta" (1966-67) 12:4 *McGill LJ* 476.

300 Dale Gibson, "The Fulton-Favreau Formula in Manitoba" (1966-67) 12:4 *McGill LJ* 485; "Constitutional Amendment and the Implied Bill of Rights" (1966-67) 12:4 *McGill LJ* 497.

301 Frank MacKinnon, "Prince Edward Island and the Amendment Formula" (1966-67) 12:4 *McGill LJ* 487.

302 AS de Smith, "The Separation of Powers in New Dress" (1966-67) 12:4 *McGill LJ* 491.

303 Geoffrey Marshall, "Parliamentary Sovereignty: A Recent Development" (1966-67) 12:4 *McGill LJ* 523.

304 Scott interview, *supra* note 278.

Sheppard Shapiro LLP; Executive Editor Jean-Paul Hubert Jr., who would become President of Rights and Democracy; Circulation Editor Gerald Nemiroff, who would become a Professor of Law Emeritus at Robson Hall; and Case Comments and Book Review Editor Armand de Mestral.

Volume thirteen published a special issue on the subject of the habitual criminal. The introduction to this issue, however, began a new tradition of prefacing the special issues of the *McGill Law Journal*. Beforehand, the editorial board had taken care of trying to synthesize the reason behind the issue. For this particular special issue, the preface was instead written by the Chief Justice of the Supreme Court of Canada, the Honourable Robert Taschereau. The preface was before his retirement, and published around the time he was to step down.

The Chief Justice wrote of the issue's topic that,

> This question is one of paramount importance and the contributors to this volume will be rendering a very great service to the profession and the public at large.
>
> In all efforts to improve the laws and their adjustments to new conditions, society needs the expert knowledge and the sympathetic understanding of the Bar. Acknowledging this to be a truism, the great work of the administration of justice and the development of the law have been entrusted to the legal profession. Changes in the law largely take place on the advice of the profession and, as a rule, such advice is followed by the legislators.
>
> A study of the criminal law as it affects the habitual criminal and preventive detention is under constant and searching scrutiny. I am confident that the views expressed in this number by the eminent academicians and practitioners will be read with much interest by the profession, legislators and the general public, *and such views may very well influence the course of future legislation.*[305]

The Chief Justice would be right. Two years after the issue was published, the *Ouimet Report* would recommend the abolishment Canada's *Habitual Criminal Act*,[306] and in 1977 the *Act* would be struck down in Parliament. Authors that were a part of the special issue that were cited by the *Report* included both Norval Morris[307] and Denis Szabo,[308] though the two-year-old issue was not specifically cited. Morris's article "The Habitual Criminal" was however cited in the 1987 Supreme Court of Canada decision *R v. Lyons*, where the Justice Gerard LaForest wrote that, "Morris ... observes that a number of countries have enacted legislation to deal with incorrigible or habitual offenders, and notes ... that generally three elements are included in the definition of the group targeted for such punishment—criminal qualities inherent or latent in the mental constitution, a settled practice in crime, and a public danger."[309] What influence the issue had beyond these very direct and on-the-record instances, was likely robust for it to the have spread this far.

The special issue included an article by George P. Springate,[310] who was a second year law student at the time as well as a long-serving police officer. He would go on to play in the Canadian Football League for the Montreal Alouettes, winning the Grey Cup in 1970, and be elected to the National Assembly of Quebec, where he served for eight years. Later he would become a founder of the Police Technology program at John Abbott College—an institution named for one of the first Deans of McGill Law.

There was also a section at the end of the issue dedicated to a comparison of different jurisdictions around the world, inviting contributors to record their own region's legislation and statutes dealing with the matter of habitual criminals. Contributors to the section included Harry P. Glassman,[311] future Justice of the Supreme Court of Maine; future Earl F. Nelson and John D. Lawson Professor Emeritus of Law at the University of Missouri School of Law Edward H. Hunvald;[312] William Royal Ferguson,[313] then a law student at the University of Texas, and now a Federal Justice with the United States District Court for the Northern District of Texas; future Director of the Australian Institute of Criminology Duncan

305 Robert Taschereau, "Preface" (1967) 13:4 *McGill LJ* 532 at 533 [emphasis added].

306 Roger Ouimet, "Toward unity: criminal justice and corrections" Report (1969) Canadian Committee on Corrections, Queen's Printer.

307 *Ibid* at 428.

308 *Ibid* at 202.

309 *R v Lyons*, [1987] 2 SCR 309 at para 33..

310 George P Springate, "A Police Officer's View of the Habitual Criminal" (1967) 13:4 *McGill LJ* 648.

311 Harry P Glassman, "The Maine Habitual Offender Statute" (1967) 13:4 *McGill LJ* 653.

312 Edward H Hunvald, "Missouri Habitual Criminal Statute" (1967) 13:4 *McGill LJ* 656.

313 W Royal Ferguson, "The Law of Recidivism in Texas" (1967) 13:4 *McGill LJ* 663.

Chappell;[314] and N.R. Medhava Menon,[315] who would become the founder/Director of the National Law School of India University in Bangalore, founder/ Vice-Chancellor of the West Bengal National University of Juridical Sciences in Calcutta, and founder/ Director of the National Judicial Academy in Bhopal, where Indian judges are trained.

Authors that contributed to the rest of the volume included Alfred Avins,[316] future Dean of Widener Law and founder as well as Dean of Delaware Law School; future Director of Research and Treaties at the United Nations Office of the High Commissioner for Human Rights Maxime Tardu;[317] future drafter of the *Nova Scotia Trade Union Act* and the *Nova Scotia Labour Standards Code*, Innis Christie;[318] René Dussault,[319] future Justice of the of the Quebec Court of Appeal; and former Dean of Law at the University of Ottawa Pierre Azard.[320]

Before looking at the Editorial Board that solicited and prepared this monumental list of authors, an overview of the volumes that would follow volume thirteen is helpful. The next few volumes were very special for the *McGill Law Journal*, both at the time and well into the future. Volume seventeen marked the first of two times that John Humphrey would publish full articles in the MLJ, with a 1971 article entitled "Main Functions of the United Nations in the Year 2,000 A.D.", which he wrote after returning to McGill Law as a professor following his twenty-year career with the United Nations (his first short piece would be a one page book review published in 1968).[321] Having spent this time in the thick of the most complicated global problems of the twentieth century, he had the following to say,

> One of the reasons why we study the past and analyze the present is to prepare for the future. It may well be, of course, that this world has no future, that we are reaching the time when, more or less rapidly, the life which eons ago began to assert himself in the slimes of the oceans, having flowered in what we call civilization, will utterly disappear and the Earth will no longer be distinguished among all the planets as the sole depositary of life. Somewhere else in the solar system the drama may be repeated or - for all we know - may be going on now. But our Earth will be as dead as the moon. A rigidly logical observer considering the evidence before him might indeed reach such a conclusion. But one of the characteristics of the kind of men and women which inhabit this planet is that they are seldom logical. Most of them, moreover, possess a spark of optimism; and this optimism has always been an important factor in helping the race muddle through its difficulties, however hopeless they may seem. It is in that spirit of optimistic illogicality that the present essay is written.[322]

It was up to the world to prove Humphrey's "logic" wrong, and in many ways, it did. From the bringing of Soviet Bloc nations into NATO, to the (perhaps rocky) democratization of Russia, to the bringing of capitalism to China and the (perhaps slow) economic liberalization of India, the world has not teetered on a threat of total global war since the late 1980s. In fact, modern globalization has produced a world where nations are in many ways intractably intertwined. It is a world that Humphrey foresaw as even more hopeful than what he saw then as our only choice, when he wrote,

> [B]arring some quite unforeseen and unlikely conjecture which would force the superpowers to unite their efforts in common defence, the overall picture is likely to be substantially the same in the year 2000 A.D. as it is now and was indeed in 1945; and it would be unwise to base our planning for the future on any other assumption. There is, in any event, no compelling reason for thinking that,

314 Duncan Chappell, "Australian Habitual Offender Legislation" (1967) 13:4 *McGill LJ* 673.

315 NR Medhava Menon, "A Note on the Law and Practice Relating to Habitual Criminals in India" (1967) 13:4 *McGill LJ* 675.

316 Alfred Avins, "Freedom of Choice in Organizations in the British Commonwealth" (1967) 13:2 *McGill LJ* 309.

317 Maxime Tardu, "L'Individu et l'Etat en Afrique Tropicale" (1967) 13:2 *McGill LJ* 277.

318 Innis Christie, "Inducing Breach of Contract in Trade Disputes: Development of the Law in England and Canada" (1967) 13:1 *McGill LJ* 101.

319 René Dussault, "Legislative Limitations on the Court's Power to Review Administrative Action in Quebec" (1967) 13:1 *McGill LJ* 23.

320 Pierre Azard, "Vers une normalisation souhaitable des rapports entre la profession et la faculté dans le domaine de l'enseignement du droit" (1967) 13:1 *McGill LJ* 152.

321 John P Humphrey, "Journal of the International Commission of Juriste: Special Issue for the International Year for Human Rights ed. by Sean MacBride" Book Review (1968) 14:2 *McGill LJ* 349.

322 Humphrey 1971, *supra* note 275 at 219.

> in the light of past and current trends, the great powers and particularly the two superpowers - there may then be three which would only compound the difficulties - will be better able to cooperate in security matters 25 years from now than they have in the past. So that however pessimistic it may be, the conclusion seems to be inescapable that in the foreseeable future as in the past, the United Nations will not be able to perform its primary function of maintaining international peace and security.[323]

Exactly what drove Canada and the world away from Humphrey's darker predictions about the world towards a more sustainable future can be seen in the article that opened the first issue of volume seventeen: a piece by future Prime Minster John Turner, the man who would take the reins of the Liberal Party of Canada from Pierre Trudeau. His article, "Law for the Seventies: A Manifesto for Law Reform", discusses how the 1960s produced many things that the MLJ would comment on over the next forty years; and like Le Dain's premier article in 1952, Turner discusses a moment of world altering change, though this time for Canada as a whole:

> It is not surprising … that some have even called the Sixties the Age of the Apocalypse. Nations stockpiled weapons in the name of peace. Political leaders yawned the rhetoric of brotherhood while waging war. Governments destroyed cities in order to save them. Economies accumulated wealth and distributed poverty. Technology controlled man rather than released him. Corporate bureaucracies denied individuality while proclaiming it. The gross national product became Marcuse's One Dimensional Man.[324]

In the face of globalization, mass social changes, and a worsening Cold War, then-Minister of Justice Turner alerted us to a "crisis of authority",[325] pointing out that, "All our institutions – the state, the university, the family, and, of particular concern to us tonight, the law – are being challenged."[326] He admitted that the past decade had created "a revolutionary climate"[327] and that law in the modern world was quickly becoming nothing more than "a false consciousness".[328] To that end, he wrote that, "The problems of the Sixties are now the legal challenges of the Seventies. Society itself has become the lawyer's client, and society will hold the law to account."[329]

Simply put, John Turner stated, "The law must never stand still again."[330]

The *McGill Law Journal* had become a Canadian institution in many ways at this point, but what future lied before it? These foreboding ideas of the future appear to have taken a wide berth from the more hope-based challenge that Chief Justice Rinfret posed in 1956, now less than fifteen years past that time. To begin finding the answer to that question, we need look no further than those that served on the editorial boards of the MLJ, for example, the board of volume thirteen—which allows us to return to our point of brief departure.

The senior board of volume thirteen included future Justice of the Alberta Court of Appeal Ronald L. Berger as Special Features Editor; future Chief Justice of the Federal Court Alan Lutfy as Articles Editor; Vincent Prager, future winner of the Queen's Jubilee Medal, as one of two Circulations Editors; Irwin Rudich, future President of the Lord Reading Law Society (2009-10), as fellow Contributing Editor; Michael Garonce, future Chair of the Commercial Real Estate section at McMillan LLP and President of the Lord Reading Law Society (1993-94), as Executive Editor; Douglas Pascal, future Vice President of Canderel, as Editor-in-Chief; Richard Pound as Managing Editor, who would go on to many prestigious positions, including Chancellor of McGill University, Vice-President of the International Olympic Committee, and President of the World Anti-Doping Agency; and Contributing Editor Lionel Chetwynd, who would be nominated for an Academy Award for Writing – Adapted Screenplay eight years later,[331] and go on to be awarded the Caucus of Writers, Producers and Directors Lifetime Achievement Award

323 Humphrey 1971, *supra* note 275 at 224.

324 John N Turner, "Law for the Seventies: A Manifesto for Law Reform" (1971) 17:1 *McGill LJ* 1 at 1-2.

325 *Ibid* at 2.

326 *Ibid* at 1-2.

327 *Ibid.*

328 *Ibid.*

329 *Ibid.*

330 *Ibid* at 9.

331 Chetwynd was nominated for his screen adaptation for the film "The Apprenticeship of Duddy Kravitz", alongside Mordecai Richler. They lost the category to "The Godfather Part II" written by Francis Ford Coppola and Mario Puzo. As an example of the incredible class of nominees that year, Gene Wilder and Mel Brooks were also nominated but lost See: "47th Academy Awards Winners and Nominees" *Oscars.com*, online: < http://www.oscars.org/awards/academyawards/legacy/ceremony/47th-winners.html >

in 2003 as well as the John Singleton Copley Medal from the National Portrait Gallery of the Smithsonian Museum in 2008.

Volume thirteen Advertising Editor Robert Vineberg, of the marquee family of Davies Ward Phillips and Vineberg LLP, would receive his first academic publication while on the board of volume thirteen, with a short article entitled "A Feasibility Study in the Computer Retrieval of the Law of Quebec or The Care and Feeding of Your Friendly Neighbourhood Legal Computer", in which the young student living on the edge of the information revolution wrote, perhaps presciently:

> Have you ever wished that there was a truly well-developed index of Quebec law that could lead you to all the jurisprudence relevant to a particular matter? Or have you ever spent hours poring through cases, searching for that one judgment directly on point? When one realizes that the jurisprudence of Quebec currently amounts to approximately 120,000,000 printed words, and is growing at a rate of 1,700,000 words per year, the enormous difficult of "thorough" legal research immediately becomes apparent. Luckily, the ultimate legal scholar is waiting on the steps of our profession ... He can read more in a minute than you can in a day, and he can print about fifteen times as quickly as the fastest legal stenographer ...
>
> Why is such a legal "wunderkind" not working for you right now? The problem is ... his education.[332]

Vineberg was talking about computers, which were not yet used in law on a very wide scale. He continues by stating that, during his time it was estimated that to create a computer that could search through all the jurisprudence of Quebec "would require approximately 15,000 man-days, at a projected cost of $250,000,"[333] and includes that "the cost of programming is at present virtually impossible to evaluate."[334] We now know that such an initial investment is a pittance compared to the gained efficiency of the computerized world—an efficiency far beyond Vineberg's early prediction of "a return on investment of approximately 25%."[335] Vineberg wrote that "computerization ... may signify a breathtaking achievement in the search for a modern and truly contemporary legal system."[336] As for that point he was spot on.

Alan Lutfy—Articles Editor for volume thirteen and future Chief Justice of the Federal Court of Canada—had his first academic publication in the prior volume, while serving on their junior board.[337] However in volume thirteen another *Journal* alumnus, Roy L. Heenan, appeared as an author in the MLJ, writing an article called, "Strikes, Picketing and Injunctions in Quebec". Heenan focuses on a subject matter where he says there is "a long history of violence and disorder"[338] as well as "[t]he mystique of the picket line"[339] within Quebec. Still, Heenan comes down against the general movement in the Province to lessen the rights of (legally) striking workers to picket.[340]

Perhaps the most storied future of all those involved with volume thirteen would belong to Managing Editor Richard Pound. In Ian Pilarczyk's history of McGill Law, Pound wrote about the atmosphere he and his fellow executives developed that year for the *Journal*, writing that, "The *McGill Law Journal* was just entering its teenage years ... We [had] as our objective getting the whole of Volume into print before Volume [12] was completed. There was a good deal of self-satisfied smirking from our team when [our objective was] achieved."[341]

In a 2010 interview, Pound took a more thorough look back at his time on the *Journal*. Discussing how he came to be selected as Managing Editor for his volume, he wrote,

> My recollection is that the various editors and staffers on the *Journal* decided on the Editor-in-Chief, the Associate (or whatever he was called) and the Managing Editor as a package, which was acceptable to all three of us. It was not as structured as it now appears to be and I had been an editor in the ordinary sense before becoming Managing Editor. The top three of us consulted regularly on both editorial and business matters. The Managing

332 Robert Vineberg, "A Feasibility Study in the Computer Retrieval of the Law of Quebec or The Care and Feeding of Your Friendly Neighbourhood Legal Computer" (1967) 13:3 *McGill LJ* 513 at 513.

333 *Ibid* at 514.

334 *Ibid* at 514-15.

335 *Ibid* at 515.

336 *Ibid.*

337 Alan Lutfy, "Creditor's Recourse for Deterioration of Immovable Security" (1966) 12:3 *McGill LJ* 327.

338 Roy L Heenan, "Strikes, Picketing and Injunctions in Quebec" (1967) 13:3 *McGill LJ* 367 at 381.

339 *Ibid* at 368.

340 *Ibid* at 371.

341 Pilarczyk, *supra* note 27at 131.

> Editor was not limited to the role of the "publisher" of the *Journal* in the classic division of responsibilities.[342]

He wrote further that,

> There are no "bad" memories at all. Some days were more challenging than others, but it was always fun ... I remember writing directly to Ian Smith of (then) Rhodesia, who had announced the unilateral declaration of independence (UDI), saying that I was certain that, as Attorney General, he would have had a legal basis for UDI and that we would be prepared to publish something on the point if he would care to submit it. He did not reply. I got several judges of the Quebec Court of Appeal to contribute articles, despite their general reluctance to publish anything besides their judgments...
>
> The usual rule of 80-20 (or 90-10) applied, in the sense that 80% of the work was done by 20% of the people. This is not at all uncommon in volunteer organizations. No academic credit was accorded to service on the *Journal*, so those of us who did it did it for fun and general interest in the law. We were having fun, so it was fun and not personally stressful at all.[343]

Credits would start being awarded to *Journal* members at some point between volume fourteen and volume eighteen. Though, according to the letter from the *Yale Law Journal* incorporated into the original MLJ Constitution, providing credits to journal members at other elite journals was commonplace even before the founding of the MLJ.[344]

Memories are in a sense all that is left of this era in the *Journal*'s history, asides of course from the printed volumes themselves. As Pound wrote, "I suspect that we were longer on enthusiasm than on having a sense of history that records of our activity should be saved for posterity."[345] To get the right picture of everything that was going on, one must envision the fashions and environment of the time. On that note, Stephen Scott recalled in a letter to Ian Pilarczyk that,

342 Interview of Richard Pound by James Cummins (23 November, 2010 - 31 October, 2011). This interview took place via email on the beginning and on the end dates cited)

343 *Ibid.*

344 See Appendix E.

345 *Ibid.*

> Armand de Mestral and I, while strolling one afternoon on lower campus, overheard one undergraduate remarking to another, "There go those law students in their three-piece suits." Yes, those Artsmen had our number! In the mid-sixties, student dress in law school was basically a business suit, maybe a sports jacket and tie if you wanted to dress down. Just before my exams in third year, however, a heat wave prompted a few—just a few—students to come to the law school in t-shirts, sweat shirts, and the like. [Maxwell] Cohen, by then Dean, paid a special visit to our class. He was virtually apoplectic, and harangued us about the traditions of student dress. Astonishingly, I don't remember him so visibly angry on any other occasion.[346]

Volume thirteen Contributing Editor Lionel Chetwynd recalled that this, however, was something quickly changing in the culture of both McGill Law and the *Journal*. He stated that,

> When someone says "*Journal*", I have in my mind an image of [Stephen] Scott and [Armand] de Mestral ... I came into law school at a very interesting time. I don't know where the dividing line is in terms of a year, but it might well have been our year ... the McGill law school had, for virtually all of its career, seen itself as (and correctly so, by the way, because it delivered the results), if you will, a "pedigreed institution". We didn't really have pedigreed institutions in Canada. We had elite schools—McGill being the principal amongst them—and in those days in the United States the Ivy [League] schools were elite, but they weren't pedigreed in the sense that Oxford and Cambridge were pedigreed. I eventually got to Oxford; I was up at Oxford [and] I was always stunned by that. The assumption was your mere presence on Broad Street meant you were going to be Prime Minister if you wished to be—it was only a matter of choice.
>
> If Canada had, for its first hundred-odd years, a pedigreed institution, it would have been the McGill law school.

346 Pilarczyk, *supra* note 27 at 130.

> It was the private domain of the barons of the "Square Mile", who had built the country—old Scottish families, with a small contingent of Anglo-Catholics. The Jewish presence at the law school had been minimal into the '50s ... it was a Cosa Nostra; it was a private kind of thing really. And the people who went to it, went on to become the captains of industry—of the legal profession certainly. Certainly a major responsibility was turning out the top tier of what would become the Bar in Montreal, which was at that time the only city of any significance in Canada ... it was the centre of gravity of public life, if you will.
>
> As Canada changed, things at the law school itself changed. There was no longer going to be a role for that kind of school ... and it was about that time that Max came: Max Cohen. And he had a broader vision for what the law school could become; and it is today what he envisioned it to be. He turned it into a major international school, he [was there at] the start of the Air and Space Institute, and so on ... Prior to Max, the role of the *Journal* was to identify the serious legal minds—the scholars; it was a matter of scholarship—and these people, a lot of them did end up in the Bar. They became the dominant Q.C.s; these were the great legal minds—not necessarily the ones that would become the "Stikemans" or the "Elliots", but they nonetheless would become the justices.
>
> Somewhere, as this all changed, the type of person who entered law school also changed. We were living through that. You had this huge population bubble coming through and for many a legal education was not the keys to the kingdom, but a trade certificate ... With the democratization of the population of the law school, it lost its exclusivity. So there came to the *Law Journal* people whose reasons for wanting to be on the *Journal* were not demonstrably scholarly. It wasn't that they were scholars or wanted to be seen as scholars, but they were laying down markers for a future career. It was, "Hey, I was on *Law Journal*!" because this was when you were gonna hear, "Hey, he was on law review; he was on law review!", from the States. And so it became an important *credential* in job seeking. And I really don't believe it had been seen [like] that prior...
>
> In all candour, I was probably [in] the second group; I wanted to be on *Law Journal* not because I was a legal scholar, truthfully I was not ... by the time I got to the second year (which was when these decisions were being made), I fairly well understood that I was never going to be a lawyer. I was temperamentally unsuited. I had a Professor called Hamish [James John] Gow ... who was from the University of Glasgow, and I once had a long talk with him and he said, "Look, law... *it's an organized system of ancestor worship, lad.* If you have no taste for that then you have no taste for law." And he talked to me candidly about the advantages to having a law degree—which was once a way to make a living, but was now a key to corporate life, all kinds of things. That was what was feeding these new people coming to law school...
>
> I knew that I wanted to move on and possibly wanted to go to the United States; I needed this credential ... I had the marks, I was on Scarlet Key; I was gathering all the things that a diligent young man trying to arm himself to take on the world had—but I needed law review.[347]

Chetwynd continued by stating that Stephen Scott and Armand de Mestral were of the old school[348] that existed before the change in McGill Law's environment, and that they were the ones most in charge of the *Journal*. He recalled that,

> I love them both. I remember with great affection that Stephen dressed like an English gentleman; Armand preferred tweeds, with knitted ties—professorial—and the *Law Journal* that they ran was probably a *high peak*, probably the peak of intellectual, scholarly, legal, juridical rigour and discipline in the history of the *Journal*. It was probably its best year. They could see what was going on ...

347 Interview of Lionel Chetwynd by James Cummins (29 November, 2011).

348 *Ibid.*

> My two closest friends in law school were Robert Vineberg, who was Laz Phillips's nephew and he was Phil Vineberg's son—Phillip Vineberg was one of the two or three most important law firms in Canada, and the one with the most important international [practice] … and Robert was the heir to that—the third generation. The other [one] was Norton Segal, and he used to make fun of Robert—there was a lot of teasing that would go on, he'd say "Ah, *you* go work for Uncle Laz, I'm gonna be the *king of the municipal court*. I'm gonna take all the guys with the traffic tickets, the immigration problems, I'm gonna have a lot of bills *this big*", you know, and he'd have us all laughing.[349]

Vineberg (as previously mentioned) was also on the *Journal*, serving as Advertising Editor during volume thirteen—Chetwynd's senior year. Michael Vineberg, of the same family, served as a Contributing Editor himself during volume fourteen.

Returning to Scott and de Mestral, Chetwynd continued, recalling that,

> They said that you [did] need to publish something in the second year in order to be an editor in the final year. So I went and I did something, something that honestly would have been published anywhere—it was a good piece! They turned it down—Armand and Stephen. Correctly so, by the way. Armand looked me in the eye, and he said "it's a fine piece" and he said "it could be published anywhere but it really doesn't rise" (I remember his words, it just stung) "it doesn't rise to the level of excellence in terms of scholarship"…
>
> There was a new Code of Procedure, and I was talking about substantive and adjectival law in the French and English systems—well that's a bullshit subject, but you can really make it sound good. They had very different systems: one was dealing with due process and one was dealing with result. The Europeans tended to judge whether a thing was fair by its outcome, the Anglo-Saxon system (in view the superior one) wanted to make sure the process was fair—if the process was fair, the outcome by definition was fair. It was a distinction, by the way, that stayed all my life in everything I do: what's more important, process or outcome?
>
> So that didn't need a lot of footnotes; that didn't need deep scholarship. That was as much an op-ed piece as it was a heavily footnoted, juridically argued point of view … It was really interesting, it was really good, but Armand said, "It does not rise to the level of competence and scholarly juridical rigour that we are going to acquire." Well if you didn't publish, you couldn't be on the Board! And we went back and forth, and back and forth, and in the end—as I recall—they excerpted part of it, and they published it (it was not really a full article) but it met the requirement for me to be called a "Contributing Editor"… and that was how I won my place on the law review …
>
> I was recently taken on a bit of a tour of the university, and I marvelled at how both Armand and Stephen maintained that kind of intellectual honesty through all their lives. I don't think it was ever as good again. They were the *last* of the era of the shirt and tie—we all wore shirts and ties and suits—that was coming to an end by the time I graduated. That time when people went to McGill as a sacred trust to be scholars of the law, and go on to be Canada's leaders, was being digested by a new ethos—which was "law is a good thing to have and you can get ahead anywhere with that."[350]

Chetwynd also recalled the culture of activism and change that existed at the Faculty in those days, remembering that,

> I was deeply involved then—the thing that was taking up my space and my time—with those students who were resisting UGEQ.[351] That was the period when

349 *Ibid.*

350 *Ibid.*

351 L'Union Générale des Etudiants du Québec—an organization of students unions exclusive to Quebec institutions of higher learning, which sought to draw the membership of Quebec student unions away from the Canadian Union of Students—whose members came from across Canada.

> [Student Society of McGill President] Sharon Sholzberg took McGill out of the [Canadian Union of Students], and moved us into the French language organization. I opposed that, as I opposed almost all influences of Quebec Nationalism … This was the period of the astringent years of Montreal, when it shrunk from a city rivalling Philadelphia—the fourth largest city in North America at that point—huge city, the center of everything; and ten years later it was comparatively a ghost town and they were building Bay Street in Toronto, all those huge skyscrapers…
>
> What all of that did was vindicate Max Cohen's foresight. Because what he did reimagined the McGill law school … but in that transition to an internationally important law school, certain things were lost. You don't build that kind of school on a student body of scholars and people who were happy to be the lawyers of affairs of business and those sorts of things …
>
> Coming to the fullness of my adulthood in that period in Quebec absolutely made it unavoidable … in Pericles's *Funeral Oration*—something I would not have read had I not gone to the McGill law school by the way, he warns the Athenians; he says "You who say you have no interest in politics, keep in mind, the politics *always* has an interest in you"[352] … I realized that at the end of the day, it all depended upon your willingness to engage in the battle for the Body Politic. You had to be engaged … That was the stuff we argued about all day long; it was probably the most interesting time to go to the McGill law school.[353]

Armand de Mestral had a bit more tempered view of how things had changed as the years move along, stating that, "I wouldn't say that things have changed so much, if you think about the people who over the years have gone on to clerk and gone into academic life or professional life; you see the same mix."[354] It is, however, arguable that the kind of academic rigour that went into volume twelve, and to much the same extent volume thirteen, is something not entirely common to every single Board. While all Board's have consisted of very dedicated and smart individuals, there have been some Boards that proved to "live the agony of the law"[355] (as Stephen A. Scott put it while describing Justice Gerald Le Dain) to a greater extent.

Bora Laskin would contribute a piece for volume fourteen: a speech before the Annual Dinner of the McGill Law Undergraduate Society on March 9, 1967 regarding the influence of FR Scott on the political use of the Constitution over the preceding forty years.[356] During the speech Laskin spoke of how Scott's insistence that the Supreme Court of Canada needed to become the final court of appeal in Canada—until 1949 the final court of appeal was controlled by the British—had a deep impact upon him as a student.[357] Beyond this, Laskin wrote that from Scott's work, he had determined that "constitutional decision could not be based on abstract principles; the constitution [can] not remain a living document if the courts [insist] on separating it from the social, political and economic changes that [are] reflected in almost all phases of Canadian life."[358]

Professor FR Scott was in the audience that evening, and yet another meeting of iconoclasts was incorporated into the history of the MLJ. The words in Laskin's speech, as it would be within the words of Pigeon's and Morin's volume twelve pieces, forecasted some of the most important historical moments in Canadian history. There would soon be a new constitution—and Laskin would reside on the bench of the Supreme Court of Canada for its preceding *Patriation Reference* in the same year that FR Scott would win the Governor General award for a collection of poetry, many years later.

Returning to the group of students slogging through such complex pieces as Laskin's, in the "teenage years" of the *Journal* there was a great deal of camaraderie, but everything could be quite formal. When Articles Editor for volume fourteen Robert Leclerc[359]—future CEO of Milner Fenerty (now part

352 This is a paraphrasing of the quote, "Just because you do not take an interest in politics doesn't mean politics won't take an interest in you." See: UNESCO, *Engineering: Issues, Challenges, and Opportunities for Development* (Paris: United Nations Educational, Scientific and Cultural Organization, 2010) at 176. The quote is commonly attributed to Pericles, though its exact origin text is disputed.

353 Chetwynd interview, *supra* note 346.

354 De Mestral interview, *supra* note 258.

355 Scott interview, *supra* note 278.

356 Bora Laskin, "Canadian Federalism: A Scott's Eye View in Prose and Poetry" (1968) 14:3 *McGill LJ* 494.

357 *Ibid* at 497.

358 *Ibid* at 498.

359 Leclerc would find his first academic publication in the *McGill Law Journal* as well, within the bounds of volume thirteen as a member of their junior board, see: Leclerc, Robert, "Beim v.

of the law firm Frasier Milner Casgrain), CEO of Echo Bay Mines Limited, and Chairman of Minefinders Corporation—was asked why he joined the *Journal*, he replied that he was asked, and that it "was something that seemed the right thing to do – if you are studying law at McGill and are invited to join the *Journal* staff or Board, you ought to respond and do your part."[360] Leclerc says that by this time, for the editors, "There was a sense of institutional knowledge and the idea was to build on that foundation."[361]

Leclerc's senior board also included a person for whom institutional knowledge would become very important as an author himself in the future—as Executive Editor Douglas H. Tees would become the author of the 1979 book recording the one-hundred-year history of the law firm Ogilvy Renault;[362] as well as Contributing Editor Michael Vineberg, who like his brother, is partner with Davies Ward Phillips & Vineberg LLP.

Contributors to the volume, alongside Laskin, included future Justice of the Court of Quebec Raoul P. Barbe;[363] future founder of the Laboratory for Legal Sociology at Paris II University Jean Carbonnier;[364] and future Professor Emeritus of Marketing at York University Donald N. Thompson.[365] Book reviews were contributed by James E. Beaver,[366] future Professor Emeritus of Law at Seattle University; Dean of Law at Windsor University, future Vice-President (Academic) at York University, and future Justice of the Ontario Court of Appeal Walter S. Tarnopolsky;[367] and (as previously noted) John P Humphrey's first appearance in the MLJ as an author.[368]

In volume fifteen, former Associate Justice of the Supreme Court of the United States Tom C. Clark contributed to the *Journal* two years after resigning his position due to the appointment of his son to the same court. In his article "Improving the Administration of Justice", Justice Clark comments on another trend moving into the future. In the article he writes, "I believe it my duty to speak up for change. Everyone agrees that judges should be selected on merit. Politics should have no part in their selection."[369]

Like with Chief Justice Rinfret, Justice Clark's words rung out almost uncensored within the pages of the *Journal*. He wrote further that,

> It is not my purpose to paint the failings of the judicial system with a heavy brush. Nor do I intend to deride the courts, criticize the judges nor tell anyone how to improve the judicial system. We have good judges—many great ones. And so do you. But I ask you: "Is every appointment the best?" Does the system lend itself to the appearance of political preference and manipulation? ... Even the appearance of a judge must be the best. If, through the system, some believe that politics is the predominating factor in the selection of judges, that is bad. We in the United States suffer from the same problem and are endeavouring to correct it. Indeed there is a mighty crusade in the United States today to correct such "appearances".
>
> Many years ago Chief Justice Marshall said: "The greatest scourge of angry Heaven ever inflicted upon ... a people was ... a dependent judiciary".[370] This means that no judge can be beholden to either a political party or to a politician. The judge is the only guarantee of justice. He must therefore be responsible only to God and his conscience. His independence is the bulwark of public liberty and the great security to private property. The very nature of his service prevents his enjoyment of widespread public favour. It is not enough that we keep the doors of the courthouse open, the floors clean, counsel table and bench polished ... When it starts from politics it ends with politics in the minds of the multitude, particularly the dissatisfied. We must

Goyer" Case Comment (1967) 13:3 *McGill LJ* 516.

360 Interview of Robert Leclerc by James Cummins (30 November, 2010).

361 *Ibid.*

362 Douglas H Tees, "Chronicles of Ogilvy, Renault, 1879-1979: Published on the Occasion of the One Hundredth Anniversary of its Founding" (Toronto: Ogilvy, Montgomery, Renault, CLarke, Kirkpatrick, Hannon & Howard, 1979).

363 Raoul P Barbe, "Le Statut des juges de la Cour des sessions de la paix" (1968) 14:1 *McGill LJ* 84.

364 Jean Carbonnier, " Quelques remarques sur l'esprit de la loi francaise du 13 juillet 1965 portant réforme des régimes matrimoniaux " (1968) 14:4 *McGill LJ* 590.

365 Donald N Thompson "French Regulation of Exclusive Distribution Agreements and Refusal to Sell" (1968) 14:4 *McGill LJ* 598.

366 James E Beaver, "The Insanity Defense by Abraham S. Goldstein" Book Review (1968) 14:4 *McGill LJ* 757.

367 Waler S Tarnopolsky, "The International Protection of Human Rights ed. by Evan Luard" Book Review (1968) 14:2 *McGill LJ* 343.

368 Humphrey book review, *supra* note 320.

369 Tom C Clark, "Improving the Administration of Justice" (1969) 15:1 *McGill LJ* 1 at 6.

370 Ellipses found in the original text; not added.

avoid these connotations. The appearance of the judge and his staff must be above suspicion.[371]

Clark ended his piece by imploring all Canadians—involved in the legal community or not—to end the march towards politically-oriented appointments, or election, of justices.[372] Whether or not the world heeded this claim can be seen all around us today.

Other contributors to the volume included Ron C.C. Cuming,[373] future Chairperson of the Saskatchewan Law Reform Commission; future assistant to the Solicitor General of the United States Harry R. Sachse;[374] future Professor Emeritus of Law at Stockholm University Jan Hellner;[375] past Charles H. Stockton Professor of Law at the United States Naval War College Richard B. Lillich;[376] future Dean of the Joseph M. Bryan School of Business and Economics at The University of North Carolina at Greensboro James K. Weeks;[377] the first of two articles future Canadian Ambassador to the United States Allan E. Gotlieb would publish in the *Journal*;[378] and a review of one of Gotlieb's books from future Chichele Professor of Public International Law at Oxford University D.P. O'Connoll.[379] The Editorial Board included Notes and Recent Cases Norman Saibil, now Partner Emeritus at the Montreal office of Blake, Cassels & Graydon LLP.

Herbert Marx published in volume sixteen. The future Minister of Justice and Attorney General of Quebec and Justice of the Superior Court of Quebec, wrote an article entitled "The Emergency Power and Civil Liberties in Canada". The article was published nine years before his election, and published almost immediately after the beginning October Crisis.[380] At the time Marx was a Professor of Law at the Université de Montréal.

In a snapshot of history, Herbert writes that,

> Since the outbreak of the First World War, Canada has been subject to "emergency" legislation for about forty percent of the time. During both World Wars and for a period after, as well as during the Korean War, legislation was in effect that at times virtually allowed the Federal Government to rule by Order-in-Council. Generally the emergency power had permitted the Federal Government to override fields normally reserved to the provinces.[381]

Today, Trudeau's actions of enforcing the *War Measures Act* can seem like something out of a different world—human rights and calm mediation have become a hallmark of the Canadian way—but under this context provided by Herbert Marx, reaction to the Crisis can almost seem perfunctory. Prime Minister Trudeau's now famous words when a reporter asked him what he would do in response to the kidnapping—"Just watch me"—do not seem quite as radical with such a background.

The context Marx gives to the problem could not be covered in the space of this book—with his history of emergency powers from several different relevant jurisdictions.[382] From this context, he provides a warning for the future that appears to have only become more pertinent over the last thirty plus years. He writes that,

> A war legally ends when the executive or the legislature makes a determination that it has ended. It is also clear that the war power is not extinguished with the cessation of hostilities. However, the effects of a war can "continue for centuries", and if the federal government could legislate on changes caused by a war, its jurisdiction would know no bounds. The question then arises as to when the Canadian judiciary would be justified in overturning emergency legislation because the emergency had seemingly passed.[383]

371 Clark, *supra* note 368 at 7-8.

372 *Ibid* at 8.

373 Ron CC Cuming, "The Credit Consumer in Trouble: Remedies of Canadian Consumer Creditors" (1969) 15:1 *McGill LJ* 48.

374 Harry R Sachse, "Purchase Money Security in Common Law and the French System of Civil Law" (1969) 15:1 *McGill LJ* 73.

375 Jan Hellner, "Prospects for the Unification of Sales Law at the Regional or International Level: A Scandinavian View" (1969) 15:1 *McGill LJ* 83.

376 Richard B Lillich, "Intervention to Protect Human Rights" (1969) 15:2 *McGill LJ* 205.

377 James K Weeks, "The Future of Investment Controls" (1969) 15:2 *McGill LJ* 244.

378 Allan E Gotlieb, "Recent Developments Concerning the Exploration and Exploitation of the Ocean Floor" (1969) 15:2 *McGill LJ* 260.

379 DP O'Connell, "*Canadian Treaty Making* by A.E. Gotlieb" Book Review (1969) 15:2 *McGill LJ* 357.

380 The October Crisis occurred in October of 1970, when the *Front de libération du Québec* kidnapped British Trade Commissioner James Cross for sixty-two days. In response, the *War Measures Act* was put into effect on 16 October 1970. The events that followed inspired the reasoning behind Herbert's article—fifteen years before his appointment as Minister of Justice.

381 Herbert Marx, "The Emergency Power and Civil Liberties in Canada" (1970) 16:1 *McGill LJ* 39 at 40.

382 *Ibid* at 44-56.

383 *Ibid* at 62.

In the present context of the War on Terror, Marx's words have special import. While the original *War Measures Act* has since been replaced by successor legislation, the crux of what Marx wrote about is still a hotly contested issue: the question of how far a state can impinge upon established social boundaries under the pretext of public protection.

Additional articles of interest in volume sixteen included a contribution from Vice-President of Bell Canada A.J. de Grandpré,[384] two pieces from the Director of the Institute of Comparative and Foreign Law at McGill, Herman Hahlo;[385] the now famous Finnish and Swedish Professor Tore Modeen;[386] other articles by Rene H Mankiewicz[387] and Maxell Cohen,[388] as well as a piece by Editor-in-Chief of volume fourteen Ronald I Cohen,[389] future Chairman of the Canadian Broadcast Standards Council; and a book review by W.R. Lederman,[390] whose importance as an author we will visit later on in the book. Future luminaries from the board included future Dean of the Faculty of Law of the University of Alberta Lewis N. Klar as Notes and Recent Cases Editor.

Authors of interest published in volume seventeen included Melvin L. Rothman,[391] future Justice of the Quebec Court of Appeal and namesake of the Hon. Melvin L. Rothman BA'51, BCL'54 Entrance scholarship in Law; Franciszek Przetacznik,[392] former Head of the Section of International Public Law at the Polish Ministry of Foreign Affairs; and future Bonython Chair of Law at the University of Adelaide Adrian Bradbrook.[393] John Turner and John Humphrey's articles, discussed previously, were also published within the volume. The editorial board included Articles Editor Julius Grey, future President of the Canadian Foundation for Individual Rights.

Volume eighteen then published future Justice of the Supreme Court of Canada John Sopinka (one of the first judges to be appointed to the Court directly from private practice without prior judicial experience), who at one point quotes three full paragraphs from Albert Camus' novel *The Outsider*.[394] Sopinka spends his article pointing out the trivialities and cross-purposes of the subject matter he is investigating, and presses the legal public to end the practice of non-correlative character referencing in the courts.[395]

The volume also published authors including future Canada Council on International Law (CCIL) founding member and President Donat Pharand;[396] future Justice of the British Columbia Court of Appeal P.D. Lowry;[397] Professor of Jurisprudence Peter Brett of the University of Adelaide,[398] who was defence counsel in the famous *Tait v. R* (1962) before the Australian Supreme Court; and John D Honsberger,[399] who would become the inaugural recipient of the Ontario Law Society Medal.

Volume nineteen then included a contribution from future Chief Justice of the Federal Court of Canada, Justice of the Supreme Court of Canada, and President of the University of Toronto Frank Iacobucci on the *Canada Business Corporations Act*, a piece of legislation that was in draft form at the time. Iacobucci accuses the *Act* of being "rather complicated and inelegant"[400] at times, and in so doing, showed his clear vision of the law that would lead him throughout his illustrious career. Very much in the spirit of future Justice Sopinka, as well as future Justice Laskin several more volumes before him, Iacobucci calls out the legislative and judicial standard of his day on its

384 AJ de Grandpre, "Fair Return for Utilities--Concept or Reality" (1970) 16:1 *McGill LJ* 19.

385 Herman Hahlo, "The Privy Council and the Gentle Revolution" (1970) 16:1 *McGill LJ* 92.

386 Tore Modeen, "Situation of the Finland-Swedish Population in the Light of International, Constitutional and Administrative Law" (1970) 16:1 *McGill LJ* 121.

387 Rene H Mankiewicz, "L'Unification Du Droit Aerien Organes Et Techniques De L'Unification Du Droit Aerien (public et prive)" (1970) 16:3 *McGill LJ* 419.

388 Maxwell Cohen, "The Judicial Process and National Policy--A Problem for Canadian Federalism(1970) 16:2 *McGill LJ* 297.

389 Ronald I Cohen, "The Transmissibility of Damage Claims" (1970) 16:4 *McGill LJ* 676.

390 WR Lederman, "Judicial Review of Legislation in Canada by B.L. Strayer" Book Review (1970) 16:4 *McGill LJ* 723.

391 Melvin L Rothman, "Insider Trading, Proxy Solicitation and Take-over Bids under the Canada Corporations Act" (1971) 17:3 *McGill LJ* 521.

392 Franciszek Przetacznik, "Les pouvoirs découlant pour l'Etat accréditaire de l'inviolabilité personnelle de l'agent diplomatique" (1971) 17:2 *McGill LJ* 360.

393 Adrian Bradbrook, "A Reassessment of the Scope of the Gift Mortis Causa" (1971) 17:3 *McGill LJ* 567.

394 John Sopinka, "Character Evidence in Civil Cases" (1972) 18:2 *McGill LJ* 246 at 247.

395 *Ibid* at 257.

396 Donat Pharand, "The Continental Shelf Redefinition, with Special Reference to the Arctic" (1972) 18:4 *McGill LJ* 536.

397 PD Lowry "The Shipowner and Oil Pollution Liability" (1972) 18:4 *McGill LJ* 577.

398 Peter, Brett, "The Implications of Science for the Law" (1972) 18:2 *McGill LJ* 170.

399 John D Honsberger, "The Need for a Rapprochement of the Bankruptcy Systems of Canada and the United States" (1972) 18:2 *McGill LJ* 147.

400 Frank Iacobucci, "Shareholders under the Draft Canada Business Corporations Act" (1973) 19:2 *McGill LJ* 246 at 252.

apparent inconsistencies. The erosion of public faith in the Constitution represented by Stephen Scott in his early exchange with Justice Kellock appears, in this context, to be spreading.

Other authors published in volume nineteen included future founder and President of the Washington Consulting Group, Armando C. Chapelli;[401] William V. O'Brien,[402] Chair of the Institute of World Policy at Georgetown University; and future Dean of Law at Université Laval, Pierre Verge.[403] A book review was also contributed by President of the International Court of Justice Manfred Lachs.[404]

To get a sense of the people at the *Journal* during this era, the secretary for volume eighteen Lois C. Dubin, then an undergraduate student at McGill and now an award winning author and Professor of Religion at Smith College, recalled that the MLJ offices at the time had started to transition to a more informal place. Professor Dubin even recalls that, "[O]ne day as I sat in the *Law Journal* office, the star goalie of the Montreal Canadiens Ken Dryden—then a law student at McGill—came in. I was thrilled!"[405]

Volume eighteen Editor-in-Chief Michael David Kaylor—now a partner with Lapointe Rosenstein LLP—discussed other things that had begun to change by the time he took the reins of the *Journal* in 1972. He wrote that, "There were many competing law journals as well as other sources for the publication of erudite articles and there always seemed to be a shortage of willing authors who had sufficient time available to make a contribution. Accordingly, considerable time was devoted by myself to simply persuading authors to write."[406]

Other members of volume eighteen included Executive Editor Stuart H. Cobbitt, who would become Chair of the McGill University Board of Governors and senior editor David W. Flicker, who would become Vice-President of Government and Public Affairs at Canadian Pacific Railways. During this time major changes were coming to not only the *McGill Law Journal*, but to the Province of Quebec and Canada as well.

In volume twenty-one (1975), David Matas wrote an article entitled, "Can Quebec Separate?" The author, who in 2010 was nominated for the Nobel Peace Prize for his investigation of organ harvesting crimes against the Falun Gong in China, wrote that,

> The separation of Quebec from Canada is a primary plank in the platform of the Parti Quebecois, the official opposition in the legislature of the Province of Quebec. If one day the P.Q. should form the government of Quebec, it will propose to the National Assembly a law authorizing it to request from Ottawa the transfer of powers to Quebec. Until recently, the position of the party was that if Ottawa should oppose separation, Quebec would separate unilaterally, without a referendum on the issue of separation. Whether separation occurred unilaterally or by agreement with Ottawa, the party would submit to the Quebec electorate, by way of referendum, a proposed constitution for its approval.[407]

It was still a time when, as Matas writes, separation would be unconstitutional if enacted outside the British Parliament.[408] Much was to change. We know now that in the year following Matas' article, the PQ did indeed form the official government of Quebec. And it did so under the leadership of the Jacques-Yvan Morin, now Leader of the Official Opposition in the National Assembly, as Matas placed his article in the publication Morin founded.

Morin assumed the leadership of the PQ in 1973, which was a monumental event considering that only fourteen years earlier McGill university professors and graduates had been under enormous political pressure from the Premier at the time due to the actions of FR Scott and other faculty members in the face of political corruption. The best example of this is the *Roncarelli v. Duplessis* Supreme Court case, against a Premier whose reign was referred to by many as The Great Darkness, and who would die in office seven months later, over a series of days where the Premier ordered a total media blackout in the region.[409] Some associated with the

401 William V O'Brien & Armando C Chapelli, "Law of the Sea in the Canadian Arctic: The Pattern of Controversy (Part I)" (1973) 19:3 *McGill LJ* 322; "Law of the Sea in the Canadian Arctic: The Pattern of Controversy (Part II)" (1973) 19:4 *McGill LJ* 447.

402 *Ibid.*

403 Pierre Verge, "De la souveraineté décisionnelle de l'arbitre" (1973) 19:4 *McGill LJ* 543.

404 Manfred Lachs, "Explorations in Aerospace Law (Selected Essays by John Cobb Cooper) by Ivan A. Vlasic" Book Review (1973) 19:4 *McGill LJ* 593.

405 Interview Lois Dubin of James Cummins (17 November 2010).

406 Interview of Michael David Kaylor by James Cummins (22 November, 2010).

407 David Matas, "Can Quebec Separate?" (1975) 21:3 *McGill LJ* 387 at 387.

408 *Ibid* at 389.

409 Norman DePoe & KingsleyBrown, "Duplessis Nears Death" *Newsmagazine*, CBC Television (6 September 1959).

Faculty and the *McGill Law Journal* were even victims of serious threats and violent physical assault as a result of their scholarship and Scott's work on *Duplessis*, forcing them out of the province in some cases.[410]

Another specific example of such threats came from volume six Case Comment and Book Review Editor Roy Heenan, who according to a 1960 article in *The McGill Daily*, was one of student Presidents that were invited to speak with Premier Maurice Duplessis to give a presentation on the need for Quebec universities to accept grants from the Federal government in addition to the Quebec government, a meeting held on December 2, 1958. The report, written by future Executive Producer of *W5* Peter Rehak (at the time an undergraduate student at McGill), stated that,

> It seemed the students hadn't even settled into their chairs when Duplessis started to tongue-lash them. They, he said, were not qualified to discuss problems of universities. Such things were up to administrators and principals. In a monologue that took most of the two hours [of the meeting], Duplessis listed his government's education improvements such as loans to students and grants to universities. He warned the six not to make unfavourable comments to the press after the meeting. Waving a $300,000 cheque which Sir George Williams College was to receive, he threatened to tear it up if anything was said to the press ...
>
> While glancing around the room, Heenan said, he saw a dossier with each student's name on it ... Heenan's observation is partially supported by Pierre Laporte ... in his book, "The True Fact of Duplessis", Mr. Laporte writes: "He (Duplessis) had a well-organized police. It is said he had secret files on every leading political, civic or church authority in the province." It can therefore be reasonably assumed that Duplessis asked his police to investigate each student he invited to the conference.[411]

Despite this, the meeting was front page news the next day, held up as evidence that the Premier cared about the common man and what they had to say in articles with titles like "Students, Premier Parlay Two Hours—Delegates' View to Help Guide Legislation".[412] Within less than a decade and a half, however, McGill Law scholars had gone from being castigated, intimidated, beaten, or run out of town for their work, to being anointed the new leadership of the Province. McGill Law professors and both current and former *Journal* members, however, would remain a constant thorn in the side of the successive generations of new political power.[413]

People all over the country were standing up and taking notice, including one undergraduate student in particular. When asked why he had applied to McGill Law in the late 1970s, a school all the way across the country from where he had been living, he replied that,

> Well, it was 1978, it was right after the election of the Parti Quebecois in 1976. At the time, I was living in British Columbia, although my parents and the

410 Castel interview, *supra* note 44.

411 Peter Rehak, "Students Brief Duplessis", *The McGill Daily* (Autumn 1960).

412 Herbert Lampert, "Students, Premier Parlay Two Hours—Delegates' View to Help Guide Legislation" *The Montreal Gazette* (3 December, 1958) 1.

413 For just one example of this, I point to the advocacy of minority rights, as well as the Constitutional responsibilities of both the Provincial and Federal governments, during the Quebec secession debate, by volume twelve Editor-in-Chief and then-Professor of Law at McGill Stephen A Scott. Scott became a vocal reminder that the secession of Quebec from Canada—the main goal of the PQ—could also lead to the secession of northern Quebec and the Montreal area from Quebec, if they wished to rejoin Canada. See Elizabeth Thompson, "Sovereignty could cost Quebec north, political adviser says" *Montreal Gazette* (2 December, 1991).

Beyond his private scholarship, Scott also served as counsel for the interveners Roopnarine Singh et al in the Quebec Secession Reference before the Supreme Court of Canada (*Reference re Secession of Quebec*, [1998] 2 SCR 217) regarding the legalities of unilateral secession. Here, Scott argued that,

> Under the Constitution of Canada, neither the National Assembly of Quebec, nor the Legislature of Quebec, nor the government of Quebec (in any sense of the term), has any power or authority whatsoever to effect the secession of Quebec from Canada unilaterally. Accordingly neither Quebec as a political or legal entity, nor any of its executive or other institutions, nor the whole or any part of its population, whether acting as an electorate or otherwise, has any power or authority to effect the secession of Quebec, or any part of Quebec, from Canada unilaterally.

(See Stephen A Scott, "Factum of the Interveners: Roopnarine Singh, Keith Owen Henderson, Claude Leclerc, Kenneth O'Donnell, Van Hoven Petteway" for the *Reference by the Governor in Council concerning certain questions relating to the secession of Quebec from Canada, as set out in Order in Council P.C. 1996-1997*, 30 September, 1996 at 30.)

rest of my family were here in Quebec. And I thought it was the most exciting time possible to be in Quebec, and law school was something that attracted me after I had done my BA.[414]

That student was Patrick Healy, who would become Editor-in-Chief of volume twenty-six, Faculty Advisor for the MLJ from volume thirty-six through forty-one, long-time Professor at the McGill Faculty of Law, and now Judge of the Superior Court of Quebec.

The *Journal* itself had changed radically by the time Healy had been admitted to McGill Law. Whereas Leclerc spoke of volume fourteen's formalities, within six years the spirit of revolution discussed by future Prime Minister John Turner had taken a hold of the Faculty of Law. Just how different the Faculty and the MLJ had become is easily construed from a comparison of volume twelve Editor-in-Chief Stephen A. Scott's anecdote about the dress code at the Faculty, to the following words of volume twenty's Editor-in-Chief Frank H. Buckley—now Associate Dean and Director of the Law & Economics Center at the George Mason University Faculty of Law.

One thing was the same as it was surrounding Scott's year. Buckley writes that,

> We were at that time very much in retard. Only one number of volume 18 had come out, and it seemed volume 19 had the slows. There was talk of a faculty take-over ... Really that was the last thing the faculty wanted, but the delay was an embarrassment. We put a push on, however, and brought out 10 numbers in one year, thanks in no small measure to Graham Nevin, my predecessor. By the time I left we were up to date. Mistakes were made. One of Nevin's numbers had an article by a certain "H. Patrick Gleen", our then faculty advisor. The problem might have been cured had Glenn changed his name, but he stubbornly refused to do so.[415]

The Glenn that Buckley is referring to is Professor H. Patrick Glenn, Faculty Advisor of the MLJ from volume eighteen to Buckley's volume twenty, and now Peter M. Laing Chair at the McGill Faculty of Law. It

Annual Senior Board photo for volume twenty. Front row (left to right): senior editor Adelle Fruman; Editor-in-Chief F.H. Buckley; Faculty Advisor H. Patrick Glenn; and senior editor Fran Norych. Back row: Advertising Editor Larry Moroz; senior editor R.G. Doumani; senior editor Jack Zwicker; Managing Editor Issie Fishman; Jurisprudence Editor Eric Nadler; senior editor Berl Nadler; senior editor Charles Schmidt; and Assistant Editor-in-Chief Georges Djandji. (Courtesy of F.H. Buckley).

414 Interview of Patrick Healy by Omar Soliman (3 December, 2010).

415 Interview FH Buckley of James Cummins (17-23 November, 2011). The interviewed occurred over a series of emails sent between these dates.

appears that the struggle with keeping the volumes of the MLJ coming out on time that is experienced to this day is at the very least fifty years old. Professor Glenn described his memories of the time as well, recalling that like Jean-Gabriel Castel, he started with the *Journal* in his first year of teaching:

> I was called by then-Dean Durnford into his office one day in the Fall of '71—I had started in January of '71 as a professor, so I was in my first full year of teaching; I had taught for a term and a half. He called me in and said, "Glenn, the *Journal* has fallen very much in arrears, I'm receiving complaints from many people; I'm appointing you Faculty Advisor and I want you to do something about it." So this was my first experience with the *Journal* ... So there I was, and we had some serious problems at that point, and I had to be rigorous—more than a Faculty Advisor should usually be.[416]

Dean Durnford had been taking a strong view of the situation at the *McGill Law Journal* for some time at that point. For example, in a letter dated June 9, 1971 (as volume seventeen came to a close) from the Dean to Chief Librarian at the McGill Faculty of Law Marianne Scott, he wrote:

> I am please to know that you are going to continue investigating the situation. My own assessment of the situation is that the Journal is in danger of ceasing publication, and I am already faced with having to make emergency arrangements to resuscitate the as yet uncompleted issues from the year before last. It must therefore be Faculty policy, which I am going to vigorously carry out this year, to forcibly encourage the production of the Journal on time ... Consequently, all possible steps will have to be taken for the carrying out of this policy.[417]

This would have been in the summer before Glenn came onto the Faculty, and was subsequently called into Durnford's office.

Glenn, however, when asked of the apparent Faculty take-over in his 2011 interview, responded by saying that there was no organized effort of that sort that he could recall.[418] He stated that,

> It was not suggested to me by the Dean. And that maybe had something to do with that fact we were probably only fifteen or sixteen faculty members at the time. It was quite small, and it probably was the case that the Dean felt that the Faculty couldn't do that. I mean, it's such a major enterprise in terms of time and expertise—and the Faculty was struggling along at that point. There was no doubt that the Faculty was struggling along. I did a study in about '73 on the national programme as it then was, and discovered correspondence between the Dean and the university administration about its survival.[419]

Glenn recounted again that, "There was one Editorial Board that had gotten into serious difficulties, but the succeeding ones managed to turn it around ... it was an indication that we really didn't need to think more drastically."[420]

What Glenn did do at the time was put substantial pressure on Graham Nevin and the Board of volume nineteen. On January 2, 1973, he wrote to Nevin (cc'ing Dean Durnford) that,

> As you know, a considerable effort has been made in the last eighteen months to bring the Journal up to date. Since July 1971 nine numbers of the Journal have appeared and I think the quality of these numbers has been good...
>
> Since such progress has been made to date I think it is important not to lose any ground. I am therefore rather concerned with the fact that little measurable progress appears to have been made in the last three months. This is clearly not attributable to anyone in particular, but I do feel it necessary to say that I do not regard the granting of credits for Journal work as a simple formality. In order to assist me in deciding to whom credits should be given, I am, therefore, asking all persons who have registered for obtaining credits by means of Journal work to present to me by January 12th, 1973, a

416 Interview of H Patrick Glenn by James Cummins (16 November, 2011).

417 Letter from John Durnford to Marianne Scott (9 June, 1971). See McGill Archives file 3930; RG40 r.335 Law Library, *McGill Law Journal*.

418 Glenn interview, *supra* note 415.

419 *Ibid.*

420 *Ibid.*

> written report, indicating the nature of their responsibilities with the Journal and what progress they have made in carrying out those responsibilities …
>
> I hope that all members of the Senior and Junior Boards will agree with these objectives, which will enable the Board of Vol. 20 – whom I think should be elected before the end of January – to continue the excellent efforts which have been made by previous Boards.[421]

The letter was a cannonball shot across the bow of the *Journal*. Faculty pressure on the *Journal* saw a major effort to catch-up on past volumes, and threats to remove credits from editors that did not help make up the delay were issued. The Faculty was not technically in a position to do anything substantial, but they were definitely struggling to keep the MLJ afloat by any means necessary—a very different view from that of Dean Meredith on the importance of keeping the *Journal* alive twenty years prior.

Over the next three weeks, Glenn met frequently with the Board of volume nineteen, after which time he issued a report to the entire McGill Law Faculty. In it, Glenn stated that he and the Editor-in-Chief had agreed to review—together—reports from each of the members of the Board at the end of each academic term to review whether or not someone had not been pulling their weight, at which point the Faculty Advisor would use the threat of credit revocation to try and persuade them to continue on in better form. The Editor-in-Chief agreed to submit an Annual Report for the files of the *Journal*, copying the Faculty Advisor.[422]

The Advisor in turn agreed to make a greater effort to keep the Faculty informed as to where the *Journal* was in need of help, specifically that the Advisor should be responsible for placing pressure on the Faculty to "give the Journal a preferred place as publisher of your own writing and indicate to them any noteworthy student writing which comes to your attention," as well as suggesting other sources of material.[423] The Faculty Advisor also convinced volume nineteen to push its election of the new Executive Board up to the first of February, much earlier than it had ever been—and the approximate date that the election has been held ever since. The reason for this was so that the Executive Board could start working on their volume earlier,[424] even though additional credits had not yet been afforded them. The language used was less deferential than had been used in the past, however such candour should be expected for a letter between colleagues at the Faculty and not directly to those that owned and operated the *Journal*.

It should be said though that Leo P. Martinez once pointed out, as regards the idea that a Faculty could do much better at running a large scale journal operation than students, that, "To expect a handful of faculty to cull through twenty or thirty articles for the purpose of selecting five or six for publication is unrealistic. If, as is the case with many of the more elite law reviews, the number of submissions is on the order of hundreds, the task becomes impossible. That student editors keep up is astounding."[425] In the end the results of everyone's efforts overall was that things were back on track, thanks to all involved.

Like Richard Pound, Buckley also had a run-in with the supporters of a would-be dictatorship from foreign lands. As Buckley recalls, "We rejected an article by a white law professor at Makerere Law School, who celebrated the move to one-party rule under Idi Amin. The author was outraged and took the matter up with John [Brierley], who found it all vastly amusing. Wouldn't have been so funny in Kampala, I expect."[426] Buckley included that, "One of the nicest things about the *Journal* was that it permitted me to become friends with some faculty members, and especially Dean John Brierley."[427] Brierley, Executive Editor of volume five, no doubt still remembered the strip that Dean Meredith had torn off him fifteen years prior. As Buckley states, his relationship with Brierley "helped, on occasion".[428] Authors that volume twenty did publish included Albert S. Abel,[429] namesake of the Albert S. Abel Graduate Award at the University of Toronto, and one of Bora Laskin's favourite friends and influences;[430] and Colin Tapper,[431] who would go on to

421 Letter from H Patrick Glenn to Graham Nevin (2 January, 1973). See McGill Archives file 3930; RG40 Co.335 Law Library, *McGill Law Journal*.

422 Letter from H Patrick Glenn to the Faculty Members of the Faculty of Law at McGill University (23 January, 1973). See McGill Archives file 3930; RG40 C.335 Law Library, *McGill Law Journal*.

423 *Ibid.*

424 *Ibid.*

425 Leo P Martinez, "Babies, Bathwater, and Law Reviews" (1995) 47:6 *Stan L Rev* 1139 at 1144.

426 Buckley interview, *supra* note 414.

427 *Ibid.*

428 *Ibid.*

429 Albert S Abel, "Re Official Languages Act: A Comment" (1974) 20:1 *McGill LJ* 136.

430 Darrel Abel, ML Friedland & Bora Laskin, "In Memoriam: Albert S. Abel 1906-1978" (1978) 28:3 *UTLJ* 364 at 366-67.

431 Colin Tapper, "Legal Information Retrieval by Computer:

become a full professor at the Oxford Faculty of Law. There was also a special issue, which will be discussed later on in this chapter.

The environment the *Journal* was very different then that it was before. Buckley recalled that,

> Our offices were on the ground floor, near the stairs of [Old Chancellor Day Hall]. First door on the left. A smallish office, yet it suited us well.
>
> No Lexis [Nexis] of course.[432] Research as done in the dark ages... People ... Jean Hale, Paul Crepeau's sister, as different from him as night is to day. She was from Saskatchewan and he from the sixth arrondissement, I believe. She was effectively the Associate Dean and very effective she was too. Unfortunately her office (first door on the left, ground floor) gave her a view of the parking lot; from which she would emerge, shaking her finger, when she caught me parking there. A dear lady.
>
> On occasion we received submissions from students. A few were good, most bad, but one was in a class by itself. It was by a 3L LL.B student, a lady, and concerned the difference between transsexuals and transgendereds ... She had written it by hand on yellow-lined legal size paper; and was very upset when I rejected it. She was a friend, and indeed once took me to a Theodorakis concert, for which I am eternally grateful.
>
> She ended up in practice abroad, but not before, upon graduation, taking the President of the Law Students Association into the bushes at a reception at John Durnford's house, and giving him a most energetic f___.[433]

The excess formality of years past appears to have been somewhat eroded by this point. But not everything was happy then. The first thing Buckley had to say was, "I should never have become editor-in-chief. The job should have gone to Joey Treiger, who unlike me was a civilian, and who moreover was a Montreal boy. But Treiger died of leukemia, tragically, and the job devolved upon me. I think I was the first common law editor-in-chief, as I never took the B.C.L."[434]

Buckley added that, "Joey and I were on the junior board and it was understood that he was the Dauphin. He sickened around Christmastime, however, and withdrew from school shortly thereafter."[435] After his passing in 1973, during his final year of studies, the Law Undergraduate Society founded the Joseph Treiger Memorial Award in his honour. According to Stephen A. Scott, who was a professor at McGill during the period, a colleague remarked to him at the time that, "He showed extreme courage about his condition, and his imminent death. He was without complaint."[436] There is also a tree that was planted in front of the Law Faculty dedicated to his memory. It remains there to this day.

Beyond the new professional informality, the tenure of volume twenty also marked the introduction of two important aspects of the MLJ's future: electric typing and an MLJ cite guide. To begin with the new technology, Buckley wrote that,

> In 1974 the *Law Journal* bought an IBM Selectric, operated by Maria Wehm, our secretary.
>
> We largely rewrote the articles submitted to us. Maria typed them up, and when they came back we sent them to Eugene Doucet Ltée, our printer. We went through galleys, then page proofs. The final stage was the approval of the last set of pages. This was done at the Doucet plant, on Papineau just below Sherbrooke. Only Editors-in-Chief of a certain vintage would remember this. We were met by M Roy, the chief printer. Each page had been set in lead by a linotype machine, and blocked so that we could not make any but the slightest changes at that point. I would approve each page, and that was the last we saw of them before we received the bound journal.
>
> I still remember well my last visit there, June 1974...
>
> The Harvard Law Review president who visited us, [Barry Simon], explained that they had a computer on which they typed their papers.[437]

This visit from Simon led unto the other major event that volume twenty brought forth. Buckley and his

Applications and Implications" (1974) 20:1 *McGill LJ* 26.

432 As a side note, Quicklaw—of LexisNexis—would be founded by the same individual that founded the *Alberta Law Review*.

433 Buckley interview, *supra* note 414.

434 Buckley interview, *supra* note 414.

435 *Ibid.*

436 Scott interview, *Supra* note 278.

437 Buckley interview, *supra* note 414.

executive had the foresight to invite Simon to Canada two years before the *Harvard Law Review* was about to produce the twelfth edition of the *Bluebook*—the legal citation bible in the US. During the visit Buckley showed Simon the MLJ's style guide—twenty to thirty pages long at the time—which had been substantially revised during his tenure. Buckley stated that after the meeting with Simon "the Blue Book came to adopt our method of citing Canadian materials."[438] The context of this achievement is significant, as we must consider that alongside this, volume twenty was creating the first full index of the MLJ from volume one through volume twenty (basically a fifth issue)—though this took two years to complete.[439]

the job still demands today. As Buckley stated, "[T]he editor-in-chief should assume, on taking the job, that he has left the school. He should be overjoyed about this."[440] No doubt this was a message he passed on to the next volume's Editor-in-Chief: Laura Falk Scott, the first woman to ever hold the position. Indeed, Scott would carry the torch well, even working late into the evenings during the summer following her tenure.[441] Scott would later become the first ever in-house council for the Canadian branch of The Seagram Company, at the time the world's largest distillery, setting up its legal division and eventually becoming Vice-President of Legal Affairs.

THE McGILL LAW JOURNAL

Published by LAW STUDENTS OF McGILL UNIVERSITY

Editor's Office, 3644 Peel Street, Montreal 112, Canada

Tel. 845-8824

6 September, 1973

To: All members of Faculty

From: F.H. Buckley
Editor in Chief

Re: Harvard Law Review

Members of Faculty are invited to a meeting at 2:00 Friday, 7 September in the Common Room in Old Chancellor Day Hall, when Mr Barry Simon, President of the Harvard Law Review, will discuss the organization of his journal.

Source: McGill Archives file 3930; RG40 C.335 Law Library, McGill Law Journal.

Other members of the volume twenty Editorial Board included Assistant Editor-in-Chief Georges Djandji, future Senior Vice-President at Gulf International Bank; senior editor Fran Norych, who would have the S. Frances Norych Memorial Scholarship at McGill Law named in her honour after her early death in 1991; and future Justice of the Alberta Court of Appeal and Nunavut Court of Appeal senior editor Adelle Fruman.

The workload of the Editor-in-Chief, at this point, had already reached the legendary proportions

The *McGill Law Journal* is perhaps unique among institutions that were begun before 1960. The first woman to ever hold a senior position at the MLJ was Natalie Fochs Isaacs—who would take over as marquee partner in the firm started by Morris Fish, Harvey Yarosky, and Fred Kaufman (today named Yaroksy Daviaul Isaacs). As mentioned previously, Fochs served as Book Review Editor for the very first issue of volume one. Kathryn H. Mason was then on the masthead of issues two and three as an Editorial Associate. However, as volume thirteen Contributing

438 *Ibid.*

439 Louise Pelly, "Preface" (1974) *Cumulative Index Volumes 1-20 McGill LJ* ii.

440 Buckley interview, *supra* note 414.

441 Letter from Laura Falk Scott to Marianne Scott (23 June, 1975). See McGill Archives file 3930; RG40 C.335 Law Library, *McGill Law Journal.*

Editor Lionel Chetwynd stated of the general era at the Law Faculty leading up to Scott's election,

> There were only two women in my class, this was not a place where women... they were not made unwelcome—that is the best thing that can be said about the attitude at the time ... We argued about it in school—we had a big argument in my third year class; in Brierley's class. I engaged him in a long discussion in front of the class... I felt his attitude was very pre-modern; that he still looked upon the law school as having the function of turning out "gentlemen of a certain sort"; I had been a corporal and a sergeant at the Black Watch, not an officer, and I never wanted to be like those people. [I said], "Those are your people, and that's one way to be, but Canada is many things."[442]

It took twenty-three years until a female Editor-in-Chief was elected—though thirty-five percent of all Editors-in-Chief have been female since her 1975 tenure, in addition to fifty percent of the last twelve, from volumes forty-seven to fifty-eight. Laura Falk Scott was elected three years earlier than Susan Estrich, who was the first female President of the *Harvard Law Review* and two years before the *Alberta Law Review* elected its first female Editor-in-Chief. The *University of Toronto Faculty of Law Review* had previously set the standard though, by selecting Gloria Carpenter as the first woman to become a law review Editor-in-Chief back in 1944.

The executive positions at the MLJ were also not something women had held until 1973, when Claudette Bellemare became the first woman to hold an executive position during volume nineteen—the position of Executive Editor. When Falk Scott—now residing in San Francisco as a professional artist—was asked about the process of becoming Editor-in-Chief for volume twenty-one, she recalled,

> [B]eing asked by Editor in Chief of Volume 20 Frank Buckley and his Executive Editor George Djandji if I would consider taking on the job. I don't know if it's still the case, but at that time the senior board chose the Editor-in-Chief for the following year from the junior board. I said yes, and it was not a big deal that I was the first woman. There was no particular atmosphere surrounding the event other than perhaps a general feeling that it was about a time. It is also noteworthy that between the senior and junior boards, we probably had the greatest number of female MLJ staff ever.[443]

442 Chetwynd interview, *supra* note 346.

Falk Scott also wrote that,

> My main memories are of sitting in the basement office for hours on end, reading submissions, editing manuscripts, composing letters to contributors and potential contributors, and proofreading galleys. On the junior board, there was lots of fact checking. I spent a lot of time in the so-called cafeteria which had some poor-quality vending machines. Much coffee got consumed and quite a few pizzas delivered. A challenge was keeping our people motivated to get the work done and on time, when we all had so many other commitments and pressures. My Executive Editor David Trezise recently commented to me that he was surprised we didn't all flunk out.
>
> For me, MLJ was a sort of life line. While I did very well academically, I didn't particularly enjoy my classes (with some exceptions, such as Constitutional Law taught by the always-entertaining Stephen Scott), or the subject matter in general, which I found rather dry. I had previously enjoyed work in communications, so working on the *Law Journal* made the rest of the law school experience more tolerable.[444]

The turnover of editorial boards is made all the more astounding when considering that Stephen Scott, Laura Falk Scott's favourite professor (no relation), held the same position as her only nine years prior.

The tentativeness of the Faculty towards the MLJ still remained after Buckley and Graham Nevin got the *Journal* back on track. Laura Falk Scott remembers that, "this was the first year at McGill for our Faculty Advisor, David Jones. It was a new experience for him to be working with an entirely student-run, professional organization. [Though in] time he became very respectful and supportive of what we did."[445]

Falk Scott also discussed how the position

443 Interview of Laura Falk Scott by James Cummins (31 December, 2010).

444 *Ibid.*

445 *Ibid.*

changed her life, writing that, "My decision to take on the editorship of MLJ actually was a potentially life-changing decision, as I realized I couldn't pursue the four-year dual degree program and be EIC at the same time, yet still do the quality job at MLJ I felt needed to be done. So that in effect eliminated common law for me: Who knows what impact that may or may not have had on my life?"[446] This decision is something that those who have attended McGill Law since the advent of the transsystemic program of 1999 (implemented by former *McGill Law Journal* Editor-in-Chief Stephen Toope) no longer face.

When asked about her main vision for her volume as Editor-in-Chief, she thought of—as is common—the special issue she included in her volume:

> The main vision I had was for No. 4, the special issue on Women and the Law in Canada. This had to my knowledge never been done before, and was inspired by my attendance (along with some other of our board members, including Joyce Gilden and Roz Levine), at the 1974 first-ever Women and the Law conference held at the University of Windsor. In fact some of the writers we ended up soliciting, including I believe June Menzies,[447] were presenters at that conference.
>
> As we proceeded, we added elements not covered by articles solicited from professors and practitioners, including a Chronology of Legal Landmarks by a couple of students, Susan Altschul and Christine Carron,[448] one of whom was on the junior board; and an article by another of our junior board members, Frances Freedman, on Partnership of Acquests in Quebec.[449]
>
> In general, I thought it was important to include contributions by students and recent graduates so long as they were of law journal level. Hence we published articles by fellow senior board member David Trezise[450] on Environmental Quality in Canada and a case comment by Alan Hilton,[451] among others.
>
> Given the focus on the special issue, I wanted to be sure to represent a broad range of topics, both common and civil law, in the other issues. I was especially drawn to exploring the more controversial topics of the day, such as Geoffrey Marshall's piece on "Right to Privacy"[452] and David Matas on "Can Quebec Separate?"[453]

Falk Scott worked alongside another female editor that would go on to bridge into art from her career in law: Circulations Editor Suzanne Coupal. Not only did Coupal serve as a Justice at the Court of Quebec for twenty years, but afterwards she became a professional artist herself in the field of painting. After taking several art classes in Paris and Montreal, she discovered a true passion. The links she saw between art and judging drew her mind further and further towards the world of art and away from her courtroom. After spending several years living a double-life, staying awake past midnight in her art studio on Rachel Street in Montreal after finishing her days at the courthouse, she left the judicial world to become an artist full time.[454]

As for additional connections: Christine Carron, the student mentioned by Falk Scott in her interview (and who has consistently ranked as one of the best Canadian lawyers in the world according to *Lexpert*, *Chambers Global*, and *The National Post* over the last decade) may not have been on the *Journal* yet, but the following year she would become a member and the year following that she would become the Special Issue Editor for volume twenty-three.

The special issue that year was entitled "The Environment" issue. According to Carron, the idea came from either Falk Scott or her successor as Editor-in-Chief Louise Pelly.[455] Carron added that, "Back then

---

446 *Ibid.*

447 June Menzies, "Uncounted Hours: The Perception of Women in Policy Formulation" (1975) 21:4 *McGill LJ* 615.

448 Susan Altschul & Chistine Carron, "Chronology of Some Legal Landmarks in the History of Canadian Women" (1975) 21:4 *McGill LJ* 476.

449 Frances Schanfield Freedman, "Juridical Capacity of the Married Woman in Quebec: In Relation to Partnership of Acquests and Recent Amendments to the Civil Code" (1975) 21:4 *McGill LJ* 518.

450 David Tresize, "Alternative Approaches to Legal Control of Environmental Quality in Canada" (1975) 21:3 *McGill LJ* 404.

451 Alan Hilton, "*Trottier v. J. L. Lefebvre Ltee*: Fault or Risk as Basis of Employer Liability" (1975) 21:2 *McGill LJ* 307.

452 Marshall, Geoffrey, "The Right to Privacy: A Sceptical View" (1975) 21:2 *McGill LJ* 242.

453 Laura Falk Scott, *supra* note 442; Matas, *supra* note 406.

454 Éric Clément, "Suzanne Coupal: madame la juge se tourne vers l'art" *La Presse* (28 May 2011), online : < http://www.cyberpresse.ca/arts/arts-visuels/201105/28/01-4403824-suzanne-coupal-madame-la-juge-se-tourne-vers-lart.php >

455 Interview of Christine Carron by James Cummins (24 November, 2010).

environmental law was a relatively new field, compared to what it is today."[456] Her inside view on the culture that surrounded the fact that the last two Editors-in-Chief before her senior *Journal* year were female was that they "unquestioningly commanded respect"[457] so much so that,

> it never struck me that there was anything "novel" about the *Journal* being run by women. In fact, it seemed quite natural. What seemed less natural (and less equitable) was the perception of the role women were expected to play, and the jobs they were expected to get, upon graduation.[458]

The issue Carron was involved with was the fourth in a spurt that began in volume twenty, issue three: the Labour Law Special Issue. Whereas the previous special issues had focused more purely on the legal and legislative aspects of the law, Assistant Editor-in-Chief Georges Djandji wrote in the Preface to the volume twenty special issue that,

> Labour law is not merely a codification of basic guarantees, rights and recourses in the realm of labour relations, but also an all-embracing regime of human relations in perpetual change. For this reason, some of our authors have emphasized the sociological ramifications rather than the legal factors pertaining to labour law.[459]

Authors in this special issue included the future Justice of the Supreme Court of Canada Louis LeBel in the first of the two articles she would contribute to the MLJ over her career, writing about the application of the rules of procedure within Article 134 of the *Labour Code of Quebec*.[460] Other authors that appeared in the special issue included future Professor Emeritus of Social Sciences at Université Laval Fernand Morin.[461]

An additional highlight of the issue is that after the introduction by Georges Djandji, one of the Honourable John Turner's fellow cabinet ministers provided an opening statement for the issue. John Munro, the Federal Minister of Labour at the time (and namesake of Hamilton's John C. Munro International Airport), wrote the piece in recognition of the Labour Department's seventy-fifth anniversary: discussing the problems of clashing unions, management groups, and other interest groups. He stated, "We in the Department of Labour can in no way guarantee that confrontation between groups will not at times be unreasonable, and even damaging. But neither can we calmly accept the premise that disruptive conflict and the resulting social and economic strains will always be with us."[462]

Achieving this kind of direct communication, if rhetoric-filled, between members of the Cabinet and the kind of people interested in reading about the topics they legislate on is a difficult thing to arrange outside of vehicles like law journals and their special issues. These issues gather readers over the span of decades into the future—and while readers may reach for the issue to review one article in particular, they can flip to a different point of view with ease. Especially before the advent of the Internet, this kind of anthological convenience was of great importance to someone looking for a wide variety of perspectives.

After the advent of the Internet, the importance of special issues continued, but in a different manner. The advent of a greater number of specialized legal journals also diminished the quasi-monopoly held by special issues, as most topics that a special issue of great public interest could cover were already covered on a bi-annual or quarterly basis by a different publication. The nexus of high quality articles in a special issue, sometimes based on an outside conference, other times based on articles solicited directly by the *Journal*, now provide a mountain above the over-saturated Internet. Word searching in any one of the online scholarly databases for a specific term can land you thousands of articles—many of them irrelevant. But stumbling upon a special issue provides a haven of well thought out, cohesive, and challenging material revolving around contemporary sources. They still provide an important platform for engaging in progressive scholarship, rather than a mere rehashing of old ideas.

The examples of Labour Minister Munro, Dr. Morgentaler, or Chief Justice Taschereau using the MLJ as a platform for political or philosophical exposition are representative of what has become a hallmark of the MLJ. The special issue for volume twenty-one, under the leadership of Laura Falk Scott, was on "Women and the Law". The preface written by the Editorial Board

456 *Ibid.*

457 *Ibid.*

458 *Ibid.*

459 Georges Djandji, "Preface" (1974) 20:3 *McGill LJ* 339 at 339.

460 Louis Le Bel, "La Procedure D'Appel Au Tribunal Du Travail Et L'Application De L'Article 134 Du Code Du Travail Du Quebec" (1974) 20:3 *McGill LJ* 364 at ff.

461 Fernand Morin, "Pour un titre deuxième au Code du travail portant sur la relation individuelle de travail" (1974) 20:3 *McGill LJ* 414.

462 John Munro, "Message from the Minister of Labour" (1974) 20:3 *McGill LJ* 340 at 340.

reads that, "It is ... our hope that further discussion of the law as it affects women and of the perceptions behind the law, will be stimulated by our efforts."[463] Authors included future Justice of the Ontario Superior Court Edythe I. MacDonald, who wrote of the struggle for equality that was persistent within her decade that,

> One of the most important challenges to reformers ... is the diversity of interests and needs inherent in our pluralistic society. The sure determination of what are the most pressing claims to be satisfied at any given time is made more difficult when the demands are expressed in a federal jurisdictional framework. Thus, even when the need for reform in a particular field is recognized ... comprehensive solutions to the problem [do not find] their way into legislative form.[464]

Though volume twenty-one Editor-in-Chief Laura Falk Scott had found her way to the top of student body at McGill Law, a glass ceiling still awaited all female graduates upon their entry into the workforce. Though MacDonald did write further that,

> as social attitudes become more attuned to the demands of social justice, the law will be better able to discharge its obligations as an instrument for effecting social change. It is to be anticipated that the law, while continuing the serve as the "backbone of civilization", will in time cease to appear to any segment of the population as ... a "barrier".[465]

Another author within the special issue was future President of the National Farm Products Marketing Council S. June Menzies (mentioned before by Falk Scott), who writes that creating a society free of discrimination "is an elusive goal"[466] and that at the time "the economic significance of the work women do"[467] was not adequately compensated in either income or within government run social programs. Her piece is perhaps most representative of the ideas behind the issue. Menzies writes that it was very clear during this moment in time that "policies that appear fair in form may be discriminatory in practice,"[468] including tax laws that basically made husbands pay for up to forty-three percent of his wife's income through tax increases on their own income.[469] Yet, as she writes, a woman's unpaid work was "rewarded only by lip service,"[470] thus,

> Women cannot attain economic equality as long as the major economic role they perform is outside the economy and is disregarded in policy formulation. As long as we exclude the household and the labour performed within it from the legitimate economic framework of our society, women cannot attain equality and they will not be able to share in the benefits of society proportionately to the contribution they make to it ... It is a matter of hard-core economic and social policy for which a government has primary responsibility.[471]

The special issue also marks the first article published in the MLJ by former Faculty Advisor to the MLJ Professor H. Patrick Glenn;[472] the author that has published more times in the *Journal* than any other author, with his name appearing in the various MLJ tables of contents issues thirteen times as author since 1975, not to mention his various MLJ book reviews—he also eventually became a member of the MLJ Board of Advisors. The full range of debate throughout the issue very much represents the importance that David O'Brien had said special issues held.

Other authors in volume twenty-one's special issue included Roy L. Heenan,[473] and more generally, the volume included contributions by Daniel Mettarlin[474] (namesake of McGill Law's Daniel Mettarlin Memorial Scholarships); future Cecil A. Wright Chair of the University of Toronto Faculty of Law Ernest Weinrib;[475] future Justice of the Quebec Court of Appeal Allan R. Hilton;[476] Faculty Advisor of the MLJ

463 "Preface" (1975) 21:4 *McGill LJ* 475 at 475.

464 Edtyhe I MacDonald, "View from Ottawa: The Role of the Federal Goverment as Regards the Status of Women" (1975) 21:4 *McGill LJ* 601 at 609-10.

465 *Ibid* at 614.

466 Menzies, *supra* note 446 at 615.

467 *Ibid* at 618.

468 *Ibid* at 621.

469 *Ibid* at 625.

470 *Ibid* at 627.

471 *Ibid* at 630.

472 H Patrick Glenn, "The Constitutional Validity of Abortion Legislation: A Comparative Note" (1975) 21:4 *McGill LJ* 683-84.

473 Roy L Heenan, "Women under Quebec Labour Law" (1975) 21:4 *McGill LJ* 594.

474 Daniel N Mettarlin, "The Quebec Trust and the Civil Law" (1975) 21:2 *McGill LJ* 175.

475 Ernest Weinrib, "The Undisclosed Principle of Undisclosed Principals" (1975) 21:2 *McGill LJ* 298.

476 Hilton, *supra* note 450.

during that year and future acting-Dean of the Faculty of Law at the University of Alberta David P. Jones;[477] future Justice of the Ontario Supreme Court Maurice C. Cullity;[478] Daniel Ish,[479] future Dean of Law at the University of Saskatchewan and Chief Adjudicator of the Indian Residential Schools Adjudication Secretariat in Canada; and future Dean Emeritus of the University of British Columbia Faculty of Law Peter Burns.[480]

Volume twenty-one also included a contribution from Morris C. Shumiatcher, who in 1947 (at the age of thirty) drafted Canada's first Bill of Rights as assistant to the Premier of Saskatchewan: the "Saskatchewan Bill of Rights". In his MLJ article, Shumiatcher makes as accurate a future prediction as any author in MLJ history. Writing in response to the not too removed 1973 Middle Eastern war, he states that,

> What the policy of the Middle Eastern states promised, and what Canada's present policy and complicity in such a policy seems likely to produce, is that our use and enjoyment of oil and gas will hereafter depend not upon the marketplace or the desires and demands of citizens as consumers, but upon political considerations, domestic and international.[481]
>
> Soon the National Energy Policy would be implemented in Canada, marking the beginning of the path towards the global oil market of the future. Shumiatcher added that at the time people were and would be witnessing a departure from the traditional role of government. There is here not merely an orthodox attempt to enhance public revenues through taxation, nor even the usual competition between provincial and federal legislative authority over a field in which there is obvious overlapping. The legislative scalpel cuts far deeper. The devices that are being adopted are unequivocally designed to wrest legal and physical ownership of petroleum and petroleum resources from their private owners and to vest them in the state ...
>
> If the governments of Canada succeed in ousting the private entrepreneur from developing and marketing the oil and mineral resources of Canada, it will be because the developers have failed to be vigilant in the protection of their interests.[482]

Another important author to publish in volume twenty-one was future Justice of the Supreme Court of Canada Gerard V. La Forest. La Forest wrote about the delegation of legislative power in Canada, commenting that his future place of employment—the Supreme Court—was in a position to settle simmering arguments about the proper balance of legislative powers across the provinces and the federal government.[483]

Volume twenty-two's special issue was supervised by Special Issue Editor Michael Prupas. Prupas would go on to become the owner of MUSE entertainment and win both Gemini and Emmy Awards as an Executive Producer of television programming. The issue was entitled the "Access to Justice" special issue, and Prupas introduced the issue by writing that, "While law reform and the advent of government programmes such as Legal Aid have in theory made the law available to all, in practice 'equality before the law' remains an elusive goal. We do not pretend to have found all the answers, but we hope that the articles in this Special Issue will illuminate some of the problems which still exist."[484] Herbert Marx contributed yet again with an article to this issue,[485] alongside future Deputy Attorney General for Ontario Larry Taman;[486] future Dean of Robson Hall Christopher S. Axworthy;[487] and future Vice-Dean of the Faculty of Law at the University of Ottawa Bradford W. Morse.[488] Authors that contributed to the volume more generally included

477 David Phillip Jones, "Howarth v. National Parole Board: A Comment" (1975) 21:3 *McGill LJ* 434; David Phillip Jones, "Some Problems with RHOSPs" (1975) 21:3 *McGill LJ* 442.

478 Maurice C Cullity, "*Law of Trusts In Canada* by D.W.M. Waters: Book Review" (1975) 21:3 *McGill LJ* 461.

479 Daniel Ish, "Some Aspects of the Taxation of Canadian Co-Operatives" (1975) 21:1 *McGill LJ* 42.

480 Peter Burns, "Private Prosecutions in Canada: The Law and a Proposal for Change" (1975) 21:2 *McGill LJ* 269.

481 Morris C Shumiatcher, "Canda's Constitutional Curmudgeons, or a Tale of Three Cities" (1975) 21:1 *McGill LJ* 113 at 114.

482 *Ibid* at 128-29.

483 Gerard V La Forest, "Delegation of Legislative Power in Canada" (1975) 21:1 *McGill LJ* 131 at 142.

484 Michael Prupas, "Preface" (1976) 22:3 *McGill LJ* 351 at 351.

485 Jean Hetu & Herbert Marx, "Les Defavorises, Le Code Civil Et Les Juges" (1976) 22:3 *McGill LJ* 352.

486 Larry Taman, "Legal Aid in Ontario: More of the Same" (1976) 22:3 *McGill LJ* 369.

487 Christopher S Axworthy, "Controlling the Abuse of Small Claims Courts" (1976) 22:3 *McGill LJ* 480.

488 Bradford W Morse, "Native People and Legal Services in Canada" (1976) 22:3 *McGill LJ* 504.

André Rousseau, former Minister of Industry of Commerce in the National Assembly of Quebéc.[489]

During the tenure of volume twenty-two the first specialized legal publication at McGill Law began publishing—the Faculty-run *Annals of Air and Space Law / Annales de Droit Aérien de Spatial.* It had been sixteen years since a Faculty-run journal had been housed on campus, as after Professor Castel took the *Canadian Bar Review* to Osgoode Hall there was no other successful attempt to create or move a journal onto campus. Founding Editor-in-Chief Nicolas Mateesco Matte (then-Director and now Director Emeritus of the Institute for Air and Space Law) prefaced the first volume of the *Annals*, writing,

> The *Annals* are not the materialization of a spontaneous commendable enthusiasm: the decision to publish was reached after a number of basic elements had been taken into consideration. Indeed, within a few weeks, 25 years will have elapsed since the Institute of International Air Law was created as a post-graduate school of knowledge for a rapidly developing aviation technique: a technique which was followed by an equally speedy developing law...
>
> The *Annals* benefits from decades of silent but serious and progressive work in the Institute, and the geographical location of this publication makes possible the utilization of English and French. Articles can, therefore, be published in one of the two very important languages in which air and space law developed its rules and extended itself towards maturity ...
>
> The world-wide nature of the inter-dependent consequences for all nations resulting from rules yet to be globally accepted – as a result of increased flights of supersonic or subsonic aeroplanes, space satellites activities ... and from their consequences oblige mankind to strive unrelentlessly towards a world peace in the shadow of possible general destruction. Towards this effort, the *Annals* will try to bring, in the field of air and space law, its modest but steady contribution.[490]

The Institute that would house the *Annals* was one of the first major supporters of the MLJ, thus the appearance of the *Annals* represents a coming-of-age for both the Institute and the *Journal* itself, as the MLJ had become more and more independent of any and all connections with McGill University—a brief period of friendly prompting by the Faculty in the early 1970s aside. While the *Journal* had always technically been independent, most contributions for many years came from permanent or temporary McGill Law faculty members and the McGill student body. This was, of course, one of the goals of Morin's original vision. But over the coming decades, the MLJ would emerge as something different—an intellectual meeting place for not just members of the Quebec and Canadian legal communities, but for the world.

In volume twenty-three, future Chief Justice of the Supreme Court of Canada Antonio Lamer contributed a note three years before his promotion from the Superior Court of Quebec.[491] As is historically usual with those that will one day serve on the highest court in the land when they write within the pages of the MLJ, Lamer wrote about law reform. Lamer and his co-author wrote that "we all know that the law *has* grown in the last century. But, because of the formal consignment of policy to Parliament, the changes that have occurred have been concealed under the doctrine that judges only 'find' law, not make it. We agree with [the] view that this is 'a childish fiction'."[492] They follow this idea up by saying that, "In pursuit of democracy we have created a system whereby the courts do not, in theory, legislate, yet where they sometimes must in fact, without official acknowledgment, make substantial changes in the social fabric through law."[493] However, they do warn that "the public interest does not always coincide with the interests of lawyers or of judges for that matter."[494]

It is a debate that has raged for several decades—how to place the role of the judicial branch of our government into the paradigm of a public that is more and more engaged with the *idea* of democracy, and not just voting. As Lamer and his co-author wrote, "We can no longer afford the misleading comfort of continuing to build for the 21st century using 19th century tools."[495] This is an especially fitting comment, considering that the issue prior to that in which Lamer was published, was Carron's special issue on "The Environment".

489 Claude D'Aoust, André Rousseau, & François Delorme, "Considérations sur le degré de preuve requis devant l'arbitre de griefs" (1976) 22:1 *McGill LJ* 71.

490 Nicolas Mateesco Matte, "Preface" (1976) 1:1 *Ann Air & Sp L* vii at vii-viii.

491 Edward F Ryan & Antonio Lamer, "The Path of Law Reform" (1977) 23:3 *McGill LJ* 519.

492 *Ibid* at 522.

493 *Ibid* at 523.

494 *Ibid* at 529.

495 *Ibid* at, 534.

Cally Jordan, Editor-in-Chief of volume twenty-three and future Associate Professor of International and Comparative Law at the University of Florida Fredric G. Levin College of Law, wrote the introduction to the issue. In it she described the issue as a collection of pieces developed by Quebec delegates to the Henri Capitant Society conference of 1976[496]—a society whose conferences would contribute several additional special issues and sections to the MLJ moving into the future.

The President of the Society's Quebec Chapter from that time through to 2011 was volume four Comment Editor Jean-Louis Baudouin. In addition to the other honours bestowed on Baudouin already highlighted earlier in the book, he has been the recipient of seven honorary degrees, including one in 2007 from McGill. Baudouin is one of just a dozen or so former *Journal* members who would receive honorary degrees in their future, a list that includes (but is not exclusive to): Jacques-Yvan Morin, Morris J. Fish, Richard Pound, David P. O'Brien, Irwin Cotler, Yves Fortier, Jean-Paul Hubert Jr., Lionel Chetwynd, and Roy L. Heenan.

In his interview, Baudouin stated that the Henri Capitant Society always asked presenters at their conferences to always provide a publishable law review article alongside their presentation.[497] In a short preface of his own for the special issue, following Jordan's, Baudouin writes that by this point the environment was becoming one of the world's greatest concerns, and that it had "now become common place to insist upon the protection of our environment as evidenced by the recent efforts of the vast majority of governments in the Western World."[498]

Authors for the special issue included future President of the Canadian Association of Law Teachers, Professor Jean-Denis Gagnon;[499] future Professor Emerita, jointly of the Faculty of Law and the School of Urban Planning, at McGill, as well as Faculty Advisor for the MLJ for volume twenty-five, Jane Matthews Glenn;[500] and Lorne Giroux,[501] future Justice of the Quebec Court of Appeal. Other authors that contributed to volume twenty-three more generally included Peter MacKinnon,[502] future Dean of Law at and President of the University of Saskatchewan. A book review was also contributed from Professor Ian Brownie,[503] world renowned author on public international law. As Christine Carron wrote in her interview regarding the special issue, the very best part of her job "was getting to speak to the authors who were 'famous' professors and lawyers."[504]

Another senior editor of the MLJ that year was Elaine Feldman, who would serendipitously go on to become President of the Canadian Environmental Assessment Agency, though Feldman insists that she came about her future position through pure "happenstance".[505] Feldman also served as the Assistant Deputy Minister of North America at the Department of Foreign Affairs and International Trade. In her years with the *Journal*, Feldman relates that the MLJ editors were interested most specifically in publishing and learning more about ideas "not seen as the bread and butter of legal practice."[506] Other members of the Editorial Board for volume twenty-three included senior editor and future Justice of the Quebec Court of Appeal Brigitte Gouin.

The following volume, twenty-four, saw its own share of high profile authors and alumni. Book reviews were contributed by Carl Q. Christol, future USC Distinguished Professor Emeritus of International Law and Political Science;[507] Gerard FitzGerald,[508] namesake of the Gerald F. FitzGerald Memorial Prize awarded by the Canadian Council on International Law; Edgar Bodenheimer,[509] Professor Emeritus at the UC Davis Faculty of Law; John P Humphrey;[510] as well

496 Calle Jordan, "Editorial Note" (1977) 23:2 *McGill LJ* 161.

497 Baudouin interview, *supra* note 142.

498 Jean Louis Baudouin, "Preface" (1977) 23:2 *McGill LJ* 162 at 162.

499 Jean-Denis Gagnon, "La Protection Des Travailleurs Contre Les Maladies Industrielles Et Les effets De La Pollution" (1977) 23:2 *McGill LJ* 225.

500 Jane Matthews Glenn, "L'Amenagement Du Territoire En Droit Public Quebecois" (1977) 23:2 *McGill LJ* 242.

501 Lorne Giroux, "L'Interet a Poursuivre Et La Protection De L'Environnement En Droit Quebecois Et Canadien" (1977) 23:2 *McGill LJ* 292.

502 Peter MacKinnon, "Conspiracy and Sedition as Canadian Political Crimes" (1977) 23:4 *McGill LJ* 622.

503 Brownie, Ian, "*Canadian Perspectives on International Law and Organization* ed. By R. St. J. MacDonald, Gerald L. Morris, and Douglas M. Johnston" Book Review (1977) 23:2 *McGill LJ* 152.

504 Carron interview, *supra* note 454.

505 Interview of Elaine Feldman by James Cummins (22 March, 2011).

506 *Ibid.*

507 Carl Q Christol, "*Aerospace Law : From Scientific Exploration to Commercial Utilization* by Nicolas Mateesco Matte" Book Review (1978) 24:1 *McGill LJ* 158.

508 Gerard F FitzGerald, "*Ratemaking in International Air Transport. A Legal Analysis of International Air Fares and Rates* by Peter P.C. Haanappel" Book Review (1978) 24:3 *McGill LJ* 509.

509 Edgar Bodenheimer, "*Modern Legal Philosophy: The Tension between Experiential and Abstract Thought* by Cornelius F. Murphy" Book Review (1978) 24:4 *McGill LJ* 661.

510 John P Humphrey, "*The Law of Habeas Corpus* by R.J. Sharpe" Book Review (1978) 24:4 *McGill LJ* 674.

as several other authors previously highlighted in this book. Articles were contributed by the likes of Geoffrey Marshall, a renowned British constitutional expert and former Sheriff of Oxford, who wrote a short note on cultural sovereignty;[511] Alastair Bissett-Johnson,[512] future Chair of Private Law at the Dundee University; and future Justice of the Quebec Superior Court, senior editor for volume twenty-four Brian Riordan.[513]

The Editorial Board of volume-twenty four also produced individuals that went on to do significant things in their future in a true diversity of fields: from Executive Editor Bartha Knoppers—future Chair of the International Ethics Committee of the Human Genome Project and Canada Research Chair in Law and Medicine—to senior editor Donald R. McCarthy, future Vice-President at Imperial Tobacco.

As the year 1980 neared, so did the *Journal*'s twenty-fifth anniversary celebrations—though technically the anniversary was during the 1977-78 academic year, the MLJ waited until its twenty-fifth volume to acknowledge it. Opening the twenty-fifth anniversary volume, MLJ alumnus then-Dean John Brierley wrote that, "In addition to a host of distinguished Canadian authors who have made significant contributions in these pages to the study of law and legal scholarship, there has been a steady series of contributions by eminent writers from France, the United Kingdom, Germany and the U.S.A. Subjects treated have ranged over most aspects of local, national and international interest."[514] And while Brierley had applauded the *Journal* for not taking the time to rest on its laurels to idly reflect, he himself offered the following:

> The *Journal* has not always been able to function under the best conditions. After many years spent in a crowded attic room of Old Chancellor Day Hall (which I remember well from my own time on the board), it has migrated to the basement of the same building in only slightly more spacious accommodation. Financial conditions, too, have been modest; the *Journal* – and this is not generally known – has survived, indeed flourished, with no direct financial support from McGill University or the Faculty of Law itself (save for "special" projects such as the cumulative index to volumes 1-20) and only occasional support from outside agencies. To their credit, successive editorial boards have always wished to retain this financial independence as well as their managerial and editorial autonomy. The *Journal* is, then, in my view, a source of real distinction for the students who have served on it and it is a distinction which inures to the Faculty and the University. In no sense is it an "*in* house" publication…
>
> The law itself, increasing in volume and in complexity, will put the editorial skills of future editors to new challenges. I am confident that our students will meet these challenges because I know how very profoundly they believe in the value of their publication. Over the past twenty years – as a member of the junior and then senior Boards, as a former faculty adviser, and now as Dean – I have been involved in the welfare of the *Journal* and I have seen this belief and pride in the publication grow. This is good. It will be a strength for the future.[515]

Stories of the cramped offices of the early MLJ must of course be tempered with the memory that McGill Law itself did not have much space in the early days. As Maxwell Cohen wrote during his own deanship, "Only in 1950 did the Faculty acquire a building of its own when it moved into Chancellor Day Hall, formerly the home of Mr. J.K. Ross. For sixteen years the Ross house, now named Chancellor Day Hall after McGill's first Chancellor – and one of the Commissioners appointed to draft the Quebec Civil Code of 1866 – was the home of the Faculty."[516] That first acquisition of property was but two years before the *McGill Law Journal* first opened its doors.

Dean Cohen wrote a piece in the MLJ upon the opening of the New Chancellor Day Hall, during the tenure of volume thirteen. It was a spectacular event, including the conferring of honorary degrees upon Chief Justice Robert Taschereau of the Supreme Court of Canada, Chief Justice Earl Warren of the United States Supreme Court, and The Right Honourable Lord Alfred Thompson Denning, among others who were present at the opening ceremony.[517] During this era, there was no perennial student newspaper at the

511 Geoffrey Marshall, "Cultural Sovereignty in the U. K.: A Glance Ahead" (1978) 24:1 *McGill LJ* 112.

512 Alastair Bissett-Johnson, "Damages for Personal Injuries--The Supreme Court Speaks" (1978) 24:2 *McGill LJ* 316.

513 Brian Riordan, "The Currency of Suit in Actions for Foreign Debts" (1978) 24:3 *McGill LJ* 442.

514 Brierley 25th, *supra* note 47.

515 *Ibid* at 1-2.

516 Maxwell Cohen, "The Opening of the New Law Building: A Message from the Dean" (1967) 13:2 *McGill LJ* 197 at 197.

517 *Ibid* at 198-99.

Faculty of Law. The *McGill Law Journal*, until this point, had served not only to publish the legal scholarship of the day, but also to detail important events at the Faculty of Law.

From the decision to publish an announcement of the death of former Chancellor of McGill University and Chief Justice of the Superior Court in Montreal Orville S. Tyndale in the second issue of volume one onwards,[518] the MLJ served partly as student body crier. The use of editorial notes in volume seven and in several issues appearing in later volumes was just one way in which the MLJ performed this function. Another way was in the publication of speeches given at the Faculty of Law by rare guests—such as the speech Bora Laskin gave in honour of FR Scott noted earlier in this book.[519] This particular dinner was covered in two different ways: both in the publication of Laskin's speech and in a tribute to the guests of honour—FR Scott and L.M. Baudouin—who were retiring from academia.[520] Professor Baudouin had himself honoured a late-colleague within the pages of the MLJ as well two years prior—with a short piece on Justice Bernard Bissonnette of the Quebec Court of Appeal following his death.[521]

The MLJ also announced the appointment of each new Dean to its national readership.[522] In volume twelve, Stephen Scott even took it upon himself to write a full history of Canada's efforts to find a new method of amending its constitution—replete with the most scintillating of choices of language from those involved.[523] The care taken to put this together ensured all those reading the articles of the special issue following it had the greatest of context. Context and meaning was also given on the occasions that the MLJ published an obituary of legal figures.

For example, in the *Journal's* announcement of the death of Justice George Swan Challies—former Chief Justice of the Quebec Superior Court and McGill Professor—the editors tried to ensure the importance of the man's life was recorded alongside notification of his death, writing:

> Men cannot live together without law, and the extent of a society's civilization may be measured in part by the degree of perfection attained by its legal system. Western society has, over the centuries and through the efforts of many, developed an advanced legal system. Among those who devoted themselves to its furtherance in Quebec must be counted George Challies.[524]

Challies had published four articles within the MLJ during his time, alongside several book reviews.

In volume twenty-three, Dean Brierley took to the MLJ to make a statement of a similar nature. While the *Journal* may have been the first place of publication for future Dean Brierley, he now wrote, "There appears, in the following pages, the last published work of a distinguished jurist of Quebec and Canadian law whose untimely death has left stricken the several communities with which, in a short but brilliant career, he was associated … his many contributions to the science of law are well known in his own province and beyond."[525]

The colleague Brierley was writing about was McGill Professor of Law Yves Armand Caron, who died at the young age of thirty-eight. The Yves Caron Memorial Award was named in his honour in the year following his death. Caron's work would, though, be published once more in the *Journal* after the article published in the year of his death. In 1973 a paper based on a presentation Caron had given was edited by Brierley and prepared for publication in the *Journal's* anniversary volume, volume twenty-five.[526] Over all, Professor Caron had eight articles published within the MLJ—including an article in each of the volumes between volume thirteen and seventeen, and one other article in volume twenty-three (the volume in which his memoriam appears) prior to his death.[527] Through these actions and articles, the MLJ helped to not just play a part in history, but also to preserve it.

Soon after the twenty-fifth anniversary of the MLJ there would be another publication to take over some aspects of this secondary function of the MLJ: the *Quid Novi*, founded in 1981 by its first Editor-in-Chief Peter Dauphinée and his fellow students. As Professor of Law Richard Janda at McGill University—the second Editor-in-Chief of the *Quid*—recalls, before

518 Fred Kaufman, "Chief Justice O.S. Tyndale" (1953) 1:2 *McGill LJ* 108 at 108.

519 Laskin 68, *supra* note 355 at ff.

520 "The End of an Era" (1967) 13:3 *McGill LJ* 349 at 349.

521 Louis Baudouin, "In Memoriam: Monsieur le Juge Bernard Bissonnette" (1965) 11:1 *McGill LJ* 1.

522 $152, *supra* note 203; FR Scott retires, *supra* note 239.

523 Scott's Diary, *supra* note 288.

524 "George Swan Challies, 1910-1973" (1973) 19:3 *McGill LJ* 321 at 321.

525 JEC Brierley, "Yves Armand Caron 1939-1977 Professor, Faculty of Law McGill University 1967-1977" (1977) 23:3 *McGill LJ* 379 at 379.

526 Yves Caron, "The Trust in Quebec" (1980) 25:4 *McGill LJ* 421.

527 Yves Caron, "La Vente Et Le Nantissement De La Chose Mobiliere D'Autrui: Premiere Partie" (1977) 23:1 *McGill LJ* 1.

the founding of the *Quid* student newspapers at McGill Law only "came out sporadically",[528] however the *Quid* represented a firm effort on behalf of the students association of the Faculty of Law to take a more active role in the "news and views" of the Faculty. The publication took over the function of the student association's regular newsletter to the students of the Faculty, but asserted a weekly regularity to the newsletter's function and started the publication on the path to becoming a true student newspaper.

The first issue of the *Quid Novi* was published on March 4, 1981 and its first volume lasted only about a month—until the end of the scholastic year. The issue consisted of a three page long newsletter, with one of the pages dedicated to the photocopies of an editorial from the March 2, 1981 *Montreal Gazette* newspaper with several passages underlined by the editors and a three frame *The Wizard of Id* comic strip.[529] One of the other pages included a letter from Editor-in-Chief Dauphinée placing pressure on the other students of McGill Law to participate in a "day of silence" at the Faculty of Law, where the student body would say nothing—stay silent—all day, in all classes, to protest of a lack of student representation at the school. In fact, this first issue of the *Quid Novi* was released on the very day that the day of silence was taking place. Page two also advertised an upcoming "Social Law Conference" to be held later in the week, with panellists including MLJ alumnus and Dean of Law at the time JEC Brierley.[530] Page one of the issue included notices for an upcoming moot, a notice from the book store, a notice about upcoming elections, and a notice from the *McGill Law Journal* advertising an information seminar to be held on March 18, 1981, writing for students to, "Come and meet the present Editorial and Management Boards and see how the Journal is put together."[531]

In terms of the day of silence, Dauphinée elaborated on its significance to both the Faculty and the *Quid* in a 2010 email to then editor at the *McGill Journal of Health Law* Simone Bittman, writing that,

> Whatever may be the subtle influence o[f] *Quid Novi* on the course of legal history, certainly the protest and day of silence (winter of 1981 I think) shook a number of us out of our customary apathy to do something to "make a difference". I think that must have had some influence, perhaps imperceptible, on the law faculty and on the students that participated. It's certainly part of the story of *Quid Novi* … Probably the day of silence was just a last gasp of the sixties, a peep in history.[532]

In a 2012 statement regarding the greater history of the *Quid*, Dauphinée also wrote that,

> Some time during the 1980-81 school year, the student body at McGill University's Law Faculty became agitated. Students were displeased about some aspects of the administration and wanted changes. Thirty-one years later, the particulars of those complaints reside in the fading memories of those present at the time and may be forever lost to the world.
>
> There were issues and there were opinions, but there was no convenient forum where these could be brought together in a way that might constitute a discussion and point to solutions. During that year, one or two students began to publish a broadsheet of sorts, a weekly sheet of happening events printed on one or two sheets of legal paper. Its mission was aptly captured by its title, *Quid Novi*. There may have been one or two substantive articles published, but a paper given to one-line announcements, jokes, lost and found items, and the like groaned under the weight of the controversy roiling the Law Faculty.
>
> The Law Undergraduate Society (LUS) convened an assembly in the Moot Court. The LUS President addressed a packed roomful of students, and then Campbell Stuart delivered a barnburner of a speech. He outlined our grievances and delivered our demands. Little stands out now other than a surprising demand that we receive increased hours of class teaching time (!) and a need for greater student representation on Faculty Council.
>
> Campbell concluded by proposing a day of protest to inform the faculty of our serious intent. On a selected day, students would register their discontent by refusing to utter a word in class. The

528 Pilarczyk, *supra* note 27 at 135.

529 "First issue" (1981) 1:1 *Quid Novi* 3.

530 *Ibid* at 2.

531 *Ibid* at 1.

532 Interview of Peter Dauphinée by Simone Bittman (21 July, 2010). Bittman was an Editor for the *MLJH* at the time and interviewed Dauphinée, and interviewed him as a part of a school project. The interview response was sent to James Cummins on 30 May 2012.

"Day of Silence" was effective at least in creating a notably strained atmosphere throughout the faculty as a majority of students withheld participation in class while glaring at the few who were as usual fully primed for class and eager to engage in legal repartee.

In LUS elections that followed the Day of Silence, students elected a radical slate of candidates led by Campbell Stuart. The one exception was Treasurer. I ran, but of course no one wants a radical Treasurer. Free of that burden, I could better contribute to the budding revolution by starting a newspaper as a forum for dialogue about issues of relevance to the Law Faculty.

The following year, a small group of us set up shop in a tiny room in the basement under a staircase in Chancellor Day Hall. There was a brief moment in time when we considered alternative names, but *Quid Novi* had brand recognition and we quickly became overwhelmed by production issues. Our enthusiasm was taxed by the effort of hammering out eight pages of text on an old IBM Selectric typewriter, now extinct, cutting and pasting articles on 11 by 17 sheets, and sprinting down McTavish Street to have it printed at the McGill Printing Service.

Law students tend to be wordy opinionated individuals so generating 8 pages of material a week for 26 weeks was not a problem. More challenging was finding a way to turn all that verbiage into neatly stapled and stacked booklets while passing law school. We were greatly supported by the LUS with funding and the Faculty administration who granted us the keys to the office. We graduated from the single Selectric in the basement to the pair of high-tech daisy-wheel word processors upstairs. By the end of the year we had raised some additional funds to afford typesetting by McGill Printing – and a professional looking product.

The crowning achievement of *Quid Novi*'s first year as a newspaper was on the LUS Election Day, 1982. No, we did not uncover robocalls or election fraud of any sort. We secured the future of the newspaper, and countless more nights of sleep for future *Quid Novi* volunteers, by asking students in a referendum to increase student fees by $5.00 per year, dedicated to *Quid Novi*. The student body said yes.

Much as is occurring today, these events marked a change of era. Student revolt came and went at McGill Law School almost purely symbolically, in the blink of an eye. The gender balance was shifting rapidly, and a great many younger students were entering the Civil Law program directly from CEGEP with more conservative views than the grizzled graduates who still retained some passing memories of the sixties.[533]

It was during the sixties that the MLJ had served this function itself; the function of allowing a platform for student dissent, however the main function of the MLJ—to borrow from Dauphinée—generally overwhelmed any urgency that may have been behind maintaining a steady platform for localized opinion. Thus the *Quid Novi* assumed with greater regularity and reach around the Faculty what was once a part of the MLJ's mission. The launch of the *Quid* marked the end of the *Journal*'s participation in faculty politics, at least within the pages of its volumes.

Now twenty-seven years into its history, when asked what aspects of the *Journal*'s history were most at risk of being lost over time, senior editor for volume twenty-five Peter D. Nesgos wrote that it was "[h]ow MLJ editors functioned year-by-year relative to teamwork, activities, administration and available technology."[534] Now a partner with Milbank, Tweed, Hadley & McCloy LLP in New York City, Nesgos wrote of the importance of "[c]omparing how things were done in the past versus today."[535]

Looking back on his time with the *Journal*, he added that:

> A lawyer's tools are words. How we express them and use them in drafting contracts or court pleadings reflects indelibly on our proficiency, persuasiveness and professionalism. Over the years, it is noticeable how education and technology have affected our attitudes towards the use of words. Those of us who were

533 Interview of Peter Dauphinée by James Cummins (30 May, 2012).

534 Interview of Peter D Nesgos by James Cummins (24 November, 2010).

535 *Ibid.*

> fortunate enough to serve on law journals were imbued with the significance of precise expression at the very start of our careers. Those lessons remain and those experiences are applied every day.[536]

The next twenty-five years would indeed by impacted significantly by the advent of new technologies—from how the *Journal* itself was produced to the pieces it published inside its volumes. The next twenty-five years would also be greatly impacted by the coming globalization of the world economies and the international focus this would put on the importance of comparative and multi-jurisdictional law. The special issue for volume twenty-five focused on just that: multi-jurisdictional issues, within the recent Supreme Court of Canada decision *General Motors v. Kravitz*.

Gathered from articles presented at a conference held by the *Colloque de l'Association québécoise pour l'étude comparative de droit*, contributors to the issue included future Wainwright Emeritus Professor of Civil Law at McGill Pierre-Gabriel Jobin,[537] and future Dean of the UCL Faculty of Arts at the London School of Economics Professor Michael G. Bridge. Bridge wrote plainly that the *Kravitz* decision under a common law jurisdiction would have failed the plaintiff.[538] Though he added that while the decision "may appear radical in the present Anglo-Canadian common law world ... the picture in ten or fifteen years' time is likely to be very different."[539] We see here, upon the occasion of the MLJ's twenty-fifth anniversary volume, that Bridge and his fellow contributors are focused upon the dawn of a world of jurisdictions about to become irrevocably intertwined.

Other contributors to the twenty-fifth anniversary volume generally included Thomas E. Carbonneau,[540] future Samuel P. Orlando Distinguished Professor of Law at the Dickinson School of Law at Penn State; and the first of thirteen articles to be contributed over the years by Professor Roderick A. MacDonald,[541] whose achievements were discussed previously. There were also articles by Ronda Bessner,[542] future Assistant Dean at Osgoode Hall; and the poet Lazar Sarna discussing tax law.[543] Interesting members of that volume's Editorial Board include Executive Editor Peter Chepya, future President of the Faculty Senate for Post University; junior editor Philip Girard, future Acting Dean of Law at Dalhousie University; and senior editor Claire Gohier, who would become a noted Montreal philanthropist and fundraiser.

The first quarter century of the *McGill Law Journal* established an institution far more influential and impressive than its founders ever imagined it would be. In only a few short years it had outpaced all of its contemporaries in terms of the quality of articles and editorial staff. During the following quarter century, the MLJ began to outpace even its faculty-run competitors. That story, of volumes twenty-six through today, is the tale of how what started out as a small, independent student project with big aspirations turned into what the Washington and Lee University Law School official global law school index ranked in 2012 as one of the ten best law journals outside of the United States, and the number one non-US student-run law journal, *in the world*.[544]

536 *Ibid.*

537 Pierre-Gabriel Jobin, "L'Arret Kravitz Sous Les Feux Du Droit Compare" (1980) 25:3 *McGill LJ* 296.

538 Michael G Bridge, "A Common Lawyer Looks at Kravitz" (1980) 25:3 *McGill LJ* 335 at 335.

539 *Ibid* at 364.

540 Thomas E Carbonneau, "The French Legal Studies Curriculum: Its History and Relevance as a Model for Reform" (1980) 25:4 *McGill LJ* 445.

541 Roderick A MacDonald, "Judicial Review and Procedural Fairness in Administrative Law: I" (1980) 25:4 *McGill LJ* 520.

542 Ronda Bessner, "Condonation as a Bar to Divorce in Canada" (1979) 25:1 *McGill LJ* 64.

543 Lazar Sama, "Federal Continued Corporations and the Deemed-Resident Provisions of Section 250(4) of the Income Tax Act" (1979) 25:1 *McGill LJ* 111. Sarna is also a practicing attorney.

544 "Law Journals: Submissions and Ranking, 2005 - 2012" *Washington and Lee University School of Law* (15 February, 2012), online: < http://lawlib.wlu.edu/LJ/index.aspx > According to the website, rankings are based upon the amount of citations to a periodical over the last eight years, the number of American cases cited to the periodical over the same period, and the length of time between an article's publication and its citations.

Chapter Three:

A Canadian Institution

In 2010 David L. Johnston would become the twenty-eighth Governor General of Canada, but in 1980 Johnston was serving as Vice-Chancellor and Principal of McGill University—a job in which he served from 1979 to 1994. The article he contributed to the MLJ, cited earlier in this book, was published in volume twenty-seven. In addition to the history of McGill Law, he also wrote of his present time (1980), writing that,

> [T]he existence of the two first-degree programs, the LL.B. and B.C.L., reflects the fact that life is always a little harder at McGill because one is not content to do the conventional. By presenting the two Canadian legal traditions side by side – traditions which mirror the two great European legal systems – and by insisting that they inform and refine one another in fruitful co-existence, one begins to fulfill in law the rich destiny of Canada. [545]

Johnston would also help open the second quarter century of the MLJ by contributing a book review to volume twenty-six, discussing within the review his opinions on such hot-button issues as the lack of national legislation in Canada dealing with markets and securities,[546] and of what he saw at the time as "fractious intergovernmental relations that do not augur well for the adoption of" positive proposals for change.[547] The issue was also graced with a contribution from the Chief Justice of the Quebec Superior Court at the time, Justice Jules Deschênes,[548] who would also go on to become President of the Royal Society in 1990.

The fourth issue of volume twenty-six would serve as the first special issue of the MLJ's second quarter-century. That issue, "Issues in Medical Law in Canada", would include contributions from former long-time Dean of the University of Alberta Faculty of Law W.F. Bowker;[549] future Justice of the Alberta Court of Appeal Ellen Picard;[550] as well as often-time contributor Margaret Somerville, future Samuel Gale Professor of Law at McGill University. Somerville would go on to become the Founding Director of the McGill Centre for Medicine, Ethics and Law five years after the special issue was published. Only two years into her professorial career, her trademark style is already put on display in this early article. She writes, appropriately in the historical context of her work, that the questions in the issue had, "raised complex and interesting legal, ethical and policy issues. This development is far from finished."[551]

Fellow Professor in both Law and Medicine Bernard M. Dickens of the University of Toronto also published a contribution. Dickens, the future President of the American Society of Law, Medicine and Ethics, and Vice-President of the World Association for Medical Law, wrote about the limits of a person's right to refusal of medical care when death is imminent.[552] The issue also included the *Journal*'s one and only section of Theatre Reviews, based on a production of the play *Whose Life is it Anyway?* by Brian Clark—a play that centered on the subject of deciding between suicide and a life of impairment.[553] Each of the reviews came from a different philosophical perspective: an "ethical perspective" given by the Director of the Centre for Bioethics Clinical Research Institute of Montreal David J. Roy;[554] a "juridical perspective" from Professor Jean-Louis Baudouin;[555] and a "psychiatric perspective" from Dr. Maurice Dongier,[556] who was Chairman of the McGill Department of Psychiatry and future namesake

545 Johnston & Frost, *supra* note 113.

546 David Lloyd Johnston, "*Proposals for a Securities Market Law for Canada* by Philip Anisman" Book Review (1981) 26:3 *McGill LJ* 637.

547 *Ibid* at 642.

548 Jules Deschênes, "L'Affaire Marier" (1981) 26:3 *McGill LJ* 556.

549 WF Bowker, "Minors and Mental Incompetents: Consent to Experimentation, Gifts of Tissue and Sterilization" (1981) 26:4 *McGill LJ* 951.

550 Ellen Picard, "The Liability of Hospitals in Common Law Canada" (1981) 26:4 *McGill LJ* 997.

551 Margaret A Somerville, "Structuring the Issues in Informed Consent" (1981) 26:4 *McGill LJ* 740 at 808.

552 Bernard M Dickens, "The Right to Natural Death" (1981) 26:4 *McGill LJ* 848.

553 "Whose Life is it Anyway?" (1981) 26:4 *McGill LJ* 1068.

554 David J Roy, "Whose Life is it Anyway?" Theatre Review (1981) 26:4 *McGill LJ* 1069.

555 Jean-Louis Baudouin, "Whose Life is it Anyway?" Theatre Review (1981) 26:4 *McGill LJ* 1076.

556 Maurice Dongier, "Whose Life is it Anyway?" Theatre Review (1981) 26:4 *McGill LJ* 1080.

of the Maurice Dongier Training Award at the Douglas Mental Health University Institute. Other contributors to the volume more generally included future Justice of the Quebec Superior Court Mark Schrager.[557]

Volume twenty-six had another first—there were two different Editors-in-Chief. Editor-in-Chief Patrick Healy wrote the preface for the special issue, whose interview we discussed earlier in the book.[558] Healy inscribes that one of the issue's other authors, Bernard Starkman, discusses the *E. (Mrs.) v. Eve* Supreme Court case five years in advance of the decision.[559] *Eve* would become a landmark case in the field—ruling against the rights of parents to sterilize their mentally handicapped children—and Starkman would represent the Attorney General of Canada during the Supreme Court appeal.[560]

Healy wrote further that "the province of medical law remains largely undetermined, and new categories are continually opened as problems in medical care force the law to provide reason and guidance."[561] On a note related more to the process behind getting the issue out, Healy wrote further that, "This special issue was long and hard in gestation, partly as a function of its size. The Editorial Board extends sincere thanks to its contributors, some of whom have been waiting more than nine months to see the publication of their work."[562]

In his interview, Healy wrote further of the process of getting the *Journal* out for volume twenty-six, stating that they all,

> [P]ut in very, very long hours: everybody did. You have to remember that at that time we had word processors, but nothing like what they are now; also the *Journal* was printed with hot lead—it was the old style of printing. So it was a very intensive process to bring something from a manuscript to final readiness. And then, once it was in proofs, they had to be read and re-read, and re-read, several times over. And we had to go to the printer—it was on Papineau Street—to supervise the corrections to the proofs.[563]

Like Executive Editor of volume eight Arnold Isaacson, Healy became close friends with his Faculty Advisor Professor Yves-Marie Morrisette. Healy stated that, "I felt that we had very good relations with all of the faculty, not just with the Faculty Advisor. When I was the Editor-in-Chief, I think we published four or five papers by faculty members, and so clearly there were close relations with those, as well as with the Faculty Advisor."[564]

The reason for his volume having two Editors-in-Chief appears not to have a particularly scandalous backstory. Healy explained that,

> If you look at the masthead for volume twenty-six, you'll see that there is an apparent doubling of the staff, and the reason for that is not what it appears. It was done—that masthead was presented that way—because the *Journal* had fallen into arrears. There was one year when I don't think even a single issue was published. And so in order to put the *Journal* back in the position where the masthead identified the people who actually produced the volume in question, this fiction was created of doubling up the masthead for that one particular volume. [So] my predecessor ... has her board and my board together. That was the reason ... the problem was that the thing had gotten out of synch.[565]

It appears that it only took five years for the efforts of volume twenty—putting out ten issues in one year—to have been completely wiped out.

Healy would go on to be one of only five individuals to serve as both a member of the senior Editorial Board of the *Journal* and as future Faculty Advisor: along with Professor John E.C. Brierley, Professor Stephen A. Scott, volume twenty-eight Editor-in-Chief Stephen J Toope, and volume thirty-four Executive Editor David Lametti. Returning to the subject of his special issue, Healy also spoke about the reason behind putting the issue together:

> [A]t the time, we thought, as a board, that the subject of medical law or medical aspects of the law was becoming increasingly important, both academically and practically. We wanted very much to contribute to that, so that was the reason we had a special issue on that subject. It

557 Mark Schrager, "Recent Developments in the Law Relating to Confessions: England, Canada and Australia" (1981) 26:3 *McGill LJ* 435.

558 Healy interview, *supra* note 413.

559 Patrick Healy, "Preface" (1981) 26:4 *McGill LJ* 671.

560 *E (Mrs) v Eve*, [1986] 2 SCR 388: beginning.

561 Healy preface, *supra* note 558.

562 *Ibid* at 672.

563 Healy interview, *supra* note 413.

564 *Ibid.*

565 *Ibid.*

> dealt with quite a variety of topics. It was also—it wasn't specifically about abortion, but that was also one of the things that was in the air at the time. And if I remember correctly, there was one article in there dealing with section 45 of the Criminal Code, which had been raised in *Morgentaler*.[566]

The same Morgentaler that had found support in the MLJ near the beginning of his activist career.

In the end, in the context of the thirty years that had elapsed since his time on the *Journal*, Healy related that,

> The circumstances of the *Journal*, I think, have changed. I don't know what it costs now, but I remember that the production costs were very substantial when I was the Editor-in-Chief. It was always a concern. The volume that I edited, I think that we came in at the end around a thousand pages for the four issues, which is certainly much longer than the *Journal* was when it started. I don't know what it is now, but I imagine that it is somewhere between seven-fifty and a thousand pages a year, which is a very, very demanding task to produce at a high quality. But the students who work on it are dedicated; they're committed to making it as good as it could possibly be ... The experience of the *Journal*, it always makes an impression on everybody who works there. I certainly feel very grateful for having had the opportunity to do what I did. I have no idea what it's like now, with modern technology.[567]

Healy's volume was indeed longer than things had been in the beginning. The first volume of the *McGill Law Journal* was 291 pages long, with volume two coming in at 176 total pages. Volume twenty-six, under Healy's command, was the first volume to have published more than one thousand pages. It is a standard that would—as Healy pointed out—continue into the future, and considering the quality of scholarship found in volume twenty-six, it appears that Morin's envisioned permanent meeting place was now abuzz with a voluminous amount of enlightening and insightful thought.

566 *Ibid.*

567 *Ibid.*

Alongside Healy sat several other editors that went on to do things of particular note. Associate Editor Pierre Legrand Jr. became the Director of Postgraduate Comparative Legal Studies at l'Université Paris-Sorbonne; Executive Editor Thomas M. Davis went on to become the Chairman of Health Partners International of Canada; Executive Editor Marguerite Brien went on to become a Senior Instructor at The College of Law in New Zealand; Managing Editor Deborah Berlach went on to become a marquee partner of Stieber Berlach LLP; Comment Editor Margriet Zwarts went on to become General Counsel and Secretary of Telesystem International Wireless Inc; and Book Reviews Editor Peter Carver went on to become a cross-appointed Professor of Law and Rehabilitation Medicine at the University of Alberta. In addition, senior editor Andrew Szemenyei would become a marquee partner of Szemenyei MacKenzie Godin LLP; senior editor Elo Tulving-Blais went on to become the founder and Editor-in-Chief of *Canadian International Lawyer*; and senior editor Sydney John Isaacs became Chief Legal Officer of Ace Aviation Holdings Inc.

Alongside David Johnston, contributors to the following volume (twenty-seven) included another piece by Justice Gerald Le Dain—sitting on the Federal Court of Appeal at the time—who like Laskin before him (who was also an Appeals judge at the time he gave his speech about Scott), wrote about his memories and relationship with FR Scott.[568] Le Dain's piece came from a presentation as well, this time held on February 21, 1981 before the Conference on the Achievements of FR Scott held at Simon Fraser University.[569] Le Dain reminds us of the context of the 1950s, when the *Journal* was just coming into the world, writing that it was a time "when legal education was on the threshold of the important break-through that was to open the way to the great development of the 1960s."[570] In this simple phrase, we can appreciate even more the context given in the volume twenty-seven by the piece from Johnston and Frost on the history of McGill Law.

Johnston himself offered yet another book review on the revision of securities law, in which he welcomes the increased attention to a cause he truly stood behind.[571] Healy added a book review as well[572]—

568 Gerald Le Dain, "F. R. Scott and Legal Education" (1981) 27:1 *McGill LJ* 1 at 1.

569 *Ibid.*

570 *Ibid* at 12.

571 David Lloyd Johnston, "*Ontario Securities Law* by Victor P. Alboini" Book Review (1981) 27:1 *McGill LJ* 123.

572 Patrick Healy, "*A Modern Legal History of England and Wales 1750-1950* by A.H. Manchester" Book Review (1981) 27:1 *McGill LJ* 125.

marking his first academic publication—as did future Professor Emeritus of the University of Calgary Faculty of Law Eugene Dais,[573] and Maxwell Cohen, now a Justice of the International Court of Justice.[574] A particularly long book review was also contributed by Canadian Senator Arthur Tremblay.[575] Authors contributing articles to the issue beyond the pieces by Johnston and Le Dain, included M.H. Ogilvie,[576] who was appointed the first ever Chancellor's Professor at Carleton University in 2002, as well as several prestigious authors noted in prior volumes.

There is one other author of note who, at the time, was only on the junior board of the *Journal*. That author is Stephen J. Toope—who would become the youngest Dean at the Faculty of Law of McGill to ever hold the position, founding Dean of the transsystemic program at McGill Law, and future President of the University of British Columbia. Writing at a young age in his first legal academic publication, he speaks on a subject matter that would become a real concern of his later on, as it is with all high ranking university administrators: the consideration of information privacy. As if speaking with full knowledge of the world to come in twenty years time, he wrote that, "Some… have suggested that it is more important to know to whom information is being released than to know that it will not be released. This highly debatable assumption implies that freedom of government information is valued more highly than personal privacy."[577]

On the staff of volume twenty-seven, alongside junior editor Toope, was Associate Editor Bernard Amyot, who went on to become National President of the Canadian Bar Association and Governor of the National Theatre School of Canada; Advertising Editor Elaine M. Kierans, who went on to become Acting-Chair of the Canadian Artists and Producers Professional Relations Tribunal; and Circulation Editor Ronna Brott, future Justice of the Ontario Superior Court.

Stephen Toope would go on to become Editor-in-Chief of the following volume. In an interview, Toope related that upon taking on the position there was an "incredible sense of responsibility. There was already a tradition at the *Journal* and it was very highly regarded; to make sure that it got out on time and with the appropriate quality felt like an important thing to be able to do."[578] The efforts of Healy and his team were still in effect, as Toope remembers that:

> I actually graduated and so [I was] quite fortunate, and everything came out pretty much on time. I think what I remember most is just reading articles again and again and again. I remember the proofreading and how I'd sit there with one or another of the editors and I'd feel that I had probably read the article at least ten if not fifteen times previously, making sure at the end that there were no mistakes. I can tell you that you really had to concentrate a lot because it was not fresh material … I had a really wonderful team.[579]

The teams by that point had changed from the time F.H. Buckley was Editor-in-Chief. Toope relates that during his time it was "a very intense experience, especially for the editing team. So I would say that it was very collegial in my year. We got along with each other; it was fun in that sense. We certainly had loads of time together having pizza while we were working but in some ways it really wasn't a social culture: it was a work culture,"[580] though it was still very friendly. By that point, the MLJ had also developed an established peer review practice. As Toope remembers,

> It was pretty established I think by the time we got there. That occupied a lot of time. That's one place where I would say that email and everything would have made things a lot easier. I mean we were sitting there photocopying actual articles and then sending them out and having to get them back by mail – the whole thing took a long time and that was a very nerve-wracking period, because people aren't always on time when they do these reviews and that could actually [cause] delays and of course if you were really trying to solicit the article and you'd sent it out and then someone was late in reviewing it, ah, it was

573 Eugene Dais, "*In Defence of Fundamental Rights* by William E. Conklin" Book Review (1981) 27:1 *McGill LJ* 133.

574 Maxwell Cohen, "*Anticombines and Antitrust*[,] *The Competition Law of Canada and the Antitrust Law of the United States* by R.J. Roberts" Book Review (1982) 27:2 *McGill LJ* 387.

575 Arthur Tremblay, "*Continuing Canadian Constitutional Dilemmas* [:] *Essays on the Constitutional History Public Law and Federal System of Canada* by W.R. Lederman" Book Review (1982) 27:3 *McGill LJ* 569.

576 MH Ogilvie, "Reception of *Photo Production Ltd. v. Securicor Transport Ltd* in Canada: *Nec Tamen Consumebatur*" (1982) 27:3 *McGill LJ* 424.

577 Stephen J Toope & Alison L Young, "Confidentiality of Tax Returns under Canadian Law" (1982) 27:3 *McGill LJ* 479 at 503.

578 Interview of Stephen J Toope by James Cummins (20 December, 2010).

579 *Ibid.*

580 *Ibid.*

really a nightmare…

It did take a lot of time. Although the biggest amount of time was in the checking of the footnotes. There's no doubt that that was the big time sink and I mean at that point we had not done the [official] citation guide. In fact, the citation guide came just after us and it was built a lot on a lot of decisions that we were making in volume twenty-eight and twenty-nine…

We had our own internal guide. The difficulty in my year was that Disarmament Issue, because we actually started using a whole bunch of international law materials that hadn't been used that much by the *Journal* before; so we actually had to really come up with our own style—obviously looking at what other journals were doing, what the UN itself was doing, etc. That took a lot of time and I know that that piece ultimately did inform a lot of what went on subsequently in the first iteration of the *Cite Guide.*[581]

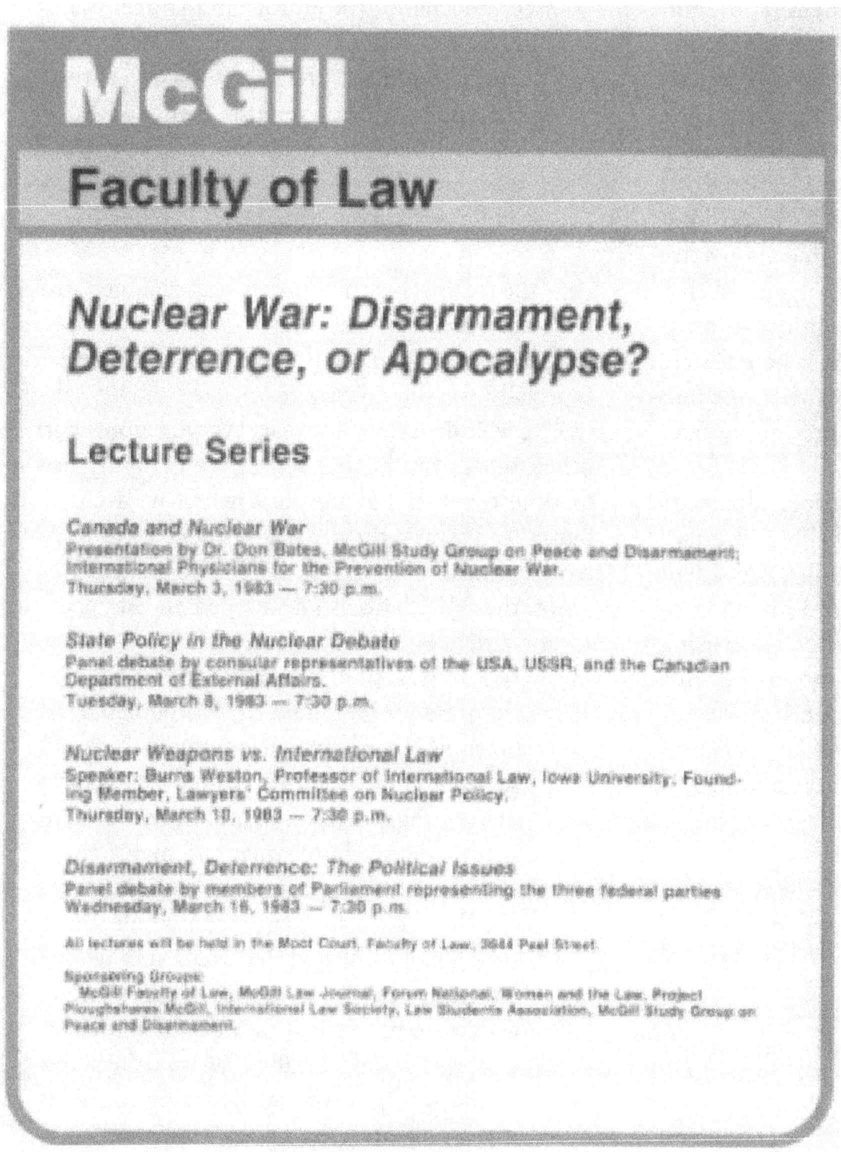

Poster for the 1983 "Nuclear War: Disarmament, Deterrence, or Apocalypse" conference, used to advertise around McGill University (Courtesy of Marc Barbeau)

Keeping Toope's words about the citation guide alongside those of Buckley for our discussion about the citation guide later on in this chapter, the "Disarmament Issue" Toope discusses was the special issue for volume twenty-eight. Talking about that specifically, Toope related that,

> The big thing in my year was doing special issues. So we did a special issue on disarmament, which was a fun topic in the early 80s, and so that was where we focused our energy … [I]t was a very major topic at the time and there was a lot of concern that there had just been the conclusion of the "Disarmament Decade", as the UN had declared, and we wanted to do an assessment of where things stood; and my interest at the time, and still is, international law. We also had strong support from Professor [Ivan A.] Vlasic, a real specialist in disarmament. So he was incredibly helpful to me in making sure that we could get top quality people …
>
> [W]e actually did a lot of direct solicitation for that special issue. We wrote letters to people that; we drew up a "wish list" of people that we would like to participate and then we just went after them—and professor Vlasic helped us a lot. We actually got almost all of the people that we wanted, so it was very exciting to work on at the time … we were writing letters and making phone calls and we tried to plan out the special issue in some detail, then give people an

581 *Ibid.*

> overview of what we were trying to achieve and asked them specifically to contribute in certain areas, so it was quite targeted.[582]

There was no preface to the issue, but at nearly four hundred pages there wasn't likely enough room. Of those no doubt on their wish list that contributed to the article, we can count Richard Falk—Professor Emeritus of International Law from Princeton University—who wrote on the subject of developing a new legal regime for nuclear weapons. Writing in 1983, he believed that there was at that time just recently a climate "in which to argue the case for the relevance of international law to nuclear issues ... For reasons of state policy, the Soviet Union seems prepared to lend its official support to most efforts to delegitimize nuclear weapons."[583] Eleven years after Humphrey published his doomsayist piece on the future of the world, Falk was pointing out the slow evolution of global hope.

Falk was not entirely assured of the world's future, however, as he points to a "continuing predominance of a Machiavellian tradition of political leadership"[584] on the global stage. Yet he still gives a proscription for what he sees as an effective method of creating international law that could do something about the nuclear problem,[585] with the following warning:

> If this disarmament effort fails to materialize within this decade, then the burden of persuasion would seem to shift in support of the unconditional prohibition of the threat, use and possession of nuclear weapons, almost regardless of national security claims ... The interim position ... here, in effect, provides governments with a final opportunity to get their normative house in order.[586]

Considering that after the decade he was discussing—the 1980s—a worldwide campaign to end nuclear proliferation, culminating in wars over who could have weapons of mass-destruction, would come to fruition, it appears that this special issue was well timed. As volume twenty-eight Associate Editor Marc Barbeau wrote in his own interview,

> There was nuclear disarmament, the nuclear issue, the arms race and all that, and in the early 80s, you had Reagan at the head of the US, the Soviet Union still in full swing, and frankly, most of us were convinced that it was nice to be educated but it was a futile exercise because in all likelihood we'd blow ourselves up before the end of the decade. That was kind of the mindset.[587]

Falk was published alongside future Bessie Dutton Murray Distinguished Professor of Law Emeritus at the University of Iowa, Burns H. Weston—world renowned human rights lawyer—who wrote that "while no treaty or treaty provision forbids nuclear warfare *per se*... almost every use to which nuclear weapons might be put ... appear to violate one or more of the laws of war that serve to make up the contemporary humanitarian law of armed conflict."[588] Other authors included Simone Courteix,[589] future President of the European Centre for Space Law; and future Mike and Teresa Baker Law Center Professor at the University of Houston, Jordan J. Paust.[590]

One of the most important authors at that time was Eugene V. Rostow, who was Director of the United States Arms Control and Disarmament Agency under US President Ronald Reagan as well as being appointed the Sterling Professor of Law and Public Affairs Emeritus at Yale University in the year following the issue's publication. He was also Under Secretary of State for Political Affairs under US President Lyndon Johnson. He wrote the article with Mary Elizabeth Hoinkes, who would go on to become General Counsel of the Arms Control Agency. They wrote that new Soviet policy had been to "make detente irreversible"[591] as the "task [was] indispensable in the name of humanity."[592]

Rostow and Hoinkes were less in favour of a complete eradication of nuclear arms than Falk was, however. They wrote that,

> It is evident that an impregnable wall cannot be erected between nuclear

582 *Ibid.*

583 Richard Falk, "Toward a Legal Regime for Nuclear Weapons" (1983) 28:3 *McGill LJ* 519 at 529.

584 *Ibid* at 534.

585 *Ibid* at 537-8.

586 *Ibid* at 541.

587 Interview of Marc Barbeau by Omar Soliman (3 December, 2010).

588 Burns H Weston, "Nuclear Weapons versus International Law: A Contextual Reassessment" (1983) 28:3 *McGill LJ* 542 at 589.

589 Simone Courteix, "Le Controle De La Proliferation Des Armes Nucleaires" (1983) 28:3 *McGill LJ* 591.

590 Jordan J Paust, "Controlling Prohibited Weapons and the Illegal Use of Permitted Weapons" (1983) 28:3 *McGill LJ* 608.

591 Eugene V Rostow & Mary Elizabeth Hoinkes, "The United States Approach to Negotiating Arms Limitation Agreements with the Soviet Union" (1983) 28:3 *McGill LJ* 750 at 751.

592 *Ibid.*

and conventional war. A nuclear standoff is meaningless to the victims of the many eruptions of hostilities waged with conventional arms. Foreswearing the use of nuclear weapons, thereby increasing the possibility of ever more devastating conflicts with conventional arms, would be a mockery of arms control … The struggle to save mankind from nuclear catastrophe must be seen in the context of a wider struggle to establish world public order … The issue is not "colonialism" or "capitalism" or "communism" or "democracy" or the so-called "arms race". It is aggression. The motives for aggression are irrelevant. We live in a shrinking world, a world which is increasingly dangerous. The arms race is a symptom, not the cause, of the breakdown in world public order.[593]

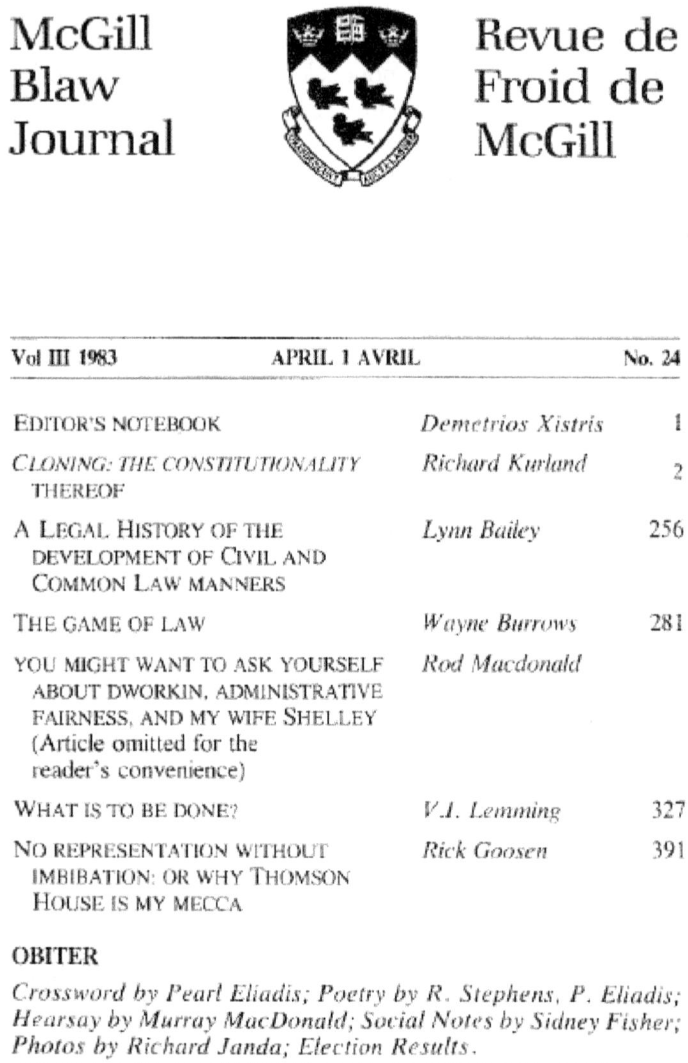

McGill Blaw Journal

Revue de Froid de McGill

Vol III 1983	APRIL 1 AVRIL	No. 24
EDITOR'S NOTEBOOK	*Demetrios Xistris*	1
CLONING: THE CONSTITUTIONALITY THEREOF	*Richard Kurland*	2
A LEGAL HISTORY OF THE DEVELOPMENT OF CIVIL AND COMMON LAW MANNERS	*Lynn Bailey*	256
THE GAME OF LAW	*Wayne Burrows*	281
YOU MIGHT WANT TO ASK YOURSELF ABOUT DWORKIN, ADMINISTRATIVE FAIRNESS, AND MY WIFE SHELLEY (Article omitted for the reader's convenience)	*Rod Macdonald*	
WHAT IS TO BE DONE?	*V.I. Lemming*	327
NO REPRESENTATION WITHOUT IMBIBATION: OR WHY THOMSON HOUSE IS MY MECCA	*Rick Goosen*	391

OBITER

Crossword by Pearl Eliadis; Poetry by R. Stephens, P. Eliadis; Hearsay by Murray MacDonald; Social Notes by Sidney Fisher; Photos by Richard Janda; Election Results.

Front page of the 1 April, 1983 *Quid Novi* (Courtesy of Marc Barbeau; permission from the *Quid Novi*)

Here we see the struggle augured by John Humphrey at the start of the 1970s taking hold of the 1980s. How to deal with the ticking time bomb of its nuclear arsenal before tragedy strikes was perhaps the most significant issue the world had faced since the Second World War that brought nuclear arms into existence.

From the Soviet side of the issue, leading Soviet diplomat Victor L. Issraelyan contributed to the issue as well. Issraelyan (normally spelled Israelyan, though not in the article) was First Deputy Permanent Representative to the United Nations during the height of the Cold War, and the Director of the USSR Foreign Ministry's Department of International Organizations during the 1970s. Issraelyan wrote that disarmament was at the core of the Soviet ideology going back to the time of Lenin.[594]

The article now reads like a relic from long ago—filled with propaganda (like linking Lenin to the idea of nuclear disarmament) and accusations that in the West "[n]umerous channels of propaganda are very active in exaggerating the myth"[595] of the military threat of the Soviet Union. All the while, stressing that "Soviet military doctrine has a strictly defensive orientation"[596] aimed at "repelling any aggression or threats aimed at the Soviet Union and its allies,"[597] while castigating the United States for a "a programme of military build-up which is in no way justified by the defensive needs of the country,"[598] and insisting that "the U.S.S.R. and other countries of the

593 *Ibid* at 753.

594 Victor L Issraelyan, "Arms Limitation and Disarmament Talks: Soviet Approach" (1983) 28:3 *McGill LJ* 757 at 757.

595 *Ibid* at 761.

596 *Ibid.*

597 *Ibid.*

598 *Ibid* at 762.

socialist community possess tremendous economic potential which continues to grow steadily."[599] Eight years later the Soviet Union would, after a stunning economic collapse, cease to exist.

Another UN Ambassador contributed to the issue as well—Inga Thorsson, Sweden's UN Ambassador from 1970-1982. Thorsson is also noteworthy for her role in bringing about the world's first intergovernmental conference on the global environment in 1972.[600] One of the world's leading experts on disarmament, Thorsson spoke to the perspective of the neutral nation, unaligned with either the USSR or the US.[601] Thorsson writes of the two nations that "[b]oth powers prefer secret bilateral talks behind closed doors."[602] Such words speak to the importance of this special issue during the time in which it was published, especially as Thorsson writes of "a race with time ... we are losing."[603]

The wish list candidates of this special issue go on and on. John Alan Beesley, Canada's first UN Ambassador for Disarmament contributed a piece about the future of Canadian arms policy.[604] Canada's Ambassador to the United States Allan Gotlieb at the time then contributed an article with future Canadian Ambassador to the European Union Jeremy Kinsman as co-author, on Canada's position in the global disarmament movement.

Gotlieb and Kinsman wrote that, "Canadians judge their security to be very much affected by world events. We feel vulnerable."[605] To that end, they offered their own proscriptions on dealing with the problem.[606]

The special issue would be accompanied by a conference entitled "Nuclear War: Disarmament, Deterrence, or Apocalypse?" between March 3 and March 16, 1983, where several of the authors from the issue spoke. Though not solely sponsored by the *McGill Law Journal* as future conferences would be, this marked the beginning of another role the MLJ would take on in the Faculty—provider of high profile lecturers from around the world. During the four lectures that composed the conference, the living history of the special issue was brought to life through live debate.

Like Healy's volume, volume twenty-eight also published more than one thousand pages. The solidification of this new standard was starting to become etched in historical stone. Again, the quality of scholars attracted to the volume was high. Beyond the special issue, the Dean of Law at the University of New Brunswick Edward Veitch[607] contributed a piece; as did future Professor Emeritus of the Faculty of Law at the Université de Montréal Ejan Mackaay;[608] and John J. Robinette,[609] who was lead counsel in the *Patriation Reference* before the Supreme Court of Canada.

Toope's second-in-command, Associate Editor Marc Barbeau, was asked about the editing staff behind volume twenty-eight's achievements. By this time there was an elections process for selecting the new Executive Board, instead of the appointment process that existed towards the end of the MLJ's first quarter century. In his interview, Barbeau remembered that he and Toope had ran against each other for the position of Editor-in-Chief: "We actually [both] ran for the Editor-in-Chief position. And then we worked together ... Frankly, [Stephen] was the right guy to take that job. It wouldn't have been the same thing. I learned a lot from Stephen; a great deal from Stephen."[610]

Barbeau stated further that,

> I remember that the last issue would tend to draw well into the summer. And that was always, that was kind of an issue just in terms of getting things out, moving things along...
>
> The first summer was less of an impact on me, but then I was kind of the Associate Editor-elect, so you were starting to look forward to the next issue. I don't have a specific recollection of the timing of it all. I do remember there was always this question that you had to get the issue out so that the next board could take over... One thing that comes to mind is—funding was always an issue. Funding particularly, because we had funding from a variety of sources, but one of the sources

599 *Ibid.*

600 Douglas M Costel, "Women and the Environment" *EPA Journal* (November/December 1978), online: <http://www.epa.gov/aboutepa/history/topics/perspect/women.html>

601 Inga Thorsson, "Negotiating Arms Limitation Agreements: Non-Aligned Perspectives" (1983) 28:3 *McGill LJ* 770 at 770.

602 *Ibid* at 771.

603 *Ibid* at 781.

604 Alan J Beesley, "1984 and Beyond: Canadian Policy on Arms Control and Disarmament" (1983) 28:3 *McGill LJ* 783.

605 Allan Gotlieb & Jeremy Kinsman, "A Political Agenda for Arms Control: A Canadian View" (1983) 28:3 *McGill LJ* 794 at 795.

606 *Ibid* at 799-801.

607 Edward Veitch, "The Implications of Lindal" (1982) 28:1 *McGill LJ* 116.

608 Ejan Mackaay, "Le Droit Civil Aux Prises Avec l'inflation" (1982) 28:2 *McGill LJ* 284.

609 John J Robinette, "Report and Record of the Committee of Investigation into the Conduct of the Hon. Mr. Justice Berger and Resolution of the Canadian Judicial Council" (1982) 28:2 *McGill LJ* 378.

610 Barbeau interview, *supra* note 586.

> was the Quebec government. For reasons that currently I don't remember exactly, it was always difficult to get the Quebec government; to convince them that this was appropriate.
>
> As I recall, one of the reasons is that they had funding for law journals or scientific journals that had to be faculty journals, and our journal is a student-run journal. This was not a box that was easily checked on a form for the Quebec government's funding. As I recall, the year before us it got through, my year it got through, but every year it was kind of a—it was a struggle. There was a lot of discussion around that, how we were going to convince the Quebec government, the agency, and have them stick with us, and make them understand that in fact, this was a tradition that exists in other faculties in North America …
>
> The quality of the *Journal* was not affected … I do remember very vividly that we had, in the early 80s certainly, that never-ending discussion with the Quebec government … I remember the forms, and of course being the French-side editor I think, quite naturally, I would take more of an interest although the funding would go to the entire *Journal*, not just the French side.[611]

Barbeau archived several items from his days with the *Journal*. As was stated before, the *Quid Novi* had just started being published at the Faculty of Law. Barbeau provided two of the *Quid*'s old issues that were of particular interest to the MLJ. The first of the issues revealed something of the financial situation at the *Journal* at the start of the MLJ's second quarter century. According to an advertisement printed in that issue, volume twenty-six held what was at the time an "annual book sale", selling the books they had received from publishers around the world at discounted prices to students, between March 26 and April 4, 1981.[612] The second issue Barbeau had saved was one that followed the age old tradition of satire, with an issue entitled the "McGill Blaw Journal", filled with inside-jokes about a range of items, from the graduate student house and bar to well-known professors at the Faculty.[613]

The "Editor's Notebook" at the beginning of the mock issue read as follows:

> So you think we're not funny at the Quid. Well we don't think that the Law Journal is any funnier. What's so funny about a bunch of preppy koala bears walking in and out of an office whose door is never opened? How would you like to talk about footnotes and standard form abbreviations during your lunch hour? Or even publish articles on mundane topics by professors whose only motivation is to answer the question: If the Charter came into force at 8 a.m. in Canada was that 8:30 a.m. in Newfoundland? Ah, the constitutionality of time zones and time warps!
>
> Well, you might ask, "Why a parody on the Law Journal?" Good Question.
>
> You see, at the Quid Novi we have been labeled as pretty serious dudes. We take exception to that. We're not half as serious as the Law Journal … These MLJ types think that excitement in the library is to figure out whether in 1844 there was a King or a Queen (you know, K.B. or Q.B.). Standard trivia for the Editorial Board… their idea of weekend excitement is to count the number of typo's and spelling mistakes in the Journal when Stephen Scott was editor…
>
> If the MLJ thinks that we're picking on them then they can surprise us with a Volume 28:2 Quid Novi joke issue. Now that really would be funny.[614]

Historically situated, the April Fool's Day article appears to mark the official divergence of the MLJ from its previous place as a sometimes-soapbox for the student body.

Those items that the MLJ did still have to worry about caused daily concern. For example, when it came to the finances, there was no backup plan.[615] Either they got funding from the government or there would be no *Journal*. Many things were changing at a rapid pace for these young students. Barbeau recalls that,

> At the time, our year, I think it would've been our year, or maybe the year before us … We started getting these huge

611 *Ibid.*

612 "Advertisement" *The Quid Novi* (26 March, 1981), 2.

613 "McGill Blaw Journal" *The Quid Novi* (1 April, 1983), 1 at ff.

614 *Ibid* at 1-2.

615 Barbeau interview, *supra* note 586.

AES machines.[616] They were ugly beige things about the size of a mini fridge, and they had these black screens with the green letters on them, you know? At the top of them there were these roller things that would print out, continuous paper as I recall. The thing was like a mini fridge. You had big diskettes, probably 6 inch diskettes, that you would swap in, and basically you would have an article on there …

[The production assistant] would type in the articles onto these disks, and then we would edit. I think our year would have been one of the first years [we did something] instead of going straight to the printer … the costs of printing are not really the costs of producing the paper itself … [Instead] we would delay sending the disk to the printer as much as we could, and then when the disk would go it was as close to final… I don't know when they replaced the AES machines, but there certainly was a mainframe computer in the Faculty … it had a number of monitors that could be used but it was a single computer. I think the *Quid* was produced off that somehow. I think in '85 … they brought Macs into the library. It gives you a sense of the timeframe. So you are looking at a timeframe when you gradually get migrated off typewriters, even electronic typewriters, and you're going towards PCs during those years…

It sounds tough, but three years before us, people would've been operating off typewriters, and then sending this to the printers, who would then typeset—and then every change you made, the printer would charge you.[617]

Barbeau had a very clear memory of the late nights and long hours put into this time of technological transition, relating further that:

We had a key to the law library… I remember I would go up and it was actually fun because you didn't have to worry about getting up there and doing what you have to do. And I guess now you do more and more electronic stuff. But at the time, the only way to check the source, to check the quote, whatever, is to go upstairs. So you would ride up the elevator, and to have a key was great because you didn't have to worry, of course, about getting there before the cut-off time. I gotta tell you, a couple of times, I would find myself up there, arrive upstairs, turn on the lights—literally because it's eleven-thirty, it's twelve, whatever the time is—and kind of walk my way through the library, go to the spot, work for fifteen minutes, and then after a while it just kind of; I would just become aware.

I would say, "Oh my god I'm in the middle of an empty library. And there's dark everywhere around me except where I am." I don't scare that much, but inevitably I would say, "Maybe I should just pack it in now" … Every rational bone in you says, "Come on, what's the issue?" But there's this kind of sense of complete and utter silence, and darkness around you, and you say, they are horrible these things. You spook yourself and you leave. Now I would never have confessed to this twenty-five years ago because we don't, we're tough guys. I tell you something now though, I've spooked myself more than once in that library.[618]

Other members of Toope and Barbeau's Editorial Board included Book Review Editor Martine Turcotte, who went on to become Vice-Chair of Quebec for Bell Canada Enterprises.

Barbeau's board would be one of the last boards to deal with a sense of impending financial doom. The following year, in volume twenty-nine, one of the most innovative and important events in MLJ history occurred. After this event, nothing would ever be the same—for the MLJ or for the legal system in Canada. The project that would change everything was the *Canadian Guide to Uniform Legal Citation*.

Previous attempts at a Canadian legal style or citations guide had come before the *McGill Guide*. The *Alberta Law Review* had been nationally distributing a legal publication style guide since at least 1969 (the year of the *Alberta Law Review Style Guide*'s fourth edition), which the MLJ itself had used as a reference point in the past. In addition, former Member of the Quebec

616 AES machines were early programmable word processors.

617 Barbeau interview, *supra* note 586.

618 *Ibid.*

National Assembly and Member of Parliament Daniel Turp wrote that there was "the *Protocole de référence* of the *Revue québécoise de droit international (RQDI)* that was prepared when the *RQDI* was first published in 1984."[619] Turp also recalled that, "At the very beginning of my teaching career, I also wrote a book that contained information on how to cite legal documents,"[620] in reference to his 1981 book *Sources et méthodologie du droit québécois et canadien : notes et documents*. The book had been well received critically as the beginning of better referencing and stylistic standards for legal research and publishing in Canada.[621]

The main competitor for McGill was Chin-Shih Tang's citation work *Canadian Guide to Legal Citation: a Canadian Perspective in Common Law Provinces* published in 1984, two years before the MLJ's work, and which changed its name to the *Guide to legal citation and sources of citation aid: a Canadian perspective* for its second edition in 1988.[622] A 1987 book review of the MLJ's work appeared in the *Canadian Law Library Review* that also mentioned Tang, and writes that,

> The editors of *McGill Law Journal* have produced this first bilingual edition of the *Guide* in the hope that it will form the basis for a nationally accepted standard for legal citation achieved through consensus. Some might wonder whether practically or conceptually a uniform standard is worthwhile. None will, I think, question that the *Guide* is the most useful work of its kind yet produced in Canada both for quick reference and for use as a teaching tool.
>
> Unlike Tang's learned and discursive *Guide to Legal Citation* there is no prose to sift through to find an answer and when you find the answer, again unlike Tang, there is only one alternative presented without discussion. In this way it resembles the Harvard Law Review's *A Uniform System of Citation*.
>
> Coverage is broad, extending to a wide range of secondary sources, and organization logical. Each chapter is devoted to a different type of legal resource: each facet of the exemplified recommendation is highlighted in bold print before the governing rule is set out. Access through either detailed table of contents or index is efficient. In short it would be difficult to improve on the clarity of presentation.[623]

The review was not entirely glowing, however, as the tradition of allowing for alternate citations by authors shone through when the reviewer criticized the students of the MLJ for not discussing alternative forms of citations against its purported standard forms. Though as volume thirty Managing Editor Brian Pel—future Tax Partner with McCarthy Tétrault in Toronto and long standing member of the MLJ Boards of Trustees and Advisors—put it, professors may not have seen all of the benefits behind standardization, stating that among the other reasons for creating the *Guide* they were looking "to make some sort of process to make it easier for us to do our job—force people to provide something in a particular format and it'll save a lot of time. Standardize things."[624]

The *Guide*'s reviewer also wanted to eliminate *supra*'s from legal citation in Canada, in favour of an English equivalent—English, not bilingual. Tang did not favour full standardization, nor did he focus much on the civil law jurisdiction of Canada in his first edition, which gave the MLJ a leg up regardless of style. And considering that both Turp (in Quebec) and Tang (in common law Canada) had made an impression on the the legal systems of Canada with their prior works, there is no telling whether or not a fully national system of citations standardization could have been achieved without the effort of those young McGill students who put forward their first edition of the *Guide*.

The person who first conceived of the idea and developed it from the beginning was volume twenty-nine Associate Editor Robert Metcalfe, during his junior year with the *Journal*. In an interview he recalled that,

> When I started at the *Law Journal*, under Stephen Toope, one of my first jobs was to check footnotes and so on. So I asked him what style manual they used and he said, basically they didn't have one.

619 Interview of Daniel Turp by James Cummins (8 December, 2011).

620 *Ibid.* See also Daniel Turp & James Leavy, *Sources et méthodologie du droit québécois et canadien : notes et documents* (Montréal : Éditions Thémis, 1981).

621 Michel Filion, "Daniel Turp et James Leavy, Sources et méthodologie du droit québécois et canadien — Notes et documents" Book Review (1982) 23:1 *C de D* 249 at ff.

622 Chin-Shih Tang, *Guide to legal citation and sources of citation aid : a Canadian perspective: 2nd Edition*. (Toronto: Don Mills, 1988) at 95.

623 Martha L Foote, "Book Reviews" (1987) 12:1 *Can L Libr* 94 at 95.

624 Interview of Brian Pel by James Cummins (17 May, 2012).

You had to flip through all their journals and find out what was done; that's how you did it. You just flipped through old articles until you found a way that someone had done it, and copy that.

Which sort of amazed me. I was a literature student before and we had all kinds of guides—the PLMA guide to citation in literature, and the Chicago guide. It surprised me that there was no similar instrument for legal research and citation. So I looked around a bit and found the Harvard guide, which was very complete but didn't really work for Canadian sources. So basically what I started to do was just to keep a hand-written list of how things were done, and trying to figure out why they were done that way; how to adapt them. I think once it got up to about twenty pages I realized—one, there was a lot of work to do and, two, there was not a lot of consistency in the way things were done.

So we talked about it… I believe it was Brian Pel or [volume twenty-nine Managing Editor] Demetrios G. Xistris—two of the business guys on the *Journal*—who said "well, why don't we apply for a summer work grant, so we can hire some people and maybe we could do something that would be good for the Faculty.". And to our great surprise, we got the grant to hire some people. Sonia Struthers was one of the first people to work on it as a summer student, Jill [Frank], and others.

We gave them all a bunch of tasks, and we used to sit around and argue about the rules of citation the whole summer. And the idea was eventually to see if we could produce some sort of publication and get it accepted by the Faculty, and people like the Supreme Court or other authorities. It was a bit of a difficult road there. There was a fellow at the Université de Montréal—[Professor] Didier Lluelles—who had a little book that he used for his courses in legal writing, and so they weren't interested in following us or discussing anything. We visited the Supreme Court, and I think we were probably just a bit premature in our exercise, because they weren't initially interested.

But it progressed quite well. We had quite a document by the end of the summer and work continued as we went along and we did the second summer's work, I believe, on more obscure things. And Brian Pel had the great idea of going to see Canada Law Books and discussing the idea of printing this or publishing it. And again to our great surprise, they did accept—and I think the rest is pretty much history.[625]

When asked about how long Metcalfe had kept his legal pad of citations as a personal project before sharing it with others or gaining help from the rest of the *Journal*, Metcalfe replied,

> Probably a couple of months. We kind of used it informally amongst ourselves, and I guess I became kind of a repository. I had started to do it as a junior member of the *Law Journal* just for myself, and I showed it to Stephen Toope, who said it was interesting, but it wasn't until we got on the senior board that we started to apply it a bit more methodically. So probably over six to nine months, as it got up steam, and then the summer after that [we got the grant]—which would have been a year or eighteen months after I started to work as a junior member on the board.[626]

When asked how long it took for him to know that this would be more than just a personal project for his own editorial work, he replied,

> That's hard to say. It was pretty apparent from the beginning, to me at least, that something like this was necessary. The law school didn't have anything like that, so there was [only] this process of assimilation that you were supposed to learn while you were writing—there was no manual, no nothing. Where I came from, that's just insane. People shouldn't have to think about this stuff, you should just be able to open a book and find it. To understand the principles and so on is one thing, but to have to retain and continually be researching and thinking

625 Interview of Robert Metcalfe by James Cummins (26-27 June, 2012).

626 *Ibid.*

> about this is just too horrible. Plus it was never really consistent, so even if you tried to understand, it wasn't really clear what the reasoning was for the way things were done.[627]

So the *Guide* originated as a list kept by Metcalfe over his junior year. It really is amazing to think that if he had for some reason decided halfway through the year to discontinue writing things down because he had gotten the hang of things a bit more, or just felt it was too much work on top of his studies, or something else, that the *Guide* would never have been born. If Metcalfe had not made it onto the Executive Board, again who knows if he would have had as much contact with the Managing Editors of the *Journal* or enough influence over the editorial processes for his list to be used in the same way. Like the previous attempts spoken of by volume twenty Editor-in-Chief F.H. Buckley or even Morin with his conflict with Professor Cooper, there may have never been anything more than a temporary in-house document typed out in hard copy and difficult to alter. Metcalfe's original list was written in blue ink with a fountain pen on a white legal pad. After converting it into the more substantial project, however, the original was not kept.[628]

It also helped that Metcalfe's year was the first in which they used computers, which made the integration and saving of data—something unheard of before—an actual reality. As Metcalfe put it,

> I don't remember [the *Alberta Law Review Style Guide*] and I never had seen Didier Lluelles', which probably pre-existed the *Cite Guide*, but was only used inside the Université de Montréal for its own writing courses. These things were not commercially or publicly available. We didn't have the Internet, so you couldn't find them on the Internet. Originally we thought of just doing up something for our own purposes. But as evident as it was that one was needed, it was also equally clear that it wouldn't be useful or of any authority or value beyond the *Law Journal* or in the community unless everybody else was adopting the same conventions. It wouldn't be of any use to have a system that only we used.[629]

It is also interesting to note that according to Metcalfe, the editors that worked on the project had no knowledge of any prior style guide along the lines of what Buckley had shown to the *Harvard Law Review* ten years beforehand. He was actually very surprised to hear of the longer, if disconnected, history of the MLJ's efforts to bring some standardization to Canadian legal citations. However it was the efforts of Metcalfe in his reaction to Toope that is the original seed of the *Cite Guide*'s genesis. At the time of Metcalfe's hiring to the junior board, there was really nothing in place—all prior efforts had been lost over time.

Around the time the *Journal* began developing the idea for what would become the *Guide*, volume twenty-nine was publishing a piece by future Supreme Court Justice Marie Deschamps on the subject of undivided co-ownership.[630] The *Guide* itself would benefit from an ownership that transcended not only the individual members of that first board, but the members of each editorial board moving forward. And perhaps the best way of viewing the immediate and widespread impact the publishing of the *Guide* had on the Canadian legal system can be seen by observing the opinions of Deschamps's future employer over the span of 1983 (the year the writing of the *Guide* began) and 1987 (after the *Guide* was published).

For example, in 1983 there was only a loose standard method of citation within the opinions of the Supreme Court of Canada. Taking the citation of MLJ articles specifically, in the 1983 case *Citadel Assurance v. Johns-Manville Canada*, the MLJ was cited with the following in-text citation:

> In *La Rivière Inc. v. Canadian Surety Co.*, [1973] C.A. 150, the failure by an unpaid material man to preserve privileges under the *Civil Code* of Québec was held not to discharge the surety from its obligations under a labour and material payment bond. That case is the subject of a helpful article, *Labour and Material Payment Bonds* (1973), 19 McGill L.J. 433, by N.H. Salomon.[631]

This citation, though largely similar, is still different than the way in which another 1983 decision—*Cement LaFarge v. B.C. Lightweight Aggregate*—cited a different MLJ article:

> Professor Fridman, on the other hand, in *The Wrongdoing Plaintiff* (1972), 18

627 *Ibid.*

628 *Ibid.*

629 *Ibid.*

630 Marie Deschampes, "Vers Une Approche Renouvelee De l'Indivision" (1983) 29:2 *McGill LJ* 215.

631 *Citadel Assurance v Johns-Manville Canada*, [1983] 1 SCR 513 at 523. Added Emphasis.

> McGill L.J. 275, argues that the question of whether the plaintiff's conduct should deprive him of his remedy can only be determined by weighing three factors: causation, remoteness, and blameworthiness.[632]

Once the *Guide* was published in 1986, citations shifted. Looking to the 1987 citation of Norval Morris in *R. v. Lyons*, which we discussed earlier, the citation was as follows:

> Norval Morris, in "The Habitual Criminal" (1967), 13 *McGill L.J.* 534, also observes that a number of countries have enacted legislation to deal with incorrigible or habitual offenders, and notes, at p. 536, that generally three elements are included in the definition of the group targeted for such punishment--criminal qualities inherent or latent in the mental constitution, a settled practice in crime, and a public danger.[633]

We can see between the *Citadel* and *Lyons* cases that an important standardization has occurred. The name of the journal becomes italicized; the use of authors' names has changed; and the title of the articles are no longer italicized—they are in quotation marks, distinguishing them from the title of the journal they appear in.

Every SCC opinion from that day forward would adhere to the rules set by the *Guide*, bringing true standardization to the Court for the very first time. In addition, a new aspect of each decision, the "Authors Cited" section, was introduced at the same time talks between the Court and the MLJ were taking place over how the *Cite Guide* would impact the writing of decisions and vice versa; a bibliography of all articles and books cited in each decision, putting more focus on the place of periodicals and books as a basis of decisions. Beforehand you would have to scan the entire article to see whether or not something had been cited.

This change is made all the more radical in the context of how the SCC viewed legal periodicals up until the 1950s. By the time the first *Guide* was published, the MLJ had more Supreme Court of Canada citations that any other university-based law journal in the world—faculty- or student-run. Between 1985 and 1992, the MLJ was cited thirty-three times by the SCC, and the next most cited university-affiliated law journal was the faculty-run *University of Toronto Law Journal* with twenty-six citations.[634]

The study producing these numbers was presented in the article by Gordon Bale, who earlier informed us of Chief Justice Rinfret's 1950 comments on the *Canadian Bar Review*. A broader review and original research of Supreme Court of Canada decisions since the founding of the MLJ reveals an even more impressive picture. Between volume one and volume fifty-six, nearly eighty-six percent of all MLJ volumes have had at least one article in them cited by the Supreme Court of Canada—that's forty-eight volumes out of the MLJ's first fifty-six. Over the last fifty volumes specifically, the average has been eighty-eight percent. Twenty-three different volumes of the MLJ have had at least three Supreme Court of Canada citations during this timeframe—which is over forty percent of all MLJ volumes. Twelve MLJ volumes have had at the Supreme Court cite them five times or more—amounting to twenty-one percent of all MLJ volumes.

As of April 2012, twenty-nine percent of these citations came from French articles, meaning seventy-one percent came from English articles. The split is essentially the same when looking only at the number of articles cited. It is a surprisingly healthy split, considering that only just north of twenty percent of all articles published in the MLJ have been written in French, whereas nearly eighty percent of articles appearing in the tables of contents have been English through the end of volume fifty-six. While French articles have only taken up one-fifth of the *Journal* over the last six decades, the strength of the scholarship within those articles has been impressive.

Out of the approximately 1400 English articles and nearly 370 French articles (from volume one through fifty-six), 6.6% of all articles had been cited by the Supreme Court of Canada. Five and a half percent of all English articles have been cited, and just north of eleven percent of French articles have been cited. That means that over one in every ten French articles published by the MLJ is likely to be cited by the Supreme Court of Canada during this period. The *McGill Law Journal*, overall, was cited by the Supreme Court of Canada between volumes one and fifty-six a grand total of 142 times, accounting for 116 articles (as of January 2013)—well over one hundred articles printed in *McGill Law Journal* have been cited by the Court.

This is far and away the most articles or citations out of any university-affiliated law journal in the world

632 *Cement LaFarge v BC Lightweight Aggregate*, [1983] 1 SCR 452 at 478.

633 *R v Lyons*, [1987] 2 SCR 309 at point 33.

634 Bale, *supra* note 20 at 62.

to appear in Supreme Court of Canada decisions. The highest cited volume was volume thirty-five with nine different citations. Now, according to the Washington and Lee University Law School ranking methodology, it is also important to note the length of time between the publication and the citation of an article—after all, if all the citations came from only one era of the *Journal*, then this would point to a certain level of inconsistency in the quality or importance between volumes.

On this point, the MLJ also ranks at the top. If taking into account every citation since the *Journal* came into being until 2011, the average length of time between the publication of an article and its citation by the Supreme Court is about ten years. However, this number is deceiving, as the Court did not begin citing Canadian university-affiliated law journals until 1971—and even then, it was only a slowly adopted process.

Taking this into account and looking only at articles published from 1981 onwards, the seventy-eight articles cited in the thirty years between then and 2011 have taken an average of only five and a half years to be cited by the Supreme Court—about half the original figure. Further considering that many cases and issues take between five and ten years before the Supreme Court decides on them, the MLJ average sees its articles used as quickly as could possibly be imagined. In addition, forty percent of the MLJ citations over this period (representing thirty-one articles) occurred within two years of the publication of the cited article, and thirteen percent were cited within less than one year of the article's publication. For the most recent snapshot, only looking at SCC decisions published since the year 2000, we see that the old volumes of the MLJ are still relevant as well. Seven volumes eighteen years or older were cited within decisions from the year 2000 forward, including four volumes thirty-five years or older.[635]

Ten English articles and five French articles published in the MLJ have received two distinct Supreme Court of Canada citations. Three English articles and one French article have received three distinct citations, and one English article has received four. That article was "Is There a Right against Self-Incrimination in Canada" by Ed Ratushny, who was at the time of publication a professor at the Windsor University Faculty of Law. Ratushny introduced his article writing about "[o]ne of the leading Canadian scholars in the area of criminal procedure and evidence,"[636] and due in part to this article, he himself was to become one too. The article was published the year after Ratushny was called to the bar. He would go on to be cited, as either the author or the editor of publications by the Supreme Court of Canada more than twenty-five times in his career. This was his first.

The only other author to have four citations by the Supreme Court of Canada for a combination of articles they wrote appearing in the *McGill Law Journal*, is Professor W.R. Lederman.[637] Mentioned once before in this book, Lederman was the focus of the article by Gordon Bale. In his article, Bale talks about some of the reasons for the change in the attitude of the Supreme Court of Canada towards citation practices other than the appearance of the *Guide*, namely the appointment of Robert (Brian) Dickson as Chief Justice[638] and the influence of the work of Lederman.[639] Bale sees the appearance of the "Authors Cited" section of SCC decisions as the result of Dickson's promotion, and it certainly appears serendipitous that Dickson would take the reins around the same time the MLJ was beginning to speak with the Court about the establishment of nation-wide citation standards.

Besides Lederman and Ratushny, the other authors with either two distinct MLJ articles cited by the Supreme Court or more than two citations are: Giuseppina D'Agostino (with two decisions citing one article); Jean-Louis Baudouin (with two separate articles cited); Jean Gabriel Castel (with two articles cited); H. Patrick Glenn (with two articles cited and three decisions citing them); Patrick Healy (with two articles cited and three decisions citing them); Pierre Legrand Jr. (with two articles cited); José Woehrling (with three decisions citing his one cited article); Tim Quigley (with three decisions citing his one cited article); Stephen A. Scott (with two articles cited and three decisions citing them); Sébastien Grammond (with two articles cited and three decisions citing them); and Ernest J.Weinrib (with two separate articles cited). In all, there have been nine authors with three or more Supreme Court citations and nine authors with more than one MLJ article cited by Supreme Court. Comparing these numbers to the overall citation statistics reveals that the MLJ has received its citations over a large range of articles and authors, with a select few appearing multiple times. H. Patrick Glenn is the only author with multiple articles cited to have had one of those articles published in French and one in English. No author has ever had more than two MLJ articles cited by the Court.

635 SCC citations search, *supra* note 194. These specific statistics do not include citations after 2011.

636 Ed Ratushny, "Is There a Right against Self-Incrimination in Canada" (1973) 19:1 *McGill LJ* 1 at 1.

637 See Appendix A.

638 Bale, *supra* note 20 at 60.

639 Bale, *supra* note 20 at 63.

Professor Ziegel's article, the first article ever cited by the Court from a Canadian university-based journal, had been accompanied by citations to both the *Yale Law Journal*[640] and the *Harvard Law Journal* in the same decision,[641] however neither of these publications had enjoyed much support from the Court beforehand either. The only other university-affiliated journals cited by the Court before 1972 occurred with a 1964 citation to the *University of Queensland Law Journal*[642] and a 1969 citation to the *Stanford Law Review* in another decision also citing the *Harvard Law Review*.[643] Before 1971, even the *Canadian Bar Review* had only ever been cited twice. As Peter McCormick wrote, "[P]ractices began to change under Laskin [1973-84], became more formalized under Dickson [1984-90], and were revolutionized under Lamer [1990-2000]. The Lamer Court cited academic authorities in roughly half of its decisions, to a total of more than 400 citations per year."[644]

Former Editor-in-Chief of the *Canadian Bar Review* and Faculty Advisor to the MLJ Jean-Gabriel Castel concurred, stating of the change of attitude within the courts towards legal periodicals that, "Starting in the seventies [they] became quite significant."[645] The work of professors at McGill University, period, was only mentioned in Supreme Court of Canada decisions twice in the Court's entire history before 1971.[646] Ziegel's citation was the beginning of an exponential movement. It did not start out quickly. During whole of the 1970s, the *McGill Law Journal* would be cited by the Supreme Court five times. During the same decade, the *University of Toronto Law Journal* received four citations (three to a single article), and there was but one citation afforded to the volumes of each of three other Canadian university-affiliated journals: the *University of British Columbia Law Journal*, the *Osgoode Hall Law Journal*, and the *Alberta Law Review*. As volume four Case Comments Editor Jean-Louis Baudouin recalled of how the courts viewed law journals, in light of both his years as a student writing or selecting unwelcome comments about the courts and his twenty years as a justice himself, "It progressed very slowly, but by the 1970s" the real confrontationalism that courts employed towards law journals "was out".[647]

The domination of the *McGill Law Journal* in this field would continue over time. Between the year 2000 and November 2011, the MLJ would be cited forty-two times by the Court. As we can see from the appended chart, this is nearly double most of the other university-affiliated law journals in the country and substantially ahead of the *Journal*'s nearest competitor. The MLJ also received more citations than the four top cited American university-affiliated law journals combined. The *Canadian Bar Review* is still clearly the most cited though, having been cited by sixty-seven cases (let along how often it was cited in each) over the same period.

Moving on to other contributions the MLJ and its editors have made to the Court, the first former member of the *McGill Law Journal* to receive a clerkship with the Supreme Court of Canada was volume fifteen Editor-in-Chief Léonard Serafini (now a partner with the Montreal office of Gowlings LLP). He began his clerkship in 1970, during a time when far fewer clerks were hired and many of them were already lawyers or academics. Clerks were first taken on in the Supreme Court only in 1967—that first year there were only five, and only nine served in Serafini's year (as compared to the twenty-seven that serve annually now). Since Serafini's clerkship there have been over forty more former *Journal* members that also served as clerks to the Supreme Court. Most impressively, in 1991, 2008, and 2012 there were four different former *Journal* members clerking for the Court at the same time.[648] In 2008 and 2012, the former MLJ members represented one half and then two thirds of clerks selected from McGill University, during a period where McGill was placing more clerks with the Court than any other university in Canada.[649]

McGill LJ	42
Queen's LJ	26
Alta L Rev	24
UTLJ	22
C de D	18
Ottawa L Rev	17
Osgoode Hall LJ	16

640 *McKeown SCR* at 472.

641 *Ibid* at 478.

642 *Jarvis v Associated Medical Services Inc*, [1964] SCR 497 at 524.

643 *Freeborn et al v Goodman*, [1969] SCR 923, at 934 and 931 respectively.

644 Peter McCormick, *Supreme at Last: the evolution of the Supreme Court in Canada* (Toronto: James Lorimer & Company Ltd, 2000) at 142.

645 Castel interview, *supra* note 44.

646 *Marleau v People's Gas Supply Co Ltd*, [1940] SCR 708 at 723; *Preload Co of Canada v City of Regina et al*, [1959] SCR 801 at 806.

647 Baudouin interview, *supra* note 142.

648 For a complete list of former *Journal* members that went on to clerk with the Supreme Court, see Appendix D.

649 Pascal Zamprelli, "McGill Law Faculty keeps Supreme Court streak going" *McGill Reporter* (5 May, 2010), online: < http://publications.mcgill.ca/reporter/2010/05/mcgill-law-faculty-keeps-supreme-court-streak-going/>

Harv L Rev	16
UT Fac L Rev	13
Sask L Rev	12
UBC L Rev	9
Man LJ	9
Dal LJ	8
Yale LJ	7
UNBLJ	6
Stan L Rev	5
Colum L Rev	5

Figure 2: Number of Citations by the Supreme Court of Canada to University-Affiliated Law Journals, 1 January, 2000 to 12 November, 2011.

As for articles authored by people who would either go on to served as a Justice with the Supreme Court, were sitting Justices at the time, or had retired from a judgeship with the Supreme Court, there have been nineteen in all. Sixty percent of all judges since the appointment of Justice Antonio Lamer to the court have published in the *McGill Law Journal*, as have four out of the last seven Chief Justices (with a fifth providing an unpublished *McGill Law Journal* Annual Lecture in 1991). Of all the Justices that have been alive at some point during the existence of the *McGill Law Journal* since 1952, forty percent were published by the *Journal*.[650] Still others—future Chief Justice Beverley McLachlin (as was already mentioned), Justice Willard Zebedee Estey, and Justice John Majors—would come to provide lectures for the MLJ that were not published. Taking this into account, nearly three quarters of the Justices since the appointment of Lamer have contributed in some way to the scholarship of the *McGill Law Journal* in written or spoken form. Over thirty contributions have been published by future, current, or past Supreme Court judges in the pages of the MLJ since Le Dain's first article in 1952—an average of about one every two volumes. There can be no doubt that the members of the Court have come to embrace the MLJ since its founding sixty years ago in a way that is unique among Canadian legal publications.

On the subject matter of citations, those who write them, and those that standardize them, Arthur D. Austin once wrote that:

> A cursory survey indicates that unpublished manuscripts provide the most fertile source of fugitive literature. Access to non-public material makes the author an "insider" to a mysterious clique or a ferocious archaeologist of buried scholarship. There is, moreover, a curiosity factor: is the material too "hot" or controversial to publish? Trial transcripts are also impressive, especially from old and obscure trials. The message is thoroughness; the author gets credit for plowing through pages of dusty transcripts to flush out gold nuggets...[651]
>
> The quality of the footnotes reveals the author's range and comprehension of the topic. In a notoriously risk averse discipline, footnotes are the accepted forum for risk-taking. Footnotes leave permanent passages and landmarks to obscure information. As literary submarines, footnotes can torpedo established doctrine with frontier perspectives. They serve as embryos for new ideas and an underground source for humor, fugitive nuggets, and candor...[652]
>
> Using a citation that frustrates law review editors because it cannot be accommodated by the *Bluebook* or conventional guidelines merits positive recognition from discriminating peers...[653]

While American law review editors had their *Bluebook* in hand since its first publication in 1926—exactly sixty years before the *Guide*—Canadian law review editors were suddenly thrust into a much more heated battle between student and professor over the formatting of an article's footnotes in 1986. Then again, what has become known as the *McGill Guide* had a much more rapid transformative effect on the national community of scholars it pertained to than the *Bluebook* had in its own country. The first edition of the *Bluebook* was inscribed with the following: "This pamphlet does not pretend to include a complete list of abbreviations of all the necessary data as to form. It aims to deal with the more common abbreviations and forms to which one has occasion to refer."[654] The manuscript contained only twenty pages of citation directions, followed by six pages of common abbreviations. The *McGill Guide* entered the world with broader ambitions than this.

In terms of the creation of the *Guide*, volume thirty Editor-in-Chief Peter Oliver, now a Full Professor of Law at the University of Ottawa, wrote that,

650 These statistics, pertaining the Supreme Court Justices, are from the period between September of 1952 to August of 2011.

651 Arthur D Austin, "Footnotes as Product Differentiation" (1987) 40:5 *Vand L Rev*, 1131 at 1148.

652 *Ibid* at 1153.

653 *Ibid* at 1152.

654 *A Uniform System Of Citation: Abbreviations and Form of Citation*, (Cambridge: Harvard Law Review, 1926) at 1.

The McGill Law Journal / Revue de droit de McGill

Alumni Newsletter / Bulletin des Anciens

Introduction

In a few months time, Volume 30 of the McGill Law Journal will appear. We felt that this anniversary would be an appropriate occasion on which to renew contact with the Journal's alumni.

Our goal in reviving alumni interest in the Journal is threefold. First, we hope to take advantage of the knowledge that alumni have acquired in their various fields of legal work. At any given time, the Journal might be in need of legal advice, notarial service or insights into new activity in a particular area of law. We hope that we will have to look no further than our own alumni for help. Second, we would like to stabilize Journal finances through the regular solicitation of alumni contributions to our trust fund. Finally, we sincerely hope to encourage renewed interest in the continuing activities of the Journal and to stimulate contact between past and present Journal collaborators.

On the occasion of the Journal's anniversary and in order to promote renewed alumni interest in the Journal, we are planning a reception and lecture for late October, 1984. Details and invitations will follow as soon as a date has been confirmed. The evening will combine a brief but very stimulating lecture with cocktails and good company. We hope that all of you will take time out from your busy schedules to attend.

We think it unfortunate that so many Journal alumni have lost touch with their *alma mater* publication. Those few who have had occasion to drop by our offices in the basement of Old Chancellor Day Hall have discovered new technology — word processor, McBee billing system, air conditioner and radio — placed in the familiar, almost unchanged law journal atmosphere. For those of you who have not had time or cause to return, we set out a brief description below.

1. Production of the Journal

The production of the Journal has changed remarkably since the first issue appeared in 1952. The advances in computer technology in recent times have taken us a further large step beyond Gutenberg. The Journal was one of the first Canadian learned publications to use a combined word-processor and disk-photocomposition technique. The time savings are gratifying, as are the cost savings (approximately eight dollars per printed page).

After an article has been accepted and preliminary discussions with the author are underway, the edited text is recorded on word-processor disks. While further editing is a relatively easy task on the word-processor screen, the process inevitably stalls as all-too-human Junior Board members struggle with obscure footnote references. Technology has its limits. Once the completed text with footnotes is recorded, it is printed and proofread. A complex code of printing instructions (for italics, bold type, indentations, etc.) must be verified with care as it provides

Introduction

Le trentième volume de la Revue de droit de McGill verra le jour dans quelques mois. Cet événement nous paraît être le moment opportun pour permettre aux anciens de reprendre contact avec la Revue.

Trois raisons nous motivent à solliciter les anciens de la Revue. D'abord, nous aimerions connaître les divers secteurs de droit dans lesquels ils oeuvrent afin de faire éventuellement appel à leurs services. La Revue pourrait ainsi s'adresser directement à eux pour obtenir un avis juridique, les services d'un notaire ou pour des précisions dans un domaine de droit. Ensuite, nous espérons, grâce aux contributions des anciens, pouvoir améliorer les finances de la Revue. Enfin, nous souhaitons faciliter les rencontres entre les collaborateurs d'hier et ceux d'aujourd'hui, et ainsi promouvoir l'intérêt des premiers dans les activités contemporaines de la Revue.

Afin de célébrer cet anniversaire, nous préparons une conférence qui se tiendra à la fin du mois d'octobre prochain. La soirée débutera par un brève allocution et sera suivie d'une réception. Les invitations et d'autres détails suivront. Nous espérons vivement compter sur votre présence lors de cette rencontre.

Il est regrettable qu'un grand nombre d'anciens ait perdu contact avec la Revue. Ceux et celles qui ont récemment visité notre local au sous-sol du *Old Chancellor Day Hall* ont fait la découverte d'un appareil à traitement de texte, d'un système de facturation McBee, d'un climatiseur et d'une radio, le tout mêlé à l'atmosphère d'autrefois. Pour le bénéfice des anciens qui n'ont pas pu nous rendre visite dernièrement, nous proposons le court aperçu qui suit.

1. Production de la Revue

Depuis la parution du premier numéro en 1952, le processus de production de la Revue a été largement modifié. Les progrès dans le domaine de l'informatique nous ont menés bien au-delà de l'ère de Gutenberg. La Revue fût l'une des premières publications académiques canadiennes à combiner la technique de traitement de texte à celle de la photocomposition sur disque. Ce procédé offre le double avantage de permettre une économie de temps et d'argent (le coût par page est estimé à huit dollars).

Après avoir accepté un ouvrage et discuté des modifications préliminaires avec l'auteur, le texte est mis en mémoire sur disquettes. Des remaniements additionnels peuvent alors s'effectuer rapidement sur l'écran de l'appareil. Toutefois, le processus ne peut être complété sans l'effort acharné du comité de rédaction adjoint aux prises avec des sources parfois lointaines, rapportées aux notes infrapaginales. La technologie a ses limites. Le texte, accompagné des renvois est ensuite imprimé et corrigé par

3644 rue Peel, Montréal, Québec H3A 1W9 Téléphone (514) 845-8824

(Courtesy of Marc Barbeau)

> I can remember meetings where the first rules were laid out, leading to extended discussions, veering between stimulating and exasperating, over things like the double bracket rule. I think we all had the sense that the key people, Robert [Metcalfe] and Sonia [Struthers], were committed to this, and that they and the others around the table were all bright and energetic enough to produce something really good. And that of course proved to be the case.
>
> One personal memory I have was being assigned the job of recommending how to do constitutional citations. There wasn't a lot to it, there being far fewer constitutional acts than legislative acts, but it was not at all obvious how to do it. I tried to find everything that others had written about it, and looked at emerging practices, settling I think on something pretty close to what librarian Margaret Banks had recommended. So that is how we came up with the fairly cumbersome, though historically accurate "Constitution Act, 1982 being Schedule B of the Canada Act, 1982 (U.K.)". I subsequently wrote my PhD thesis on the Patriation and Amendment of the Constitution of Canada and have for some time wished to write a McGill Law Journal note recommending that we have one citation for regular use – simply Constitution Act, 1982 – and another for historical purposes, the one I cited above. I should say that I of course handed my constitutional law work to Robert [Metcalfe] and Sonia, and later Sonia and Kathy Szabo, I believe, and they and the full committee may have made changes to what I recommended, but I think that it is pretty close to what I originally proposed.[655]

Other members of the volume twenty-nine editorial board included Editor-in-Chief Daniel Gogek, who would go on to become the Managing Partner of Hogan Lovells in Moscow; Advertising Editor William R.C. Tresham, who would become President of Global Investments of Ivanhoé Cambridge; Alan S Alexandroff, future Co-director of the G20 Research Group at the Munk School of Global Affairs; and Donna Kaufman, future Corporate Director of Bell Canada Enterprises.

655 Interview of Peter Oliver by James Cummins (17 March, 2012).

The last crop of authors whose footnotes would be done without the influence of the *Guide*, those of volume twenty-nine, alongside future Justice Deschamps, included future Distinguished Professor of Law Emeritus at Washburn University Banks McDowell;[656] future Justice of the Ontario Court David M. Paciocco;[657] future Professor Emeritus of Political Studies at Queen's University C.E.S. Franks;[658] future President of the International Law Association Cecil J. Olmstead; [659] and future co-director of the Center for Human Rights and Humanitarian Law and Director of the War Crimes Research Office at Washington College Law, Diane F. Orentlicher.[660] A book review for volume twenty-nine was also contributed by future Executive Director of Centre for Women in Politics and Public Leadership at Carleton University, Clare Beckton.[661]

In other Canadian legal publishing news, the end of this volume (early 1984) occurred within the same timeframe as Jean-Gabriel Castel—the first ever Faculty Advisor to the *Journal*—stepped down after spending twenty-seven years as Editor-in-Chief of the *Canadian Bar Review*. Over his tenure he had built the institution up from a small Canadian publication into one of the most well-respected legal periodicals in the world. Recalling his time with the *Bar Review*, Castel recalled that,

> At Osgoode [Hall] ... I had two offices. I had one for myself and then one for the *Bar Review* with my secretary. That was one of the advantages, as it was very difficult to get secretarial help. When I started at McGill we only had one secretary for seven people and she was also the secretary of the Dean, so there were

656 Joel Levin & Banks McDowell, "The Balance Theory of Contracts: Seeking Justice in Voluntary Obligations" (1983) 29:1 *McGill LJ* 24.

657 David M Paciocco, "Proposed Canada Evidence Act and the Wray Formula: Perpetuating an Inadequate Discretion" (1983) 29:1 *McGill LJ* 141.

658 CES Franks, "Parliamentary Control of Security Activities" (1984) 29:2 *McGill LJ* 326.

659 Cecil J Olmstead, Edward J Krauland & Diane F Orentlicher, "Expropriation in the Energy Industry: Canada's Crown Share Provision as a Violation of International Law" (1984) 29:3 *McGill LJ* 439.

660 *Ibid.*

661 Clare Beckton, "Lawmaking By The People[:] Referendums and Plebiscites in Canada by J. Patrick Boyer" Book Review (1984) 29:2 *McGill LJ* 365.

> a lot of things you had to do yourself… having the *Bar Review*, I had my own secretary.[662]

Castel stated that it had come time to leave when "I felt that twenty-seven years was more than enough, and you needed some new blood."[663] Upon leaving the *Review*, Castel was awarded the Order of Canada for his service.[664] There have also been over a half dozen actual editors for the MLJ that received the Order in Canada later in life as well, including Armand de Mestral, Fred Kaufman, Yves Fortier, Richard Pound, Roy L. Heenan, Irwin Cotler, and David P. O'Brien.

Volume thirty saw the beginning of yet another new tradition—the Alumni Newsletter. As the introduction to the first edition of the newsletter explained:

> In a few months time, Volume 30 of the McGill Law Journal will appear. We felt that this anniversary would be an appropriate occasion on which to renew contact with the Journal's alumni.
>
> Our goal in reviving alumni interest in the Journal is threefold. First, we hope to take advantage of the knowledge that alumni have acquired in their various fields of legal work. At any given time, the Journal might be in need of legal advice, notarial service or insights into new activity in a particular area of law. We hope that we will have to look not further than our own alumni for help. Second, we would like to stabilize Journal finances through the regular solicitation of alumni contributions to our trust fund. Finally, we sincerely hope to encourage renewed interest in the continuing activities of the Journal and to stimulate contact between past and present Journal collaborators.
>
> On the occasion of the Journal's anniversary and in order to promote renewed alumni interest in the Journal, we are planning a reception and lecture for late October, 1984. Details and invitations will follow as soon as a date has been confirmed. The evening will combine a brief but very stimulating lecture with cocktails and good company. We hope that all of you will take time out from your busy schedules to attend.[665]

The newsletter was mailed out just after the election of the incoming board and before the summer of 1984.

The newsletter then went on to give a brief history of the changes that had happened to the *Journal* over its first thirty volumes. Of technology they wrote that, "[A]dvances in computer technology in recent times have taken us a further step beyond Gutenberg. The Journal was one of the first Canadian learned publications to use a combined word processor and disk-photocomposition technique."[666] Indeed this was the first volume of the *Journal* to purchase for itself computers and printers for the office.[667] It is surprising to see that electronic editing was taking place so long ago, as for a long time the *Journal* ended up returning to handwritten redlines. However, according to the newsletter, initial footnote editing occurred within the word processor itself and not by hand as long ago as volume twenty-nine and thirty.[668] The creation of the final version of the manuscript sent to the printer was filled with computer coding—for example "R. V. Wray" would be written as "*#R. $$ Wray@*".[669]

Editor-in-Chief Peter Oliver recalled of the time that,

> Brian Pel, our Managing Editor, was a prime mover in most of what followed. I credit myself with having the good sense to recognize that so many of Brian's idea were worth following up on. For example: Computers were still quite a new thing at the Journal. We had a dedicated word processor that was about the size of my present washing machine. It also sounded at lot like my washing machine when it was turned on. Brian thought that we needed to move into the world of PCs and these PCs had to be networked. We visited some private sector companies like Imperial Tobacco, went to computer fairs and tried to work out what hardware and software combination would work.

662 Castel interview, *supra* note 44.

663 *Ibid.*

664 "Order of Canada citation for Jean-Gabriel Castel", *Governor General of Canada* (24 June, 1985), online: <http://archive.gg.ca/honours/search-recherche/honours-desc.asp?lang=e&TypeID=orc&id=270>

665 "Alumni Newsletter" MLJ Editorial Board (1984) 1.

666 *Ibid.*

667 Interview of Brian Pel by James Cummins (17 May, 2012). Pel stated that, "I was one of the group that introduced computers, *Word Perfect*, and printers into the office so we could have versions of drafts … By today's standards, they were pretty basic."

668 *Ibid.*

669 Newsletter 84, *supra* note 664 at 2.

> Eventually we bought 4 IBM PCs all networked together. We hesitated between Word, Wordstar and WordPerfect and went with WordPerfect. There were regular crashes, as was common with all systems in those days, but on the whole it all worked well. I remember we had an incredibly complicated set of keystrokes that had to be entered into journal text to indicate things like bold, italics, footnotes etc.[670]

The *Journal* was receiving between two and three hundred unsolicited pieces a year, and a developing system of blind peer review was in place.[671] On top of that, they were attempting to produce the first edition of the *McGill Guide* from the citations research done by the prior volume. The newsletter reported on their progress:

> The Journal has been awarded a Summer Canada grant by the Ministry of Employment and Immigration to begin the production of a comprehensive national style guide for legal publications. This work will involve the collation and editing of an enormous quantity of material. We must collect extant variations of citation style for the thousands of different sources which are used in legal writing. We will then edit these into a uniform system in both French and English. Our aim is to produce a long-needed reference work sensitive to the particular problems of both civil and common law Canadian publications…
>
> For this project we have mobilized the resources of both the outgoing and incoming editorial boards. The outgoing Editor-in-Chief and Associate Editor are organizing the work, while the incoming Board is lending a hand. The grant has allowed us to hire six or seven law students for the summer to help with the initial collection and analysis of data. We hope to have a preliminary working edition ready by the end of the summer to circulate to other journals for comment and criticism. We will, before publication, endeavour to obtain the support of other major journals, so that the finished product can serve as a standard Uniform Guide to Legal Citation in Canada.[672]

Managing Editor Brian Pel recalled that,

> I think I'm the one that saw there was a business case for it, and that it might be a long-term stable source of funding the *Journal*'s other activities … we got Carswell to publish it and to pay a pretty good royalty for a Canadian publication, and that in the slowness of time has turned out to have worked pretty well … there may have been one or two books dealing with legal citations—Tang comes to mind … I think we were looking at the Harvard *Blue Book* frankly as a manual that had been adopted by law students in the United States, and [saying] "geez, couldn't we do something like that, and put it into the hands of most law students in Canada?"[673]

Volume thirty was very busily helping to change the *Journal* into something closer to what it looks like today. In addition to the citation guide, Managing Editor Brian Pel developed the first annual alumni fundraising campaign and the trust fund these donations would go towards.[674] In an interview, Pel stated that the campaign and the newsletter went hand in hand, saying that they were "an attempt to figure out who our constituency was, and to bring them back into the fold."[675]

Brian Pel is today the longest serving Trustee/Advisor in the history of the MLJ. In the 2012-13 academic year Pel surpasses the previous mark, with his single year as Trustee during his tenure as Managing Editor combined with a continual length of service on the Board of Trustees, then Advisors, from 1995 to present (eighteen years). Pel's early efforts though, along with the *Cite Guide*, would become the cornerstone of future MLJ finances and allow the *Journal* to finally stabilize itself financially.

Also mentioned in the introduction to the newsletter was the "brief but stimulating lecture" they were planning to hold in the fall. That lecture would launch yet another important MLJ tradition—the *McGill Law Journal* Annual Lecture (though there would be an extended hiatus of the event during a later period of time). On October 29, 1984, the first "McGill Law Journal Lecture" would be provided by Jacques-Yvan Morin: the institution's founding

670 Oliver interview, *supra* note 654.
671 *Ibid.*
672 Newsletter 84, *supra* note 664 at 3.
673 Pel interview, *supra* note 666.
674 Newsletter 84, *supra* note 664 at 4.
675 Pel interview, *supra* note 666.

Editor-in-Chief. The topic of his lecture, subsequently published in the *Journal*, was on the need for a formal Constitution in Quebec—and how to go about creating one that respected the traditions and culture of the province.[676] The piece was also anything but "brief", coming in at a full forty-seven pages in print—again the MLJ had taken a small idea and turned it into a grand event. Managing Editor Brian Pel discussed the lecture, stating that it was, "Again, an attempt to create something that the former members could coalesce around." However in the beginning the lecture was not intended to be an annual event, for as Pel recalled, "The thought was that it would be *ad hoc*; we wouldn't necessarily have to have it every year."[677]

Volume thirty's fourth issue was also a departure from the past. Containing no articles, the issue instead recorded two distinct histories. The first was the full bibliography of FR Scott, who died earlier that year; and the second was of legislative texts[678] and other related documents[679] relating to the *Constitution Act of 1982*. The format was similar to Stephen A. Scott's "Editorial Diary" published back in volume twelve, who also helped contribute to this new issue's creation. As Peter Oliver recalled,

> Because the delay in the previous volume had put us under time pressure, and because we were determined to choose our material by May at the latest (we amended the Journal Constitution to that effect) we needed to have a Special Issue which could be produced on that tight schedule. Professor Stephen Scott suggested just the thing. He proposed that we publish Legislative Texts and Documents relating to the Constitution Act, 1982. He provided us with the various Legislative texts and I went to Ottawa and Quebec City locating the rest. Some of this material is now available in other locations, but we were the first, most accessible version.[680]

Then Dean Roderick A. MacDonald prefaced the issue by eulogizing FR Scott, stating that, "It is especially fitting that this bibliography should preface an issue devoted to recent constitutional documents and legislative texts."[681]

In discussion of volume thirty, senior editor Nicholas Kasirer—who would later in life become Dean of Law at McGill and then a Justice of the Quebec Court of Appeal—shed an abundance of light on many of these achievements, as well as the culture of the *Journal* at the time. He stated clearly that, having been both a Dean of one of Canada's leading faculties of law and a high ranking justice, "The *Law Journal* is, I think, one of the most important institutions in legal Canada, I really believe that very strongly."[682] The recent Dean even went so far as to say of the MLJ that "it's interesting that it's now every bit one of the pillars of intellectual life at the Faculty. It's not just an 'add on' ... this is one of the things that the Faculty thinks of as one of its defining qualities and characteristics."[683]

He remembered his fellow editors strongly, and their dedication to the *Cite Guide* project, stating that: "[They're] people who are just content to work hours way ... not count their hours, and not saying, 'Oh, I want more credits than the person beside me.'"[684] Kasirer remembered that, "It is a collaborative and non-competitive environment, the *Journal*."[685] Then, on another great contributor to the future of the *Journal*, Managing Editor Brian Pel, Kasirer wrote of the impact of his developing the alumni and cite guide trusts and continual dedication to the *Journal*:

> Brian's an exceptional figure—if you put his picture on the front of this book it wouldn't be too small a tribute to his role in the health and happiness of the *Law Journal*. When we were working on the *Journal* together, he was—much as he is now—this kind of quiet, solid as a rock figure who steadied the ship along the way. He was a really terrific presence. We met through the *Journal* and we've been friends ever since, in fact I think of him as one of my very closest friends from law school thanks to the *Journal*. There were a few others: Alain Roberge ... there was Hélène [Guay] who was on the executive, there were some people that were just absolutely extraordinary.
>
> Brian's unbelievably quiet yet constant

676 Jacques-Yvan Morin, "Pour Une Nouvelle Constitution Du Quebec" (1985) 30:2 *McGill LJ* 178.

677 Pel interview, *supra* note 666.

678 "Legislative Texts Relating to the Constitution Act," (1985) 30:4 *McGill LJ* 753.

679 "Documents Relating to the Constitution Act" (1985) 30:4 *McGill LJ* 645.

680 Oliver interview, *supra* note 654.

681 Roderick A MacDonald, "Francis Reginald Scott 1899-1985" (1985) 30:4 *McGill LJ* 635 at 635.

682 Interview of Nicholas Kasirer by Omar Soliman (25 March, 2011).

683 *Ibid.*

684 *Ibid.*

685 *Ibid.*

> commitment to the *Journal* through the establishment of the Trust ... and that was really Brian ... the combination of Brian and the *Cite Guide*, the good fortune of the *Cite Guide* and that very close group of people who worked around the *Cite Guide* [elevated the *Journal*]. That was one of the really big themes of the time that I was there. It was mostly volume thirty and volume thirty-one that did the *Cite Guide*, but there was a group of people in volume twenty-nine who were involved and then thereafter the people that followed.
>
> Brian to me is one of the reasons that you can think of the *Law Journal* as something more than a publication, but as an institution for both McGill and Canadian legal literature. Brian is a big reason for that.[686]

The MLJ established its first trust in 1978. According to memorandum issued to the Board of Trustees in 2000 on the history of the trust fund, that first trust consisted of,

> a board of four trustees: the Dean of the Faculty of Law, the Faculty Advisor to the Journal, the Editor-in-Chief of the Journal and the Managing Editor of the Journal. The underlying rationale for creating the fund was to: (a) Provide a basis for the long term financial independence of the Journal in anticipation of possible declines in public funding; (b) Create a reserve fund to which access would be restricted; and (c) Remove surpluses from the Journal's operating accounts.[687]

The memorandum then notes the changes effected by Pel.

> The Trust was reconstituted by a new deed of trust on 21 January 1985. The number of trustees was expanded to nine members, including the *ex officio* trustees named in the 1978 deed. Pursuant to article 8 of the new deed of trust, at least three trustees must be alumni of the Journal. The three trustees who are appointed by virtue of their status as alumni of the Journal serve a three-year renewable period. The remaining two trustees are appointed for a four-year renewable term.[688]

According to the original Deed of Trust, the money in the trust was to be placed in a McGill University Endowment Fund.[689] Governing this fund would be the first nine trustees of the new 1985 Trust:

Dean of the McGill Faculty of Law: Roderick A. MacDonald
Faculty Advisor to the *McGill Law Journal*: Yves-Marie Morissette
Editor-in-Chief of volume thirty: Peter Oliver
Managing Editor of volume thirty: Brian Pel
Volume five Executive Editor: John E.C. Brierley
Volume four Advertising Editor: Yves Fortier
Volume one Editor-in-Chief: Fred Kaufman
Volume twenty-two Editor-in-Chief: Louise Pelly
Justice Claire L'Heureux-Dubé[690]

Though Pel would only serve one term in the beginning—as student terms on the Board were for only one year—he would return as an alumni member to the Board of Trustees during volume forty and remain in that position to this day (with the caveat that the Trust has now been dissolved, and the Board replaced with a Board of Advisors on which Pel sits). L'Heureux-Dubé would retain her trusteeship even after her appointment as a Justice of the Supreme Court of Canada—she was the first of the trustees to simultaneously hold a trusteeship and Supreme Court judgeship. Brierley would retain his position until 1992, as would Fortier until 1991. Kaufman would stay until 1994 and Pelly until 1996. Morissette would only serve one year as well, but would return in 1990 for his tenure as Dean of McGill Law.

Brian Pel recalled of the Trust that, "The idea was to sequester funds for a 'rainy day'; if the funds are available, too easily available, they're going to get spent. So we needed to create a sort of barrier." As was stated before, as of 2012 Pel becomes the longest serving member of the trustee/advisory body in MLJ history—perhaps only fitting as he was the man to initiate the board in the first place. As the person with perhaps the best perspective on the history of the board he recalls,

> That body has sort of evolved. It was strictly, originally, just to perform

686 *Ibid.*

687 "Memorandum from Trent Mell to Professor David Stevens regarding the McGill Law Journal Trust" (18 April, 2000) 1.

688 *Ibid.*

689 "1985 Trust Deed for the McGill Law Journal" (25 January, 1985) 2.

690 *Ibid* at 3-5; see also Appendix C for a historical list of the Board of Trustees from 1985 to its dissolution.

> the financial supervisory function on the surplus funds, and then morphed into something more. It has no official jurisdiction I suppose, but it seems to be a sort of 'lightning rod' or a reporting body; the body to which the management reports on an informal basis. It's been good in that sense because it's created this record on an annual basis of what's happened and what plans were.[691]

Generally this change appears to have been taking place since far before it switched from the Board of Trustees to the Board of Advisors that will be discussed later. When asked why he remained as a Trustee/Advisor for so long, Pel replied that "I have a big thing about institutional memory, so to the extent that I could I helped with that aspect of it. [The *Journal*] was important to me in law school—I thought it was just a great, great learning experience, really one of the highlights of my law school tenure. I was happy to be allowed to continue to be involved."[692]

The bond between editors was substantial during the era of Pel and Kasirer. Kasirer talked further of his fellow student colleagues, and what drew him to the *Journal*:

> I liked the idea that the *Journal* was a bilingual venture … and I joined with one of my very, very great friends, someone who has been a friend of mine since we were children together … Peter Oliver, who was Editor-in-Chief of volume thirty…
>
> It was a funny period. This was the advent of computers at the *Law Journal* … I remember when the *Law Journal* bought its first computer—and this was a moment of great excitement, because prior to that (this would have been volume twenty-nine) there was an unbelievably laboured process where you had to get it typed by someone, and then retyped, and then have to go to some off-site place where changes to the text would be made, and then it's sent to the printers, and then you'd have to go to the printers to proof read, and so on. So the beginning process of using computers was a big moment.
>
> Peter Oliver was a very, very key figure [in all this] … he was my roommate at the time (we lived with two other law students) and I spent an awful lot of time working hard on the *Journal* in large part because of him … To the point that—one funny story—I went to graduate school right after I finished at the Faculty in Paris and Peter went to Oxford, and volume thirty, number four, the last number of our volume, was a special issue on the *Constitution*. And like many volumes of the *Journal* we were late … so in November of the year following our graduation—long gone from the Faculty (both metaphysically and physically; we were over in Europe)—I crossed the Channel and spent two weekends in Oxford working, I expressly remember, right through the night trying to finish … We were kind of at once celebrating and cursing the *Law Journal* … But that was a very, very happy memory.
>
> It was a close senior board. The *Law Journal* offices were downstairs in the basement … It was dark; we had one window, and we would spend thousands of hours going over footnotes in that room. It sounds like a bit of a right of passage, but it was a very, very happy time.[693]

Kasirer also spoke about other moments that brought his board close together, as well as the evolution from type setting to computers, and a story from Morin's speech-turned-article:

> Pre-email, pre- a lot of stuff, there was a kind of a physical dimension on work at the *Law Journal* that you can't really imagine today, whereby you would get proofs and the proofs would be something that was generated by the printer and it would have to be delivered back to the printer—and "my god there's a typo in footnote seven hundred and forty-three." So there was a kind of fastidiousness and a timeline that was quite different than today.
>
> The idea that today you could just sit at a computer and do corrections at the last minute and then send it by email to the printer; that you can control a print run in the way it's done today … I mean, we worried about things like page sequence,

691 Pel interview, *supra* note 666.
692 Pel interview, *supra* note 666.
693 Kasirer interview, *supra* note 681.

in really a very big way, and today nobody even thinks a second about it. The combination of [our] technologies, which ran right through to how you contacted authors, was extremely labourious—we would, generally speaking, get manuscripts that had no electronic form whatsoever, not even discs. They were typed scripts, so we'd have to retype them … [then] you would have to proofread a manuscript to make sure the *Law Journal* had a viable copy to work from. So all of this meant hours for *Journal* people …

I remember one of the articles I worked on as an editor was [by] Jacques-Yvan Morin … who had quite strong political views, atypical for a McGill Law graduate. Anyway, he gave the first *Law Journal* Lecture—now you think of them as an annual event, but we had the first one—and I was editing his paper … I remember going to his office and sitting down with him, because you couldn't do this by email, and for about four hours I went over the manuscript with him. And he would do manual corrections that I would record on our copy; I'd have the copy in my hot little hand and be terrified that I would lose it—because it was the only version of it until I got photocopies…

[These were] very much "on site" labours. You were in the office to get things done; they weren't done at a distance, and that led to bonding between people, and eating at three in the morning, and all of those kinds of things.[694]

Kasirer also talked through the lens of both Dean and former editor of what characterized the relationship between the Faculty and *Journal* from his time hence:

The general rule has been over the years, a posture of deference to students by the Faculty Advisor to the *Law Journal*. That's historically been the role: deference to the idea that this is a student-run publication … the Faculty definitely shouldn't have any claim to editorial decisions—who gets published in the *Journal*, that kind of thing … [they're there] to handle a crisis if necessary … That's frankly because the *Law Journal* student board is so engaged, and it's such a contrast from the model that one finds just about everywhere else … The University of Toronto, they have two journals, but the flagship U of T journal is unequivocally a faculty enterprise.

I'm on the board, and have been over the years, of different law journals … right now I'm on the *Revue internationale de droit comparé* board in Paris—there's not a student to be seen anywhere near that operation … I'm on the board of the *Revue de Droit de l'Universite d'Chambord*, which is a journal that has actually been around for quite a while—for forty years—but was for a long, long time an absolutely faculty-run endeavour. Only recently there's been made room for students on the theory that this is a wonderful site for learning.[695]

The beginning of PC computing at the MLJ, the start of a new and permanent financial regime, the start of the *McGill Guide*, and a special issue largely gathered and refined by the editors of the *Journal* without authors—upon the thirtieth volume of the MLJ, it appears the now "institution" as Kasirer called it, was in good hands. Other members of the MLJ board during volume thirty included Associate Editor Grant McCrea, who went on to be named by the Euromoney Guide as one of the world's leading litigators and a finalist for the Crime Writers of Canada's Arthur Ellis Award for his first crime novel in 2007, published by Random House.[696]

As for articles published by the volume, they also included pieces by Daniel J. Arbess,[697] published three years before Arbess became the youngest person ever to make partner at White and Case LLP; future Honourary Lifetime President of the International Academy of Law and Mental Health Professor David Weisstub;[698] future Dean of Law at the University of Ottawa Bruce Feldthusen;[699] and Jacques Béguin, future

694 *Ibid.*

695 *Ibid.*

696 Grant McCrea, *Dead Money* (New York: Random House, 2006).

697 Daniel J Arbess, "The International Law of Armed Conflict on Light of Contemporary Deterrence Strategies: Empty Promise or Meaningful Restraint" (1984) 30:1 *McGill LJ* 89.

698 David N Weisstub, "Le Droit Et La Psychiatrie Dans Leur Problematique Commune" (1985) 30:2 *McGill LJ* 221.

699 Bruce Feldthusen, "City of Kamloops v. Nielsen: A Comment on the Supreme Court's Modest Clarification of Colonial Tort Law" (1985) 30:3 *McGill LJ* 539.

Professeur Emeritus at l'Université Paris-Sorbonne.[700] Book reviews were contributed by, among others, Justice G. Arthur Martin[701] of the Ontario Court of Appeal; recently retired Justice of the Supreme Court of Canada Louis-Philippe Pigeon;[702] and Stephen J. Toope, then a Ph.D. candidate at Cambridge.[703] The *Journal* also published a very rare "Letter to the Editor" from Harry H. Almond—a professor at Georgetown University—in response to the article by Arbess.[704]

Volume 32 Marc Lemieux and Managing Editor Holly Nickel in *McGill Law Journal* offices, 1986. (Courtesy of Marc Lemieux)

While the stories of the many volumes of the MLJ are often best told as units in time congregated by a certain set of personalities and events, the production of the *Cite Guide*'s first edition spread itself over several volumes. As the summer work grants rolled in and Metcalfe graduated from law school, the reins of the project were handed to Sonia J. Struthers, associate editor to begin with during volume thirty and senior editor of volume thirty-one, and Donald Lawrence Munn—Case Comments Editor of volume thirty-one. They took the research gathered over several years and integrated the notes into the final published version. Today Struthers is currently a senior partner with the Business Law Group of McCarthy Tétrault in Montreal and Munn is Chair of the Privacy Law Group at Clark Wilson in Vancouver.

In an interview Struthers stated that, "Daniel Turp ... had a book out, but what we wanted—what we thought was necessary—was very similar to what we called the 'Harvard Blue Guide'... so we thought we'd publish the McGill 'Red Guide'. Did you notice it's always been in red and white?" When asked if the coloration was a conscious effort to mimic the *Blue Book* with Canadian colours and produce a "Red Book" standard, Struthers replied,

> It was—and we thought that we were ideally placed to do it because we were bilingual and we were bijuridical—so both the common law and the civil law. We already had our own style—we published articles in both English and French, and had developed a style ... It was myself and Larry Munn who did the first edition. We drafted the first one. With a lot of help we led the whole project ... We had lots of people working on different chapters; we gave different chapters to different people to work on.
>
> We sent a hundred letters with the drafts of various styles for different documents to, say, the Supreme Court editor, and to different law faculties and professors, and we obtained feedback. This process took a year and a half or two years,

700 Jacques Béguin, "La Developpement De La Lex Mercatoria Menace-t-il L'ordre Juridique International" (1985) 30:3 *McGill LJ* 478.

701 G Arthur Martin, "*A Century of Criminal Justice: Perspectives on the Development of Canadian Law* by Martin L. Friedman" Book Review (1985) 30:3 *McGill LJ* 619.

702 Louis-Philippe Pigeon, "*Vocabulaire bilingue de la Common Law : Droit de la preuve* by Association du Barreau canadien" Book Review (1985) 30:2 *McGill LJ* 302.

703 Stephen J Toope, "*The Structure and Process of International Law: Essays in Legal Philosophy Doctrine and Theory* by R. St J. MacDonald and D. Johnston" Book Review (1985) 30:2 *McGill LJ* 355.

704 Harry H Almond Jr, "Correspondence: The International Law of Armed Conflict" (1985) 30:3 *McGill LJ* 629.

and then we negotiated a publishing contract with Carswell—that took quite a while too. We thought that this really should benefit the *McGill Law Journal*. We went back and forth with Carswell because we knew it would be a bestseller. Right after we started to get feedback—everyone was just craving this.

Tiré de R.-L. Séguin, *L'esprit révolutionnaire dans l'art québécois : De la déportation des Acadiens au premier conflit mondial*, Montréal, Parti-Pris, 1972. Le croquis, daté du 18 janvier 1839, montre la pendaison des Patriotes Joseph-Jacques Robert, François-Xavier Hamelin, Pierre-Théophile Décoigne, et Ambroise et Charles Sanguinet.

The introductory picture to 32:2 [Source: (1987) 32:3 *McGill LJ* vi.]

At this point there was a great deal of confidence at the *Journal* that the project would be a success. Struthers continued, stating, "We knew it would be a best-seller and we wanted to get a higher percentage of royalties, so there was a lot of work done there as well. It was a labour of love—it truly was, because we signed away our royalties to the *McGill Law Journal* ... That was the genesis."[705]

When asked about the interactions that she and Munn had with the Supreme Court specifically, she stated that, "We sent it to them and they commented on the various styles. They were among our most active commentators."[706] The timing here appears to fall into place with the theories of Professor Bale about Justice Dickson's early impact on the Court—as he would have taken over the position of Chief Justice between when Metcalfe first approached the Court and later on when Struthers and Munn did. Struthers added, "We also sent it to the Federal Court and the Court of Appeal, many courts. The outpouring, the craving, this hunger, to have something in place—it was really extraordinary. It was a great project, and it was all our initiative too. The professors supported us, but we came up with the idea and did it all."[707]

Struthers was involved with the *Cite Guide* for several years following her graduation from McGill Law. She stated that, "I was in an advisory role. We renegotiated the royalties agreement; I helped with that. The institutional memory is not so strong at the *Law Journal*—students come and go, so I helped put things in perspective ... You know, Larry and I published a book."[708] She also mentioned that the French and English parts of the *Guide* were assembled at the same time, stating that, "Every citation, when we developed a style for that particular document, we did it in English and French simultaneously."[709] Hélène Guay, Executive Editor for volume thirty, was heavily involved on the French side of developing the *Guide*, but in terms of managing the project Struthers stated that, "It was really the three of us leading: Robert Metcalfe, Brian Pel, and myself ... it just goes to show you what a bunch of students can do when they set their minds to it."[710]

In addition to the coming to fruition of the *Cite Guide*, volume thirty-one also saw a return of The *McGill Law Journal* Lecture—now labelled as the Annual *McGill Law Journal* Lecture—held on October 30, 1985. As Morin was both the first Editor-in-Chief and the first lecturer, it was perhaps only natural to invite Fred Kaufman—the second Editor-in-Chief of volume one—as the second *Journal* lecturer. An article based on a portion of his speech was published under the title "The Canadian *Charter*: A Time for Bold Spirits, Not Timorous Souls". In the article, Kaufman stated that the *Bill of Rights* was not being embraced quickly and strongly enough by the courts of Canada or by Parliament,[711] and that the *Charter* required pressure to ensure its full and permanent

705 Interview of Sonia Struthers by James Cummins (25 June, 2012).

706 *Ibid.*

707 *Ibid.*

708 *Ibid.*

709 *Ibid.*

710 *Ibid.*

711 Fred Kaufman, "The Canadian Charter: A Time for Bold Spirits, Not Timorous Souls" (1986) 31:3 *McGill LJ* 456 at 458-60.

impression upon Canadian society.[712]

During the speech itself there was a power outage, plunging the moot court into darkness—causing quite a stir.

Future Justice of the Supreme Court of Canada Michel Bastarache also contributed to the volume, who in an ironic turn of events, wrote critically of recent Supreme Court decisions (over ten years before his appointment to the high court)—specifically about their efforts to end the problem of legislative unilingualism in Manitoba.[713] Among the other authors that contributed to the volume included then-recent McGill Law graduate and now popular author Richard J. Goossen with his first academic publication;[714] future University Research Chair at the Faculty of Law of the University of Ottawa, Constance Backhouse;[715] Nicholas Kasirer with his first academic publication;[716] the man who would replace Nicholas Kasirer as Dean of the Faculty of Law at McGill Daniel Jutras;[717] namesake of the Margaret A. Banks room at the University of Western Ontario Faculty of Law, Margaret A. Banks;[718] and James M. Spence,[719] future Justice of the Superior Court of Ontario.

Book reviewers for the volume included Susan B. Boyd,[720] future Chair in Feminist Legal Studies at the University of British Columbia; and Christophe Jamin,[721] future Dean of the Law Faculty at Sciences Po in France. The process of acquiring book reviews from such luminaries, as had been occurring for years at the MLJ, was described in an interview with Book Review Editor for volume thirty-one Gary Nachshen. He wrote that:

> My recollection is that I would look over the various books which the legal publishers sent us, choose those which seemed worthwhile and then try and find someone from my circle of acquaintances (professors, practising lawyers, etc.) who would be willing to review those for us – ideally, two or three per issue. I think that my predecessor explained to me how he operated, and then I more or less followed suit. I don't remember accepting many, if any, unsolicited book reviews or innovating too much in how I went about the process. One of the things I enjoyed about the Book Reviews "portfolio" is that it was a discrete and not overly voluminous part of the *Journal*, and so I could operate in autonomous fashion.[722]

Commission chargée de la codification des lois du Bas-Canada. La photographie, prise entre 1863 et 1865, montre, de gauche à droite, Joseph-Ubalde Beaudry (secrétaire), l'honorable Charles Dewey Day (commissaire), l'honorable René-Édouard Caron (président), l'honorable Augustin-Norbert Morin (commissaire) et Thomas McCord (secrétaire). Cette photographie se trouve à la bibliothèque de droit de l'Université McGill.

The closing picture to 32:2 [Source: (1987) 32:3 *McGill LJ* 710.]

Sadly, Mr. Nachshen would pass away at the age of fifty-two less than two months after providing his interview to this project. He was, according to his long-time firm Stikeman Elliot,

> the driver behind the development of the firm's Pensions and Benefits practice, and he was

712 *Ibid* at 463-5.

713 Michel Bastarache, "Commentaire Sur La Decision De La Cour Supreme Du Canada Dans Le Renvoi Au Sujet Des Droits Linguistiques au Manitoba, Judement Rendu Le 13 Juin 1985" (1985) 31:1 *McGill LJ* 93 at 93.

714 Richard J Goosen, "Canadian Business Negotiations in Post-Mao China: A Progress Report on the New Foreign Economic Legislation" (1985) 31:1 *McGill LJ* 1.

715 Constance Backhouse, "Pure Patriarchy: Nineteenth-Century Canadian Marriage" (1986) 31:2 *McGill LJ* 264.

716 Nicholas Kasirer, "Equine Business Organizations" (1986) 31:2 *McGill LJ* 159.

717 Daniel Jutras, "*Dedman c. R.*: Pouvoir Et Fonction Se Confondent" (1986) 31:2 *McGill LJ* 333.

718 Margaret, A Banks, "Defining Constitution of the Province--The Crux of the Manitoba Language Controversy" (1986) 31:3 *McGill LJ* 466.

719 James M Spence, "Current Approaches to Foreign Investment Review in Canada" (1986) 31:3 *McGill LJ* 508.

720 Susan B Boyd, "Child Custody and Divorce: The Law in Social Context by Susan Maidment" Book Review (1986) 31:2 *McGill LJ* 349.

721 Christophe Jamin, "Dictionnaire de droit privé by Paul-André Crépeau et al" Book Review (1986) 31:2 *McGill LJ* 722.

722 Interview of Gary Nachshen by James Cummins (4 January, 2011).

> widely regarded by clients, peers and the international legal community as one of Canada's finest practitioners in the sector... The respect of his clients and peers led to his recognition in a number of prominent legal publications.[723]

Another member of Nachshen's board who provided an interview was Managing Editor Raj Pande, who wrote that while he was on the MLJ he,

> learned a great deal about *Journal* tradition, the importance of team work, and the value and importance to the legal community of a high quality academic legal publication ... I recall that my interest in the *Journal* was initiated through a suggestion by a good friend on the *Journal*. I think I visited the *Journal* office and spoke with a number of the students on the *Journal* and became excited about being part of the *Journal* and its activities. I really do not recall the application process that well but think there was a written submission and an interview process.[724]

Other members of their board included Associate Editor Jill Frank, who went on to become an Associate Professor of Political Science at the University of South Carolina.

Volume thirty-one also marked the first year of employment for the woman who would act as the backbone of *Journal* tradition for the next twenty-seven years: Nicole Leger. She started out as a typist for the volume, but over time Leger has turned into one of the most important parts of the MLJ. She serves as mentor to incoming executive board members and a shoulder to cry on for student editors that have reached the end of their rope; she has become the source of two and a half decades of anecdotal and professional history that exists only within her, though she is willing and able to dole out the best possible advice at every turn. She is the crutch many editorial members relied on to get through the beginning, or middle, or end of their tenure. And she was well remembered by the Editor-in-Chief of the following volume, Marc Lemieux (now a partner at the Montreal office of Fraser Milner Casgrain LLP), for her wizardry with technology.

Volume thirty-two was the beginning of a very successful generation of scholarly publication at the MLJ. Over the six volumes from volume thirty-two through thirty-seven, the MLJ has averaged six Supreme Court of Canada citations per volume since their publication. Future Executive Editor of volume thirty-four David Lametti remembered that the newness of the *Charter* at the time definitely added to the likelihood of citations—as there was something very new and important on the legal scene that would have an impact people were just beginning to understand.[725]

Volume thirty-two Editor-in-Chief Marc Lemieux remembers that many other things were changing. He wrote that, "Vol. 31 was one of the earliest boards (if not the first) to adopt word-processing technology. Back then, personal computers were as unfamiliar to us as spaceships. I remember countless hardware meltdowns tempered by the good nature, patience and expertise of Nicole Leger in what was then the early years of a brave new world."[726]

It was during volume thirty-two that the MLJ finally moved offices. It started in the attic, then moved to the basement, and now finally—after over thirty years—had an office on one of the floors. As Lemieux recalls, "Vol. 31 was headquartered in a room in the basement of Old Chancellor Day Hall. The following year, vol. 32 of the *Law Journal* was moved to room 204 of New Chancellor Day Hall. The former headquarters had become the Faculty's smoking room in the wake of provincial legislation containing and ultimately banning smoking from campuses."[727]

Lemieux continued recounted his times with the *Journal*:

> [We] published the first doctoral thesis survey. I note that the *Revue du Barreau* has since picked up on this idea, which promotes the work of graduate students in law.
>
> [A] big disappointment came with Gérard Mémeteau's article on loss of chance (*perte de chance*)[728] in medical malpractice under the civil law. Prof. Mémeteau was a visiting professor and we were very excited to be able to publish a piece on what was then a leading-edge legal theory. There are no words to describe our emotions when we discovered, upon

723 "Gary Nashchen" *stikeman.com* (26 October 2011), online: < http://www.stikeman.com/cps/rde/xchg/se-en/hs.xsl/15055.htm >

724 Interview of Raj Pande by James Cummins (5 January, 2011).

725 Interview of David Lametti by James Cummins (2 December, 2011).

726 Interview of Marc Lemieux by James Cummins (13 October, 2011).

727 *Ibid.*

728 Gérard Mémeteau, "Perte de chance en droit médical français" (1986) 32:1 *McGill LJ* 125.

The McGill Law Journal
Revue de droit de McGill

le 18 septembre 1986

Me Marc Barbeau
apt. 225
3421 rue Drummond
Montréal, Québec
H3G 1X7

Maître Barbeau,

En 1984, la **Revue de droit de McGill** mettait sur pied la conférence annuelle des anciens. Nous avions alors le plaisir de présenter une allocution de monsieur le professeur Jacques-Yvan Morin. L'an dernier, notre conférencier d'honneur était l'honorable Fred Kaufman, juge de la Cour d'appel du Québec.

Nous sommes très heureux d'annoncer que le conférencier invité cette année est l'honorable Alan B. Gold, juge en chef de la Cour supérieure du Québec. Sa conférence portera sur "Le juge en chef en tant qu'administrateur des tribunaux", et elle se tiendra à l'heure et au lieu suivants:

Mercredi, le 15 octobre 1986
Conférence - 6:00 p.m.
Moot Court
Réception - 7:00 p.m.
Common Room
Faculté de droit de McGill
tel. 845-8824

Vous êtes cordialement invité à assister à la conférence de monsieur le juge en chef Gold et à la réception qui suivra. Nous espérons recevoir la confirmation de votre présence d'ici lundi le 6 octobre 1986.

Bien à vous,

Revue de droit de McGill
per Christian Allard

3644 rue Peel, Montréal, Québec H3A 1W9 Téléphone (514) 845-8824

Invitation for Marc Barbeau to the third *McGill Law Journal* Annual Lecture (Courtesy of Marc Barbeau)

> making our routine verifications, that the article was in fact a poorly-enhanced copy of a chapter in a book which the professor had published in France. There was a similar disappointment when we realized a note by Prof. Magnet[729] had already been published elsewhere.
>
> On a positive note, articles by Professors [H Patrick] Glenn ("Persuasive Authority"),[730] [Christian] Atias ("*La Mort de la littérature juridique?*"),[731] and [Phillippe] Rémy ("*Les civilistes français vont-ils disparaître?*"),[732] among others, were remarkable contributions to Canadian legal scholarship that still read well today.[733]

On the subject matter of articles, Lemieux also wrote about volume thirty-two's special issue, stating that they had

> published a special issue on Quebec legal history that began with an editorial preface and a drawing of the hanging of the *Patriotes*, and ended with a picture of the codifiers of the 1867 Civil Code of Lower Canada. From rupture to continuity – a little naïve but what a daring statement for the *Journal* to make! One article in that special issue had pie charts, bar charts and line diagrams[734] – I recall what headaches that gave to Nicole and our printer Trendek! All the articles of that special issue were tendered on invitations sent by the Board.

The preface to the special issue written by the Executive Boards read with the same energy with which Lemieux wrote in his interview, stating that,

> It may seem surprising to contribute to the development of legal history with a special issue. In France, the United Kingdom and the United States, a number of societies and journals have been devoted to the subject since the mid-nineteenth century. Legal history forms an integral part of the law school curriculum in European and American law schools. What was *special* for the Osgoode Hall Law Journal in 1983, for the Dalhousie Law Journal in 1985, and for our journal in 1987, is in fact *usual* for journals in other countries. It is difficult to understand the hesitation on the part of Canadian and Quebec legal scholars to institutionalize the historical study of their own discipline.[735]

The authors that contributed to that special issue included Sylvio Normand,[736] future Dean of the Law Faculty at the Université Laval. Authors that contributed to the other issues of volume thirty-two included Professor Udo Reifner,[737] future Chairman of the European Coalition for Responsible Credit; H. Wade MacLauchlan,[738] future President and Vice-Chancellor of the University of Prince Edward Island; and Roger Bilodeau,[739] future Registrar of the Supreme Court of Canada. Book reviews for the volume were contributed by, among others, future Nathan Nemetz Chair in Legal History at the University of British Columbia W. Wesley Pue;[740] future Justice with the Quebec Court of Appeal Allan R. Hilton;[741] and future President and CEO of Air Canada Calin Rovinescu.[742]

What might be considered the "fifth issue" of the *McGill Law Journal* volumes twenty-nine through thirty-one was also released during the tenure of volume thirty-two: the first edition of the *Canadian Guide to Uniform Legal Citation*. Published in 1986, its impact has already been discussed. A brief history

729 Joseph Eliot Magnet, "Collective Rights, Cultural Autonomy and the Canadian State" (1986) 32:1 *McGill LJ* 170.

730 *McGill Law Journal* (1986) 32:2 *McGill LJ* 261.

731 *McGill Law Journal* (1987) 32:4 *McGill LJ* 751.

732 *McGill Law Journal* (1986) 32:1 *McGill LJ* 152.

733 Lemieux interview, *supra* note 725.

734 Evelyn Kolish, "Imprisonment for Debt in Lower Canada, 1791-1840" (1987) 32:3 *McGill LJ* 602 at 616-28.

735 "Preface" (1986) 32:1 *McGill LJ* i at ii.

736 Sylvio Normand, "Un Theme Dominant De La Pensee Juridique Traditionnelle Au Quebec: La Sauvegarde De l'integrite Du Droit Civil" (1987) 32:3 *McGill LJ* 559.

737 Udo Reifner, "The Bar in the Third Reich: Anti-Semitism and the Decline of Liberal Advocacy" (1986) 32:1 *McGill LJ* 96.

738 H Wade MacLauchlan, "Of Fundamental Justice, Equality and Society's Outcasts: A Comment on *R. v. Tremayne* and *R. v. McLean*" (1986) 32:1 *McGill LJ* 213.

739 Roger Bilodeau, "Une Analyse Critique De L'Affaire Societe Des Acadiens Du Nouveau-Brunswick Et L'avenir Precaire Du Bilinguisme Judiciaire Au Canada" (1986) 32:1 *McGill LJ* 232.

740 W Wesley Pue, "Law & Justice in a New Land: Essays in Western Canadian Legal History by Louis A. Knafla" Book Review (1986) 32:1 *McGill LJ* 254.

741 Allan R Hilton, "Righting the Balance: Canada's New Equality Rights by Lynn Smith: Book Review" (1987) 32:4 *McGill LJ* 972.

742 Calin Rovinescu, "The Proxy System in Canadian Corporations: A Critical Analysis by R. Crête" Book Review (1987) 32:2 *McGill LJ* 452.

of the development that took place over volume thirty-one was explained in the *McGill Law Journal* alumni newsletter of August 1986—the month prior to the *Guide*'s release. In a section delightfully subtitled "The Art of Footnoting", the editors explained:

> The *Guide* will appear as a bilingual edition, dealing with five major areas: Legislation, Cases, Secondary Materials, Government Documents, and Treaties.
>
> The project, begun by the *McGill Law Journal* in 1984 to establish a uniform system of citation across Canada, benefited greatly from the aid of the Canadian Law Information Council and the Department of Employment and Immigration. Comments regarding earlier drafts of the *Guide* were considered and incorporated into a revised version, which was adopted by the McGill Legal Research and Writing Program and the Mooting Program. The regional Law Journal Conference hosted by the *Queen's Law Journal* in February 1986 offered an additional opportunity to discuss citation form and to reach greater consensus.
>
> The publication by Carswell of this first edition of the *Guide* is only the beginning: research is continuing in preparation for a second edition. At the present time, work is progressing in the areas of municipal by-laws, administrative tribunals, gazettes, European courts and French legislation, jurisprudence, doctrine and encyclopedias. The rules concerning these areas will be incorporated in a second edition and we hope to distribute them for comment as a draft supplement to the *Guide* before the appearance of the second edition.[743]

When finally published the first edition of the *Guide* began with a preface that encapsulated what was then a two and a half year process, which read:

> In the spring of 1984, the editors of the McGill Law Journal began a process of research and discussion on citation form which has resulted, two years later, in the publication of this Manual. The incentive for the citation project developed out of the recognition that although several citation systems had been proposed over the years, no one system was accepted as standard. The editors believed that the formulation of a citation system which mirrored our bilingual and bijuridical legal community would have the greatest chance of providing a nationally acceptable standard …
>
> In order to achieve our aim that the citation project result in a negotiated consensus on citations style across the country, in March 1985, we distributed for comment a limited number of copies of a preliminary draft of the Guide in English and French. We also began to apply the new system, in the Journal in September 1984 in order to determine whether the system was workable. Reasons supporting the rules were included in the initial draft in order to provide a basis for discussion.
>
> The draft received tremendous response. Editors of law reviews, journals and publishing houses, university law librarians, members of the Canadian Association of Law Libraries (CALL), judges of the courts of various jurisdictions, legislative counsel, research directors and law firms and others expressed support for the project and submitted detailed comments …
>
> Preliminary drafts of the newly-researched citation forms with supporting reasons were distributed in the fall of 1985 in both English and French. As well, a limited number of copies of the Guide [were] printed for use by the McGill Legal Research and Writing and Mooting programmes. The regional Law Journal Conference hosted by the Queen's Law Journal in February 1986, provided us with an op[p]ortunity to discuss citation form with several journals and to reach greater consensus. Response to the new sections of the Guide was considered and incorporated into the manuscript which was finally submitted for publication in April 1986.[744]

Other members of Marc Lemieux's board that initiated this new era in Canadian legal history included Circulation Editor Farrel G. Miller, who

743 "Alumni Newsletter" MLJ Editorial Board (1986) 2.

744 McGill Law Journal Editorial Board, *Canadian Guide to Uniform Legal Citation* (Toronto: Carswell, 1986) at v-vi.

went on to become the owner of the Club de Hockey Junior de Montréal hockey team of the Quebec Major Junior Hockey League; and Book Reviews Editor Janet E. Henchey, future Director of the International Assistance Group at the Federal Department of Justice. Lemieux wrote fondly of the time he spent with his board:

> The publishing process involved two or three communications between the *Journal* and the publisher Trendek. Ultimately we would receive boxes of printed copies of the *Journal*. Upon receipt of the physical copies of the journals we would always skim the pages looking for a typo which we unfailingly would find, notwithstanding the long hours reviewing the references in the library and editing manuscripts. We would then manually insert the printed copies in envelopes to be mailed to our subscribers. When the work was completed we would treat ourselves with pizza and beer (on occasion we may have started on the beer during the process). Some of those mailing sessions I remember warmly, the satisfaction of sending off the finished product, the celebration of work well done, the precious sense of forming part of a team.[745]

A third *McGill Law Journal* Lecture was held on October 15, 1986, featuring Chief Justice of the Superior Court of Quebec Alan B. Gold, a man who would also go on to become Chancellor of Concordia University. In its announcement the alumni newsletter for that year joked that, "The building director has assured us he will double-check the fuse box before the *Lecture*, in order to avoid a repetition of last year's mid-speech power blackout."[746] Gold spoke on the subject of court administration in the office of Chief Justice[747]—the office he then held. The tradition of publishing the Lecture, however, was discontinued—Gold's presentation did not appear in the pages of the MLJ, even though volume thirty Editor-in-Chief Peter Oliver recalls that the idea from the beginning was to treat each lecture as a *Journal* publication.[748]

The newsletter also made mention of a new trend developing continent-wide in law reviews that would continue to this day: specialization. One of the publications of particular concern to the editors was *La Revue québécoise de droit international*.[749] The journal was founded in 1984 by none other than Jacques-Yvan Morin himself—still looking to continually innovate the industry he revolutionized over thirty years earlier. While the MLJ would never specialize *per se*, this era did mark the beginning of a shift in editorial policy. The newsletter read that the board was starting to "seek to explore a number of particular editorial viewpoints: foreign and comparative law, international law, and multidisciplinary studies in law"[750] writing further that, "with the modern impact of specialization, it may become necessary to focus on a number of more closely defined objectives."[751] This signalled a shift that would lead the MLJ into the next century. The newsletter also reported on the stage of computerization at the MLJ, stating that,

> [C]onstant use of the word-processing function has now been putting the computer to the test for two years. Though the integration was not always "bug free", the system has improved the editorial quality of the *Journal* and increased its administrative efficiency. A forthcoming addition to the system is a customer records database, which will allow computer invoicing and facilitate each biannual billing. Distribution and special projects necessitating mass mailings have become more manageable... Happily, there is no IBM software which automatically stuffs the journal into the envelope, so that the "mail-out assembly line" in the cafeteria has not yet become obsolete.[752]

Today, as it is with many things, the packaging and shipping of issues has been outsourced. It appears, however, that such a move outsources more than just the task at hand—perhaps, when considering the words of Lemieux, it also outsources a bit of the community.

While peer review had been around in a general sense, volume thirty-one and thirty-two instituted the first blind refereeing system. Lemieux wrote that, "All the articles of that special issue were tendered on invitations sent by the Board. Most if not all of these articles were refereed – which was then new for the Journal."[753] The newsletter commented on this as well, writing of "the *Journal*'s newly adopted outside referee

745 Lemieux interview, *supra* note 725.

746 Newsletter 86, *supra* note 743 at 2.

747 Letter from Christian Allard to Marc Barbeau (18 September, 1986).

748 Oliver interview, *supra* note 654.

749 Newsletter 86, *supra* note 743 at 1.

750 *Ibid.*

751 *Ibid.*

752 *Ibid.*

753 Lemieux interview, *supra* note 725.

system"[754] in response to "the preference given by university tenure committees to publications in refereed journals."[755] At this point the *Journal* was focusing mostly on academics outside the Faculty, in order to create the kind of double-blind system that is now standard among legal academic publications worldwide.

The newsletter read further on the decision to move in this direction:

> At the same time, valid reservations were expressed, such as the protection of student editorial control and the avoidance of delays in the publishing schedule. After a series of discussions, the *Journal* voted last March to adopt a referee system which reflects concern for these conflicting perceptions. Under the adopted system, all material received by the *McGill Law Journal* is first evaluated internally by the student Editorial Board. Where a preliminary decision favours publication, the article is forwarded to one or two outside evaluators who are asked to comment upon its strengths and weaknesses. The evaluator's comments will serve not only to confirm (or question) the publication decision, but also to offer guidance in the editorial process. There will be no permanent board of referees; rather, the *Journal* will match each article with a suitable outside evaluator on the basis of the latter's interest and expertise in the subject area.[756]

This system would remain intact from that day forward—absolutely no different in 2012 than it was then. It may now seem commonplace, but such a decision by the students running the *Journal* during this time was not only innovative, it was also sacrificial. It would mean even more work hours, and even more tasks, just as computers were starting to make their lives a little bit easier. It was, however, a decision that kept the MLJ at the forefront of legal scholarship in Canada.

---

754 Newsletter 86, *supra* note 743 at 1.

755 *Ibid.*

756 Newsletter 86, *supra* note 743 at 1-2.

Chapter Four:

The Permanent Meeting Place

The initiatives put forward by volumes thirty-one and thirty-two continued over the following volumes. The following year's alumni newsletter reported that the external evaluation system had proven a great success in terms of the willingness of academics to review articles.[757] The *Guide*, in its first year of publication, had already received official support from *The Manitoba Law Review*, the *Osgoode Hall Law Journal*, the *Ottawa Law Review*, the *Queen's Law Journal*, the *University of British Columbia Law Review*, and the *University of Toronto Faculty of Law Review*.[758] In addition, a publication date for the second edition had already been set. The *Journal* was now running three IBM computers,[759] and the doctoral thesis survey became an annual addition to MLJ volumes.[760] In fact, volume thirty-three expanded the survey to also include graduate theses alongside those for doctoral programs.[761] The *McGill Law Journal* also became a registered charity in 1987, as part of a major restructuring of the MLJ's management and finances that was begun by Brian Pel.

The *McGill Law Journal* Lecture continued, but was renamed the "Alumni Lecture". The lecture that year featured Stephen Lewis, at that time the Canadian Ambassador to the United Nations, though he had led the New Democrat Party as Leader of the Official Opposition in Ontario for several years.[762] The lecture was held on February 10, 1988 on the subject of international law through the lens of Canadian foreign policy.[763] Once again, the lecture was not published, as would become the custom again during the later reinstitution of the annual event.

One thing that did separate volume thirty-three from previous volumes, was the rising concentration the MLJ was starting to have on "becoming a truly bilingual and bijuridical institution."[764] It was only in 1987 that the constitution of the MLJ was also adopted in French instead of just English, perhaps a representative move considering the constitutional status of Quebec at the time (and today).

To get some context of the efforts that would be needed to accomplish the raising of the French aspects of the *Journal* to the level of the English, consider the following. From volume one through volume ten, less than ten percent of articles and comments published by the MLJ were French. Between volumes eleven and twenty, only fourteen percent of articles and comments published were in French. In fact within the four volumes composing volume fifteen through eighteen, only six French articles saw publication out of the total ninety-six articles and comments published by the MLJ—a paltry six percent! It was only in between volumes twenty-one and thirty that the MLJ saw its percentage of articles and comments published in French reach over twenty percent.[765]

In the beginning, there was only one French article published in all of volume one (by the father of a future editor),[766] though there were two French book reviews.[767] The masthead only began putting the name of each executive editorial position in both French and English during volume twenty,[768] and the French name for the *Journal—Revue de Droit de McGill*—has only been in use since 1977.[769] The practice of placing both a French and English abstract at the beginning of each article only started during volume twenty-eight.[770] In

757 "The *McGill Law Journal* Alumni Newsletter" MLJ Editorial Board (1987) 1.

758 *Ibid* at 2.

759 *Ibid.*

760 *Ibid* at 3.

761 "Doctoral and Masters Thesis Survey—1988" (1988) 33:4 *McGill LJ* 815.

762 Newsletter 87, *supra* note 757 at 4.

763 Letter from M Kevin Woodall and Roderick A MacDonald to Marc Barbeau (11 January, 1988).

764 Newsletter 87, *supra* note 757 at 1.

765 All statistics produced by a double counting of the articles within the various volumes' mastheads.

766 Louis Baudouin, "Immuntabilite ou Mutabilite des Conventions Matrimoniales ?" (1954-55) 1:4 *McGill LJ* 259.

767 André Forget, "*Du Droit des Biens à la Théorie Générale des Obligatore et des Contrats Livres IV, V et VI* by Louis Baudouin" Book Review (1953) 1:2 *McGill LJ* 164; Raymond Lachapelle, "Les Successions, Donations et Testaments, la Preuve, l'Order Public, l'Abus des Droits Livres XI, XII, XIII by Louis Baudouin" Book Review (1953) 1:2 *McGill LJ* 167.

768 "Editorial Board" (1974) 20:1 *McGill LJ* iii.

769 "Editorial Board" (1978) 24:1 *McGill LJ* i; Brierely 25th, *supra* note 47.

770 Robert Martin, "Criticizing the Judges" (1982) 28:1 *McGill LJ* 1.

contrast to this, volume thirty-two saw a full third of all its articles published in French—something that had not occurred since volume twenty-three. Volume thirty-three continued this tradition, and saw about thirty percent of its articles published in French. This new initiative pushed the MLJ towards a modern era where volume fifty-four (2009) published forty-six percent of its articles in French, and volume fifty-six (2011) dedicated forty-five percent of its total page count towards either French or bilingual articles, comments, and book reviews.

This was a struggle throughout all legal periodicals in Canada. The only other truly bilingual law review in Canada is the *Canadian Bar Review*, as is shown later on in this book. The man behind bringing bilingualism to that publication was, of course, Jean-Gabriel Castel. He recalled of his efforts at the *Review* that,

> I went about that with the support of Renault St. Laurent and Prime Minister Louis St. Laurent, who became friends of mine. Renault, who was President of the Bar Association at the time, had gone to McGill too. He felt that it was time to become bilingual. They supported me in the endeavour to press for a bilingual type of scholarly journal that would appeal to both common law and civil law lawyers.[771]

Castel also pushed for bilingualism at the MLJ during his tenure as Advisor.

Considering the success that French articles published in the MLJ have had over the years in terms of citations, volume thirty-three's new push for bilingualism was an intelligent move for more than cultural reasons—it was sound business to bring up this often sagging end of the *Journal*'s mandate. This was, very much so, a new endeavour to increase the *Journal*'s inclusiveness of French scholarship. It was not likely due to historical bias, however. The truth is that the civil law society of scholars in Quebec had never really accepted the idea of a student-run law review as valuable. As of the late 1980s, the *McGill Law Journal* was the only student-run law review in the province, despite the province having several outstanding law schools—though student-run law reviews were the norm throughout the rest of the country. Nicholas Kasirer attested to that in his interview regarding volume thirty: that in the French legal community, a student-run law journal was not exactly the best place to publish. But given that Jacques-Yvan Morin and his board's original goal was to create a permanent meeting place for scholars *in Quebec*, the lack of French scholarship that appeared in the MLJ is more than an oversight.

Authors that published within volume thirty-three included future Osler Professor of Corporate Law at the University of Alberta Richard W. Bauman;[772] future Chair of the Board of Directors of the International Centre for Human Rights and Democratic Development, Kathleen E. Mahoney;[773] and future Dean of Law at Hong Kong University, Albert H.Y. Chen.[774] Book review contributors included Frederick Harhoff;[775] future Justice of the International Criminal Tribunal for the former Yugoslavia; future Professor of Law Emeritus at Ohio State University P. John Kozyris;[776] recent MLJ Book Review Editor Gary Nachshen;[777] and then-Professor of History Emeritus at the University of Toronto Kenneth McNaught.[778]

The volume thirty-three board that edited the volume included Associate Editor Nathalie Vézina, who would go on to become a Full Professor of Law at the University of Sherbrooke and member of the MLJ Board of Advisors; and Circulation Editor Howard Greenspoon, who went on to become a founding partner of Greenspoon Perreault LLP. Citations Editor Michael Waterson and senior editor Randall Hofley would serve as editors for the second edition of the *McGill Guide*, and Stephen Toope returned as Faculty Advisor to the MLJ four years after his tenure as Editor-in-Chief. He would remain as Faculty Advisor for three years. Toope said of his time as Faculty Advisor that:

> I was lucky in that it was good teams overall when I was advising, and the advising role is pretty minimal quite frankly, at least it was in my experience simply because; I guess it would not be

771 Castel interview, *supra* note 44.

772 Richard W Bauman, "The Communitarian Vision of Critical Legal Studies" (1988) 33:2 *McGill LJ* 295.

773 Kathleen E Mahoney, "Defining Pornography: An Analysis of Bill C-54" (1988) 33:3 *McGill LJ* 575.

774 Albert HY Chen, "The Development of Immigration Law and Policy: The Hong Kong Experience" (1988) 33:4 *McGill LJ* 631.

775 Frederick Harhoff, "Law and Institutions of the European Communities, 4th Edition by Dominick Lasok and John W. Bridge" Book Review (1988) 33:4 *McGill LJ* 842.

776 P John Kozyris, "Conflict of Law in the European Community by D. Lasok and P.A. Stone" Book Review (1988) 33:3 *McGill LJ* 628.

777 Gary Nachshen, "Business Law and Practice in the People's Republic of China by Richard J. Goossen" Book Review (1987) 33:1 *McGill LJ* 245.

778 Kenneth McNaught, "The Politics of the Imagination: A Life of F.R. Scott by Sandra Djwa" Book Review (1988) 33:2 *McGill LJ* 422.

> minimal if things were collapsing or were in crisis. I was in luck: no crisis. Generally people were getting their work done so I just had to try to give moral support to the editing team more than anything else…
>
> I must say that I like the model of a student-run, student-edited journal … I just think it's a fantastic opportunity as a young professional to be able to really take on something that matters and to have a direct impact in your field and to try to do the very best you can to make it work.[779]

Volume thirty-four would see not one but two different future Justices of the Supreme Court of Canada published within its pages. Michel Bastarache published his second MLJ piece in three years on the effects of the *Meech Lake Accord* constitutional amendments on the French community outside of Quebec.[780] The second future Justice was Rosalie Silberman Abella, who wrote on the consistency of the judicial role in public policy both before and after the *Charter*[781]—in spite of a public feeling that existed at the time that the judicial role had become more influential in this regard. This is the first of four article contributions she would make to the MLJ over the years.

Opening her article, Abella—a woman who would one day sit on the highest court in the land in Canada—stated clearly that:

> Judges have always been involved with public policy. And judges, in their role either in the interpretation of statutes or in the selective application of precedent, have always been involved in the development of law. Why then is there now an unfolding drama about the appropriate limits to judicial power and an intense curiosity about the backgrounds of the men and women who wield it? … When the *Charter* was added to this country's Constitution, what came prominently into the nation's consciousness was the realization that public policy, far from playing a minor role in the judicial script, had in fact been a co-star all along.[782]

Abella did provide the context that the public policy role of the courts were "interpretive and not blatantly political,"[783] and wrote of why it was important for the public to understand the apolitical public policy influence they had by stating that, "Absolute justice, to paraphrase Bentham, may be unattainable… but we can certainly attempt to reduce injustice by, among other things, acknowledging that judges have operational intellectual, moral, cultural and social perceptions which my guide, as opposed to dictate, their legal conclusions."[784]

Another key part of volume thirty-four's legacy came through its continuance of the tradition of publishing speeches given around the McGill Law campus, as a method of recording history when it was unlikely to be recorded otherwise. The particular speech preserved in this volume was given as the first annual John P Humphrey Lectureship on Human Rights, and provided by none other than John Humphrey himself on November 16, 1988.[785] Despite all his achievements through life, Humphrey still opened his address in saying, "That my Alma Mater should have created during my lifetime an annual lectureship in my name is something that I still have difficulty believing."[786]

Professor Humphrey was more than humble, stating that the person who introduced him had just mentioned his part in writing the first draft of the *Universal Declaration of Human Rights*. He commented however that, "This is true. It was part of my job. Somebody must start a ball rolling. I must say, however, that I have never attached the importance to what I did that some people do now."[787] Instead, he saw his actual contribution to the history of global human rights as "the role that I was able to play in keeping the United Nations human rights programme alive when it was under attack."[788] He recalled that on occasion, some of the most powerful men in the world would warn him that they "wanted to keep the human rights programme going at the slowest speed possible"[789] in rather forward detail.

When called up by his friend Henri Laugier at the United Nations to become the first Director of the Human Rights Division at the UN, Humphrey had just been named the next Dean of the Law Faculty

779 Toope interview, *supra* note 577.

780 Michel Bastarache, "L'Accord Constitutionnel De 1987 Et La Protection Des Minorites Francophones Hors Quebec" (1989) 34:1 *McGill LJ* 119 at ff.

781 Rosalie Silberman Abella, "Public Policy and the Judicial Role" (1989) 34:4 *McGill LJ* 1021 at ff.

782 *Ibid* at *1022.*

783 *Ibid* at 1025.

784 *Ibid* at 1029.

785 Humphrey 1989, *supra* note 119 at 192.

786 *Ibid* at 194.

787 *Ibid.*

788 *Ibid.*

789 *Ibid* at 195.

at McGill[790]—which is where the title of his speech/article came from, "The Dean Who Never Was". Soon after, the first drafting committee was assembled to draft the *Declaration*, but Humphrey was not on it. Instead, the committee consisted of Eleanor Roosevelt (former First Lady of the United States), P.C. Chang of China, and Charles Malik of Lebanon. Humphrey recalled that:

> This committee only met once, in Mrs. Roosevelt's Washington Square apartment. Chang and Malik were so far apart in their philosophical approach that it very soon became obvious that the committee would never itself prepare a text. Chang had studied under John Dewey and called himself a pluralist. Malik was a Christian Lebanese who seemed to believe that St. Thomas Aquinas had had the answers to all questions. In the result, the committee asked me to prepare a text.[791]

He called his role the result of "pure luck"[792] and admitted that, "It turns out … that the adoption of the *Universal Declaration* was a much more important even than anyone could have dared to imagine in 1948. The *Declaration* is now binding on all states."[793] Similar to the conversation between Le Dain and Morin in early 1952, there was no way for anyone to know what the future would hold in those early days of 1948. If it was not for the argument between Chang and Malik, the *Declaration* may well have been written by somebody else—likely Roosevelt—and the universality of the document may never have been so clearly and thoroughly expressed.

Though the scepticism of Humphrey's 1971 piece appears to have diminished in his worldview—the November 1988 date of his speech would have allowed him to see many of his thin hopes for the world come to fruition—he still added the same pressure to those who would listen to him speak:

> The generation to which I belong has successfully enunciated international legal standards in the matter of human rights. But that is not enough. The challenge of the future – and I mean the immediate future – is how to set up efficient mechanisms for the enforcement and implementation of these standards. This will not be an easy thing to do, but it is something that has to be done if this planet is to have any future.[794]

That year the annual *McGill Law Journal* Alumni Lecture, again unpublished, was provided by Justice Willard Zebedee Estey of the Supreme Court of Canada in his last year of office[795]—he was also one of the two trustees (each given a lifetime tenure) of the Stanley Cup, replacing Clarence Campbell (one of only nine such trustees in the 118 year history of the trophy).

Volume thirty-four Executive Editor David Lametti—future Associate Dean of Academics at McGill University—recalled the lecture, stating that,

> He was a "Bay Street" judge in the way that Sopinka was and the way that Ian Binnie was. He was appointed from Bay Street [Toronto], and he said a number of things that were relatively controversial. I remember him saying that *Morgentaler* wasn't the most difficult case that the Court had to decide, which was interesting that he would say that of the Court at the time, because it was one of the landmark decisions it had made.[796]

Other authors in the volume included Kent Roach,[797] future Professor of Law and Prichard-Wilson Chair of Law and Public Policy at the University of Toronto, as well as future *McGill Law Journal* lecturer himself; Lorna A Turnbull,[798] future Dean of Law at Robson Hall; and Andrew Petter,[799] future President of Simon Fraser University. Book reviews were contributed by, among others, future Gordon F. Henderson Chair in Human Rights at the University of Ottawa Faculty of Law Lucie Lamarche;[800] future Justice of the Federal Court of Canada Johanne Gaultier;[801] as well as a sort of "guide to the *Guide*" written by volume thirty-three Editor-in-Chief Kevin M. Woodall that overviewed the changes to the second edition of the *Canadian Guide to*

790 *Ibid* at 196.
791 *Ibid.*
792 *Ibid* at 195.
793 *Ibid* at 198.
794 *Ibid* at 202.
795 "Alumni Newsletter", MLJ Editorial Board (August 1990), 4.
796 Lametti interview, *supra* note 724.
797 Kent Roach, "The Administrative Law Scholarship of D. M. Gordon" (1989) 34:1 *McGill LJ* 1.
798 Lorna A Turnbull, "*Brooks, Allen & Dixon v. Canada Safeway Ltd*--A Comment (Bliss Revisited)" (1989) 34:1 *McGill LJ* 172.
799 Andrew Petter, "Legitimizing Sexual Inequality: Three Early *Charter* Cases" (1989) 34:2 *McGill LJ* 358.
800 Lucie Lamarche, "Equality and Judicial Neutrality by S.L. Martin and K.E. Mahoney" Book Review (1989) 34:3 *McGill LJ* 705.
801 Johanne Gaultier, "*Marine Cargo Claims* by W. Tetley: Book Review" (1989) 34:3 *McGill LJ* 724.

Uniform Legal Citation, alongside how the guide fit into some of Canada's other premiere legal research writing handbooks.[802]

This, in particular, is of interest—there are very few people in Canada who spend as much time perfecting citation methods and referencing than the Editor-in-Chief of a law journal; and most, once done, are very often so sick of citations that they never want to see another footnote again. Of course, for most, their life is still filled with footnotes of some kind moving forward, but for Woodall to contribute such a service reveals a real dedication to enhancing the nation's understanding of how clear legal writing is best done.

Volume thirty-four was led by Editor-in-Chief Gary F. Bell, who would go on to become the Director of the Asian Law Institute at the National University of Singapore. One of his colleagues that year, Executive Editor David Lametti, recalled of volume thirty-four that,

> As a student I guess what I remember most was the hard work, and just I think the quality of the writers. I look back at the articles that we published and there were some fabulous people who were at various stages of their career. Kent Roach published his first major article with us, and then came back to publish with us on a number of different occasions—who had a long standing career at the University of Toronto. Whereas others were sort of mid-career, and still a few others towards the end—John Humphrey … Pierre Trudel,[803] a very famous French language writer here in Quebec who wrote in communications law …
>
> We were in room 204 for the two years that I was on the *Journal*—so we were in New Chancellor Day Hall. It probably wasn't the best room, but it was surprising how big the room could be, given the fact that it was just a rectangular box. The three "senior" editors were Scott Diamond, Gary Bell, and myself—Gary was the Editor-in-Chief and Scott was the Managing Editor—and we got along fabulously; we've remained good friends ever since those days.
>
> I think we had fun. There were a lot of late nights; a fair bit of pizza consumed in the old days when we were getting stuff ready to ship, and for other reasons. We had the usual dinners and whatnot for new board members, and potlucks.[804]

When asked about why he joined the Executive, Lametti recalled that,

> While we were junior members of volume thirty-three I was the [Law Students Association] President and Gary was one of the Vice-Presidents … we were moving into our last year of law school and certainly I thought I wanted to put a bit more work into the *Journal*—I thought I had some pretty good administrative and people skills—and being Executive Editor I thought I would be able to use those skills effectively. The Executive Editor in those days was the one managing the work load of all the various board members. Gary was looking for a larger leadership role and I certainly supported him in that—I thought he was fabulous as an Editor-in-Chief.[805]

Lametti further recalled that at the time there wasn't much communication between Executive Boards. He and Gary Bell where friends with Peter Oliver—Editor-in-Chief of the Board four years before they were on the Executive—so discussed *Journal* tradition with him quite a bit.[806] But other than this happenstance connection, Executive Boards were fairly isolated within the knowledge passed down from the Board immediately behind them. Thus there was still a fair amount of reinventing the wheel, despite the new technology-centric *Journal* that had been developing in recent years.

The following volume (thirty-five), hired by Bell, Lametti, and his fellow executives, brought even more future luminaries to the *Journal*. Senior board members of volume thirty-five included: Editor-in-Chief Daniel Torsher, future managing partner of Kinstellar LLP in Bucharest; Citations Editor Timothy M. Egan, future

802 M Keving Woodall, "Canadian Guide to Uniform Legal Citation by The McGill Law Journal; La recherche documentaire Juridique au Quebec by D. LeMay and D. Goubau; Using a Law Library: A Guide for Students and Lawyers in the Common Law Provinces of Canada by M. Banks; Legal Research Handbook by D.T. MacEllven; and Legal Writing and Research Manual by M.J. Iosipescu" Book Review (1989) 34:3 *McGill LJ* 727 at ff.

803 Pierre Trudel, "Le standard e programmation de haute qualité dans la législation sur la radio et la télévision" (1989) 34:2 *McGill LJ* 203.

804 Lametti interview, *supra* note 724.

805 *Ibid.*

806 *Ibid.*

President and CEO of the Canadian Gas Association; and Mayo Moran. Moran would become the James Marshall Tory Chair and Dean of the Faculty of Law at the University of Toronto in 2006. In an interview, Moran said of her time with her volumes that:

> I knew at the time that I was on the law journal what a great privilege it was and my sense of that has only increased in the years that have passed since then. I was fortunate to work with other students who were just fantastic, and as someone who later became an academic, the early insight I got there was invaluable. Also, since I was a former English teacher when I went to law school, it was terrific to be able to find a whole group of people who loved nothing more than debating language, grammar, punctuation and, of course, ideas. Being on the law journal also engaged us as students very profoundly in the great legal events of our time which supplemented our legal education in an extremely stimulating way.[807]

The *Journal* had a strong impact on Moran, as she further recalled that:

> The very first article I edited was a wonderful piece on the special morality of tort law by Professor Ernie Weinrib.[808] That piece, and my outstanding torts professor Stephen Perry (who was also faculty advisor to the journal at that time), had a profound effect on me. I went on to specialize in tort law, which I now teach. I wrote a doctorate which I later turned into a book that [Oxford University Press] published on the reasonable person. Tort law was central to my thesis and my doctoral supervisor was none other than Professor Ernie Weinrib![809]

The academic integrity of her volume is perhaps represented best in the fact that since its publication, six articles within it have been cited, and between them cited a total of nine separate times, by the Supreme Court of Canada in its decisions—the most citations ever for a single volume of the MLJ. For this volume Richard Pound—Managing Editor of volume thirteen—who was the Vice-President of the International Olympic Committee at the time, provided the *McGill Law Journal* Alumni Lecture on February 14, 1990.[810] The topic of his speech was on the legal issues and implications surrounding mandatory drug testing,[811] nearly a decade before the founding of the World Anti-Doping Agency, which he would one day serve as President. Pound was one of the world's most vocal and influential advocates of stronger drug testing at the time, and as a former Olympic athlete himself (he swam the 100m freestyle and relay at the 1960 Summer Olympics in Rome). His perspective prefaced one of the most controversial issues of the two decades since—the use of performance enhancing drugs by professional and amateur athletes alike.

The volume was also the first to publish an annual "Books Received" list within its volume[812]—a tradition that would continue into the future, though the per-issue format of the Books Received list would be converted to a per-volume format three years later, during volume thirty-eight.[813] While the volume thirty-four board had intended for one to be published within its bounds,[814] volume thirty-five published both the received list for its own volume and that of its predecessor.[815] Books Received lists had been printed in the *Journal* since as early as volume seven,[816] but only sporadically.

This was truly a sign of the times. Whereas the books that would flow in from publishers would once be put up for sale by the *Journal* as a source of revenue, the MLJ was now running an overall surplus thanks to the revenues from the *McGill Guide* and successful alumni donation drives.[817] In turn, the books began to be donated to other McGill institutions like the McGill Legal Information Clinic.

MLJ editors at the time wrote about the reason behind the establishment of the "Books Received" list, stating that,

> The section consists of a listing of books received from publishers for which a full review has not been written. We hope that readers will appreciate an overview of the latest in legal publications. In turn, this

807 Interview of Mayo Moran by James Cummins (25 January, 2011).

808 Ernest Weinrib, "The Special Morality of Tort Law" (1989) 34:3 *McGill LJ* 403.

809 Mayo interview, *supra* note 807.

810 Newsletter 90, *supra* note 795 at 4.

811 Pound interview, *supra* note 341.

812 *Ibid.*

813 "Books Received" (1993) 38:4 *McGill LJ* 1104.

814 Newsletter 90, *supra* note 795 at 4.

815 "Books Received" (1990) 35:1 *McGill LJ* 301; "Books Received" (1990) 35:4 *McGill LJ* 1013.

816 ie; "Books Received" (1961) 7:2 *McGill LJ* 178.

817 "Minutes of the *McGill Law Journal* Board of Trustees meeting" (14 February, 1990).

> will prompt publishing houses to continue sending their new books to us. Most of all, we hope that the listing will prompt our readers to undertake full reviews of the books which are of interest to them.[818]

Still, in a nod to the continued pressures of running a progressively more complicated and broad venture, the Progress Report of volume thirty-five to the MLJ alumni—published halfway through their tenure—read that,

> Noting the exhausted but triumphant mood of the outgoing Volume 34 Board and the impressive results of its labours, it was hard for Volume 35 members not to be daunted. However, this year's Board has had some consolations. Rows of pictures of solemn-faced alumni remind us that publishing four issues is possible if improbable. Our bookcase, long shelves of bound copies from Volume 1 onward, shows that the prize is worth winning. The temporal element – after all, how long can a year be? – forces us to make and adhere to concrete deadlines. Finally, it is wonderful how panic focuses the mind.[819]

The second edition of the *McGill Guide* had already sold over four thousand copies in its first year of publication—as nearly every law student, lawyer, and judge in the nation was now looking to McGill as the standard for Canadian legal citation. Considering that in 1990 there were only about 53,000 lawyers and Quebec notaries in Canada[820] and 2,000 law students,[821] that would mean that that one in every thirteen lawyers and law students owned a copy of the new edition within a year of its coming out.

Authors of interest published by volume thirty-five included Professor Brian R. Cheffins[822] of Cambridge University at the Faculty of Law; Peter W. Hogg,[823] future Professor Emeritus at Osgoode Hall Law School; Donna Greschner,[824] future Dean of the University of Victoria Faculty of Law; future Justice of the Federal Court of Canada Yves de Montigny;[825] Nicholas Kasirer's first MLJ article;[826] and future Greenberg Chair at the University of University of Ottawa Faculty of Law, Martha Jackman.[827] Contributors of book reviews included future Justice of the Superior Court of Ontario Alison Harvison Young;[828] and one from Stephen Toope.[829]

Volume thirty-five had "a record number of initial applications"[830] for its junior board—the editors that would comprise the senior board of volume thirty-six. Since publication, that following volume has had eight distinct citations in decisions by the Supreme Court of Canada, only one less than its predecessor volume. However, while volume thirty-five had six distinct articles cited by the Court, volume thirty-six has had seven different articles cited: a record for volumes of the MLJ. The legal community certainly had a lot of articles to pick from as well, as volume thirty-six was 1518 pages long, another *Journal* record that has stood the test of time. It is a full 278 pages longer than any other volume published by the MLJ—in fact, only three other volumes have ever exceeded 1200 pages in length. Their legacy was punctuated by only running a few months overdue in terms of publishing schedule and publishing before the end of the calendar year—only one volume (fifty-six) in MLJ history would publish over 1200 pages while still publishing on time (defined as before the start of the next school year, beginning in September).

The Board of Trustees meeting for this year saw Justice Claire L'Heureux-Dubé (then of the Supreme

818 Newsletter 90, *supra* note 795 at 4.

819 Newsletter 90, *supra* note 795 at 1.

820 Mathieu Charron, Rachel Nemar & Roxan Vaillancourt, "Aging of Justice Personnel", *Statistics Canada* (5 October, 2011), online: < http://www.statcan.gc.ca/pub/85-002-x/2009001/article/10782-eng.htm >

821 David S Cohen, "How Many Lawyers and Law Students?" *BarTalk* (August 1998), online: < http://www.cba.org/bc/bartalk_95_00/08_98/guest_cohen.aspx >

822 Brian R Cheffins, "U.S. Close Corporation Legisaltion: A Model Canada Should Not Follow" (1990) 35:1 *McGill LJ* 160.

823 Peter W Hogg, "Jurisdiction over Telecommunications: Alberta Government Telephones v. CRTC" (1990) 35:2 *McGill LJ* 480.

824 Donna Greschner, "Abortion and Democracy for Women: A Critique of *Tremblay v. Daigle*" (1990) 35:3 *McGill LJ* 663.

825 Yves de Montigny, "La Protection Contre l'Auto-Incrimination Au Canada: Mythe Ou Realite" (1990) 35:4 *McGill LJ* 746.

826 Nicholas Kasirer, "Canada's Criminal Law Codification Viewed and Reviewed" (1990) 35:4 *McGill LJ* 841.

827 Martha Jackman, "Cabinet and the Constitution: Participatory Rights and Charter Interets: Manicom v. County of Oxford" (1990) 35:4 *McGill LJ* 943.

828 Alison Harvison Young, "Doctors and the Law: Some Aspects of the Legal Regulation of Abortion in England from 1803-1982 by J. Keown" Book Review (1990) 35:4 *McGill LJ* 976.

829 Stephen J Toope, "Doctors Lawyers and the Nuclear Debate: Proceedings of the Canadian Conference on Nuclear Weapons and the Law by M. Cohen and M.E. Gouin" Book Review (1990) 35:1 *McGill LJ* 285.

830 Newsletter 90, *supra* note 795 at 1

Revue de droit de McGill

RECEIVED JAN 3 0 1991

Le 21 janvier 1991

Me Marc Barbeau
1155, Boul. René-Levesque ouest,
Suite 4000
Montréal, QC
H3B 3V2

Monsieur,

Il me fait plaisir de vous inviter à la septième conférence annuelle des anciens et anciennes de la Revue de droit de McGill qui aura lieu au pavillon Chancellor Day, dans le Moot Court, le mardi 19 février 1991 à 19h30.

Nous aurons, cette année, le plaisir d'accueillir Madame le juge Beverley McLachlin; sa présentation s'intitulera «The Demystification of the Judiciary».

Vous êtes également invité à une réception qui aura lieu après la conférence dans la Common Room.

Nous apprécierions une réponse avant le vendredi 6 février 1991. Vous pouvez nous rejoindre au (514) 398-7397.

En attendant de vous voir le 19 février prochain, veuillez agréer, Monsieur, l'expression de mes sentiments les plus distingués.

La rédactrice en chef,

Julia E. Hanigsberg

3644, rue Peel, Montréal, Québec H3A 1W9 Téléphone (514) 398-7397

Invitation from the McGill Law Journal to attend the 1991 Annual Lecture to Marc Barbeau (Courtesy of Marc Barbeau)

Court of Canada) pushing for changes to the annual meeting that would bring its format close to what the Board of Advisors meeting still looks like today. Recommendations were made to permanently move the meeting to later in the year, provide trustees with several months notice for the meeting, bring in both the incoming and outgoing executives of that particular calendar year, and develop a more thorough meeting package for the trustees to review before the meeting[831]—all things that were implemented and have continued until today. Also, Stephen Toope was replaced by another *Journal* alumnus as trustee and Faculty Advisor to the MLJ: volume twenty-six Editor-in-Chief Patrick Healy.

In his interview, Healy commented on the experience, saying

> Well, the Faculty Advisor is an administrative task that is assigned by the Dean. And frankly it's a very pleasant task, because there isn't very much to do. The *Journal* runs itself. And, unless there's a real problem that arises, the Faculty Advisor really doesn't have very much to do. There was a problem when I was the Editor-in-Chief, that arose from this – what I described as – overly-aggressive editing, and the Faculty Advisor got involved with that, as well as several other faculty members, including the Dean. But when I was Faculty Advisor, I don't recall doing anything, other than taking a genuine interest in what the *Journal* was up to.[832]

At the beginning of the year the MLJ offices were moved once more—though this time it was more than a simple shift between rooms. The new office space for the *Journal* consisted of four offices—an executive room, library and conference room, and two computer work rooms.[833] The spacious and open offices were a complete change from the *Journal*'s environment at its origin. The executive was even going one step further with their book collection—and began to build a reference library of court reporters solely for *Journal* member use.[834] The second edition of the *McGill Guide* sold another two thousand copies, pushing the number of lawyers and law students across Canada with their own copy to one in ten, and the third edition was in production.[835]

831 "Minutes of the *McGill Law Journal* Board of Trustees meeting" (24 May, 1991).

832 Healy interview, *supra* note 413.

833 "Alumni Newsletter", MLJ Editorial Board (November 1990), 1.

834 *Ibid.*

835 *Ibid* at 2.

The Alumni Lecture for volume thirty-six featured Justice Beverly McLachlin of the Supreme Court of Canada and was held on February 19, 1991.[836] Other highlights of the volume included a special issue on "The Greening of Environmental Law"—the second special MLJ issue dedicated to the environment (the first was in volume twenty-three). The preface was written by future Governor General David Johnston, still the sitting Principal of McGill University, who wrote of the focus and intent of the issue: "No small ambitions here."[837]

Writing further on the subject matter of sustainability efforts, he expressed that,

> As these essays so clearly illustrate, this pioneering work demands extensive interdisciplinary co-operation, innovative and imaginative solutions, and an underlying appreciation of the interconnection and interdependence of all natural as well as socioeconomic systems. A legal framework for sustainability must be derived from a recognition that the health of our economic and social order is directly related to the health of our environment.
>
> The evolution of a legal system that champions sustainability must be driven by the primary fiduciary duty imposed upon each generation to ensure the environment is protected for future generations. Simply put, we do not receive our environment as beneficiaries but as trustees.[838]

Johnston also wrote that,

> we must fix our attention on sustainability within a global context in our quest for justice and not limit ourselves to the rearrangement of rules implementing conservation strategies ... as the parameters and content of environmental law and sustainable development become both more comprehensive and better understood, there will be an increasing need for the type of scholarship shown in this issue. Critical thinking built on transdisciplinary knowledge will mould the innovative legal frameworks necessary to meet the challenges posed by sustainability. Empirical research, testing

836 *Ibid* at 1.

837 David Johnston, "Preface" (1991) 36:3 *McGill LJ* 737 at 738.

838 *Ibid* at 740.

> doctrine against scientific and social reality, will have new prominence and impact. What a good start is made in the pages which follow.[839]

Echoing the excitement of Justice Taschereau back in volume thirteen, Johnston's ringing endorsement of the issue is an important point in MLJ history. Authors that contributed to the issue included future Metcalf Chair in Environmental Law Jutta Brunnee;[840] future Chief of the MoCreebec Council of the Cree Nation Randy Kapashesit;[841] founder of the *Canadian Journal of Administrative Law and Practice* Michael I Jeffrey;[842] and Chair of Asia-Pacific Legal Relations from the University of Victoria Douglas M. Johnston,[843] who contributed a book review.

Other authors that contributed to the volume included future Professor Emeritus of Université Laval's Faculty of Law Patrice Garant;[844] future President of John Hopkins University Ronald J. Daniels;[845] future Justice of the Saskatchewan Court of Appeal Robert G. Richards;[846] future William C. Graham Chair at the University of Toronto Faculty of Law, as well as future MLJ annual lecturer, Patrick Macklem;[847] Thérèse Leroux,[848] future Director of the Ethics Office at the Canadian Institutes of Health Research; and future Cary C. Boshamer Professor of Philosophy and Professor of Law at the University of North Carolina, Gerald J. Postema.[849] Book review contributors include future Secretary-General of Bishop's University Victoria Meikle[850] and future Wainright Professor of Civil Law at McGill Law Madeleine Cantin Cumyn.[851]

The editorial staff behind this goliath-sized volume included Citations Editor Elizabeth Massey, namesake of the memorial Elizabeth Massey Award given by the Canadian Federation of University Women; and future Associate Dean of Academics at McGill Law, senior editor Geneviève Saumier. It is actually through the *Journal* and McGill Law that Saumier met her future husband, who wrote of the encounter in Pilarczyk's history of McGill Law:

> [W]e were still in the early stages of the "law partners" programme … I was asked by the coordinator, John Relton, to participate but I told him I was too busy to participate that year, and he initially respected my decision. Two weeks into the semester he approached me and told me that they didn't have enough people and that I absolutely had to be a law partner and wouldn't take no for an answer. It ended up that I was paired up with a woman. It so happens that at that time the programme was structured so that men were paired with men and women with women … By Christmas time we were a couple. The next year, the organizers of the law partners programme decided that from that time on they would pair women with men and vice versa. That whole year, I had to defend myself, saying that I hadn't in fact orchestrated the match-up. Geneviève and I were married in 1994 in Montreal, with a reception in the Common Room as well as the Faculty Club. But for the record—I had absolutely nothing to do with the pairing of partners, but was in fact conscripted to participate in this programme under duress. It was just fate.[852]

The author of these words is none other than

839 *Ibid* at 741.

840 Jutta Brunnee, "The Baltic Sea Area and Long-Range Atmospheric Pollution—How Regional Cooperation Fits Into the Larger Picture" (1991) 36:3 *McGill LJ* 853.

841 Randy Kapashesit, "Aboriginal Group Rights and Environmental Protection" (1991) 36:3 *McGill LJ* 925.

842 Michael I Jeffrey, "New Canadian Environmental Assessment Act--Bill C-78: A Disappointing Response to Promised Reform" (1991) 36:3 *McGill LJ* 1070.

843 Douglas M Johnston, "Global Regimes and Nation-States: Environmental Issues in Australian Politics by Robert Boardman" Book Review (1991) 36:3 *McGill LJ* 1140.

844 Patrice Garant, "La Justice Municipale au Regard des Chartes: Quelques Observations au Lendemain de la Grande Reforme" (1991) 36:1 *McGill LJ* 39.

845 Ronald J Daniels, "Should Provinces Compete? The Case for a Competitive Corporate Law Market" (1991) 36:1 *McGill LJ* 130.

846 Robert G Richards, "*Mahe v. Alberta*: Management and Control of Minority Language Education" (1991) 36:1 *McGill LJ* 216.

847 Patrick Macklem, "First Nations Self-Government and the Borders of the Canadian Legal Imagination" (1991) 36:2 *McGill LJ* 382.

848 Thérèse Lereux, "Les Enfants, Les Incapables et la Genetique" (1991) 36:2 *McGill LJ* 457.

849 Gerald J Postema, "On the Moral Presence of Our Past" (1991) 36:4 *McGill LJ* 1153.

850 Victoria Meikle, "Rawls "A Theory of Justice" and Its Critics by Chanran Kukathas and Philip Pettit; Realizing Rawls by Thomas W. Pogge" Book Review (1991) 36:2 *McGill LJ* 692.

851 Madeleine Cantin Cumyn, "Traité de droit civil : Les successions by Germain Brière" Book Review (1991) 36:2 *McGill LJ* 715.

852 Pilarczyk, *supra* note 27 at 136.

<u>**Volume One, Issue One**</u>

Jacques-Yvan Morin (Editor-in-Chief): "Enseigne le droit international et le droit constitutionnel comparé des deux côtés de l'Atlantique; a été élu membre correspondant de l'Institut de France (à l'Académie des Sciences morales et politiques); prépare un cours à l'Académie de droit international de La Haye."

Natalie Fochs Isaacs (Book Review Editor): "My firm has changed its name to Yarosky, Daviault, La Haye, Stober & Isaacs."

The Hon. Perry Meyer (Senior Editor): "Since leaving my position as Professor of Law at McGill in 1975, when I was appointed to the Quebec Superior Court, I have acted as an *ad hoc* Judge of the Quebec Court of Appeal; gave a doctoral course at the U. of Ottawa; was a sessional lecturer for several years at the Faculty of Law at McGill; and continue to act as a Deputy Judge of the Supreme Court of the Yukon Territory. I will become a supernumerary judge of the Superior Court in May, 1993."

The Hon. Melvin L. Rothman (Senior Editor): "I left the Law Faculty in 1954, practised law for 17 years, was appointed to the Superior Court in 1971 and the Court of Appeal in 1983. Having exhausted all I learned at the McGill Law School in the 1950's, I will be returning to McGill for a sabbatical leave this January."

<u>**Volume One, Issues Two and Three**</u>

The Hon. Fred Kaufman, (Editor-in-Chief): "After 18 years of practice and another 18 years as a judge of the Quebec Court of Appeal, I have returned to practice, as counsel, with my old firm, now called Yarosky, Daviault, La Haye, Stober & Isaacs – found I like it!"

Nicholas Vlahos (Articles Editor): "In this my 37th year of practice, what in retrospect I consider my greatest achievement is that I spawned a lawyer, Nicholas A. Vlahos practising in his 3rd year trial law in B.C. and a notary, Esmé Anastasia Vlahos, who is not practising but pursuing a U. of M. Philosophy Masters/PHD. Money, I have not made, but existential experience, I have plenty of."

<u>**Volume One, Issue Three**</u>

Oscar Respitz (Advertising Editor): "I am still doing in the second half of this century what the Law Faculty and the Law Journal prepared me for during the first half ... with the same zeal and with only slightly diminished energy."

<u>**Volume One, Issue Four**</u>

Peter D. Walsh (Book Review Editor): "Age and attrition have allowed me to stumble to senior levels at Ogilvy Renault. A lively corporate/commercial practice keeps me awake during most office hours. I saw a mountain lion in the townships. Top that for interesting!"

A. Earl Kimmel (Editorial Assistant): "I'm a real stick-in-the-mud member of the same firm, Poirier, Leroux, Kimmel & Côté, notaries, for 16 years. I [have also been] a representative on the governing Bureau of the Order of Notaries for 23 years and a lecturer in the Diploma of Notarial Law programme at the University of Montréal for 29 years."

<u>**Volume Two**</u>

John E.M. Lawrence (Editor-in-Chief): "I am practising Communications law with the Ottawa office of Blake Cassels and Graydon. Previously I was Vice Chairman (Telecommunications) at the CRTC (80-87) and Counsel to the Privy Council Office (76-80)."

Lawrence Capelovitch (Book Review Editor): "Since 1958, I have been practising law in Montreal defending the poor and raising the down-trodden."

The Hon. John Gomery (Advertising Editor): "I have been a Judge of the Superior Court for the past ten years, after twenty-five years of active practice with Martineau Walker. My daughter Sally followed me onto the editorial board a few years ago – are there other instances of two generations working for the *Journal*?"

<u>**Volume Three**</u>

Irving I. Finkelberg (Managing Editor): "Practising general commercial law in Montreal and enjoying every minute of it."

L'Honorable Jean-Louis Baudouin (Comment Editor): "Publiera le 4 février 1993 aux Presses universitaires de France un livre intitulé: < Droit à la mort et éthique à la mort > en collaboration avec la Professeure Danielle Blondeau des Sciences infirmières de l'Université Laval."

<u>**Volume Four**</u>

Yves Fortier (Advertising Editor): "Aprés une affectation de 3 1/2 ans à New York à titre d'Ambassadeur du Canada auprès des Nations Unies, je suis revenu à Montréal en janvier 1992 où j'exerce à nouveau le droit comme associé principal au cabinet Ogilvy Renault dont je suis le président. En octobre 1991, j'ai été promu au sein de l'Ordre du Canada au niveau de Compagnon (C.C.), le plus haut niveau de l'Ordre."

Yoine Goldstein (Articles Editor): "I am continuing to delude my clients into believing that I am practising law. Because of the esoteric nature of the work I do, most people think I know what I am doing but there are a few who really understand the realities. I am, at the moment, involved in the Olympia & York restructuring and therefore spending the bulk of my time in Toronto, but I expect my Montreal confreres to forgive me and allow me to come back to Montreal in due course, when I undertake to be as obtuse with them as I have been this past number of months with my Ontario colleagues."

<u>**Volume Five**</u>

Clive V. Allen (Advertising Editor): "I have served as the chief legal officer of Northern Telecom Limited and its subsidiaries since 1974, and have the title Senior Vice-President and General Counsel. I moved from Montreal to Toronto in 1979. I have two sons currently attending McGill University, the elder currently in second year law."

<u>**Volume Six**</u>.

Georges Rosenberg (Articles Editor): "Partner in the law firm of Rosenberg, Levinson, Yanay & Co. Hiafa, Israel. The firm carries on an extensive international practice. In addition, I am also associated with a private trust company ('fiduciare'), based in Brussels, dealing in the formation and management of offshore companies and trusts, international tax planning, and portfolio money management."

Volume Eight

Gerald Postelnik (Advertising Editor): "HATCHED Yes in 1992: Postelnik's Son Aaron now a top Litigation Atty. with Spencer, Romberg in T.O., hatched the idea of founding new Federal Political Party called "Prosperity Party of Canada"; MATCHED Yes in 1992: Postelnik married off his son Aaron to Jennifer Ciemiega and his daughter Elissa to Stephen Feldman; DISPATCHED Yes in 1992: Postelnik saved in excess of 500 good souls from being deported to fates unknown thereby saving the good name of Canada and our noble profession."

W. David Angus (Managing Editor): "Still going strong after 30 years at Stikeman, Elliott and practising maritime (admiralty) and Marine insurance law! Not so many ships in port these days though!"

The Hon. Justice Morris Fish (Articles Editor): "Twenty-five years (to the day) after being sworn in at the Bar, appointed to the Quebec Court of Appeal – just in time to learn the new Civil Code!"

Volume Nine

Mark M. Rosenstein (Editor-in-Chief): "The law part is relatively easy but I am trying desperately and unsuccessfully to stay young to keep up with my six- and four-year-old sons."

Graham Nesbitt (Editor): "Dan Quayle during the recent presidential campaign singled out for particular opprobrium trial lawyers engaged in mass tort litigation concerning the Dalkon Shield, asbestos, and breast implants: I am pleased to say that for several years much of my practice has been devoted to the first two subjects, with considerable success if I may say so, representing the corporate defendants."

Volume Eleven

Larry S. Sazant (Editor-in-Chief): "I left Canada in 1978 and reside in Miami, Fla. I am a member of the Florida Bar and am involved in finance and real estate matters. I act as a General Partner of several major investment funds."

Jean Elie (Co-ordinatin Editor): "Suite à l'obtention du M.B.A. de l'Université de Western Ontario en 1968, je me suis joint à la société Rolland Inc., dont j'étais au moment de mon départ, en 1981, Vice-président administration (incluant toutes les responsabilités juridiques). Depuis, je suis associé chez Burns Fry Limitée, l'une des plus importantes sociétés de courtage et d'intermédiaire financier au Canada, à titre de Vice-président et Directeur des services aux gouvernements."

Volume Twelve

Howard Bernie Shaffer (Circulation Editor): "I am alive and well and living and working in Ottawa as a Senior Counsel in the Justice Department."

Lionel Chetwynd (Contributing Editor): "He is now a terribly pretentious writer/director in Hollywood where he's actually taken seriously which should confirm your worst suspicions about the so-called media elite."

Vincent Prager (Circulation Editor): "I have been at Stikeman Elliot since passing my bar in 1968. My specialty is maritime, aviation and international trade law, which allows for a fair amount of interesting travel and related adventures!!"

Irwin Rudick (Contributing Editor): "I am a lawyer and registered trademark agent with Bell Rudick Edelstein in Montreal. My daughter Rhonda is in her first year of law at McGill in the National Program."

Volume Fifteen

Stanley Wax (Executive Editor): "I live in Toronto (since 1973) with my wife and two daughters. I am a partner and head of the real estate section with the law firm of Goodman and Carr."

Volume Seventeen

Allan A. Mass (Executive Editor): "Partner at Byers Casgrain where I have worked since second year of law school and am currently in charge of the banking and insolvency practice group. Have recently completed a 14-year stint as Adjunct Professor in the McGill Law Faculty where I taught obligations and security in property."

Volume Eighteen

Stuart H. Cobbett (Executive Editor): "After 7 years in the business world as President of the Entertainment Group of Astral Communications Inc., I am now back in the practice of law with Stikeman, Elliott in Montreal."

Volume Twenty-Two

Michael Prupas (Special Issue Editor): "Partner and Executive Committee member, Heenan Blaikie; Member of bars of Québec and B.C.; Dept. head of largest entertainment law practise in Canada, having expanded from our Montreal base, to cover Toronto and Vancouver. Credits include the sublime and powerful 'Black Robe' and the ridiculous 'Pinball Summer'."

Volume Twenty-Three

Robert A. Kasting (Jurisprudence Editor): "I have just returned to Vancouver after 5 years in Yellowknife, NWT as Director of Legal Services with the Govt of the NWT's Dept. of Justice. My time there included 2 appearances in the Supreme Court of Canada, one as an intervener in Friends of the Old Man River. I am now Director of Client Services/Field Operations with BC's Legal Services Society, the organization responsible for providing legal aid to the province."

Christine Carron (Special Issue Editor): "Partner in the litigation group of Ogilvy Renault, specializing in commercial litigation, banking and insolvency. An American with roots in Virginia who, notwithstanding the weather and politics, still prefers Montreal to any other place in North America!"

Volume Twenty-Four

Jane I. Williamson (Senior Editor): "We are living in West Vancouver and I am currently at home raising nine year old Emily. I haven't visited Montreal in over 10 years – perhaps your news letter will stir me to action!"

Volume Twenty-Five

Professor Philip Girard (Junior Editor only): "I began teaching law in 1980, came to Dalhousie Law School in 1984 and am now in my second year as Acting Dean. I am looking forward to returning to my work as a property professor and legal historian in 1993."

Kathleen Glass (Senior Editor): "I left practice in the early '80s to undertake graduate studies, receiving a Doctor of Civil Laws from McGill last June. My specialty is health law and ethics. I am currently at the McGill Centre for Medicine, Ethics and Law where I am involved in research, teaching and consultation as a clinical ethicist."

Volume Twenty-Six

Marguerite Brien (Executive Editor): "After nearly eight years of being an employed solicitor I made the decision to commence practice on my own account, which I did in late April, 1992. I advise corporate sponsors on their superannuation and pension plans and draft insurance contracts. The change has been worthwhile. My husband, Paul, (a sensible non-lawyer) has been an enthusiastic supporter and – to his relief and delight – I am incredibly relaxed and personable, much more so than I ever was as an employed solicitor. In fact, I can almost say that the old Maggie Brien, Professional Extrovert of McGill Law Journal days, has resurfaced. The joy and freedom of self-employment continues to surprise me. Although the building of a new house will occupy much of our attention for the first part of 1993, we are always happy to welcome friends and colleagues as visitors to this part of the world. (National Bank Centre, Level 17 205-209 Queen Street, Auckland, NZ)"

Volume Twenty-Seven

Bernard Amyot (Associate Editor): "Litigation partner with Lafleur, Brown in Montreal; Presided over the Young Bar Association of Montreal in 91-92; Married a McGill grad who is expecting our first child for May 93."

J. Stuart Russell (Senior Editor): "In January 1993 I commenced an appointment as Lecturer in the School of Law at Macquarie University in Sydney, Australia, after 10 tough years as a people's lawyer in Montréal. When in Sydney, give me a call!"

David B. Sinyard (Managing Editor): "I have lived in Atlanta since mid-1984. Currently, I am Vice-President Project Finance of Holiday Inn Worldwide, a subsidiary of the English beer company Bass plc.; interesting work and lots of travel."

F. Jasper Meyers (Editor-in-Chief): "In 1988, while at Fraser & Beatty in Toronto, I decided to spend one year working in Amsterdam at the law firm Loeff Claeys Verbeke. That was extended into an interesting three year stay. In August 1991 I moved to AT&T's European holding company in the Netherlands, where I work on M & A transactions and turnkey projects in the EEC and Eastern Europe."

Volume Twenty-Eight

Leslie A. Stratford (Circulations Editor): "Currently Deputy Director of Securities & Derivatives Regulation at the Securities & Investments Board in London where I have been for 4 years. Prior to that, I completed a D.E.S.S. at Université de Paris (Paris I)."

Douglas Benedon (Comments Editor): "Currently practising and living in sunny California."

Volume Twenty-Nine

Donna Soble Kaufman (Senior Editor): "I am a partner at Stikeman, Elliott in Montreal and head our antitrust practice group. I serve on the boards of TransAlta Utilities, Southam Inc. and the CRB Foundation."

<u>Volume Thirty</u>
Brian C. Pel (Managing Editor): "Presently practising tax and trade-related law at McCarthy Tétrault in Toronto. Also, part-time zoo keeper of two active children, Andrew and Adrian."
Professor Nicholas Kasirer (Senior Editor): "I am teaching at the Faculty of Law, McGill University and happily parenting (Benjamin born in May 1992)."
Peter C. Oliver (Editor-in-Chief): "I'm getting married next summer, living in Greenwich, teaching Trusts and (something like) Foundations at the University of London, and not getting across the Channel for weekends in Paris or Chamonix. The local pubs are very friendly though, and I would be very happy to buy a pint and some pork scratchings for any alumni-ae who are visiting ..."
A. Grant McCrea (Associate Editor): "Still litigating at White & Case, New York, N.Y., including death penalty appeals in Alabama and Arkansas; still married to Anne-Marie; still reproducing (Max is 5, Tess 4, Lana 2)."

<u>Volume Thirty-two</u>
Robert Spiegel (Senior Editor): "Member of the Quebec Bar (1988) and The Law Society of Upper Canada (1992). Currently reside with wife in Toronto. Presently, in-house counsel to the Toronto Stock Exchange, Market Integrity and Market Policy Divisions. Wondering what happened to colleagues who went south of the border."

<u>Volume Thirty-three</u>
Vincent Gallo (Senior Editor): "Manager of Legal Services for the Office of the Attorney in Canada for Lloyd's Non-Marine Underwriters. Married to Ingrid Gendreau. Father of Eva and expecting daughter number 2 shortly."
Michael Waterston (Citations Editor): "I was called to the Quebec Bar in 1991 and to the Ontario Bar in 1992. Having clerked for Chief Justice Antonio Lamer of the Supreme Court of Canada in 1990-1991, I am now working for Stikeman, Elliott in Toronto."

<u>Volume Thirty-Four</u>
Robert Campbell (Senior Editor): "Practising admiralty, corporate/ securities, insurance law and guitar at McMaster Meighen in Montreal."

<u>Volume Thirty-Six</u>
Evelyn Jerassy (Executive Editor): "I am presently clerking at the Supreme Court of Canada and will be finishing there August, 1993."

Figure 3: Source – Draft of "The *McGill Law Journal* Alumni Newsletter", 1993: 3. [The answer to Gomery's question (above) about his daughter, volume 35 Executive Editor Sally Gomery, is no—no other instances have occurred where the child of a former editor has also served on the MLJ.]

volume thirty-four Executive Editor David Lametti.

The Editor-in-Chief of volume thirty-six was Julia E. Hanigsberg, who would go on to become Vice-President of Administration and Finance at Ryerson University, as well as a member of the MLJ's Board of Advisors. In an interview, Hanigsberg recalled her time with the volume:

> In retrospect it is interesting to me to think of the "gate-keeping" role for publication of legal scholarship we played as young people. We also had a pretty heavy pen as editors and I suppose that might well have struck some authors as a fair amount of chutzpah. At the same time, we probably fairly represented "average" readers. Largely our authors were very tolerant and accepting of our questions and suggestions.
>
> As a junior there was so much to learn. The *Cite Guide* was my bible. I became absolutely compulsive about correct (i.e. McGill!) citation style. I was totally intimidated by having to make recommendations for or against publication.
>
> As Editor-in-Chief the *Journal* was my home on campus. I spent an incredible number of hours there. McCarthy Tétrault very generously funded a summer of work on *Journal* projects. I was deeply immersed in the work of the *Journal* and in mentoring juniors. I've stayed in touch with many including Mahmud Jamal, partner at Osler's and a fellow Fulbright Scholar…
>
> The *Journa*l has never stopped innovating. As the landscape of Canadian law journals has become increasingly full the *McGill Law Journal* has never stopped making an exceptional contribution.[853]

Soon enough those junior editors became senior editors, with Jamal going on to become Comments Editor and others taking the reins of the rest of the positions. The junior that would go on to become Book Reviews Editor, Renée Thériault, recalled her own experiences with the *Journal* in an interview. She wrote that,

> Collectively, we took great pride in crafting a product we felt was useful and in line with the Faculty's tradition and reputation. Individually, it gave me precious insight into academia, and the much-needed credentials for my future endeavours, including my clerkship at the Supreme Court of Canada and later my LL.M. at the University of London's London School of Economics. In fact, the impetus for studying international arbitration at the University of London came from Professor [Stephen] Toope, who had assisted in the elaboration of the Special Edition of the *Journal* of Volume 37 dedicated to the resolution of international disputes. On the basis of this Special Edition, Professor Toope … suggested that I make international dispute resolution (particularly in the context of NAFTA) the topic of study for my LL.M. I followed his advice, and the Faculty very generously provided me with the Thomas Shearer Stewart Travelling Fellowship on this same basis.[854]

Thériault is now counsel with the Ottawa office of Norton Rose LLP, and recently co-founded the Ottawa International Arbitration Society. She wrote further that, "My memories boil down to long nights and great friendships."[855] Those long nights would ensure the *Journal* continued to push forward into the future along the cutting edge of legal scholarship. Achievements of the volume included bringing in Ovide Mecredi—National Chief of the Assembly of First Nations—as the annual lecturer on March 31, 1992.[856] Mark Phillips, the Editor-in-Chief of the following volume (thirty-eight), wrote that:

> The timing of this speech came at a pivotal point in the constitutional debate over native rights. Mr. Mercredi had been feuding with Mr. Bourassa over the designation of distinct society. He used his speech to the *Journal* alumni, the first in Quebec since his controversial comments, to make the first moves towards conciliation with the province. Those in attendance were impressed by the power of delivery exhibited by so soft spoken an individual. The address was followed by a reception

853 Interview of Julia Hanigsberg by James Cummins (21 December, 2010).

854 Interview of Renée Thériault by James Cummins (22 February, 2011).

855 *Ibid.*

856 Timothy Mitchell, *Questions of Modernity* (Toronto: University of Toronto Press, 1994) at 199.

> where alumni and current *Journal* members mingled and had an opportunity to discuss the issues with Mr. Mercredi informally.[857]

Keeping up with their predecessor volumes, volume thirty-seven would receive six citations by the Supreme Court of Canada.

The special issue discussed by Thériault was prefaced by *Journal* alumnus John Brierley, who said of the MLJ's striving for internationalization and diversity of scholarship through this issue, that,

> Students of both private and public law will … find, in this special number, reflections of interest on a range of subjects related to arbitration. These are all the more interesting because they come from jurists with different backgrounds and professional concerns and from various countries. The diversity of matters addressed emphasizes both the wide appeal of arbitration as a legal institution and, despite the basic simplicity of arbitration as an idea, the legal complexities to which it gives rise in practice.[858]

Those writing on international dispute resolution within the issue included founding partner of the future Faskin Martineau LLP office in France (his firm was independent before merging with Faskin) Serge Gravel;[859] William C. Graham,[860] namesake of the William C. Graham Chair in International Law and Development at the University of Toronto; Charles N. Dennison Professor of Law and future Herbert and Rose Rubin Professor of International Law Emeritus at New York University, Andreas F. Lowenfeld;[861] and future Director of the Centre of Research in International Law at l'Université Paris-Sorbonne Brigitte Stern.[862] Book reviews were contributed by, among others, future Tobias Simon Eminent Scholar at the Florida State University College of Law, Fernando R. Tesón.[863]

The volume also printed not one but two special sections. The first appeared in issue one: another section similar to Stephen A. Scott's "Editor's Diary" and volume thirty-four's special issue dedicated entirely to documents relating to the *Constitutional Act of 1982*. The section was prefaced by the editorial board, who wrote,

> By publishing "Meech Lake Documents", the Journal seeks to contribute to a better understanding of both Canada's recent constitutional history and the current debate on its constitutional future. It is the Journal's hope that persons interested in exploring the rise and fall of the Meech Lake Accord will consider this section a useful and convenient research tool. Its usefulness and convenience flow from the inclusion of a short introduction which traces the broad outlines of Canada's constitutional history between April 1987 and June 1990, the reproduction of the most relevant documents from the Meech Lake episode, and the compilation of an exhaustive bibliography on the Accord.[864]

The second special section contained another selection of papers presented at a meeting of the Congrès Henri Capitant—this time from the 1992 meeting in Louisiana.[865]

Other authors published in the volume included future Associate Dean of McGill Law Rosalie Jukier;[866] alongside book reviewers Marie-France Bich,[867] future Justice with the Quebec Court of Appeal; Ronnie Warrington,[868] namesake of the Ronnie Warrington Studentships for Doctoral Students at the Birkbeck School of Law, University of London; and co-founder

857 "Alumni Newsletter (draft)", MLJ Editorial Board (1993), 3.

858 John Brierley, "Preface" (1992) 37:2 *McGill LJ* 373 at 374.

859 Serge Gravel, "French Law and Arbitration Clauses--Distinguishing Scope from Validity: Comment on ICC Case No. 6519 Final Award" (1992) 37:2 *McGill LJ* 510.

860 William C Graham, "Dispute Resolution in the Canada-United States Free Trade Agreement: One Element of a Complex Relationship" (1992) 37:2 *McGill LJ* 544.

861 Charles N Dennison, "The Free Trade Agreement Meets its First Challenge: Dispute Settlement and the Pork Case" (1992) 37:2 *McGill LJ* 597.

862 Brigitte Stern, "Un Systeme Hybride: La Procedure de Reglement Pour la Reparation des Dommages Resultant de L'occupation Illicite du Koweit par L'Irak" (1992) 37:2 *McGill LJ* 625.

863 Fernando R Tesón, "The Power of Legitimacy Among Nations by Thomas M. Franck" Book Review in *McGill L.J.* (1992) 37:2 *McGill LJ* 666.

864 "Meech Lake Documents" (1992) 37:1 *McGill LJ* 145 at 145.

865 Jean-Louis Baudouin, "Special Section: Congrès Henri Capitant—Journées Louisianaises 1992" (1992) 37:4 *McGill LJ* 1024 at 1024-5.

866 Rosalie Jukier, "*Banque Nationale du Canada v. Houle* (SCC): Implications of an Expanded Doctrine of Abuse of Rights in Civilian Contract law" (1992) 37:1 *McGill LJ* 221.

867 Marie-France Bich, "Programmes d'accès à l'égalité en emploi by Lucie Lamarche" Book Review (1992) 37:1 *McGill LJ* 325.

868 Costas Douzinas & Ronnie Warrington, "Law and Society in England 1750-1950 by W.R. Cornish and G. de N. Clark" Book Review (1992) 37:3 *McGill LJ* 947.

of the Birkbeck School of Law at the University of London, Costas Douzinas.[869]

The Editorial Board behind these issues included Associate Editor Michelle Cumyn, who would go on to become Editor-in-Chief of *Les Cahiers de droit* at the Université Laval Faculty of Law (a faculty-run law journal); Managing Editor Hanson R. Hosein, who would win an Emmy Award as a reporter for his press coverage of "The Fall of Kosovo" and become the Middle East Producer for NBC News; Solicitations Editors Adelle Blackett, who would go on to become an Associate Professor at the McGill Faculty of Law; and senior editor Eric Buzzetti, who would go on to become Principal of the Liberal Arts College of Concordia University.

The following Editorial Board, for volume thirty-eight, included Note Editor Sivan Fox, who would go on to become Vice-President at the Dundee Corporation. March 10, 1993 saw the *Journal* hold its ninth annual lecture for volume thirty-eight and feature yet another Justice of the Supreme Court, which Editor-in-Chief Mark Phillips described, writing,

> Mr. Justice John Major will be making one of his first public addresses as a Justice of the Supreme Court of Canada. Mr. Justice Major, practised law in Calgary at Bennett, Jones, Verchere before he was appointed to the Alberta Court of Appeal, where he served for a year before his recent appointment to the Supreme Court of Canada. The topic of his speech will be the state of the legal profession. The reception following his address will provide alumni with an opportunity to meet the most recent appointee to the Supreme Court of Canada on an informal basis.[870]

Most of the individuals mentioned in this book are presented with one or more of their future titles as of 2011. The draft newsletter of volume thirty-eight contained a host of updates from the year 1993 from past editors—including many from the very first volumes—and there positions as they were then. The quotes not only represent a lost history from a period of time long gone, but also the most complete set of future updates to the MLJ ever provided by its past editors at that point.

Volume thirty-eight began publishing in 1992, marking the fortieth anniversary of the *Journal*—though this anniversary would not be celebrated until volume forty, two years later. A selection of the personally addressed life updates is presented in the following inset: representing the values, professional success, and history of the *Journal* at age forty.

While the duration of this book will reveal past editors at various stages of their career more generally, this snapshot is a unique picture of what the journal alumni looked like twenty years ago. How different this work would have been at that time, before many of the editors, authors, and speakers had received the twenty years more of experience to become all the more, well, experienced. It is important to keep this in mind while moving from this point on—where the most recent twenty-odd volumes are discussed. Those editors are still working their way up the ladder of the Canadian legal system or their other chosen fields, and considering what we will read moving forward, are no less capable that those that came before them.

Volume thirty-eight was the third of seven straight volumes to include a special issue—the longest stretch in MLJ history. The issue, on the "right to competition", was prefaced by yet another Supreme Court Justice: Charles D. Gonthier, who had recently joined the Board of Trustees for the *Journal* several years after his appointment to the Court. Authors in the issue included future Chief Justice of the Federal Court of Canada Paul S. Crampton;[871] Michael J. Trebilock,[872] future Chair of Law and Economics at the University of Toronto; Margaret Sanderson,[873] future Vice-President of Charles River Associates; and future Avocat émérite of the Barreau du Quebec Yves Bériault.[874] Other authors within the volume included Professor Ronald Dworkin,[875] future Frank Henry Sommer Professor of Law and Philosophy at New York University and the second most-cited American legal scholar of the twentieth century;[876] volume twenty-three Editor-in-Chief and then Associate Professor at McGill Law, Cally Jordan;[877] and future Professor Emeritus

869 *Ibid.*

870 Newsletter 93, *supra* note 857 at 1.

871 Paul S Crampton, "Recent Developments in Conspiracy Law and Enforcement: New Risks and Opportunities" (1993) 38:3 *McGill LJ* 569.

872 Presley L Warner & Michael J Trebilock, "Rethinking Price-Fixing Law" (1993) 38:3 *McGill LJ* 679.

873 Margaret Sanderson & Ann Wallwork, "Divestiture Relief in Merger Cases: An Assessment of the Canadian Experience" (1993) 38:3 *McGill LJ* 757.

874 Yves Bériault & Madeliene Renaud, "Divulgation Volontaire au Directeur: Confidentialite et Privilege" (1993) 38:3 *McGill LJ* 778.

875 Ronald Dworkin, "Justice in the Distribution of Health Care" (1993) 38:4 *McGill LJ* 883.

876 Fred R Shapiro, "The Most-Cited Legal Scholars" (2000) 29:1 *J Legal Stud* at 424.

877 Cally Jordan, "Lessons from the Bennett Affair" (1993)

at McGill Law, as well as future member of the MLJ Board of Advisors, G. Blaine Baker.[878]

The future was here. Volume thirty-eight signed the first MLJ contracts with Quicklaw and Westlaw.[879] However, some things were put on hiatus in favour of growing financial stability and a refocusing on the editing of academic articles. There was no tenth annual lecturer. In a draft 1994 letter to the alumni, Alumni Coordinator Francis Harvey wrote that, "Due to budgetary constraints and declining interest, we have decided not to host an alumni lecture, as we have in the past."[880] And away the Lecture, that had brought in some of the most influential people in Canada over the last nine years, went—"Not with a bang but a whimper".[881] As volume thirty-four Executive Editor David Lametti explained, "Once it got dropped for a year, institutional memory was pretty short,"[882] and the idea of the Lecture faded into history—at least for a while.

The special issue for volume thirty-nine was on the topic of the new Civil Code of Quebec, which came into effect on the first of that year (January 1, 1994). John E.C. Brierley again prefaced the number, stating that, "The time for answering hard questions has therefore come. In a word, the exercise now to be undertaken will test the mettle of our general legal culture."[883] Brierley went through each of the eight articles in the issue and synopsized how the contribution added to the dawn of this new era of scholarship. This included an interesting moment in time, where he—a former Dean of McGill Law—introduced and commented upon the work of Daniel Jutras—a future Dean of McGill Law, writing that,

> Jutras uses the occasion offered to go further, that is to say, to place the new Code and that complementary law in a context in which their starkness can be attenuated by the comforting thought that, over and above the transitional provisions themselves which imply varying degrees of rupture with the past, not so much has perhaps been disturbed as we may think.[884]

Brierley was not called upon to write the preface initially, however. According to Erica Stone, Editor-in-Chief for the volume,

> I had a very good relationship with a Faculty member, for whom I had worked previously, and I had asked that Faculty member to write the preface to our Civil Code Special Issue. Very far into the process, he gave me a verbal scolding of immense proportions because we had selected an article in an earlier number whose author [Martha Shaffer] interpreted case law very differently than he did on an issue of foetal rights. He told me that because I had disappointed him and because he now realized the calibre of the MLJ, he was withdrawing from writing the Preface to the Civil Code Issue! I was furious that he would try to influence editorial selection and was very hurt that he had attacked me personally. He never spoke to me again, and I had to scramble to find a replacement. I will feel forever indebted to the late Professor John Brierley for his generosity, kindness and grace at that time – he agreed to write the Preface, no questions asked. [My husband] and I still have the blanket he gave us for a wedding present![885]

Authors in the special issue included Geneviève Viney,[886] future Professor Emeritus at l'Université Paris-Sorbonne Faculty of Law. Authors that submitted to the rest of the volume included Ian Holloway, future Dean of Law at both the University of Western Ontario and the University of Calgary, who contributed a book review.[887] Additionally, the volume published an article by future Justice of the Supreme Court of Canada Rosalie Silberman Abella, which was drawn from a speech she gave at McGill Law on March 10, 1993.[888]

38:4 *McGill LJ* 1071.

878 G Blaine Baker, "Interstate Choice of Law and Early-American Constitutional Nationalism. An Essay on Joseph Story and the Comity of Errors: A Case Study in Conflict of Laws" (1993) 38:2 *McGill LJ* 454.

879 "Managing Editor Report for the Board of Trustees (draft)" MLJ Editorial board (1993).

880 "Letter from Francis Harvey to donors to the *McGill Law Journal* trust fund" MLJ Editorial Board (1994).

881 TS Eliot, "The Hollow Men" in *T.S. Eliot - Collected Poems 1909-1962* (London: Faber and Faber, 1974) at 93.

882 Lametti interview, *supra* note 724.

883 John EC Brierley, "Preface" (1994) 39:4 *McGill LJ* 746.

884 *Ibid* at 744.

885 Interview of Erica Stone by James Cummins (29 November, 2010).

886 Geneviève Viney, "Pour une interprétation modérée et raisonnée du refus d'option entre responsabilité contractuelle et responsabilité délictuelle (article 1458, deuxième alinéa du *Code Civil du Quebec*)" (1994) 39:4 *McGill LJ* 813.

887 Ian Holloway, "*Public Law and Political Theory* by Martin Loughlin" Book Review (1994) 39:3 *McGill LJ* 725.

888 Rosalie Silberman Abella, "Equality, Human Rights, Women and the Justice System" (1994) 39:3 *McGill LJ* 489.

Executive Editor Ed Vanderberg—now a partner at Osler, Hoskin & Harcourt LLP in Ottawa—also related his experience with volume thirty-nine at the time. He wrote that,

> I had initially decided not to run for an executive position, primarily because the task appeared too daunting. But I was encouraged to run by a couple of students who were thinking of running for other executive positions, primarily Erica Stone, who later became the Editor-in-Chief. It was primarily because of that encouragement, and the knowledge that, if I did become Executive Editor, I would be working with an outstanding Editor-in-Chief and an excellent team, that I decided to run…
>
> The most important story is that I met Erica Stone, the Editor-in-Chief under whom I served. She was a year ahead of me in law school, so I likely would not have gotten to know her if not through the *Journal*. When it came to running a journal and editing articles, she had the highest level of professionalism I had ever encountered…
>
> An example of Erica's attention to detail as an Editor-in-Chief: I recall one time she asked me to go to the library to check on the name of a French author whose 1940s book showed up in a citation of an article we were publishing. She was certain the author's first name had a hyphen – something like Jean-Paul. The junior editor who had edited the article didn't include the hyphen. When I returned from the library with the news that there was no hyphen, she asked if I had checked the English translation of the book or the original French version. I responded that I checked the English translation, at which point she sent me back to check the French version. As was always the case, she was right, there was a hyphen![889]

Erica Stone, now a contract researcher in the health law field, further recalled from her experience that,

> As Editor-on-Chief I began my year with a commitment to doing what I could to have a cohesive editorial board. Some of my ideas to achieve that goal were to use better communication tools and increase the French language content in our volume and in the *Journal* offices. I focused on the way editorial information was communicated, making it a more open process with a board listing who was editing what, listing time lines etc …
>
> The editorial process during my tenure was far from high tech. Articles were received in hard copy form, and each editorial team edited on paper. Along with editing of the text, footnotes were checked by hand and citations were corrected. Our fantastic typist, Nicole Leger, typed the articles and changes into the computer and saved it all on floppy disk (!). Printouts of the edited articles were passed back to the team to review again.[890]

Apparently at this point the electronic editing system had been put on hiatus as well.

As for how she herself initially found her way onto the *Journal*, she wrote that,

> I was encouraged to apply by a friend who was a year ahead of me. I was very interested after speaking with some of the editors, and I had a feeling it would suit my "wordsmith" personality and interest in legal research. I was attracted to the idea of working together with students with similar interests. I applied, had a successful interview and went on to love my associate year, during which I was assigned to edit a great article by Sheila McIntyre.[891] I was hooked, and by the end of that year had decided to apply to be Editor-in-Chief…
>
> I think we were successful in creating a very positive bilingual atmosphere at the Journal, with meetings and all communications being bilingual. I am a bilingual Anglophone Quebecker, so I spoke English and French at work, jumping between languages depending on the mother tongue of the person with whom I was speaking. Amongst our Executive we had an almost unilingual

889 Interview of Ed Vandenberg by James Cummins (22 November, 2010).

890 Stone interview, *supra* note 885.

891 Sheila McIntyre, "Backlash against Equality: The Tyranny of the Politically Correct" (1993) 38:1 *McGill LJ* 1.

> francophone Associate Editor and almost unilingual anglophone Executive Editor, and they spoke to each other in the other's mother tongue. That really sent a message to the other Board members about the bilingual atmosphere we expected. Those two Editors are friends to this day![892]

The English Executive Editor became, in fact, far more than a friend, as Vanderberg wrote that,

> By far my best memories of working with the *Journal* come from the times I got to know the Editor-in-Chief. We used to spend a lot of time discussing *Journal* matters, and from that we often strayed into discussions about life in general. Ultimately, that led to us getting married, and we now have two children who are as adorable as my former Editor-in-Chief.[893]

The wedding gift Erica Stone received from Professor Brierley was to the two of them—she and Vanderberg, who married in 1996, very soon after graduation. Stone herself wrote that,

> Ed and I never would have met had it not been for the *Journal*. He was in the Common Law stream (I was in Civil Law), he was a year behind me and 9 years older. At the *Journal* we worked hard together, wrote an editorial manual together, and learned about our similarities in the process. I am so very grateful for the *Journal*'s existence. It gave me the chance to be part of something that brought together like-minded people, and in the process, brought me such good friends and such great love into my life.[894]

Other members of their editorial board included Managing Editor Caroline Thomassin, who went on to become the Senior Director of Legal Affairs with the Desjardins Group; Book Review Editor Caroline Ferland, who went on to become General Counsel of Imperial Tobacco; and junior editor Frédérick Têtu, who would go on to found the publishing house Résurgences.

The final issue of following volume (forty) was prefaced by the story of how the *Journal* came into being as told by Jacques-Yvan Morin—a story recounted at the beginning of this book. At the end of the issue, Editor-in-Chief Jodi Lackman, today a legal advisor with Fonds de solidarité FTQ, wrote a piece about the future of the *Journal*. Lackman writes that by this point in its history the *Journal*,

> no longer merely reflects what goes on in the legal world; it sometimes affects the law. Earlier this year, an article slated for publication in Volume 40 was included as an appendix to a factum submitted to the Supreme Court of Canada. The lawyers of two of the parties to the litigation called to confirm that the *Journal* was indeed planning to publish the article. I was pleasantly surprised that the *Journal* could have an *ex ante*, and not merely *ex post facto*, impact on the law.[895]

Lackman writes further that,

> I am certain, that whatever form the *Journal* takes forty years from now, it will have adapted and maintained its strength because its most important asset is the people who are involved in it: the thirty students who spend their spare time arguing over colons and chasing footnotes, everyone who works at McGill's Faculty of Law, the authors who submit articles, the evaluators who comment on the articles and all of the people who provide support to the involved parties. I know that my work at the *Journal* would not have been possible this year without the dedication of the Executive and of the whole Board and their uncomplaining acceptance of my nagging; without Professor Healy's patient support and calm dismantling of what seemed "tragedies" to me; without Nicole Leger, who is the *Journal*'s Person Friday; and especially without the understanding, support and good humour of my loved ones. Being at the helm of the *McGill Law Journal* has been a pleasure and an honour, and as I pass that honour to my successors, I am confident that, forty years from now, the Editor-in-Chief of Volume 80 will express the same sentiments, with the only difference being that he or she will have been running an even better *McGill Law*

892 Stone interview, *supra* note 885.

893 Vanderberg interview, *supra* note 889.

894 Stone interview, *supra* note 885.

895 Jodi Lackman, "Afterword: Forty Years Later" (1995) 40:4 *McGill LJ* 1025 at 1025.

Journal.[896]

Things continued to change for the *Journal*. During the previous year Erica Stone had not worked alongside an Advertising Editor—the first time in forty years an Advertising Editor had not been selected (though volume eighteen did not post the titles of its senior board in its masthead)—and instead had a Marketing Editor. This alteration of the management side of the *Journal* continued its metamorphosis into the first official management board to appear in a masthead, which appeared within the masthead of volume forty.[897] This division between the editorial and management sides of the *Journal* would continue until the present day. Heidi Kessner and Alexandra Kau were the first to be appointed to the senior board as "managers" instead of "editors", and together with Managing Editor Fred Purkey, they would form the MLJ's first official "Management Board".[898] A new editorial guide had been written the year before by the volume thirty-nine executive, and a management guide was written during volume forty with similar intent,[899] as beforehand management tasks had relied purely on "oral tradition".[900]

Fred Purkey—now a partner in the tax department of the Montreal office of Davies Ward Phillips and Vineberg LLP, who acted as counsel in the Molson Brothers' repurchasing of the Montreal Canadiens Hockey Club—wrote in his interview that, in contrast to the era Richard Pound recalled from his volume thirteen tenure as Managing Editor, the management side of the *Journal* had been separated from the editorial side for some time now. He wrote that "we just decided to give them the recognition they deserved."[901] Indeed, volume thirty Managing Editor Brian Pel himself recalled that more than ten years prior he did no editing in his junior year, and was hired purely for management purposes alongside his fellow associate managers.[902] The original MLJ constitution also separated the "Financial Department" from the "Editorial Department", right from the beginning.[903]

Purkey recalled other changes this first official Management Board made to the *Journal*:

> We did a lot of work to modernize the process ... Before, all our receipts/invoices were put into a shoe-box to be sorted out at year end by the accountant, invoicing of subscribers was done by hand (which was a horrible process), the law student copies were not mailed to them but handed out (which resulted in a lot of unused copies), and the publishing method was very slow and expensive (basically, an outside firm did the typesetting, and I think they charged $20-30 per page for any changes).
>
> We put into place accounting software so we could keep track of expenses and revenues, developed a subscriber database program to automatically invoice subscribers and print mailing labels, and moved the typesetting process in-house (basically doing it in Word with a template we developed, then exporting to an Adobe Postscript file which the printing company would use) to save money and enable us to make last minute changes more easily.
>
> We also started giving free coffee to *Journal* members![904]

On the editorial side, the special issue for volume forty, which also contained the addresses from Morin and Lackman, focused on the legal and ethical issues of reproductive technology. The issue was a hot topic at the time—Dolly the Sheep would be born one year later, and the first federal regulations on reproductive technology would occur at about the same time as that breakthrough in cloning.[905] Contributors to the special issue would include Professor and former First Lady of Canada (during the Prime Ministership of Joe Clark) Maureen A. McTeer, and future Justice of the Superior Court of Alberta Sheilah Martin.[906]

McTeer wrote that, "The issues looming in 1995 are ones that few foresaw a decade ago. Science and medicine will continue to use technology to push back

896 *Ibid* at 1026.

897 See Appendix E at 1. Here we see that the original MLJ Constitution separates the two boards from day one.

898 "McGill Law Journal Editorial Board" (1994) 40:1 *McGill LJ* iii.

899 "Annual Report *McGill Law Journal* Volume 40" (31 May, 1995) 6.

900 Fred Purkey, "Management Report for the *McGill Law Journal* Fundraising Campaign: Letter to MLJ Alumni" MLJ Editorial Board (1995).

901 Interview of Fred Purkey by James Cummins (2 November, 2011).

902 Pel interview, *surpa* note 666.

903 See Appendix E at 1.

904 Purkey interview, *supra* note 901.

905 Sonya Norris, "Reproductive Technologies: Surrogacy, and Egg and Sperm Donation" *Parliamentary Information and Research Service* (6 February, 2006), online: < http://www.parl.gc.ca/Content/LOP/ResearchPublications/prb0035-e.pdf >

906 Sheilah Martin & Murray Coleman, "Judicial Intervention in Pregnancy" (1995) 40:4 *McGill LJ* 947.

frontiers."[907] She further warned that,

> In the end, only an approach which allows for informed and meaningful public involvement will earn society's trust in the evolving technology and its human goals.
>
> Failure to engage in this kind of debate may lead to a situation where the public discussion of the fundamental issues involved would stagnate at the level of slogans ... We must now find new processes and contexts for the resolution of issues which profoundly affect society.[908]

McTeer viewed the issues of the day as a case of legislating morality,[909] a controversial issue that had led to Brierley's intervention with the previous volume's special issue, now in full discussion within the *Journal*'s open pages. It was an open debate about something that was many times being negotiated behind closed doors between patent-seekers, profit-seekers, and government bureaucracies. Other authors that contributed to the volume included Hans W. Baad,[910] the Hugh Lamar Stone Chair in Civil Law at the University of Texas, Austin.

Volume forty-one's special issue was on the subject of universal human rights, and dedicated to John P Humphrey who had passed away the year before. In the issue's preface Stephen Toope—now Dean at the Faculty of Law—wrote that,

> The interplay between individual and collective rights is challenging not only in the developing world, but within the so-called "North" as well. Accommodating aboriginal understandings of community has proven difficult in all states with significant indigenous populations. In Quebec, conflicts over assertions of individual rights in the face of collective cultural rights have become endemic. In numerous situations, the response has been to promote self-determination, and one particular manifestation of that idea, secession, as a solution to these conflicting rights.[911]

Toope then wrote further that, "In arguments concerning the right ordering of a political community, culture, like human-rights norms, can be a shield or a sword."[912]

Contributors to the issue included authors from all over the world, such as Simon S.C. Tay,[913] future Chair of the National Environment Agency and Member of Parliament in Singapore; Kwadwo Appiagyei-Atua,[914] future Professor of Law at the University of Ghana; and El-Obaid Ahmed El-Obaid,[915] who was schooled in law at the University of Sudan, and who subsequently became a professor at McGill Law. The volume assembled a truly diverse series of perspectives.

Senior editor Marie-Pierre Olivier—now an attorney with the International Bar Association's Human Rights Institute—wrote that, "Entering the field of human rights and international law was actually the main reason why I applied to law school and chose McGill."[916] Looking back at the issue and her time on the *Journal* in general from a future place of understanding, she also wrote that:

> Law journals play a crucial role, particularly in the field of human rights and international law. These areas of the law are in constant evolution and the analysis offered in legal articles can have an important impact on court decisions and interpretation of conventions and other legal texts. Legal articles can contribute to better protection of human rights through innovative interpretation. They also offer important comparisons between different jurisdictions and can start essential discussions and debates, that are necessary for the law to progress and stay in touch with current situations.[917]

Mary-Pat Cormier, Editor-in-Chief for the volume and now a partner with Edwards Wildman Palmer LLP in Boston, recalled her time at McGill Law more wistfully. In Pilarczyk's work, she wrote of "Stephen Toope, who as Dean ... was always interested

907 Maureen A McTeer, "Role for Law in Matters of Morality" (1995) 40:4 *McGill LJ* 893 at 900.

908 *Ibid* at 903.

909 *Ibid* at 895.

910 Hans W Waade, "*Quebec Civil Law: An Introduction to Quebec Private Law* by John E.C. Brierley and Roderick A. MacDonald" Book Review (1995) 40:2 *McGill LJ* 571.

911 Stephen J Toope, "Preface" (1996) 41:4 *McGill LJ* 741 at 741.

912 *Ibid* at 742.

913 Simon SC Tay, "Human Rights, Culture, and the Singapore Example" (1996) 41:4 *McGill LJ* 743.

914 El-Obaid Ahmed El-Obaid & Kwadwo Appiagyei-Atua, "Human Rights in Africa--A New Perspective on Linking the Past to the Present" (1996) 41:4 *McGill LJ* 819.

915 *Ibid.*

916 Interview of Marie-Pierre Olivier by James Cummins (18 January, 2011).

917 *Ibid.*

in what we had to say about the law or about the Faculty,"[918] but most of all, she remembered how in the middle of those long nights together at the Faculty and the *Journal*, ever glimmering in front of them was "the promise of things to come."[919]

On the management side of the *Journal*, the first MLJ website was under construction, with the goal of uploading abstracts and allowing keyword searches of MLJ material.[920] The MLJ also placed its issues online with LexisNexus for the first time.[921] 1996 would also be the year in which the *McGill Law Journal* was officially incorporated, with the assistance of the Montreal office of McCarthy Tétrault LLP.[922]

The volume hosted an impressive roster of authors. Contributions to volume forty-one came included articles from future President and Vice-Chancellor of the University of Regina, David E. Hawkins;[923] future Chair of The Canadian Justice Review Board, Robert Martin;[924] future Wesley Newcomb Hohfeld Professor of Jurisprudence and Professor of Philosophy at Yale University, Jules Coleman;[925] future Chair of the Philosophy Department at the University of Toronto Arthur Ripstein;[926] future Executive Partner of the Abu Dhabi office of White and Case LLP, Douglas Peel;[927] future Dr. William D. Scholl Chair in Health & Law Policy at the University of Toronto and Professor of Law at New York University, Sujit Choudry;[928] and future Robina Chair in Law, Public Policy and Society at the University of Minnesota, John Borrows.[929]

Besides Mary-Pat Cormier and Marie-Pierre Olivier, the Editorial Board included Solicitations Editor M. Craig Sheppard, future Managing Director of DRI Capital. It should be noted at this point that most editors from this point forward were not called to the bar more than fifteen years ago. Again we see a shift towards the younger, mid-career legal professionals only newly involved in the legal community. As future Justice Gerald Le Dain wrote back in 1961, it takes up to twenty-five years to produce a legal career.[930] The lists and lists of future justices, controlling partners, top-flight academics, and politicians have—given this shorter time frame for each board—yet to materialize. Though there is no doubt, given the history of the MLJ's new and continued achievements moving into the twenty-first century that will be revealed over the following pages, that such lists of luminaries could well be in the making.

Over the summer of 1996, one sole editor from the incoming Executive Board stayed in Montreal to shepherd the *Journal* forward: Editor-in-Chief Martin Valasek.[931] Following up on the memorial issue for John Humphrey, a second memorial issue in honour of FR Scott was being planned,[932] looking at how his legacy had developed since his death twelve years before.[933] In an interview, Valasek—now a partner with the Montreal office of Norton Rose and one of the *Global Arbitration Review*'s 45 under 45 out of all members of the International Bar Association—wrote that,

> I was elected Editor-in-Chief in the spring of 1996, and submitted final proofs of Issue 4 of Volume 42 at the beginning of September 1997. That makes the interval about 18 months. I was particularly pleased with the publication of the two special issues that we did during my tenure as Editor-in-Chief: Issue no. 1 (Special Issue commemorating FR Scott, on Contemporary Constitutionalism) and Issue no. 3 (Special Issue marking the hand-over of Hong-Kong to China). My greatest relief was handing in the proofs for my final issue in early September 1997. I had the best possible incentive to get everything done by that date: my wedding took place on September 13, 1997, and my wife and I left for our honeymoon in Paris on September 15, which was followed several weeks later by our move to Prague, where I completed the final year of my law studies as a visiting student at Charles University. So you see, I had no choice but to finish by early September![934]

918 Pilarczyk, *supra* note 27 at 137.

919 *Ibid.*

920 "Minutes of the *McGill Law Journal* Board of Trustees Meeting" (21 June, 1996).

921 *Ibid.*

922 Mell, *supra* note 686 at 2.

923 Richard E Hawkins & Robert Martin, "Democracy, Judging and Bertha Wilson" (1995) 41:1 *McGill LJ* 1.

924 *Ibid.*

925 Jules Coleman & Arthur Ripstein, "Mischief and Misfortune (Annual McGill Lecture in Jurisprudence and Public Policy)" (1995) 41:1 *McGill LJ* 91.

926 *Ibid.*

927 Douglas Peel, "Developing a New E.B.R.D. Product: A Case Study on Interpreting the E.B.R.D. Agreement" (1995) 41:1 *McGill LJ* 295.

928 Sujit Choudry, "The Enforcement of the Canada Health Act" (1996) 41:2 *McGill LJ* 461.

929 John Borrows, "With or Without You: First Nations Law (in Canada)" (1996) 41:3 *McGill LJ* 629.

930 Ledain 1961, *supra* note 265 at 195

931 Minutes from 96, *supra* note 920.

932 *Ibid.*

933 Michael Oliver, "Foreword" (1997) 42:1 *McGill LJ* 3.

934 Interview of Martin Valasek by James Cummins (23

Near the end of the first summer, Valasek's Executive Editor decided not to return to Montreal, leaving the volume scrambling.[935] A replacement was found for them in time though, and volume forty-two experienced mostly high points. Recalling more about his tenure, he wrote, "What surprised me was how all-consuming the position of Editor-in-Chief was. I spent many early mornings and very late nights in my office at the *Law Journal.* I knew it would be a tough job, but I never thought it was going to be as intense as it turned out to be."[936] Valasek also wrote about the then-upcoming fourth edition of the *McGill Guide.*

> We began the *Cite Guide* project (fourth edition) just after I was elected Editor-in-Chief in the spring of 1996. The task of revising the *Cite Guide* was assigned to Don McGowan, our Citations Editor. We met several times through the summer of 1996, and agreed that he would provide a draft of the revised guide by September 15, in time for the *Law Journal* to use it internally through the fall of 1996, and to have an opportunity to make suggestions for completing the draft. The draft *Cite Guide* was unveiled to the broader *Law Journal* family in January 1997. We established an advisory board of *Law Journal* alums, professors and others to assist with seeing the project through… The actual final production of the *Cite Guide* was done under the aegis of Volume 43.[937]

In his own interview, Don McGowan—future lead attorney for Microsoft Game Studios and now the General Counsel of The Pokémon Company International—recalled how he decided to join the *Journal*, and ultimately become attached to the *Cite Guide* project. He wrote that,

> For me it was Mary Pat Cormier, the Editor-in-Chief of the year before. We were discussing the *Journal* (perhaps beverages were involved) and she suggested that if I really thought it was so easy maybe I should apply so she would have the opportunity to turn me down. So I applied. It turns out that it was really hard to get in, but somehow I made it past her, and there I was …
>
> I was in a Cite Guide year: I wrote the first draft of the 4th Edition. Because I spent a lot of time trying to create a system that removed what I saw as needless formalism (*e.g.* why should there be parentheses for reporters organized by volume number but brackets for reporters organized by year?) and instead focused on what I thought was a more sensible approach (*e.g.* how can you find the thing you're looking for in the least time?), this wasn't the draft that ended up being adopted by the *Journal.* I still remember being in the meeting where I presented the draft and asking, "[W]hy should we focus on needless minutiae rather than getting on to the meat of the issue?" and hearing the response, "[B]ecause we're a law journal, we should take pride in the fact that we can get this right." I don't know who was right – I thought I did then, maybe not so much anymore.[938]

The French part of the *Cite Guide* was done by Frédérique Amrouni, the French Executive Editor from volume forty-one.[939]

Out of everything, Valasek remembered the special issues the most warmly, writing,

> My best memories include working on the special issue in memory of FR Scott, and specifically the fun I had reading and enjoying all of the selections of FR Scott's poetry that were cited in the various contributions to the special issue. It was also particularly gratifying to include a dedication in this special issue by Peter Scott, the son of FR Scott. The dedication was in the form of a section from one of Peter Scott's poems, which I found very touching and beautiful.[940]

A section of that poem went as follows:[941]

February, 2011).

935 *Ibid.*

936 *Ibid.*

937 *Ibid.*

938 Interview of Don McGowan by James Cummins (23 November, 2010).

939 Minutes of the *McGill Law Journal* Board of Trustees meeting" (25 July, 1997).

940 Valasek interview, *supra* note 934.

941 Peter Dale Scott, "Dedication" (1997) 42:1 *McGill LJ* 1 at 1.

the mindfulness
of fire-tending

taught me by my father
the importance

of not resorting to paper
how in a rainstorm

to split softwood with an axe
and kindle with splinters

from the tree's core

The special issue would be published in concert with a conference that was held to mark the inauguration of the FR Scott Chair in Constitutional and Public Law—a conference entitled "The Blasted Pine".[942] The foreword for the issue would be written by Michael Kelway Oliver: the first Federal President of the New Democrat Party as well as President of Carleton University in the 1970s (1972-78). He is also perhaps the only person to write in the MLJ to have a campus bar named after him (Carleton University's "Oliver's Pub"). Oliver called Scott "the magician who could put social as well as personal passion into the frame of verse."[943]

Authors contributing to the issue included Alan C. Cairns,[944] future Professor of Political Science Emeritus at the University of British Columbia; as well as the inaugural FR Scott Lecture from Roderick A. MacDonald[945] and second Lecture from Stephen J. Toope.[946] A book review was contributed by the past Dean of the Queen's University Faculty of Law, John D. Whyte.[947]

The second special issue within volume forty-two focused on the handover of Hong Kong from British colonial rule to the Chinese government, published in the month following the July 1997 exchange of governance. Contributors included Betty Mayfoon Ho,[948] the future founder of the first anglo-American style common and comparative law school in China; and Simon Young,[949] future Director of the Centre for Comparative and Public Law at the University of Hong Kong. Book reviews were contributed by Jonathan Ocko,[950] future Head of the History Department at Duke University; and M.J.A Cooray,[951] Head of the Department of Law at the City University of Hong Kong.

Additional contributors to the volume's other two issues included Stuart Hoegner, future Managing Director of the Gaming Counsel Professional Corporation;[952] future Chair in Business Law and International Trade at the Université de Montréal, Stéphane Rousseau;[953] and future Director of the Native Law Center of Canada James Youngblood Henderson.[954] Meanwhile, the *Journal* inaugurated a new award. For many years the Isadore Ballon Memorial Medal, once awarded at the Faculty of Law to the highest ranking student in the fourth/practical year of studies (consisting of bar preparation courses offered by the university), had since some time between volume three and six (1957-60) been awarded to the "most outstanding student on the Editorial Board of the *McGill Law Journal.*"[955] The newest award would be named the Jerome C. Smyth award, given to the member of the Management Board that gave the most outstanding contribution of that year.[956]

942 Martin J Valasek, "Acknowledgements" (1997) 42:1 *McGill LJ* 9 at 9.

943 Oliver forward, *supra* note 933 at 3.

944 Alan C Cairns, "Why Is It So Difficult to Talk to Each Other" (1997) 42:1 *McGill LJ* 63.

945 Ronald A MacDonald, "F. R. Scott's Constitution (Inaugural Lecture" (1997) 42:1 *McGill LJ* 11.

946 Stephen J Toope, "Cultural Diversity and Human Rights (F.R. Scott Lecture)" (1997) 42:1 *McGill LJ* 169.

947 John D Whyte, "A Review of Samuel V. LaSelva, *The Moral Foundations of Canadian Federalism*" Book Review (1997) 42:1 *McGill LJ* 189.

948 Betty M Ho, "Rethinking the System of Sanctions in the Corporate and Securities Law of Hong Kong" (1997) 42:3 *McGill LJ* 603.

949 Simon Young, "The Meaning of the Right to Vote in Hong Kong" (1997) 42:3 *McGill LJ* 649.

950 John D Whyte, "A Review of Geoffrey MacCormack, The Spirit of Traditional Chinese Law" Book Review (1997) 42:3 *McGill LJ* 733.

951 MJA Cooray, "Hong Kong in China: The Promise of "One Country, Two Systems. A Review of Roda Mushkat, One Country, Two International Personalities: The Case of Hong Kong" Book Review (1997) 42:3 *McGill LJ* 751.

952 Stuart Hoegner, "How Many Rights (Or Wrongs) Make a Remedy--Substantive, Remedial and Unified Constructive Trusts" (1997) 42:2 *McGill LJ* 437.

953 Raymonde Crête & Stéphane Rousseau, "De la passivité à L'activisme des investisseurs Institutionnels au sein des corporations : le reflet de La diversité des facteurs d'influence" (1997) 42:4 *McGill LJ* 863.

954 Russel Lawrence Barsh & James Youngblood Henderson, "Supreme Court's *Van Der Peet* Trilogy: Naive Imperialism and Ropes of Sand" (1997) 42:4 *McGill LJ* 993.

955 Interview of A Derek Guthrie of James Cummins, (21 November, 2011). The question asked was the reason for the awarding of the medal to Guthrie in 1960; the 1956 medal was awarded, for his fourth/practical year results, to Wolfe M Friedman. See also, "Prizes for Achievements in Courses and Subject Areas" McGill Law Student Affairs Office, online: < http://www.mcgill.ca/law-studies/information/prizes/#C >

956 Minutes 97, *supra* note 939.

While the board claimed at the time to have named the award after Smyth because he was the *Journal*'s first Managing Editor,[957] we know this to have been mistake—as the Managing Editor of the first issue of volume one was John J. Pepper (who afterwards became Advertising Editor for the following two issues). As the different issues of volume one all had different mastheads, it has been commonplace in the past to confuse one person for another, when researching the first volume only by looking at one individual masthead (not realizing there are four different ones, with different individuals at each position in each). Regardless, Smyth was the longest lasting of the Managing Editors within volume one in terms of his output of issues, and was one of the nine members of volume one, issue one to continue on in a senior editorial position for the following issue. The first Jerome C. Smyth award was given to senior manager Riva Richard, who would go on to become one of *Lexpert*'s top 40 under 40 corporate counsels in 2005, and is now Executive Vice-President of Legal Affairs and General Counsel for Pollard Banknote.

Members of the following board (forty-three) included Executive Editor Paule Morisset, future member of the MLJ Board of Advisors and senior legal counsel to Bombardier; Case Comments Editor Matias Milet, who is one of only two MLJ members since volume two to have held senior editor positions in both their years on the *Journal* (he was Case Comments Editor in both his junior and senior year, and is now a tax associate at Osler in Toronto); Solicitations Editor Ariel Deckelbaum, who would become a *Crain*'s top 40 under 40 New York City business professional and Deputy-Chair of the Corporate Division at Paul Weiss LLP in New York; and senior editor Laverne A. Jacobs, who would become an Associate Professor at the Windsor University Faculty of Law.

During their tenure, they got the first *Journal* website up and running, including electronic versions of MLJ abstracts in a searchable format.[958] A partnership was also set up with Industry Canada in order to have unemployed people in Newfoundland receive a new job through uploading all of the back issues of the *Journal* onto the Internet[959] although the issues would not be fully uploaded onto the net until Electronics Editor Waleed Bishouty of volume fifty-six would do so in 2010. However the volume forty-three special issue on the new Civil Code of Russia originally planned for their volume would have to be postponed to the following volume,[960] though volume forty-three did include a special section from the 1997 Henri-Capitant conference in Luxembourg on the subject of "outsiders".[961]

The section included an article by future President of the Quebec Human Rights Tribunal Michèle Rivet.[962] Other contributors to the volume more generally included future President of St. Catherine's College at Cambridge University J.H. Baker;[963] future President of the International Association for Genocide Scholars William A. Schabas;[964] future Harry C. Black Professor of History Emeritus at John Hopkins University, J.G.A. Pocock;[965] and former Minister of Cultural Affairs for Quebec Denis Vaugeois,[966] who sent in a reply to a previous review of his own book that was published by the MLJ.

The special issue on the *Civil Code of Russia* finally appeared in issue two of volume forty-four. In its preface, former Faculty Advisor H. Patrick Glenn wrote,

> For the last three years the Institute of Comparative Law of McGill University, the law firm Ogilvy Renault, and the Private Law Research Center Attached to the Office of the President of the Russian Federation have been engaged in a collaborative project on Russian legislative reform and its dissemination. The project has been financed by the Canadian International Development Agency. Montreal participants have provided reports and commentaries to the Russian drafters, the *Civil Code of Quebec* has been translated and published in Russian, and members of the Private Law Centre have lectured and done research at McGill. This Special Issue of the *McGill Law Journal* allows the doctrinal foundation of the new Russian legislation to be made available to

957 *Ibid.*

958 "Minutes of the *McGill Law Journal* Board of Trustees meeting" (14 August, 1998).

959 *Ibid.*

960 *Ibid.*

961 Jean-Louis Baudouin, "Préface" (1998) 43:1 *McGill LJ* 141 at 141.

962 Michèle Rivet, "Le Travailleur Etranger au Canada: A L'avant-poste de la Precarite" (1998) 43:1 *McGill LJ* 181.

963 JH Baker, "The Three Languages of the Common Law" (1998) 43:1 *McGill LJ* 5.

964 William A Schabas, "Canada and the Adoption of the Universal Declaration of Human Rights" (1998) 43:2 *McGill LJ* 403.

965 JGA Pocock, "Law, Sovereignty and History in a Divided Culture: The Case of New Zealand and the Treaty of Waitangi" (1998) 43:3 *McGill LJ* 481.

966 Denis Vaugeois, "Réplique de Deins Vaugeois à David Schulze" (1998) 43:4 *McGill LJ* 969.

> a wider audience. We are very grateful for the collaboration of the distinguished Russian and western contributors. The editors of the *McGill Law Journal* are to be congratulated for bringing the project to fruition, in spite of difficulties of communication, coordination, and translation.[967]

Glenn wrote further that,

> At the height of the Cold War, Soviet jurists argued for fundamental incommensurability between socialist and bourgeois legal orders. This appears to have been an exaggerated claim. There are still problems of communication, translation, and understanding of Russian law for western jurists, but the present Special Issue of the *McGill Law Journal* makes a major contribution to mutual understanding.[968]

Glenn's words are reminiscent of those written by Victor L. Issraelyan during the arms control issue of volume twenty-eight, who wrote—perhaps through a more political lens—that the ideals of the western world were not, at heart, all that different from their own in the USSR.[969] It is only too bad that John Humphrey, after his continual castigations of the world through the MLJ, was no longer alive to read it.

Glenn recalled the experience working with the issue in his interview, stating

> It was their [the *Journal's*] initiative, which I remember being impressed with at the time—looking to the codification of Russia as having pertinence for Quebec and generally for the codified world. It just happened that I was involved with the codification in Russia, so it worked out as a nice, happy coincidence that the people we were working with were of interest to the *Journal*.[970]

The list of authors contributing to this special issue included Rolf Knieper,[971] Director of the Reform of Private Law in C.I.S. Countries at the German Technical Corporation and future Honourary Professor for the Faculty of Law at the University of Almaty in Kazakhstan; future Clifford M. and Bette A. Carney Chair at the University of Illinois College of Law, Peter B. Maggs;[972] Evgueny A. Sukhanov,[973] future Dean of Law at Moscow State University; future Head of the Civil Code Department at the Private Law Research Center under the President of the Russian Federation Oksana M. Kozyr;[974] President of the International Commercial Arbitration Court Alexander S. Komarov;[975] Vassily V. Vitryansky,[976] future Vice-Chairman of the Supreme Arbitration Court of the Russian Federation; future Director for Innovation and Change Management at the World Bank Institute, Randi Ryterman;[977] future Chair of the Economics Department at the University of Maryland, Peter Murrell;[978] and future William Voss-Bascom Professor of Law and Political Science at the University of Wisconsin, Kathryn Hendley.[979]

Other notable authors from the rest of the volume included Timothy Macklem,[980] future Head of the School of Law at King's College London; and Roderick A. MacDonald with an epic one-hundred plus page treatise.[981] Other notable projects from the volume include the first appearance of an Electronics Editor—McShane Devlin Jones, who was, helpfully, also fluent in Russian. Jones' efforts in bringing the MLJ further into the electronic age and with the special issue led to him winning the I. Ballon Medal. He is

967 H Patrick Glenn, "Preface" (1998) 44:2 *McGill LJ* 255 at 255.

968 *Ibid* at 257.

969 Issraelyan, *supra* note 593 at 757.

970 Glenn interview, *supra* note 415.

971 Rolf Knieper, "Stability and Transition in the Civil Code of the Russian Federation(1999) 44:2 *McGill LJ* 259.

972 Peter B Maggs, "The Process of Codification in Russia: Lessons Learned from the Uniform Commercial Code" (1992) 44:2 *McGill LJ* 281.

973 Evgeuny A Sukhanov, "The Right of Ownership in the Contemporary Civil Law of Russia" (1999) 44:2 *McGill LJ* 301.

974 Oksana M Kozyr, "The Legal Treatment of Immovables under the Civil Code of the Russian Federation" (1999) 44:2 *McGill LJ* 327.

975 Alexander S Komarov, "The Legal Civil Code of the Russian Federation: General Provisions on Liability for the Violation of Obligations" (1999) 44:2 *McGill LJ* 357.

976 Vassily V Vitryansky, "Insolvency and Bankruptcy Law Reform in the Russian Federation" (1999) 44:2 *McGill LJ* 409.

977 Kathryn A Hendley, Peter Murrell & Randi Ryterman, "Regional Analysis of Transactional Strategies of Russian Enterprises" (1999) 44:2 *McGill LJ* 433.

978 *Ibid.*

979 *Ibid.*

980 Timothy Macklem, "*Vriend v. Alberta*: Making the Private Public" (1999) 44:1 *McGill LJ* 197.

981 Michael G Bridge, Roderick A MacDonald, Ralph L Simmonds & Catherine Walsh, "Formalism, Functionalism, and Understanding the Law of Secured Transactions" (1999) 44:3 *McGill LJ* 567.

now a tax litigation partner with Barsalou Lawson LLP.

Volume forty-four was produced during the final year of the old McGill Law programme. Moving forward, McGill would become the first school in the world to teach both the civil and common law programs at the same time, in what was labelled the "transsystemic programme". The program would begin in 1999 and help the school enter a new millennium fraught with change—digitization, internationalization, and a shifting of global powers away from a western-centric world. And once again, the *McGill Law Journal* would serve as one of the premiere vehicles through which the philosophy of the education of McGill's law students would be disseminated.

Chapter Five:

A Transsystemic Century

Rarely does an age-old institution manage to completely redefine itself with the times. To help us understand how the McGill Faculty of Law was able to make such a shift, Peter Strauss—the Betts Professor of Law at Columbia University—once wrote:

> To start, I'd like you to imagine an agglomeration of twenty or thirty jurisdictions experiencing a profound change in the nature of their economic realities. Their economies, and thus the transactions within them and the businesses that conduct them, have been predominantly local in character. Now, political and economic developments are producing businesses and transactions increasingly trans-jurisdictional in character. Increasingly the counseling, drafting, and litigating that goes on in lawyers' offices involves not one jurisdiction but two or three. What happens to legal education?[982]

While this is the "reason why" for the new McGill programme, which Straus is speaking about above, Straus then discusses the "how". He writes that Montreal is, of course, unique in that it straddles two jurisdictions itself in terms of business[983]—and has for far longer than globalization has been around. The development of the national programme during the 1960s was a natural offshoot of the legal environment, not a forced experiment. In fact, the necessity of a national programme, as we have seen, was noted all the way back in the 1920s. Strauss wrote that at the very least "McGill took over three and a half decades to reach the point it currently has attained, and that under the favourable conditions noted. Its leadership has self-consciously been building faculty to this end since the 1980s."[984] Thus Strauss writes that McGill's situation may be globally unique, as he compares McGill with the possibility of exporting such a programme to a school like his own in New York City:

> We cannot rely on our students to be bilingual, much less bilingual in a particular second language that fortuitously happens to be the language of one of the great legal literatures of the world. McGill too faces challenges here—both its location's politics and its language limitations work to conceal the Germanic code tradition and its extraordinary literature, as well as other legal systems. There is also a risk of confusing France with the civil law world. McGill may find even larger difficulties when it moves from the relatively comfortable juxtaposition of two legal systems that share deep cultural and social affinities to, say, aboriginal law, or non-Western systems that are neither liberal-democratic nor market oriented. Transsystemia within Western European traditions may prove much easier than transsystemia as a world proposition. But our challenges are greater; at the least, we require a full rendition of civilian sources in English.[985]

At least within the environment of the *Journal*, however, a bilingual environment *does not* come naturally at McGill—it takes real effort. As one reviews the minutes of Board of Trustees meetings, Board of Advisors meetings, and Annual General Meetings of the Editorial and Management Boards, every year there is almost the same complaint. Either there have been almost no applications for French editorial positions, not nearly enough French articles, or a serious lack of interest from French academics to do external reviews. Year after year, a significant push occurs whereby the Editorial Board looks to keep the French aspect of the *Journal* alive and well. The MLJ did not simply fall into a great situation; it took a potential situation and coaxed it to blossom. Bilingualism requires effort from each and every board; it is something that could very

982 Peter Strauss, "Transsystemia—Are We Approaching a New Langdellian Moment - Is McGill Leading the Way?" (2006) 56:2 *J Legal Educ* 161 at 161.

983 *Ibid* at 163-64.

984 *Ibid* at 170.

985 *Ibid* at 167.

easily disappear within a few years without the annual focus and concentration of *Journal* members. After all, there is no one watching them or prodding them to be any certain way.

Scott Turow wrote, within his somewhat legendary autobiographical account of the "1L" year at Harvard Law, of student editors, that "[r]eview members considered a Sunday away from law a cause for celebration."[986] When it comes purely to transsystemia, to push forward alongside McGill in its endeavour to build a new kind of legal thinking, MLJ members often had to give up even these rare occasions of rest. The new millennium had arrived. Adam M. Dodek once wrote that, "If Laurier famously quipped that the twentieth century would belong to Canada, the truth is that in Canada, the twentieth century belonged to lawyers."[987] If this is true, to whom would Canada and the world belong entering yet another new century? Transsystemic thinkers appear to be, at the very least, at the root of such a new echelon.

From the words of Chief Justice Rinfret written over forty years beforehand, the MLJ had been a consistent forum for reflection upon the mergings of culture, politics, and legal ideas and philosophies in a world hurdling towards full internationalization. The full reconfiguring of the MLJ to its modern partial focus on transsystemic philosophy (after all, it is still a generalist law journal) would not be immediate, though as the new form of education sank into the students, so did it begin to appear in the editorial philosophies of the *Journal*'s student editors.

Volume forty-five would be the one to cross the line into the year 2000. According to volume forty-five Editor-in-Chief Azim Hussain (now a partner with the Montreal office of Norton Rose LLP),

> The vision I had for Volume 45 was to get the MLJ back on track for a timely completion of the volume within the calendar year for that volume. Over the years, a backlog in the publication of the volumes had developed and it was very important to me that the volume for the year 2000 actually be completed in that same year … [My] best memory was completing the volume according to schedule.[988]

In addition to finishing on time to start the new millennium out right, volume forty-five reintroduced a new and permanent version of the *McGill Law Journal* Annual Lecture. After a seven year hiatus, Hussain recalls that, "The reason I decided to [reintroduce it was] because I wanted to create a buzz around the MLJ and give it more prominence. The selection of the speaker was based on prominence, hence Justice Gonthier, who was easy to approach since he was on the MLJ board."[989] The Board of Trustees also helped to ensure the Lecture would survive for longer this time, by passing a resolution to finance any deficits occurring from the Lecture via the MLJ trust fund.[990] The reinstituted event would no longer be seen purely as a fundraising and alumni gathering opportunity, but as an additional outlet for the *Journal* to facilitate new, groundbreaking scholarship.

The basis for Justice Charles D. Gonthier of the Supreme Court of Canada's speech can be traced back to a meeting that occurred three years earlier. During the Board of Trustees meeting, Gonthier approached the *Journal* with an idea for a special issue. He suggested an issue on the idea that while the slogan of the French Revolution—a pillar of the contemporary world and its beginnings—was often cited as a basis for modern legal philosophy, only two of the three foundations of that slogan are usually thought of. The slogan was "*Liberté, égalité, fraternité*", yet the *fraternité* aspect of the original philosophy appeared to not have entered the scholastic minds of contemporary legal scholars. Gonthier pointed out that despite this lack of scholarship, *fraternité* was still at the heart of western society and its law.[991] The *Journal* decided not to create a special issue on the subject, but the seed had been sown in the Justice's head.

The lecture based on this idea would be given on January 11, 2000 and published in June within the third issue of volume forty-five. Of his idea, Gonthier stated that,

> The first value of fraternity recognizes that there are certain people within this community who require special protection and to whom we have a commitment. Certain vulnerable groups need extra measures to play a meaningful role in the community. In one respect, this

986 Scott Turow, *One L* (New York: Farrar, Straus and Giroux, 1988) at 85.

987 Adam M Dodek, "Lawyers, Guns and Money: Lawyers and Power in Canadian Society" in *Why Good Lawyers Matter* (Toronto: Irwin Law, 2012) at essay page 17, also online: < http://ssrn.com/abstract=1656475 >

988 Interview of Azim Hussain by James Cummins (11 February and 16 August, 2011). This interview was conducted mainly in an email response on 11 February, however subsequent questions were answered in 16 August.

989 *Ibid.*

990 "Minutes from the *McGill Law Journal* Board of Trustees" (25 August, 2000).

991 Minutes 97, *supra* note 939.

imports to a liberal democracy a notion of *empathy*. In another respect, this aspect of fraternity informs our understanding of equality—the State may be discriminating against individuals by failing to accommodate their special needs. But strictly speaking, from an Aristotelian perspective, the right to equality would not recognize such inaction as discrimination. This aspect of fraternity—that of inclusion—is essential for the proper functioning of a polyethnic state such as Canada.[992]

Dear Justice Deslongchamps,

You are cordially invited to:

The *McGill Law Journal* Alumni Lecture Series

"Liberty, Equality, Fraternity—The Forgotten Leg of the Trilogy"

by

The Hon. Mr. Justice C. Gonthier

of the Supreme Court of Canada

Tuesday, January 11th, 2000

8:00 PM

Moot Court, New Chancellor Day Hall, 3644 Peel Street

(cocktail at 7 PM in the Atrium)

RSVP: Stephan Levy, (514) 398-7397

Annual Lecture Invitation for Associate Chief Justice André Deslongchamps of the Quebec Superior Court.

Gonthier's much more lengthy study on the impact of *fraternité* on Canadian law and policy provided a running start for the rebirth of the lecture series.

Soon after the end of the Annual Lecture series in the 1990s, the alumni newsletter had also fallen out of use. Volume forty-five saw a rebirth of this initiative as well.[993] The volume also carried a special issue on "Genetics and the Law", which was published in the same week that the Human Genome Project was completed.[994] In its introduction, Dr. Timothy Caulfield—Research Director of the Health Law Institute from 1993 to today—noted that during that time you could not "pick up a newspaper without finding at least one story related to the advances in genetics and biotechnology."[995] The issue was at the edge of the coming intertwining of law and the biotechnological sciences.

Other contributors to the issue included noted sociologist from New York University Professor Dorothy Nelkin. Nelkin and her coauthor Emily Marden perhaps most succinctly established the importance of the debate within the pages of that special issue by writing:

> In this era of radical biotechnology, scientific advances present profound social and ethical dilemmas ... driven by scientific hubris, commercial interests, and media hype, this technology is moving inexorably towards clinical application with minimal public discussion of these issues. Ultimately, the regulatory system, structured to address questions of safety and efficacy, effectively displaces any consideration of the social and ethical implications of scientific developments.
>
> In the past, similar social issues have generated significant and often tumultuous public debate. For example, the consequences of the possible release of genetically engineered organisms into the environment were the focus of active public discussions during the 1970s. Concerns about harming future generations prompted widespread public opposition to nuclear

992 Charles D Gonthier, "Liberty, Equality, Fraternity: The Forgotten Leg of the Trilogy, or Fraternity: The Unspoken Third Pillar of Democracy" (2000) 45:3 *McGill LJ* 567 at 574.

993 Trent Mell, "The Managing Editor Report" *McGill Law Journal Newsletter* (December 1999) at 2.

994 Minutes 00, *supra* note 990.

995 Timothy Caulfield, "Introduction" (2000) 45:2 *McGill LJ* 343 at 343.

> power and the early development of *in vitro* fertilization provoked widespread ethical debate over the potential for eugenic abuses. In recent years, however, public involvement in technological decisions has radically declined, reflecting a broader shift from public activism to personal consumerism and the ascendance of commercial interests in the biosciences. There is a growing tendency to reduce ethical issues to technical questions and to defer to scientific expertise.
>
> As a result, today, when scientists have the power to radically alter the human genetic structure, there is little public discussion or debate about the ethical and social consequences of this technology.[996]

Other authors that contributed to the volume's issues included future Albert Abel Professor of Law at the University of Toronto Alan Brudner;[997] Dean of the Faculty of Law at Queen's University and future Justice of the Superior Court of Ontario, Alison Harvison Young;[998] future Eco-Research Chair in Environmental Law and Policy at the University of Victoria R. Michael M'Gonigle;[999] future Managing Partner at Robertson Stromberg Pederson LLP Christopher J.J. Donald;[1000] former Dean of Law at the University of Western Ontario and Vice-President (Administration) of the same university, Peter Mercer;[1001] future Co-Director of the National Centre for Business Law at the University of British Columbia David G. Duff;[1002] and future Director of Legal Writing at the Fordham University Faculty of Law Rachel Vorspan.[1003]

Book reviews were also contributed by those including Head Librarian and the Chair of the Wainwright Committee of the McGill University Faculty of Law, Daniel Boyer.[1004] Over the years since, Boyer has been a significant figure of mentorship to the *McGill Law Journal*. From the recommendation of speeches around the faculty for articles to facilitating the arduous and perfectionist tasks of nailing down the minor details of every citation, he has been a significant figure of support for the *Journal* for many years. He even agreed to appear with the *Journal* members on stage at the annual law school dramatic revue "Skit Nite" with volume fifty-six as the "Good Witch of the East". As of 2011 Boyer became the first official Faculty Advisor to the *Canadian Guide to Uniform Legal Citation* at the request of the MLJ's Executive Board.[1005]

The Wainwright Collection at the Nahum Gelber Law Library of McGill, of which Boyer is the Chair, has an interesting background in terms of the *Journal* as well, as former Faculty Advisor to the *Journal* Jean-Gabriel Castel explained:

> I was a friend of, when I was a student in Paris, of [François] Olivier-Martin who was the great specialist on the Custom of Paris. At McGill I was teaching legal history, and the Custom of Paris was the basis of Quebec law. When he died I knew his wife quite well and my mother advanced me the money, and we bought the collection of Olivier-Martin—several thousand books ... you have it upstairs (in the library). It's called the Wainwright Collection because Mr. Wainwright then reimbursed my mother for the purchase ... It was good to have the collection because a large part of Quebec law is based on French law.[1006]

Other members of the volume forty-five Editorial and Management Boards included Executive Editor Andrew Comrie-Picard, who would become a bronze medalist at the 2010 X-Games in the Rally Car Racing event and an extreme-sports television commentator

996 Emily Marden & Dorothy Nelkin, "Displaced Agendas: Current Regulatory Strategies for Germline Gene Therapy" (2000) 45:2 *McGill LJ* 461 at 480.

997 Alan Brudner, "Insane Automatism: A Proposal for Reform" (2000) 45:1 *McGill LJ* 65.

998 Alison Harvison Young, "This Child Does Have 2 (Or More) Fathers--Step-Parents and Support Obligations" (2000) 45:1 *McGill LJ* 107.

999 Emily Walter, R Michael M'Gonigle & Celeste McKay, "Fishing around the Law: The Pacific Salmon Management System as a Structural Infringement of Aboriginal Rights" (2000) 45:1 *McGill LJ* 263.

1000 Christopher JH Donald, "Civil Remedies for Breach of Continuous Disclosure Obligations under Ontario's Securities Act" (2000) 45:3 *McGill LJ* 609.

1001 Margaret Ann Wilkinson, Christa Walker, & Peter Mercer, "Do Codes of Ethics Actually Shape Legal Practice" (2000) 45:3 *McGill LJ* 645.

1002 David G Duff, "Disability and the Income Tax" (2000) 45:4 *McGill LJ* 797.

1003 Rachel Vorspan, "Rational Recreation and the Law: The Transformation of Popular Urban Leisure in Victorian England" (2000) 45:4 *McGill LJ* 891.

1004 Daniel Boyer, "Recension de Denis Le May et Dominique Goubau, La recherche documentaire en droit—2000" Book Review (2000) 45:4 *McGill LJ* 1083.

1005 "Minutes of the *McGill Law Journal* Annual General Meeting" (8 February, 2012).

1006 Castel interview, *supra* note 44.

and host. Speaking of prizes, one of the first acts of the next volume (forty-six) was to enact a $1000 essay prize exclusive to French articles, in order to try and boost French submissions that year.[1007] Though it would only be held the one time, the prize went to Professor José Woehrling of the Université de Montréal, for his paper "Convergences et divergences entre fédéralisme et protection des droits et libertes: l'exemple des États-Unies et du Canada".[1008] The success of the article did not stop there—Woehrling's piece would become the only French article to appear in the *Journal* cited by the Supreme Court of Canada in three separate decisions.

Volume forty-six was led by Editor-in-Chief Robert Leckey, now a William Dawson Scholar and Associate Professor at the McGill University Faculty of Law. Of his time on the *Journal* Leckey wrote that,

> Azim Hussain sent the final issue of volume 45 to the printer in July 2000. I spent some of May and all of June working with him on the proofreading of his last issue or issues, learning from him. Then I was free to move forward with my first issue. I think my final issue went off to the printer in August or September 2001. Anyway, he deserves special credit more than I do ...
>
> Azim drilled into me throughout the summer when he was training me, as it were, that timing was a big deal and that it was critical to stay on time. Part of how I did it my year was to work out the timing carefully and realistically. My sense is that people typically underestimate how long each step will take – you underestimate by 50 per cent a few steps and in no time you're months behind.
>
> Our issue 1 was finished more or less, I think, by the time the fall term began. We knew we needed to finish issue 2 by end of the fall term. I remember that my executive editor and I were doing late proofreading of issue 3, in layout, as we called it, on Good Friday. And I think I did the layout proofreading for issue 4 myself in the summer, some of it from New York, where I had a summer job. It was all spaced out reasonably well.
>
> I tend to work quite quickly, and that probably helped ... I skipped a lot of class, too, treating the *Journal* as closer to a full-time job than a part-time one.[1009]

Leckey continued in saying that,

> I know now that the current editor in chief, Azim, was grooming me a bit. My second assignment in the fall of my year as a junior editor was the text editing, with two other juniors doing the footnotes. And then the third piece I did that fall was by Professor Healy.[1010] It came in late, and I did text and footnotes during the exam period. So by February I had had more editing experience than the average junior editor (not that anybody voting [knew] that).
>
> I decided to run, I suppose, because I thought I would enjoy it. I was considering an academic career, and I got the sense that it seemed a kind of stepping-stone thing to do. I had always liked writing and editing. To be honest, I don't think I ran on a particular vision; certainly I didn't have radical changes in mind. I had a few ideas of things we might do differently, but it wasn't a reform platform.[1011]

He then wrote further that,

> The best memories, I suppose, were simply of the time spent working closely with others on a shared project. So there was a lot of laughter, despite the hard work, spent with the French and English executive editors and the managing editor, with Nicole, and with the senior editors. The executive editors and I—Sybil and Pierre-Hugues—talked about many things in the hours reading layout in the boardroom.
>
> It was always very satisfying for me, as an Ontario Anglophone, to catch the odd error in French that Pierre-Hugues had missed.
>
> It was pretty exciting being a law student and having an office of my own. I suspect it wasn't especially healthy in the basement of 3660. But it was our space. It was also exciting, again still as a student, to

1007 Minutes 00, *supra* note 990.

1008 Robert Leckey, "Memorandum to the Trustees and Advisory Board" (15 August, 2001).

1009 Interview of Robert Leckey by James Cummins (29 December, 2010).

1010 Patrick Healy, "Automatism Confined" (2000) 45:1 *McGill LJ* 87.

1011 Leckey interview, *supra* note 1009.

> be marking up documents to be corrected by Nicole.
>
> It was a great moment holding in my hands the first issue of our volume.
>
> I learned lots from the two years at the *Journal*. One of the most important concerns big tasks that at first seem impossible: you just have to sit down, begin, and keep going. Little by little, yes, you can proofread 300 pages.[1012]

Volume forty-six senior editor Melanie J. Mortensen—now a Parliamentary Counsel (Legal) with the House of Commons—wrote that, "Our Editor-in-Chief and Executive were very hard-working and effective. In retrospect, I do not imagine that *not* publishing on time occurred to them as an option."[1013] The second lecture of the new annual lecture series was the last to appear under the name of the "*McGill Law Journal* Alumni Lecture", as from the following volume onwards the name would be changed to the "*McGill Law Journal* Annual Lecture". While the article that appeared in the MLJ as a result of the lecture was authored by two individuals, Leckey wrote that,

> We didn't have two lecturers; it was Philippe Kirsch. I guess he figured that he didn't have time to write a publishable text alone, so brought on board Valerie Oosterveld. Only he came to McGill, as far as I recollect. To be honest, I don't remember much about the lecture and the surrounding events … I remember being nervous, and *it was probably one of the first times that I had spoken French* (for half of my welcome or whatever it was) in public.[1014]

The Lecture was held on March 13, 2001. Kirsch, Canadian Ambassador to Sweden at the time, lectured on the topic of the creation and preparation of the soon to be established International Criminal Court (ICC). Two years later, Kirsch would become the very first President of the ICC, a position he would hold until 2009. Kirsch wrote in his accompanying article that, "A perfect court would be a court with universal support. This does not reflect the reality of the world today. We still face a world composed of states dealing with each other bilaterally and multi-laterally, which has a corresponding impact on what can realistically be achieved in negotiations."[1015] Soon enough, however, Kirsch would lead the way in the final development of the Court.

Volume forty-six would also contain two special sections. The first section came from papers submitted to the *Hate, Genocide and Human Rights Fifty Years Later: What Have We Learned? What Must We Do?* conference held from January 27-28, 1999 in commemoration of the fiftieth anniversary of the *Universal Declaration of Human Rights*.[1016] The section was introduced by Justice Claire L'Heureux-Dubé of the Supreme Court of Canada, who wrote that,

> Even in the developed world, there are numerous reminders of what remains to be done. Crises of homelessness, unemployment, and poverty remind us of how the rights to a home, to work, and to an adequate standard of living have not fully developed. Violence against women, sexual harassment, hate crimes, racism, and discrimination against the disadvantaged—whether minorities, women, people with disabilities, or on the basis of sexual orientation—are just some of the problems that international human rights law implores all people to confront. It demands that we pursue their elimination.
>
> In the world as a whole, the challenges—and our failures—are still greater. In recent years, war and genocide in Bosnia, in Rwanda, and now in Kosovo, and the inability of the international community to prevent or stop these deadly manifestations of intolerance, mean that what was never to happen again is happening before our very eyes. The inequality between developed and developing countries, and the vastly different opportunities and standards of living available to people in different parts of the world, show us that there is much to be done before the rights guaranteed by the *Universal Declaration* and other international conventions become a reality for everyone. The number of places where people are imprisoned for expressing their political beliefs, where torture is

1012 *Ibid.*

1013 Interview of Melanie J Mortensen by James Cummins (22 November, 2010).

1014 Leckey interview, *supra* note 1009. Emphasis not added.

1015 Philippe Kirsch & Valerie Oosterveld, "Negotiating an Institution for the Twenty-First Century: Multilateral Diplomacy and the International Criminal Court" (2001) 46:4 *McGill LJ* 1141 at 1159-60.

1016 "International Conference" (2000) 46:1 *McGill LJ* 105.

> rampant and where people live in fear of the authorities, sets off alarm bells about the monumental task ahead. For many, freedom and human rights are still just words on a distant page, words that have not yet come to have meaning in their daily lives.[1017]

Her powerful introduction began a section that included speeches turned articles from authors like future Justice of the Supreme Court of Canada Rosalie Silberman Abella;[1018] renowned columnist and author David Rieff;[1019] future Vice-President of Reporters Without Borders Francois Bugingo;[1020] another piece from Stephen J. Toope;[1021] Justice Louise Arbour of the Supreme Court of Canada[1022] (she was appointed in between the time of her speech at the conference and the article's publication); one of the founding faculty members of the City University of New York Faculty of Law Rhonda Copelon;[1023] future Edward B. Burling Chair in International Law at John Hopkins University Ruth Wedgwood;[1024] a second piece in the volume from Philippe Kirsch;[1025] former Solicitor General and Minister of Consumer and Corporate Affairs in Canadian Parliament, thirty-two year MP Warren Allmand,[1026] whose legislative leadership helped lead to the abolishment of the death penalty in Canada; Justice Richard Goldstone of the Constitutional Court of South Africa, whose judicial opinions were among those that ended Apartheid in South Africa, and who was the Chief Prosecutor of the International Criminal Tribunal for the former Yugoslavia, as well as the Tribunal for Rwanda; and one of the Chief Prosecutors of the Nuremberg War Crimes trials, Benjamin B. Ferencz.

Ferencz recalled in his speech turned article the horrors of witnessing genocides first hand. He recalled that,

> My wartime experiences led me into the concentration camps ... I was a liberator. I saw the crematoria while they were still burning. I arrested criminals, I dug up bodies with my hands. That led me to a career as a war crimes prosecutor at Nuremberg, where I got to know the murderers—the remorseless killers—personally. The trial in which I was a chief prosecutor was the *Einzatsgruppen* case, in which the twenty-two defendants were convicted of murdering over a million people, mostly Jews and Gypsies, in cold blood—men, women, and children. Thirteen of the defendants, including six SS generals, were sentenced to death. Since I was inexperienced and was only twenty-seven years old, I rested the prosecution's case after two days. That's a record for some young people to try to match. The trial itself lasted much longer, but it took that added time to rebut the lies and the denials, which came from the defendants.
>
> I learned about the mentality of intelligent German leaders—I only picked leaders to stand trial and most of them had doctor degrees! I learned that there are all kinds of people in the world, and the same mentality that made the Holocaust possible exists today. It exists in all countries. You've heard it described by other speakers at this conference. The perpetrators of the crimes in Rwanda and Yugoslavia reflect the same cruel thinking. What I saw and experienced had quite a profound effect on me. The trauma is still with me.[1027]

Richard Goldstone, Chief Prosecutor in the cases of Yugoslavia and Rwanda, and South African Justice, also spoke directly of his own experiences and lessons learned in the face of genocide, stating that,

---

1017 Claire L'Heureux-Dubé, "Introduction" (2000) 46:1 *McGill LJ* 109 at 110-11.

1018 Rosalie Silberman Abella, "The Instructive Power of Outrage: Remembering Nuremberg" (2000) 46:1 *McGill LJ* 113.

1019 David Rieff, "Are Good Intentions Enough--The Limits of the New World of International Justice" (2000) 46:1 *McGill LJ* 173.

1020 Francois Bugingo, "Rwanda : Chronique d'un Génocide Prévisible" (2000) 46:1 *McGill LJ* 179.

1021 Stephen J Toope, "Does International Law Impose a Duty upon the United Nations to Prevent Genocide" (2000) 46:1 *McGill LJ* 187.

1022 Louise Arbour, "The International Tribunals for Serious Violations of International Humanitarian Law in the Former Yugoslavia and Rwanda" (2000) 46:1 *McGill LJ* 195.

1023 Rhonda Copelon, "Gender Crimes as War Crimes: Integrating Crimes against Women into International Criminal Law" (2000) 46:1 *McGill LJ* 217.

1024 Ruth Wedgwood, "Augusto Pinochet and International Law" (2000) 46:1 *McGill LJ* 241.

1025 Philippe Kirsch, "The International Criminal Court" (2000) 46:1 *McGill LJ* 255.

1026 Warren Allman, "The International Criminal Court and the Human Rights Revolution" (2000) 46:1 *McGill LJ* 263.

1027 Benjamin B Ferencz, "Response on Receiving an Award" (2000) 46:1 *McGill LJ* 275 at 276.

> We should have learned... of the power of leadership. In this century, leaders have shown what tremendous power they can wield, for good or for evil; consider the power that Hitler wielded for evil, and the power that President Mandela and President de Klerk wielded for good. In South Africa, without good leadership, there was a grave possibility of a most terrible bloodbath. Indeed, it appeared to be inevitable, and until the beginning of 1990, we were looking into the abyss ...
>
> We should have learned, too, I would suggest, about the danger—particularly in democracies—of weak leadership, and the dangers of political decisions being taken by the military establishment. One can anticipate such decision-making happening in military dictatorships. What one does not anticipate is its prevalence in democracies, even in the most powerful democracy in the world. My own meetings in Washington, during my time as chief prosecutor of the Yugoslavia tribunal, showed me how important political decisions were made in the Pentagon rather than in the White House.[1028]

The woman who would take over from Goldstone as Chief Prosecutor for the International Criminal Tribunal for the former Yugoslavia was Justice Louise Arbour. In the same issue she recalled of her own time as Chief Prosecutor that,

> [I]t makes sense to have [a] partnership between military peacekeeping operations and criminal law enforcement in a state where there is no other alternative ... Many of the violent conflicts that occur today exist as a result of either ancient, recent, or even ongoing conflicts that were suspended but were never resolved, at least not in a demonstrably just way. And lack of accountability from powerful criminals is, I think, very much part of the unresolved nature of many of these conflicts ... it makes sense to engage NATO... in supporting the enforcement of the law of war (which is the old-fashioned way of referring to international humanitarian law) is because it is *their* law. The law that we are enforcing is the only body of law that distinguished a soldier in action from a common murderer.[1029]

Again, Justice Arbour would be appointed to the Supreme Court of Canada less than nine months after the conference came to a close.

The second special section would be on European Integration. In the introduction to the section, then-Dean of McGill Law Peter Leuprecht wrote how this section was almost interconnected with the first:

> In a rather personal vein, I am tempted to say that this special section somehow establishes a link between my earlier life devoted to the building of European unity and my present life at the helm of McGill's Faculty of Law.
>
> The building of European unity is undoubtedly one of the most fascinating and positive processes in the history of the last half century. It is an effort to build peace after centuries of European wars, two of which were to become world wars. I personally am one of those who strongly believe that, if it is to be solid, this new European order of peace has to be founded on shared principles and values, in particular those of pluralist democracy, the rule of law, and respect for human rights. Rather than dealing with purely procedural or institutional problems, the essays gathered in this special section are concerned with certain aspects of those principles and values.[1030]

Authors within this special section included Gerard Quinn,[1031] Dean of the Faculty of Law at the National University of Ireland, Galway; future Co-Director of the Center for Research on Fundamental Rights at the Université Paris Ouest Nanterre Faculty of Law, Daniel Borrillo;[1032] future Chair of Comparative Legal Studies and Internationalization of Law at the Collège de France, Mereille Delmas-

1028 Richard Goldstone, "Reflections on the Development of the Law of War" (2000) 46:1 *McGill LJ* 279 at 287-88.

1029 Arbour, *supra* note 1022 at 198.

1030 Peter Leuprect, "Introduction" (2001) 46:4 *McGill LJ* 845 at 845.

1031 Gerard Quinn, "The European Union and the Coucil of Europe on the Issue of Human Rights: Twins Separated at Birth" (2001) 46:4 *McGill LJ* 849.

1032 Daniel Borrillo, "Pluralisme conjugal ou hiérarchie des sexualités: la reconnaissance Juridique des couples homosexuels dans l'Union européenne" " (2001) 46:4 *McGill LJ* 875.

Marty;[1033] and future Jean Monnet Chair of EU Law at Cambridge University Catherine Barnard.[1034] Volume forty-six also served as a grand farewell to one of the *Journal*'s strongest supporters ever since his tenure with volumes four and five: John E.C. Brierley. As had only been done once before, in the case of FR Scott, a full bibliography of Brierley's works was published after his death on December 15, 2000. Indeed, as was noted before, the case comment he wrote on *Saint-Pierre v. McCarthy* for volume four was nestled there as his very first publication, written in his junior year with the MLJ.[1035] Strangely enough, the issue containing the memoriam and bibliography was backdated to before Brierley's death—as the issue reads that it was published in November of 2000, the month before he died. Either that, or the Editorial Board had the help of a very proficient crystal ball.

Professor Stephen A. Scott, who had Brierley as his Faculty Advisor during his year as Editor-in-Chief of volume twelve, had provided remarks that prior April 15 at the annual meeting of the *Association des professeurs de droit du Québec*, upon the occasion of the official retirement of Professor Brierley. Scott's remarks were used as a preface to the bibliography, alongside a contribution from his colleague Professor Alain-François Bisson.[1036] Scott stated that,

> The Law School is privileged to inhabit several of the fine houses of nineteenth and early-twentieth-century Montreal in the "Golden Square Mile", in particular, the James Ross House at 3644 Peel Street. John Brierley, of course, has always had a special interest in the history of Canada and Quebec, and has cherished our historic buildings, trying to ensure that they are properly preserved. About twenty years ago both of us arrived one morning at the same time, surprised to find that the Department of Buildings and Grounds—or whatever it was then called, because it seems to change its name periodically—had planted four evergreen saplings in the fine expanse of lawn just south of Old Chancellor Day Hall. We thought they had been badly placed, and John remarked that no one had bothered to consult him as Dean before planting them. Whenever I see these trees, now twenty feet in height, I become nostalgic for the years which have flown by so quickly.[1037]

And with that, the MLJ said farewell to an editor, Faculty Advisor, Dean, Trustee, and friend.

Other authors that published within the volume included future William C. Donaldson Chair at the McGill Faculty of Law Jean-Guy Belley[1038] and Ian C. Pilarczyk, author of *"A Noble Roster": One Hundred and Fifty Years of Law at McGill*, the official history of the Faculty of Law at McGill. Members of the Editorial Board, alongside Leckey, included Executive Editor Pierre-Hugues Verdier, now an Associate Professor of Law at the University of Virginia, and Managing Editor Robert Keller, now a television actor and professional stand-up comedian. By the end of the year the MLJ was offering free trial online subscriptions to its issues, as one of the only law journals in the world offering full and total access to its issues online at the time.[1039]

The dawn of a new century marked the beginning of many things, but also the end. As Leckey wrote of his time,

> The social culture varied – some people hung out in the *Journal* offices a lot, and others not. There were a handful of people who, like me, clearly enjoyed having the space. Back then before students had cell phones and laptops, it was a big deal to have an office with phones and computers that members of the *Journal* could use whenever they wanted. I wonder if it is less social now there is less advantage in those features.
>
> We used to laugh a lot at the group photos from the 1970s, the hair and clothes. It is funny to think that almost half as much time as separated them from us has now passed since my time at the *Journal*.[1040]

1033 Mereille Delmas-Marty & Marie-Laure Izorche, "Marge nationale d'appréciation et internationalisation du droit : réflexions sur la validité formelle d'un commun pluraliste" (2001) 46:4 *McGill LJ* 923.

1034 Catherine Barnard, "The Changing Scope of the Fundamental Principle of Equality" (2001) 46:4 *McGill LJ* 955.

1035 John EC Brierley "Bibliography: John E.C. Brierley" (2000) 46:1 *McGill LJ* 16.

1036 Alain-François Bisson, "Hommage à John Brierley" (2000) 46:1 *McGill LJ* 9.

1037 Stephen A Scott, "Remarks in Tribute to John Brierley" (2000) 46:1 *McGill LJ* 9 at 9.

1038 Jean-Guy Belley, "Une Justice de la Seconde Modernite: Proposition de Principes Generaux Pour le Prochain Code de Procedure Civile" (2001) 46:2 *McGill LJ* 317.

1039 Hafeez Khan, "Digital News" *McGill Law Journal Newsletter* (December 2000) at 4.

1040 Leckey interview, *supra* note 1009.

Volume forty-seven (the following volume) produced a special issue on "Legislation: Challenges and Perspectives" based on a series of roundtable meetings held by the Quebec Research Centre of Private and Comparative Law. In its preface, a team of writers including Roderick A. MacDonald, Nicholas Kasirer, volume forty-seven Editor-in-Chief Kevin MacLeod, and President of the Law Commission of Canada Nathalie DesRosiers wrote,

> There is something altogether natural in the joining of forces of the Law Commission of Canada, the Quebec Research Centre of Private and Comparative Law of McGill University, and the *McGill Law Journal* for the presentation of this special issue on legislation. Each institution shares a preoccupation with the legislative form and, in particular, with imagining the rightful place of enactment in the catalogue of legal ideas. Since its establishment in 1997, the Law Commission has identified legislation—defined in broad terms—as a central feature of its mandate relating to governance relations. From its inception, too, the Centre of Private and Comparative Law has shown an abiding scholarly interest in the manner and form of legislative enactment, particularly in respect of the fortunes of the *Civil Code of Lower Canada* and the *Civil Code of Quebec. The McGill Law Journal* has, in turn, identified legislation as a lively field of legal research over its fifty-year publication history. All share a bijural and bilingual institutional orientation and an intellectual curiosity about the fundamental nature of law that extends to the polyjural and multilingual dimensions of the legislative form. Indeed all come to legislation as a site for communicative acts in law—a view that serves to tie the papers in this collection loosely together.[1041]

Authors for the issue included future Director of the *Réseau d'études des dynamiques transnationales et de l'action collective* (REDTAC) France Houle.[1042] Authors that contributed to the rest of the volume included future Distinguished Professor Emeritus of Law at the University of South Carolina Henry S. Mather;[1043] future best-selling author Professor Michael Byers;[1044] future Dean of Law at Osgoode Hall Lorne Sossin;[1045] Justice of the Federal Court of Appeal Arthur J. Stone;[1046] and future Acting-Dean of the Faculty of Law at Queen's University as well as Justice of the Ontario Superior Court, Gary T. Trotter.[1047]

This year the annual lecture was provided by Professor Kent Roach of the University of Toronto—a former Dean of Law at the University of Saskatchewan, the Editor-in-Chief of *Criminal Law Quarterly*, and future holder of the Prichard-Wilson Chair of Law and Public Policy at the University of Toronto. Provided on March 27, 2002, his lecture focused on the legal and social impacts of the terrorist attacks of September 11, 2001 (9-11) on New York City and the Pentagon. In discussion of the Canadian *Anti-Terrorism Act* but three months after it received Royal Assent, he wrote that the *Act*,

> introduced new and potentially dangerous legal concepts such as investigative hearings, preventive arrests, broad motive-based crimes based on participation in or contribution to terrorist groups at home or abroad, as well as new powers to list terrorist groups, take their property, and deprive suspected terrorists of sensitive security information in their trials and appeals.[1048]

The full impact of the *Act* on civil society had not yet been seen, but Roach was one of the first to publicly warn of the civil rights abuses that were likely to follow. The subject of those human rights controversies as they materialized would be covered in many articles within the volumes of the MLJ to come.

1041 Nathalie DesRosiers, Nicholas Kasirer, Roderick A MacDonald & Kevin MacLeod, "Legislation: Challenges and Potentials: Preface" (2001) 47:1 *McGill LJ* 2 at 2.

1042 France Houle, "La zone fictive de l'infra-droit : l'intégration des règles administratives dans la catégorie des textes réglementaires" (2001) 47:1 *McGill LJ* 161.

1043 Henry S Mather, "Law-making and Incommensurability" (2002) 47:2 *McGill LJ* 345.

1044 Michael Byers, "Abuse of Rights: An Old Principle, A New Age" (2002) 47:2 *McGill LJ* 389.

1045 Lorne Sossin, "The Rule of Law and the Justiciability of Prerogative Powers: A Comment on *Black v. Chretien*" (2002) 47:2 *McGill LJ* 435.

1046 Arthur J Stone, "Canada's Admiralty Court in the Twentieth Century" (2002) 47:3 *McGill LJ* 511.

1047 Gary T Trotter, "Anger, Provocation, and the Intent for Murder: A Comment on *R. v. Parent*" (2002) 47:3 *McGill LJ* 669.

1048 Kent Roach, "Did September 11 Change Everything - Struggling to Preserve Canadian Values in the Face of Terrorism" (2002) 47:4 *McGill LJ* 893 at 893.

What separated Roach from many of the other vocal academics of the day was his situating of the legislative response to 9-11 within a longer, recent history of legislative philosophy, stating that, "Over the last decade, Parliament has each and every year added new crimes to what is already a thick to bursting *Criminal Code.* Crimes... have been added to the *Criminal Code* not so much because of a legal or technical need to expand its ambit, but because of a political need to respond to and denounce such harms."[1049] He also warned that, "The scary scenario of nuclear or biological terrorism should not blind us to the more likely threats of nuclear or biological accidents."[1050] Indeed, the next major release of radioactive materials onto a population would not occur through terrorism, but during the 2011 Tōhoku earthquake and tsunami.

Even though volume forty-seven occurred in a "cite guide year", where the volume is basically tasked with producing a massive fifth issue in the form of a new edition of the *Guide*, the editorial team managed to stay relatively on track in terms of deadlines.[1051] Part of the reason for this was the new technique of allowing submissions to come in via email.[1052] The Editorial Board of volume forty-seven included English Executive Editor Eric Reiter, who is now an Assistant Professor of History at Concordia University, and responsible for developing their new minor concentration in Law and Society; and Book Review Editor Grégoire Webber, who is now a Lecturer of Law at the London School of Economics.

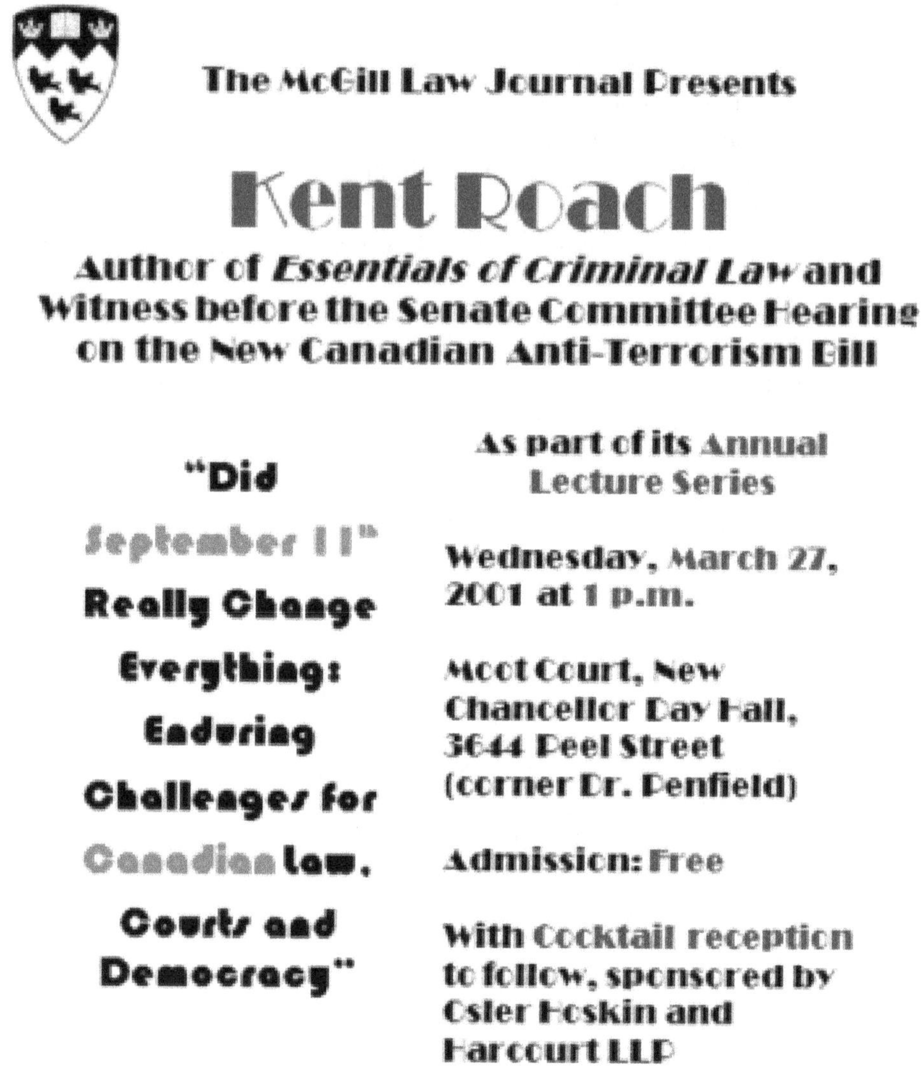

Original McGill Law Journal Annual Lecture poster, used to advertise at the McGill University Faculty of Law.

Volume forty-eight, the following volume, would begin distributing its article evaluation process over the entirety of the Editorial Board with the institution of "first reads"—a method of obtaining a full report on each piece submitted from a member of the board before making a decision on whether or not to send it out on peer review.[1053] The volume would also mark the fiftieth anniversary of the *Journal*. In commemoration of the occasion, the first pages of the volume were dedicated to a re-listing of every editor or manager to ever work for the MLJ in alphabetical order, from 1952 to 2002.[1054] A reception for alumni was also planned.[1055]

1049 *Ibid* at 900.

1050 *Ibid* at 917.

1051 "Memorandum from Kevin MacLeod to the *McGill Law Journal* Trustees and Advisory Board" (30 August, 2002).

1052 Eric Reiter, "Executive Editor—English (Report)" *McGill Law Journal Newsletter* (December 2001) at 2.

1053 Rachel Parsons, "Executive Editor—English (Report)" *McGill Law Journal Newsletter* (January 2003) at 2.

1054 "Editorial Boards / Comités de rédaction" (2003) 48:1 *McGill LJ* 1.

1055 "Memorandum from Carole Chan to the *McGill Law Journal* Trustees and Advisory Board" (13 September , 2002).

Case Comments Editor for volume forty-eight Hilary Stedwill—now associate counsel to Magna Cosma International in Toronto—recalled of her time with the *Journal* that,

> [L]earning to evaluate others' writing sounded like it could be my thing. And, I confess, the prestige of having worked on the editorial board of a law journal appealed to me too. The application process meant submitting [a] paper and attending an interview with the returning associate editors. A little intimidating, but if nothing else, I think they found me charming and appreciated that I was fluent in English and French.
>
> I was disappointed that my associate year consisted largely of checking footnotes. It seemed tedious work. That said, like Mr. Miyagi's "wax on, wax off" teaching method in the *Karate Kid* movies, the experience made me a better researcher and taught me that not all assertions in anyone's argument are equal, and just because it's been footnoted, doesn't mean that it's right or worth believing. I'd love to have another turn at the *Journal* knowing what I know now.[1056]

Executive Editor for the volume Rachel Parsons—now pursuing her PhD in Philosophy at Princeton University—remembered that "Carol Chang, the Editor-in-Chief for our volume, was a hero in that she took up the remaining slack on her own and got the job done" over the summer. She also wrote of another individual still with the *Journal* at the time, "Ultimately, she held it all together. Her stable and reliable presence was invaluable to everyone, and her experience with prior volumes enabled a transmission of knowledge from year to year."[1057] Unsurprisingly, she was speaking of Nicole Leger.

Electronic Editor Hanna Madbak—now an associate with Baker Hostetler LLP in New York City—also recalled his time with the volume, writing,

> Working at the *Journal* had its ups and downs, but none of the difficulties we faced affected the camaraderie between the *Journal* members. There is a funny incident that I will always remember. To celebrate the completion of Volume 48, we planned to have a small party and ordered a cake to congratulate ourselves. Erin Zipes, the managing editor, and I drove to the store to pick up the cake, which we pre-ordered with a "Congratulations MLJ" message. But when we looked at the cake we noticed that the message was misspelled (the "r" was missing). The manager of the store was very apologetic and offered to replace the cake immediately. Erin and I couldn't stop laughing. The manager looked perplexed when we both shouted "this is perfect" and asked her to keep the misspelling and correct it as follows:
>
> √r
>
> "Congatulations MLJ"
>
> At the *Journal* everyone thought it was a clever idea, but no one believed that it was unintentional.[1058]

Authors that contributed to their volume included future President of the Faculty Association for the University of Lethbridge and President of the Confederation of Alberta Faculty Associations, Professor Peter McCormick;[1059] Chief Justice of the Quebec Court of Appeal J.J. Michel Robert;[1060] and future Beller Family Professor of Business Law at New York University Kevin E. Davis.[1061] This volume's *McGill Law Journal* Annual Lecture was provided by Canadian Senator Gérald A. Beaudoin on the topic of judicial review as a controlling factor for the constitutionality of legislation.[1062] The speech was provided on March 21, 2003.

Beaudoin had been a Senator since 1988 and gave the speech during the year before his mandatory retirement at age 75. He was Senate Chair of the Standing Committee on Legal and Constitutional

1056 Interview of Hilary MR Stedwill by James Cummins (3 March, 2011).

1057 Interview of Rachel Parsons by James Cummins (19 November, 2010).

1058 Interview of Hanna F Madbak by James Cummins (14 January, 2011).

1059 Peter McCormick, "With Respect - Levels of Disagreement on the Lamer Court 1990-2000" (2003) 48:1 *McGill LJ* 89.

1060 JJ Michel Robert, "Hommage à L'honorable Juge Charles Gonthier à sa Retraite de la Cour Suprême du Canada" (2003) 48:2 *McGill LJ* 175.

1061 Kevin E Davis, "The Effects of Forfeiture on Third Parties" (2003) 48:2 *McGill LJ* 183.

1062 Gérald A Beaudoin, " Le contrôle judiciaire de la constitutionnalité des lois" (2003) 48:2 *McGill LJ* 325.

Affairs from 1991 to 1996. Interestingly enough, in 2005 he was succeeded as Senator by volume four Articles Editor Yoine J. Goldstein, who held the Senate seat until 2009. Goldstein was himself then succeeded by former Montreal Canadiens head coach Jacques Demers, who was the last head coach to bring the Stanley Cup to Montreal.

Original *McGill Law Journal* Annual Lecture poster, used to advertise at the McGill University Faculty of Law. As a side note, as one knows from the content of this book, though the poster claims that it was the 50th anniversary of the Annual Lecture, it was only the *Journal* that was 50 years old, not the event.

Volume forty-nine, the next volume, would be the last to hold a Board of Trustees meeting. Incoming Managing Editor Tara McPhail came into the meeting with a new investment strategy that would remove the trusteeship of the Board and place it solely with the Dean of the Faculty.[1063] In January of 2004, McPhail undertook the task of dissolving the Board and replacing it with a new Board of Advisors, in order to keep intact the *Journal*'s access to the panel of advisory it had built up over the years, writing to each of the former trustees:

> I am pleased to report that the Law Journal Trust is now officially dissolved. In its place, the Journal has created an endowment account with McGill University, which is held by the Dean of the Faculty of Law and is under the administration of McGill.
>
> Now that the Board of Trustees and the Law Journal Trust are officially dissolved, it is now appropriate to invite you – a former trustee – to become a member of the Journal's Advisory Board. Members of our Advisory Board will have similar duties to those of the former trustees, in that you will advise the Dean as to the investment and disbursement of monies within the endowment fund, and you will act as a general councilor to the executive of the McGill Law Journal through attendance at our yearly board meeting.[1064]

To kick off the year, the volume forty-nine Executive Board invited Justice Charles D. Gonthier to provide a speech at their welcome event.[1065] Gonthier had just recently stepped down

1063 "Minutes of the annual *McGill Law Journal* Board of Trustees meeting" (5 September, 2003).

1064 "Letter from Tara McPhail to Justice Charles D Gonthier" (26 January, 2004).

1065 Toby Moneit, "Editor-in-Chief's Report" *Volume 49 Newsletter* (2003) 1.

from his position on the Court, though his replacement was none other than volume eight Articles Editor Morris J. Fish—another man connected to the MLJ. Volume forty-nine would also see the official adoption of McGill Law's new official educational philosophy within the *McGill Law Journal* mandate. The mission statement within each issue up until and including volume forty-eight read that, "The primary objectives of the Journal are to assist in the scholarly study of the law, to promote original research and understanding of the civil law and common law systems, and to provide a forum for critical analysis of both private and public law issues."[1066] Starting with volume forty-nine, the mission statement would instead read: "The Journal is bilingual, bi-juridical, multidisciplinary, and *transsystemic*. While it focuses on the Canadian context, it remains international in outlook and favours a theoretical approach to legal scholarship."[1067]

The editors of the *McGill Law Journal* are pleased to correspond with new contributors and welcome papers in French or English.

The opinions expressed in the *McGill Law Journal* are solely those of the authors.

The *McGill Law Journal* is produced and published quarterly by the Journal's Editorial Board. The primary objectives of the Journal are to assist in the scholarly study of the law, to promote original research and understanding of the civil law and common law systems, and to provide a forum for critical analysis of both private and public law issues.

The *McGill Law Journal* follows the *Cana-*

Le Comité de rédaction accepte des textes rédigés en français ou en anglais, et accueille les contributions de nouveaux auteurs.

Les opinions exprimées dans la *Revue de droit de McGill* n'engagent que la responsabilité des auteurs.

La *Revue de droit de McGill* paraît trimestriellement. Le Comité de rédaction publie la Revue afin de contribuer à l'étude du droit, de promouvoir la recherche fondamentale et la compréhension des régimes de droit civil et de *common law*. La Revue sert aussi de tribune pour l'analyse critique des questions de droit privé et de droit public.

Mission Statement from Volume 48.

The McGill Law Journal is a student-run, peer-reviewed quarterly journal affiliated with the Faculty of Law at McGill University. The Journal is bilingual, bi-juridical, multidisciplinary, and transsystemic. While it focuses on the Canadian context, it remains international in outlook and favours a theoretical approach to legal scholarship.

The Journal accepts submissions of articles, case

La Revue de droit de McGill est dirigée par des étudiants et les textes qui y sont publiés sont révisés par des pairs. Elle est affiliée à la Faculté de droit de McGill et paraît trimestriellement. Elle est bilingue, bijuridique, multidisciplinaire et transsystémique. Si elle se concentre sur le contexte juridique canadien, la Revue recherche une perspective internationale et favorise une approche théorique du droit.

Mission Statement from Volume 49.

Executive Editor for volume forty-nine Regan Morris—now a legal counsel with the Office of the Privacy Commissioner of Canada—wrote of his time with the *Journal* that,

> Now that I have had more experience editing other people's work I can see why from time to time some authors would get frustrated with all the changes we wanted to make! I'm also amazed, looking back, how confident we were that, as law students, we could make substantive changes to an article written by long-tenured professors. Not to say that that confidence was always misplaced because we did often improve the article …
>
> I don't have many specific memories. What I remember is more general feelings and impressions. I remember struggling to understand an article that was heavy on philosophy with two colleagues and being exhausted (but stimulated) by the experience. I remember working at the *Journal* the summer I was an executive editor, which was fun. I basically got to spend the summer working side by side with 3 other executives, two of whom were close friends. It was fun because it was when we got to think about our plans for improving the journal and deciding what we wanted the upcoming year to be like. I remember coming to the *Journal* between classes, feeling like it was a safe haven I could come to relax and see friends. And I remember feeling pride that, for the final issue of our volume, we had put together a special issue on law and sexuality that was cutting-edge, interesting and very timely (three good criteria for any *Journal* issue).[1068]

The special issue Morris is talking about, titled "Beyond Sexuality", was prefaced by Professor Davina Cooper, Director of the AHRB Research Centre for Law, Gender and Sexuality at the University of Kent Law School. She wrote:

> The argument has been made that giving rights and respectability to some lesbians and gay men goes hand in hand with the squeezing out of others. This bifurcated political strategy is

1066 (2003) 48:1 *McGill LJ* ii at ii.

1067 (2003) 49:1 *McGill LJ* ii at ii. Added Emphasis.

1068 Interview of Regan Morris by James Cummins (9 January, 2011).

> a common one, witnessed in relation to sexual orientation regulation at many times and places. One way of reading such normative adjustments is through the resettlement and consolidation of "community standards". As both a legal term and political metaphor, this concept weaves its way through the collection.[1069]

The special issue included this volume's Annual Lecture, which was provide on March 5, 2004 by John Fisher, the founding Executive Director of Egale Canada—who, in 1993, was the first openly-gay individual to address a United Nations World Conference. The Executive Board wanted the lecture of that year to fit specifically with their special issue.[1070]

The speech, in the tradition of the renewed series of lectures, was linked to one of the hottest issues of the time—the lecture was given fourteen days before Quebec officially made same-sex marriage legal and approximately one year before Parliament passed the *Civil Marriage Act*. As of the date of the speech, only Ontario and British Columbia had yet made same-sex marriage legal. These swift legislative moves are stunning when remembering the context of that period of time. Fisher stated in his speech/article that,

> Ten years ago, I attended the 1994 International Year of the Family conference in Montreal, where, of course, there was no mention of same-sex families. Being somewhat new to LGBT advocacy in those days, I rather timidly approached the microphone and suggested that lesbians and gays have families too, which are entitled to equal recognition, only to be told that "this is a conference about families, not the promotion of homosexuality."
>
> What a difference ten years makes![1071]

However, Fisher did speak further of how far society still needed to grow, stating that,

> In my view, the responsibility of our community organizations is to maximize the opportunity of all members of our communities to celebrate their identity free from discrimination in a manner consistent with their personal aspirations, whether they be mainstream or on the margins. Those who wish to marry should have that equal choice … Whether the Charter is a sufficiently flexible vehicle to protect the full diversity of our communities, however, remains to be seen.[1072]

1069 Davina Cooper, "Introduction" (2004) 49:4 *McGill LJ* 809 at 812.

1070 "Annual Meeting of the Advisory Board of the *McGill Law Journal*—Advisor Package" (27 September, 2004).

1071 John Fisher, "Outlaws or In-Laws: Successes and Challenges in the Struggle for LGBT Equality" (2004) 49:4 *McGill LJ* 1183 at 1187.

1072 *Ibid* at 1207-08.

Other authors that contributed to the volume included Justice Louis LeBel of the Supreme Court of Canada;[1073] future Dean of Law at Dalhousie University Kim Brooks;[1074] the Tomlinson Professor of Shakespeare Studies at McGill University Paul Yachnin;[1075] future Director of the Human Rights Center at Durham University Faculty of Law Ian Leigh;[1076] and former Dean of Law at Osgoode Hall and President of York University, Harry Arthurs.[1077]

During volume fifty, the following volume, students from Osgoode Hall approached the MLJ with a new project. They had decided to develop what they called a "Guide to the Guide"; a crib-notes-like document they had produced on the subject of the *Guide* that they wanted to publish. The project was put together as a part of an Osgoode Hall legal methodology class,[1078] with the idea of making the guide more accessible to first year students.[1079] However the students involved graduated before they could really make headway and the project was abandoned[1080] before they were able produce a manuscript different enough from the *Guide* to publish.[1081]

In the meantime, volume fifty attached itself still further to the new age of the McGill Programme, by publishing a special

1073 Louis LeBel "La protection des droits fondamentaux et la responsabilité civile" (2004) 49:2 *McGill LJ* 231.

1074 Kim Brooks, "Delimiting the Concept of Income: The Taxation of In-Kind Benefits" (2004) 49:2 *McGill LJ* 255.

1075 Desmond Manderson & Paul Yachnin, "Love on Trial: Nature, Law, and Same-Sex Marriage in the Court of Shakespeare" (2004) 49:3 *McGill LJ* 475.

1076 Rex Ahdar & Ian Leigh, "Is Establishment Consistent with Religious Freedom" (2004) 49:3 *McGill LJ* 635.

1077 Harry Arthurs, "Constitutional Courage" (2003) 49:1 *McGill LJ* 1.

1078 "Memorandum from Christine Stecura to the *McGill Law Journal* Board of Advisors" (28 September, 2004).

1079 Interview of Shelley Kierstead by James Cummins (11 November, 2011).

1080 *Ibid.*

1081 Stecura memo, *supra* note 1078.

issue named "Navigating the Transsystemic". In the preface to the number Professor Shauna van Praagh—Faculty Advisor to the *Journal* that year—wrote:

> Naming this special issue of the *McGill Law Journal* was not easy. On the one hand, editors wanted to give the issue a substantive label, to suggest the content in a clear and informative way. On the other, they wanted to incorporate the dynamism and diversity of the authors' work in a way that no one term could capture. Caught in a dilemma that mirrored the one their own professors faced at McGill's Faculty of Law in 1999, the student editors could have gone the *sui generis* route. Just as the academic programme at the faculty—characterized as integrated, pluralist, and polyjural—is called simply "The McGill Programme", this issue of the Law Journal might have been named simply "The McGill Issue". After all, it is McGill students who have invited these authors and indeed the very faculty in which the Journal is housed into the reflective mode captured by this collection.[1082]

The issue contained several prestigious authors, each of which had been published before by the MLJ.

The Annual Lecture for this volume was provided on March 16, 2005[1083] by Thomas R. Berger, a former Justice of the Supreme Court of British Columbia who resigned from the court in 1982 over the lack of fairness shown by provincial law to aboriginal peoples. He was also leader of the New Democrat Party in British Columbia during the 1960s. One year after the Lecture Berger would author the *Nunavut Land Claims Agreement Implementation Contract Negotiations for the Second Planning Period 2003-2013* as Conciliator for the Nunavut Land Claims Agreement Implementation Contract—a position he was appointed to mere months after giving the Annual Lecture. The agreement represented the largest land claim in modern history.

Berger talked about his career as a lawyer and justice. Perhaps most pertinent to the university he was speaking at, he stated,

> Frank Scott became one of my heroes, and in 1963 we went to the Supreme Court together to argue the *Oil, Chemical and Atomic Workers* case against the Attorney General for British Columbia. Frank argued it and I was his junior, carrying his bags. In that period it wasn't just Premier Duplessis who brought in repressive legislation. Premier W.A.C. Bennett of British Columbia brought in a law which said that trade unions could not contribute to political parties. You can guess the political party that he did not want them to contribute to. There was no equivalent restriction on contributions by corporations. We lost by four judges to three at the Supreme Court, but it was an opportunity for me to get to know Frank. I recall as a young man still in my twenties, from the backwoods of British Columbia coming down to Montreal to work on our factum, he took me out to a lovely restaurant on Saint Helen's Island, and he did something I had never seen anyone do: when our wine was brought and he was asked to sample it, he sent it back![1084] I've never had the courage to do that myself, but it's something I've never forgotten.[1085]

Berger also spoke about his role in *Calder et al. v. Attorney-General of British Columbia*, which he also argued before the Supreme Court, stating,

> The action was brought in the name of Frank Calder, who was the president of the Nisga'a Tribal Council.
>
> When the Nisga'a first came to see me, I had a walk-up law office and my widowed mother was my secretary. I remember the Nisga'a chiefs entering my office; there wasn't enough room for all of us to sit down, and they must have wondered, "Who is this young guy that we're entrusting our case to?" The rent was $120 for the whole office. Out of that came the case that went to Ottawa and led to the judgment of the Supreme Court, resulting in treaties being made since 1973 that now cover half of the land mass of Canada.[1086]

1082 Shauna Van Praagh, "Navigating the Transsystemic: A Course Syllabus" (2005) 50:4 *McGill LJ* 701at 701.

1083 "One Man's Justice" Events release from McGill University, online: < http://www.mcgill.ca/channels/events/item/?item_id=14459 >

1084 The restaurant was called Hélène-de-Champlain, the only restaurant on the island at the time.

1085 Thomas R Berger, "One Man's Justice: My Life in the Courts" (2005) 50:4 *McGill LJ* 987 at 989.

1086 *Ibid* at 991-92.

The Editorial Board included future MLJ Board of Advisor member Fabien Fourmanoit, and Lucas Stanczyk, now an Assistant Professor of Political Science at the Massachusetts Institute of Technology (MIT). This would also be the first year where the MLJ would no longer be the only student Editorial Board at the McGill Faculty of Law. In early 2005 the first issue of the *McGill International Journal of Sustainable Development Law and Policy* (JSDLP), a fellow student-run operation, was published According to the founding Editor-in-Chief of the JSDLP Michelle Toering Sanders in her inaugural inscription:

> The JSDLP was conceived two years [prior] by McGill law students who recognized the deficiency of fora for informed debate on issues relating to sustainable development … Never has a concept generated such an aggressive exchange of ideas across so many industries, agencies, and levels of society. It is this dialogue that will hopefully enable us, as a society, to promote rather than detract from the economic, social, and environmental rights of individuals and communities across the globe.[1087]

Her words echoed the statement of future Governor General David Johnston long before in the MLJ's special issue on sustainability. Their first issue was also graced with an introductory note from Justice Charles D. Gonthier, who wrote further that,

> The creation of this journal, so timely as it is, as an encouragement to research and communication in the many fields encompassed under sustainable development law and policy, is auspicious and promising as the fruit of the initiative, intelligence and creativity of a few persons, who through their enthusiasm and commitment, have aroused and channelled the commitment and enthusiasm of many others and continue to do so together.[1088]

Dear Subscriber to the *McGill Law Journal*:

You will find enclosed the inaugural issue of a new journal being launched at McGill's Faculty of Law: the *McGill International Journal of Sustainable Development Law and Policy* ("JSDLP"). The JSDLP is an independent, student-run, peer-reviewed journal similar to the *McGill Law Journal* ("MLJ"). However, it is not run by or affiliated with the MLJ.

The editors of the MLJ are distributing this first issue to all of our subscribers free of charge as a demonstration of our support for this project; we are not, however, responsible for its content. If you wish to continue receiving the JSDLP, please contact them directly at the address provided below.

We hope that you enjoy your free copy of this exciting new contribution to the discourse on sustainable development.

Sincerely,

The Editors of the *McGill Law Journal*, Vol. 50

McGill International Journal of Sustainable Development Law and Policy

Mailing address:
McGill University, Faculty of Law
3661 Peel St.
Montreal, Quebec
H3A 1X1

Fax number: +1 514 398-8197
Email: jsdlp.law@mcgill.ca
For more information, please visit their website: www.law.mcgill.ca/jsdlp

Letter from the MLJ to its subscribers regarding the distribution of JSDLP volume one.

While only putting out a single issue in their first volume, from volume two onwards the JSDLP would produce two issues per year. In the spirit of G.V.V. Nicholls, the MLJ provided advice to the new journal whenever it was needed as the new publication was first becoming established. The MLJ even went so far as to send a free issue of JSDLP volume one to every one of its subscribers

1087 Michelle Toering Sanders, "Editor's Note" (2005) 1:1 *JSDLP* 3 at 3.

1088 Charles D Gonthier, "Introductory Note" (2005) 1:1 *JSDLP* 17 at 17.

free of charge to get the word out. As time would go by, many MLJ editors would experience their first footnoting and editorial duties with the JSDLP before joining the MLJ—as the JSDLP would allow first years students to join as associate editors, before their eligibility for the MLJ.

Those editors include volume fifty-five Solicitations Editor Justin Dubois, who was French Editor for JSDLP volume five; volume fifty-five Executive Editor (Coordinating) Sarah Walker, who was a senior editor for JSDLP volume five; volume fifty-six senior editor Andreea Vasiliu, who was also a senior editor for JSDLP volume six; volume fifty-six Editor-in-Chief Sara Ross, who was Book Review Editor for JSDLP volume six, and who in her associate year with volume fifty-five became the first student in McGill Law history to receive credits from two different journals in the same academic year; volume fifty-seven Editor-in-Chief Will Colish, who was a senior editor for JSDLP volume seven; and volume fifty-eight Citations Editor Montano Cabezas, who was a senior editor for the JSDLP volume eight. Each editor had also served on the JSDLP associate board in the year prior to their special position with the publication, and served their senior position with the JSDLP during their associate year with the MLJ.

The Editor-in-Chief of the JSDLP, at this time, was responsible for appointing all special editors to their positions, in contrast to the electoral process that occurs at the MLJ. The JSDLP does provide credits for these senior positions, though not the associate positions, which is something that began with volume six, also with the help of the MLJ. As volume fifty-six Editor-in-Chief Sara Ross recalls, "The JSDLP and MLJH were lobbying in my associate year with them to get credits, and the MLJ was helping them in terms of credits per work hours that should be dedicated per task ..."[1089]

Book Review Editor for the next volume, fifty-one, Aleksandar Zivanovic—now counsel for John Hancock Financial Services in Boston—recalled the feeling about law journals around the Faculty of Law around this time, stating that,

> For most students it is probably a purely instrumental means to career development but there's tremendous pedagogical potential that can be transformational if done right. [I]t is an opportunity to be and do much more than get 4 books out the door in record time and compile meaningless citation statistics. It can be a mode of inquiry into fresh thinking about old problems, a way to blaze frontiers of legal thought, an entrée into a sense of community. Or it can be a to-do list. It is whatever the group is motivated to make of it.[1090]

Zivanovic stated that he learned over the year that "leadership is about more than just getting the job done."[1091]

Earlier in the year, volume fifty-one invited Michael Ignatieff, future Leader of the Liberal Party of Canada and future Leader of the Official Opposition in Parliament, to speak before the *Journal* membership at a round-table event concentrating on the United States as both leader and outlier in matters of human rights discourse.[1092] The event took place on September 30, 2005,[1093] the day after Ignatieff had served as keynote speaker at the International Conference on Customary International Law held jointly by the McGill Faculty of Law and the Canadian Red Cross.[1094]

The Annual Lecture was then provided on February 15, 2006 by volume two Advertising Editor and former Justice of the Quebec Superior Court John H. Gomery. In his interview, Gomery wrote of the experience that, "I was honoured and flattered. It is most agreeable to have the approval of your peers who really know you."[1095] At the time Gomery was most famous for his role as Commissioner of what came to be known as the *Gomery Report*—investigating the Liberal Party of Canada in one of the most recent corruption scandals in Canadian history. The Lecture was given fourteen days after the final phase of his *Report of the Commission of Inquiry into the Sponsorship Program and Advertising Activities* was released to the public. In effect, Gomery and Ignatieff would be the two most poignant influences on the Liberal Party of Canada of that decade, and both came to the MLJ to share their thoughts within months of one another.

1089 Interview of Sara Ross by James Cummins (6 November, 2011; 30 December, 2011; and 14 May, 2012). Interview done in person over several dates.

1090 Interview of Aleksander Zivanovic by James Cummins (19 November, 2010).

1091 *Ibid.*

1092 "Letter from volume fifty-one Executive Board of the *McGill Law Journal* to *McGill Law Journal* alumni" (3 March, 2006).

1093 Kristin Ali, "Memorandum to the Members of the Advisory Board" MLJ Editorial Board (18 September, 2005).

1094 "Michael Ignatieff to Deliver Keynote Address of the International Conference on Customary International Law", Canadian Red Cross press release (21 September, 2005). online: < http://www.redcross.ca/article.asp?id=14767&tid=001 >

1095 Gomery interview, *supra* note 50.

Original McGill Law Journal Annual Lecture poster, used to advertise at the McGill University Faculty of Law

In his speech/article Gomery wrote, "When I was asked to deliver the *McGill Law Journal* annual lecture, I was enormously flattered, and found myself unable to refuse, in spite of my determination not to become a 'conférencier' once my duties as a commissioner had come to an end as they have, now, come to an end."[1096] Gomery, of course, could not share intimate details of the proceedings and his thoughts therein, however inside details of his work were not the most important thing Gomery could offer to posterity; his vision of the usefulness of the instrument he was just a part of, as perhaps the highest profile individual to do so in a century, was of the truest value to the study of law. On this experience he stated,

> [T]here's a danger that a judge who's presiding over a commission of inquiry will be perceived as having a political role to play and the only way he can avoid that is by acting as judges are supposed to act, which is impartially and without bias, without disclosing any preference for any side of the various arguments that are presented to him.[1097]

The magnitude and importance of this speech, given the context of the time, was reflected in the editorial choice to include not only the speech but the question and answer period that followed as well in its publication—something that would only occur with the publication of one other Annual Lecture (Carlos Fuentes in 2011).

To that end, one of the audience members asked Gomery if he had, upon being asked to Chair the Commission, "any initial misgivings and did you anticipate in any way the magnitude and the complexity and the scope of the work that awaited you?"[1098] Gomery responded, in a way reminiscent of John Humphrey's self-directed analysis provided nearly twenty years beforehand, that,

> I didn't have the slightest idea of what I was getting into. I knew that it was a major task and I thought it would take about two years, which is what it did take, but I had no idea that I would uncover, or that the inquiry would uncover some of the facts that were uncovered. I thought we were dealing with poor administration of a government program within government, and people were interested in where the money went and our inquiry pursued that line of questioning. But we certainly had not anticipated, I don't think anybody anticipated, that we'd be hearing stories about wads of money in brown envelopes being passed in bars and things like that. So, I was not prepared for that and

1096 Gomery article, *supra* note 48 at 784.

1097 *Ibid* at 795.

1098 *Ibid* at 797.

> I had not anticipated either the intense media coverage that occurred, which was in itself a source of concern.[1099]

As volume fifty-two senior editor Héloïse Robinson wrote, "I ... remember the speech given by Justice Gomery ... At the time, the Commission of Inquiry into the sponsorship program was headline news, and the speech by the judge drew a large and very interested crowd."[1100] She also added, regarding a brief part at the front of his speech and the cocktail afterwards that "it was great to hear as well of Justice Gomery's time as an editor for the *Journal*, in 1955."[1101] Other contributors to volume fifty-one included Purdy Crawford Chair in Business Law at the Dalhousie Faculty of Law Christopher C. Nicholls,[1102] and future Director of the Human Rights Centre at the University of Ottawa's Faculty of Law Karen Eltis.[1103]

Volume fifty-two, the following volume, started out with a contest, but unlike the $1000 French essay contest of volume forty-six, this contest was more in-house—to win a free lunch at Thompson House (the McGill graduate student house), MLJ members were asked to name all the computers in the *Journal* offices. The winner of the competition was the previous volume's Editor-in-Chief Kristin Ali, as volume fifty-two Managing Editor Meagan Hough wrote in the Alumni Newsletter, "with her suggestion to name each computer after a member of the Group of Seven because, in her words, 'The Group of Seven offers Canada great works of art, and so does the MLJ'."[1104] It seems that the sense of humour held by those earlier boards never did leave the institution.

By then the "development project" of the MLJ was a great success, whereby the *Journal* distributed free one-year subscriptions to countries in development and a fifty percent discount on the subscription following the first year.[1105] The project had begun with volume forty-six, when according to minutes from the March 1, 2001 Annual General Meeting of the MLJ, "Working in conjunction with faculty members and the Dean ... [we] identified 35 needy institutions in 31 different countries that would receive free subscriptions beginning with volume 46."[1106] The program began through a recommendation of the Dean—Peter Leuprecht—at the 2000 Board of Trustees meeting, who had noticed that international subscriptions to the MLJ were entirely to Western Europe and thought that free subscriptions should be sent to developing countries.[1107]

Yet this wasn't the first time that such an ethic took precedence over subscription revenues. Volume twelve Editor-in-Chief Stephen A. Scott recalled that during his tenure:

> Th[e]se were the years of the Vietnam War and the University of Hu⊠ stopped paying us ... you can look at film documentaries of war in the streets of Hu⊠, which was a prize because of its historic character, but we just decided, hell, we're gonna just keep putting a copy into the mail and not cut them off. So everything was done a little bit off-the-cuff.[1108]

Contributors to volume fifty-two included the soon-to-be Dean of the Faculty of Law at Harvard University Martha L. Minow.[1109] The Annual Lecture this volume was provided on February 28, 2007 by W.C. Graham Professor of Law at the University of Toronto Patrick Macklem on the subject of human rights law. Members of the Editorial and Management Boards of that volume included Editor-in-Chief David Sandomierski, currently a legal instructor at the Arts and Sciences Faculty of McMasters University.

During volume fifty-three, the following volume, a radical shift was made. A full vote of the *Journal* Editorial and Management boards was taken to adopt an "open access" publication model. Computers had begun to influence more than just the way the *Journal* contacted its authors, accepted submissions, and edited its first drafts. Now the Internet had forced a new methodology behind distribution down the throats of all those in the publishing business. What had occurred in the music industry a decade earlier was now happening with books and periodicals.

1099 *Ibid.*

1100 Interview of Héloïse Robinson by James Cummins (17 January, 2011).

1101 *Ibid.*

1102 Christopher C Nicholls, "Lock-ups, Squeeze-outs, and Canadian Takeover Bid Law: A Curious Interplay of Public and Private Interests" (2006) 51:2 *McGill LJ* 407.

1103 Karen Eltis, "La surveillance du courrier électronique en milieu de travail : le Québec succombera t-il à l'influence de l'approche américaine" (2006) 51:3 *McGill LJ* 475.

1104 "Managing Editor's Report in McGill Law Journal Newsletter" MLJ Editorial Board (November 2006) at 2.

1105 *Ibid* at 4.

1106 "Minutes of the *McGill Law Journal* Annual General Meeting" (1 March, 2001).

1107 Minutes August 00, *supra* note 990.

1108 Scott interview, *supra* note 278.

1109 Martha L Minow, "Living up to Rules: Holding Soldiers Responsible for Abusive Conduct and the Dilemma of the Superior Orders Defence" (2007) 52:1 *McGill LJ* 1.

So, volume fifty-three Case Comments Editor James Grohsgal (now an associate with Skadden, Arps, Slate, Meagher & Flom LLP in New York City) insisted in the MLJ Annual General Meeting "that open access is inevitable and we could be trailblazers."[1110] A vote was taken on whether or not to move the full articles of each prior MLJ volume online for free, and that vote was passed. From that day forward, the *Journal* would post issues online for free as soon as the market for immediate readership had passed. With this vote on February 18, 2008, the MLJ became the first open access general law journal in Canada.[1111] The *Harvard Law Review* would follow suit with its own vote the following month (March, 2008).[1112]

Once again, the MLJ led the way. As of the May of 2012 (four years later), the *McGill Law Journal* was one of only two general law journal in Canada to offer its entire history of back issues—right back to volume one, issue one—for free on its website. The only other journals that came close to offering this much content for free were the *Ottawa Law Review*, which was still holding back its first six issues, and the *Cahiers des Droit*, which finally made all of its issues open access in early 2012 (it had not done so as of the end of 2011) via the web service Érudit. The nation was though, slowly but surely, following the path blazed by the MLJ—with additional top-tier journals like the *Alberta Law Review* and the *Osgoode Hall Law Journal* moving to put at the very least their most recent issues up on their website.

The Annual Lecturer for this year was Justice Pierre J. Dalphond of the Quebec Court of Appeal.[1113] Other contributors to the volume included Giuseppina D'Agostino,[1114] founder and Director of the Intellectual Property Law and Technology Program at Osgoode Hall; and the future Director of the Frances Lewis Law Center at the Washington and Lee University Faculty of Law, Joshua A.T. Fairfield.[1115] Stephanie Jones, senior editor for the volume, only recently removed from the experience,

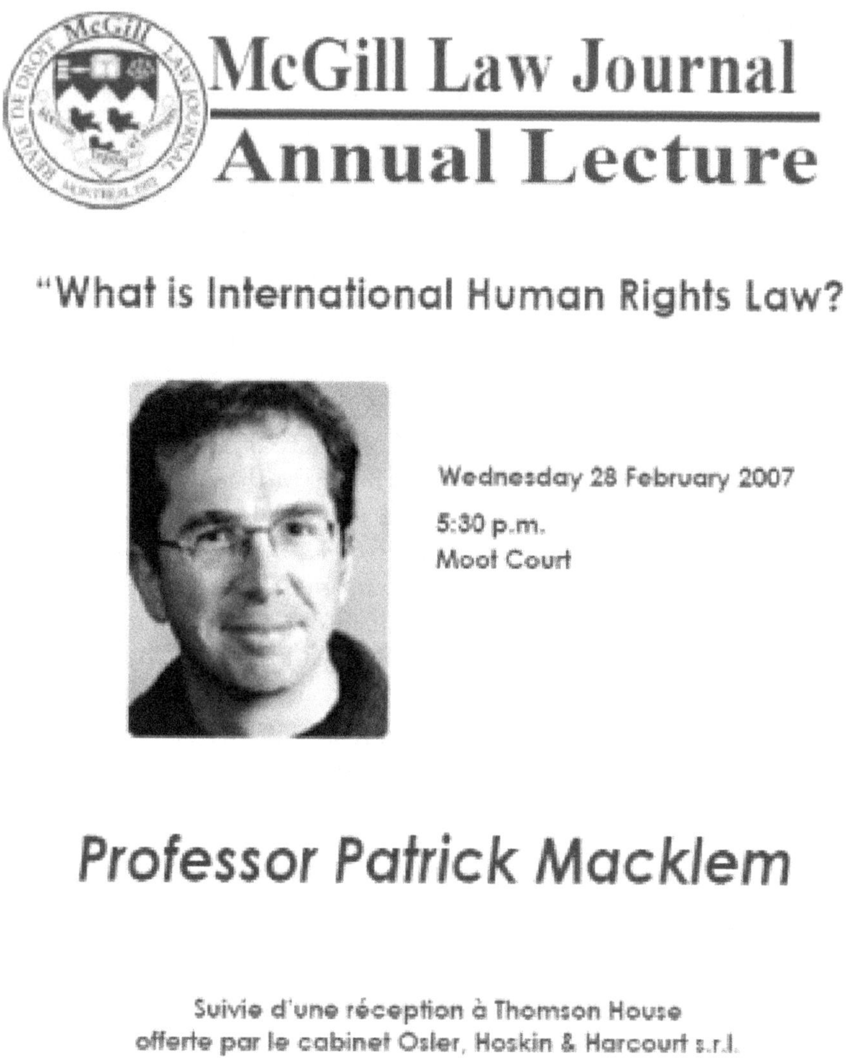

Original McGill Law Journal Annual Lecture poster, used to advertise at the McGill University Faculty of Law

1110 "Minutes of the *McGill Law Journal* Annual General Meeting" (18 February, 2008).

1111 *Ibid.*

1112 Josh Wilner, "Editors' Note – Open Access to Legal Scholarship" (2008) 2:1 *McGill JL & Health* 1 at 3.

1113 Pierre J Dalphon, "La doctrine a-t-elle un avenir au Québec" (2008) 53:3 *McGill LJ* 517.

1114 Giuseppina D'Agostino, "Healing Fair Dealing - A Comparative Copyright Analysis of Canada's Fair Dealing to U.K. Fair Dealing and U.S. Fair Use" (2008) 53:2 *McGill LJ* 309.

1115 Joshua AT Fairfield, "Anti-Social Contracts: The Contractual Governance of Virtual Worlds" (2008) 53:3 *McGill LJ* 427.

wrote that, "It is true that there were some late nights in the library and/or the law journal office. There are still late nights and, in retrospect, although my MLJ colleagues and I are now scattered around the world, we do look back on our MLJ late nights with a bit of nostalgia."[1116]

During this year yet another specialty journal began publishing at McGill Law: the *McGill Health Law Publication* (MHLP). The publication would begin as a purely online journal without printed copies and not move from one issue per year to two until 2010.[1117] First published in 2007, the founding Editors-in-Chief Daniel L. Ambrosini and Reuven Ashtar wrote at the beginning of their first issue that,

> The term "health law" is highly charged. For us, it refers to the legal challenges presented by an increasingly intricate interweaving of health, technology, and medical research as it is brought to bear on public policy and social concerns ... Eschewing a designated theme, we have assembled an intentionally diverse anthology.[1118]

Then-Dean Nicholas Kasirer—senior editor of MLJ volume thirty—also provided a foreword to their first issue, writing,

> The advent of a scholarly journal, particularly in a context where public funding for higher education and research is so severely challenged, is an occasion to celebrate. The travails associated with developing a mission statement, soliciting articles and mounting a first issue are often enough to contain the most well-meaning enthusiasm. The Faculty could not be prouder of the students who have conceived and brought to fruition this important new institution in the intellectual life of McGill University ... it is a student-run journal, and as such allies itself with a powerful and vigorous tradition at McGill ... the journal fixes on an emerging body of ideas—health law—and gives it ... new visibility and new substantive shape.[1119]

The MHLP would be renamed the *McGill Journal of Law and Health* (MJLH) in 2008.[1120]

Editors from the MJLH that would also edit on the *McGill Law Journal* included volume fifty-four senior editor Dorian Needham, who would serve as Executive Editor for MJLH volume two and Executive Managing Editor of volume three; volume fifty-four Executive Editor Sophie Tremblay, who would serve as senior editor for MJLH volume two; volume fifty-five Executive Editor Stephan Szpajda, who was senior editor for MJLH volume three; volume fifty-seven senior editor Adela Gotz, who was an editor for MLJH volume four; volume fifty-eight senior editor Michael Shortt, who was English Executive Editor for MJLH volume five; and volume fifty-eight senior editor Carmen Barbu, who was an editor for MJLH volume five. By the time volume fifty-eight had hired its new associate board, hiring MLJ editors with experience on the other McGill Law journals had become the norm—as the volume fifty-eight Executive hired four associates that had served on the MLJH and four that had served on the JSDLP. A total of more than 50% of their new hires had previously worked on one of the two specialist journals at the Faculty during their first year.

Even though, as the past few volumes have borne out, the history from this point forward has really yet to have been written, the next four completed volumes as of this book's writing accomplished some impressive achievements. Volume fifty-four included another special section dedicated to the proceedings of the *l'Association Henri Capitant*,[1121] featuring authors like Benoît Moore,[1122] holder of the *Jean-Louis Baudouin en droit civil* Chair at the Université de Montréal—a Chairship named for the previous prefacer of most of *l'Association*'s past special sections, each produced from their proceedings. Other contributors to the volume included the Thomas Pickles Professor of Law at Tulane University Vernon Valentine Palmer;[1123] and past Executive Legal Officer of the Supreme Court of Canada Robin Elliot.[1124]

1116 Interview of Stephanie Jones by James Cummins (23 November, 2010).

1117 Michael le Huynh, "Editors' Note" (2010) 4:1 *McGill JL & Health* 1 at 1.

1118 Daniel L Ambrosini & Reuven Ashtar, "Editors' Note" (2007) 1:1 *McGill JL & Health* 1 at 1.

1119 Nicholas Kasirer, "Foreword" (2007) 1:1 *McGill JL & Health*, 3 at 3.

1120 Wilner, *supra* note 1112 at 1.

1121 Erin Morgan, "Préface" (2009) 54:2 *McGill LJ* 221.

1122 Benoît Moore, "Culture et Droit de la Famille: De L'institution a L'Autonomie Individuelle" (2009) 54:2 *McGill LJ* 257.

1123 Vernon Valentine Palmer, "Quebec and Her Sisters in the Third Legal Family" (2009) 54:2 *McGill LJ* 321.

1124 Shi-Lin Hsu & Robin Elliot, "Regulating Greenhouse Gases in Canada: Constitutional and Policy Dimensions" (2009) 54:3 *McGill LJ* 463.

The Annual Lecture during this year was given by John Ralston Saul—world renowned philosopher and future President of PEN International (becoming only the second North American to serve in this position, the other being the legendary playwright Arthur Miller), and former Vice-Regal Consort of Canada, as husband of former Governor General Adrienne. His speaking was, in fact, a result of Clarkson's inability to give the lecture herself due to health reasons.[1125]

In the lecture, provided on February 3, 2009, Saul spoke in a way that well-followed Thomas R. Berger who spoke as Annual Lecturer just short of four years before him.[1126] While speaking of the central role that aboriginals have played in Canadian history and culture he asked,

> [I]s this romanticism? Do we say that the British are romantic because they keep referring to events and documents stretching back to the Magna Carta? Do we call the French romantic because they approach their current situations out of assumptions, decisions and commitments made under Richelieu or during the French Revolution? They have to go back to these roots because these are the foundations upon which they built their modern state.
>
> We built our nation-state through the treaties. You can give a cynical or ugly interpretation to that. Or you can put a pretty picture on it. Or, indeed, you can be as utilitarian as possible and simply say, "that's what happened". But without a conscious acceptance of the full role of the treaties, all we are left with are deeply colonial, deeply romantic interpretations. Without the treaties, what we have been doing here for hundreds of years is nothing more than short-term and temporary. You only have a civilization if you are willing to come to terms with its fundamental roots.[1127]

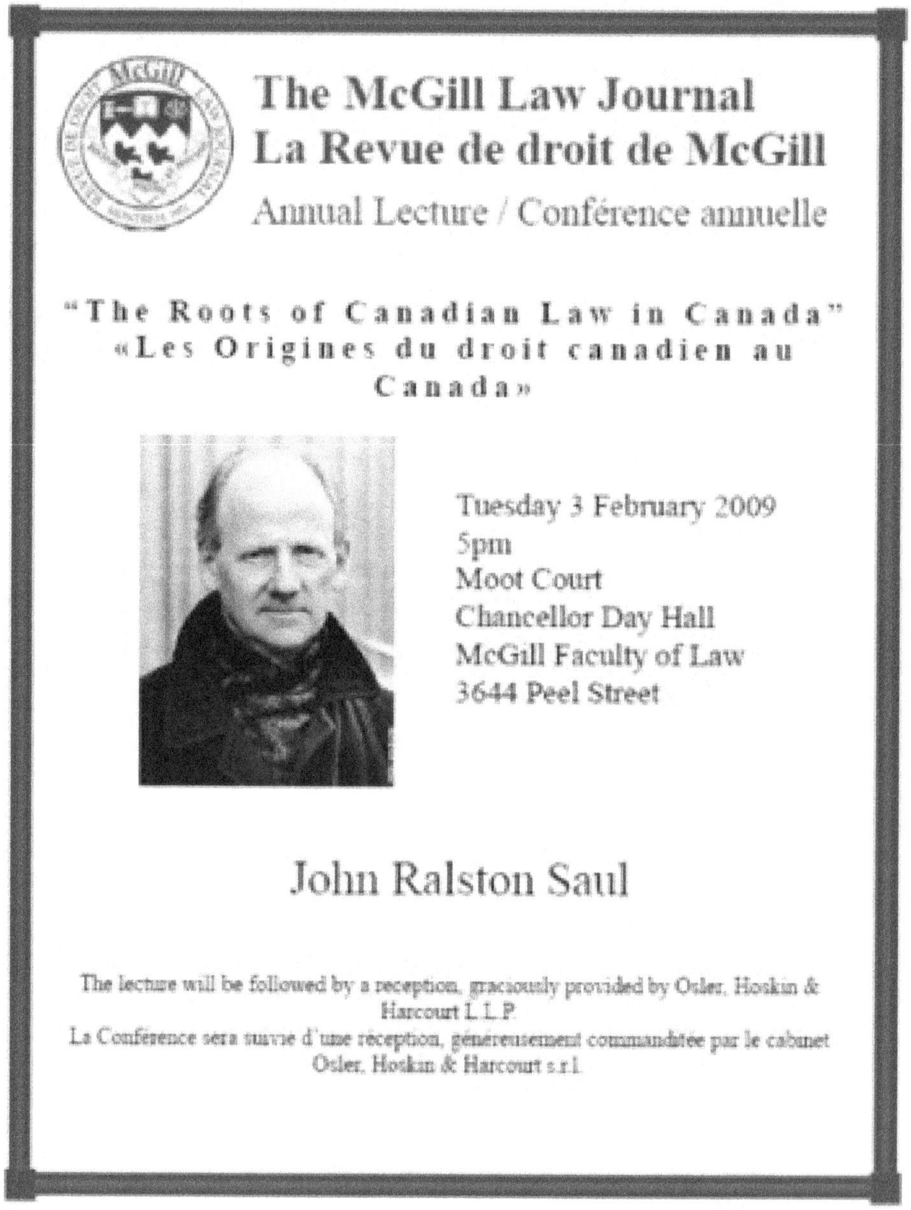

advertise at the McGill University Faculty of Law

Following up on the ideas he had written into his latest book *A Fair Country*,[1128] Saul inspired a fiery debate among his audience, which is the exact kind of shaking-free of complacency that Humphrey, Scott, and Brierley had tried to inspire long before him. The volume was also

1125 "Minutes of the annual *McGill Law Journal* Board of Advisors meeting" (7 November, 2008).

1126 John Ralston Saul, "The Roots of Canadian Law in Canada" (2009) 54:4 *McGill LJ* 671 at 675.

1127 *Ibid* at 676.

1128 *Ibid* at 671.

the first to introduce the use of social media, using the social media site Facebook to invite the McGill Law student body to the events like the Annual Lecture and recruitment events.[1129] The use of social media became ingrained within the culture, and a major method of getting people out to *Journal* events, although inter-journal communication was still carried out by email and the occasional angry telephone call. A Facebook group was also set up for this volume and the following one, allowing *Journal* members to post their thoughts on or updates for events online. The volume was also the first to look into the use of podcasts as a method of providing additional scholarly content to the academic community.[1130]

send a little joke about footnotes to one another when they start feeling nostalgic.

Senior editor for volume fifty-four Dorian Needham—one of two founding editors of the MJLH Editorial Board that would go on to be on the *McGill Law Journal* in the following year (alongside volume fifty-four Executive Editor Sophie Tremblay)—wrote about his experience editing journals at McGill Law. In a valuable comparison, he stated that,

> Working for the MLJ and for the McGill Journal of Law & Health (MJLH) provided very different experiences. The MLJ is a big operation, and despite all of the soul-searching and management restructurings and regularly missed deadlines, it runs relatively smoothly (or does a good impression of it). There are clear roles for everyone involved, the editing procedure is streamlined, and standard training is available to get everyone up-to-speed. At the MJLH, on the other hand, we had to develop all of these systems on the fly—which increased everyone's workload (writing an editing manual while you're editing a paper is a big task ...) and [this] slowed the process. But then again, there was at the MJLH the excitement of getting to start from scratch with no precedent and no baggage:

John Ralson Saul providing his lecture in the McGill Law moot court; Dean Nicolas Kasirer and Editor-in-Chief Erin Morgan at the table. (Source: McGill Law Journal website archives)

The impact of social media goes further than this, however. While in the past MLJ alumni could only really keep in touch through real effort, picking up the phone or meeting for lunch, today alumni learn about their colleagues and what they are doing with the click of a mouse. An alumni newsletter would be out-of-date before you could press print for this new generation of editors, who have all become a part of each other's deeply intertwined contact lists. It is now no longer the case that you're likely to run into somebody on the street the following year without in many cases at least knowing something about what they have been up to. Editors on exchange can message each other and meet up in the squares and taverns of remote villages, and

1129 Interview of Eytan Bensoussan by Omar Soliman (13 January, 2011) and James Cummins (11 November, 2011).

1130 "Volume 54 Management Board Work Distribution agenda" (2008).

we could be creative in a way that wasn't possible at the MLJ. The MJLH was also a very small team, produced only one issue per year, and initially had trouble attracting articles of sufficient quality, all of which made it very different from the MLJ …

I think there's no doubt that, moving forward, [the MLJ] will continue to be the Faculty's flagship journal. It has a reputation, a weight of history, and a sizeable team behind it—all of which make it incomparable. There is still plenty of space for niche journals out there, but there's also no doubt that general journals like the MLJ are many authors' venue of choice.[1131]

Clockwise: Volume 54 associate manager Wela Quan [blue top], Case Comments Editor Junaid Subhan, senior manager Maithili Sagar, Managing Editor Eytan Bensoussan, and Editor-in-Chief Erin Morgan at the 2009 Hindu Festival of Lights. (Courtesy of Wela Quan)

Volume fifty-four Managing Editor Eytan Bensoussan—clerking at the Federal Court of Canada at the time—also provided his thoughts on the volume, stating that,

What I was actually told by some professors, off the record … was until that point, there'd been a pretty giant cultural and, I guess, relationship gap between editors and management, to the point of sometimes complete boycotts of each other… I heard that there were boards that just wouldn't talk to each other, period. It was a really priority for me to make sure that we were one team and it was definitely a priority of Erin and everyone else as well.[1132]

Bensoussan was actually the first person to come up with the idea for this very book. Speaking about his moment of inspiration, he stated,

One of the things that I realized as a junior was that we had zero institutional memory. Our institutional memory at that point lived in Nicole, and a couple of the board members, and maybe some professors who were on the *Journal*. It just seemed that not only from a practical point of view … [we wanted to know] where are we coming from; why are we bilingual; why are we not fully French or fully English? How has that been working? How did that happen so long ago and not just recently … Just a whole bunch of questions …

It kind of came to my mind that there was hopefully some sort of compelling story to tell. One of the big pitches that the *Law Journal* makes is "look at all the alumni who were on the *Law Journal*." You would imagine that something pretty cool had been happening at some point in its history. It came to me … here was a long-term vision that people could rally around, and once it's done it could be part of the memory of McGill. One of the side notes to that story is that I personally felt that we were starting to hear echoes when we had our fundraising campaign. You'd have the same people giving, and a lot of them were saying: "There's nothing new. You keep on producing journals, why do you need more money, just to keep it the same?"

It's not about more or less; it's what you do with the money. So here was a way for us to use, not just the buzz but the

1131 Interview of Dorian Needham by James Cummins (22 November, 2010).

1132 Bensoussan interview, *supra* note 1129.

> intellectual capacity of all of our alumni to engage in more than just an appeal for funds … to engage and say, "Tell us about how you shaped this to the way it looks today." From that point of view, I thought that this was going to be able to engage them in many ways … There was a couple of other ideas that were on the table. That was my thing that I brought to the table and people seemed to rally around it, particularly Dean [Nicholas] Kasirer. When I was there I brought it up with him and he loved the idea. He's like: "Oh, you've gotta do it, this is fantastic: we've been waiting for something like this."[1133]

Volume fifty-four was extremely dedicated to the future of the *Journal*. Bensoussan recalled further that,

> [A]s an Executive Board, we wanted to be accountable. Everyone was saying, "You're going to go the next year once you've finished your term—you're going to give a few words to the board of advisors, and then you're done, and you're not accountable for anything." So what we did was, at the beginning of our year, Erin [Morgan] and I said, "Here are the fifteen things that we want to get done over the year. A year from now we're going to bring the same list and we're going to evaluate whether we achieved it or not."
>
> And we brought that list the next year. It was Professor [G. Blaine] Baker who said, "I've never seen a more transparent, accountable way of showing your progress."
>
> We brought that same thing and then we showed, "I failed on point seven, but I think we definitely got all the other points done and I hope that the next year will value this and take it up" … So that was a really big thing we were trying to institutionalize, and that's part of the trick: you might have a lot of really great ideas, [but] hopefully some of them live on afterwards.[1134]

Further relating his memories, Bensoussan said,

> I remember being there, sleeping at the office many nights in a row. Erin saw me there—she saw me in the night; she saw me in the morning—because I wanted to make sure that it didn't seem like I was getting the same amount of credits, or a similar type of reputation in my own right as an editor would, without putting in the weight and the sweat that was required.
>
> It definitely was required. It's not like I was there watching *South Park*[1135] all night. There was a ton of stuff to do. There were a whole bunch of different factors, starting from [something] as intangible as the culture to [something] as tangible as making sure that our decisions were made by consensus, and that we really kind of make sure that we have an institutional meeting every week—that we didn't miss it … and if we couldn't attend, that we get minutes. We all tried really hard together to make it work …
>
> I was just loving it. Every second of it was just—"Oh my god this is amazing, too bad it has to end." It was exhausting, let me be clear, but it was well worth every second that I wasn't doing something else."[1136]

In the year following his tenure, Bensoussan would undertake a 2500km bicycle ride from Savannah, Georgia to Montreal between mid-April to the end of May 2010, to raise money for the Heart & Stroke Foundation of Canada and the Intensive Care Unit of the Jewish General Hospital in Montreal.

The following volume (fifty-five) would see a continued evolution of several aspects of the *Journal*. The seventh edition of the *McGill Guide* began being constructed and altered by Cite Guide Editor Svetlana Samochkine. Taking advantage of new technology, she received over three hundred online recommendations, surveys, and other responses to changes that should be made for the next edition of the *Guide*. There was also an advisory panel of seven legal professionals and academics that provided direct insight as the project moved towards completion.[1137]

A new Executive Editor position was created in order to reorganize the institution. This position, the Coordinating Editor, would assume most of the administrative tasks that had hindered the Editor-in-Chief and other Executive Editors over the past

1133 *Ibid.*

1134 *Ibid.*

1135 *South Park* is a popular satiric comedic cartooned television show that first aired in 1997 and has experienced continual cultural importance ever since.

1136 Bensoussan interview, *supra* note 1129.

1137 "Minutes of the annual *McGill Law Journal* Board of Advisors meeting" (16 October, 2009).

decades[1138]—like determining, distributing, and receiving back editing assignments; writing to authors with editorial decisions; and keeping track of submissions from the time they arrived at the *Journal* until the point where that editorial decision was being made. This expanded the Executive Board, which had consisted of four members for nearly thirty years, to a five person board.[1139]

Continuing in the recent tradition of adding academic events to the *Journal*'s calendar, on November 17, 2009 volume fifty-five hosted a roundtable discussion titled "Reproductive Rights: Exploring the Political and Legal War Over Abortion, Surrogate Motherhood, and Embryonic Life". The event featured McGill Professors Abby Lippman (Medicine) and Angela Campbell (Law), as well as bestselling author Will Saletan.[1140] An annual roundtable discussion would take place in each of the following years as well, during volumes fifty-six and fifty-seven. The Saletan event appears (at least for now) to have been the start of a new MLJ tradition to, as Bensoussan put it the year before, make the MLJ part of the oxygen of the Faculty.[1141]

From left to right: Volume 55 English Executive Editor Stefan Szpajda, French Executive Editor Lucie Lanctuit, Coordinating Executive Editor Sarah Walker, Editor-in-Chief Seo Yun Yang, and Managing Editor Marly Ochmann St. Jean (Source: McGill Law Journal Newsletter 2009-10)

Though only recently removed from her editorial duties, volume fifty-five senior editor Mary Race, now a clerk for the Supreme Court of Canada for the 2012-13 period, wrote,

> The main impact [the *Journal* had] on my life came through my interactions with the other members of the MLJ. Getting to know the other editors and enjoying their company made the enjoyable moments even more enjoyable and helped improve some of the duller aspects of the editing process. Moreover, I made friends there who will remain close even after law school is over. Being part of the MLJ gives me a lasting link to the institution, which I will treasure...
>
> I must admit I don't particularly miss the detailed editing work, although I do miss getting to read and critique new submissions – it is a wonderful window onto contemporary legal scholarship. I also miss the sense of accomplishment when an article was finished; it's very rewarding to immerse oneself in editing and feel at the end as though one has made a small contribution, somehow helped to improve the article.[1142]

Volume fifty-five Electronics Editor Wela Quan spoke similarly of her recent experiences, writing, "Some of my best friends from law school are from my time with the journal. I especially got along well with the seniors when I was in my junior year. I am currently living in Toronto for my articling period and my roommate is a friend from the *Journal*!"[1143]

Volume fifty-five would say good-bye to another long-time supporter with the July

1138 *Ibid.*

1139 Volume twenty-six introduced the position of Associate Editor, creating an Executive Board of Associate Editor, Executive Editor, Managing Editor, and Editor-in-Chief. Then in volume forty-two, the Associate Editor lost its official title and was renamed "Executive Editor", producing a board with two Executive Editors—one in charge of French tasks and one in charge of English tasks.

1140 "Reproductive Rights: Exploring the Political and Legal War Over Abortion, Surrogate Motherhood, and Embryonic Life," McGill University press release (2 October, 2011), online: < http://www.mcgill.ca/channels/events/item/?item_id=112180 >

1141 Minutes 09, *supra* note 1137.

1142 Interview of Mary Race by James Cummins (4 January, 2011).

1143 Interview of Wela Quan by James Cummins (29 November, 2010).

16, 2009 death of Justice Charles D. Gonthier. Gonthier first joined the Board of Trustees in 1992, during his third year on the Supreme Court, and then remained on the Board of Advisors from the dissolution of the trust until the time of his death—his eighteen years with the *Journal* being the longest continuous length of service any Advisor has ever committed to the *Journal* to this day.[1144] In tribute to him volume fifty-five Editor-in-Chief Seo Yun Yang provided an Editor's Note to preface a special section devoted to Gonthier, writing,

> In 2000, when Justice Gonthier was invited to be the keynote speaker for what was then called the *McGill Law Journal* Alumni Lecture Series, he spoke about the conceptual framework of "fraternité" in the context of Canadian law. Though his lecture was shared with a limited audience at a particular event and point in time, his words and the spirit of his message resonate today among the student body—and particularly within our institution, the *McGill Law Journal.*
>
> Justice Gonthier's long-time service on our Board of Advisors is a source of great pride at the *McGill Law Journal.* He was highly committed to students and academic institutions, and we were the fortuitous beneficiaries of his wisdom and inspiration. Reading his published text on "fraternité", I now recognize that our ever-evolving student Editorial Board is a fertile ground for developing, enriching, and cherishing some of the values that Justice Gonthier spoke of: empathy, co-operation, commitment, responsibility, fairness, trust, and equity.[1145]

Jacques-Yvan Morin also wrote about Justice Gonthier within the pages of this issue. Morin wrote that he and Gonthier had known each other since their adolescence, and eventually attended McGill Law together.[1146] They were both a part of a close group of individuals that had stayed friends ever since their youth in Montreal—including the legendary Quebec filmmaker Claude Jutras, famed Quebec painter Suzanne Joubert, and Governor General's Award winning author Hélène Pelletier-Baillargeon.[1147] Of his dear friend, Morin wrote,

> *Ainsi, la vie féconde de Charles Gonthier, comme celle de tout homme sans doute, a sa source dans ses jeunes années. Les qualités dont il a fait preuve tout au long de sa carrière, soit la modestie, la recherche du dialogue et la courtoisie dans toute discussion, des qualités liées à la fois à son tempérament réservé et à la fermeté de ses convictions, étaient déjà les siennes à l'adolescence. J'ai eu le privilège de le connaître à cette époque et les années qui ont suivi n'ont fait que confirmer la haute estime que j'ai toujours eu pour lui, comme d'ailleurs tous ceux qui l'ont fréquenté.*
>
> *Malgré des cheminements ultérieurs différents et des opinions pas toujours partagées, nous cultivions cette vieille amitié. Celles qui naissent dans la jeunesse sont sans doute les plus durables.*[1148]

Though this journey of friendship had come to an end, others—like those described by Race and Quan—were just beginning.

While the prior incarnation of the Annual Lecture had only made it to nine straight lectures, the new incarnation would hold its tenth consecutive Annual Lecture during volume fifty-five. That year the Annual Lecture was provided on January 26, 2010 by Justice Rosalie Silberman Abella of the Supreme Court of Canada. She spoke of the state of international human rights law from her perspective as a "child of survivors":[1149] her parents spent four years in a Nazi concentration camp during the Second World War.[1150] After the lecture, volume fifty-six Editor-in-Chief Sara Ross—then an associate editor—remembers Abella going out of her way to speak to everybody who had shared in her lecture. Of Abella, she said, "There are some people that just have this vibrant, powerful, intense energy within them. You can feel the energy when they're walking up to you. They have so much life in them. When she walks up to you, you can just feel it. Some people ... there's just passion in their eyes."[1151]

1144 Brian Pel had one more year of service than Justice Gonthier as of 2012-13 when including his year as Managing Editor of volume 30, however in terms of continuous service, Pel will not surpass Gonthier's length of service until 2013-14. As of 2012, both men have served an equal eighteen years continuously.

1145 Seo Yun Yang, "Editor's Note" (2010) 55:2 *McGill LJ* 331 at 331.

1146 Jacques-Yvan Morin, "Charles Gonthier: L'Homme Derrière le Juriste" (2010) 55:2 *McGill LJ* 333 at 333.

1147 *Ibid* at 334.

1148 *Ibid* at 335.

1149 Rosalie Silberman Abella, "International Law and Human Rights: The Power and the Pity" (2010) 55:4 *McGill LJ* 871 at 883.

1150 *Ibid.*

1151 Ross interview, *supra* note 1089

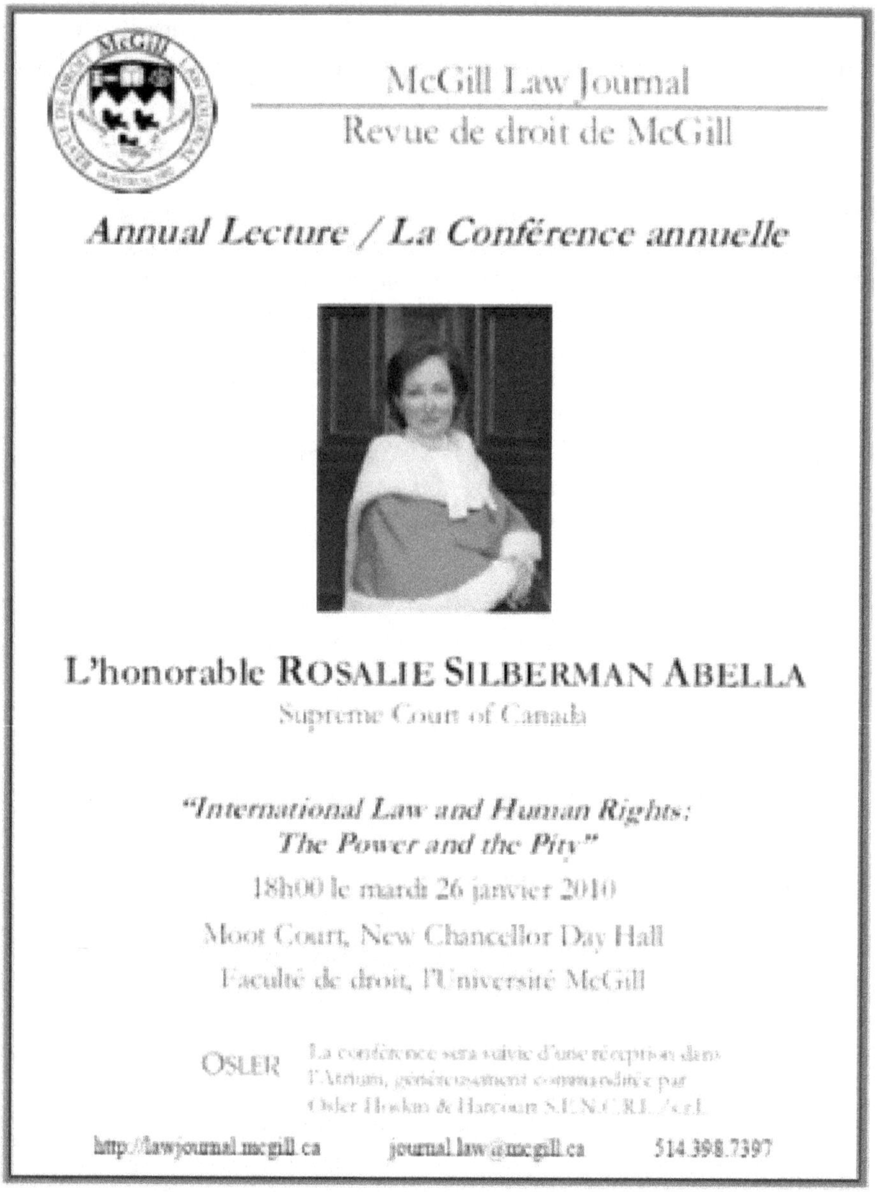

Original McGill Law Journal Annual Lecture poster, used to advertise at the McGill University Faculty of Law.

Volume fifty-five also included a special issue in commemoration of the fiftieth anniversary of the landmark Supreme Court of Canada decision in *Roncarelli v. Duplessis* entitled "The Legacy of *Roncarelli v. Duplessis*, 1959-2009"—a case in which FR Scott famously acted as counsel to Frank Roncarelli, establishing that nobody in Canada is above the rule of law. The case is considered to be one of the most influential antecedents to the 1982 creation of the *Canadian Charter of Rights and Freedoms*.[1152] The issue also contained a reprint of the original case comment that Professor Claude-Armand Sheppard wrote on the *Roncarelli* case that the MLJ had printed in volume six.[1153] The issue was based upon a conference held in the Eastern Townships between September 18 and 19, 2009 on the subject of the legacy of the verdict, during the fiftieth anniversary year of the January 1959 Supreme Court decision.[1154]

Contributions to the issue included an article from Emeritus Professor of Law at The University of New South Wales Mark Aronson;[1155] and the first MLJ publication of volume forty-six Editor-in-Chief, now Associate Professor of Law at McGill, Robert Leckey.[1156] Contributions to the rest of the volume included a review essay from Justice Louise LeBel of the Supreme Court of Canada;[1157] and articles from Marie-Claire Cordonier Segger,[1158] Director of the Centre for International Sustainable Development Law at McGill University, who was published within the special section on the achievements of Justice Gonthier; and arbitrator Emmanuel Gaillard,[1159] who is probably best known for bringing the largest international arbitration in history against the Russian Federation on behalf of the Yukos Oil Company. It was projects and articles like these that allowed the *McGill Law Journal* to be one of only three Canadian law journals to earn an A+ rating from the Australian Research Council in their seminal 2010 Excellence in Research for Australia Initiative that

1152 Joel Bakan, *Canadian Constitutional Law* (Toronto: Emond Montgomery, 2003) at 640.

1153 Claude-Armand Sheppard, "*Roncarelli v Duplessis, Art. 1053 C.C. Revolutionized*" (2010) 55:3 *McGill LJ* v.

1154 Geneviève Cartier, "Preface" (2010) 55:3 *McGill LJ* i.

1155 Mark Aronson, "Some Australian Reflections on *Roncarelli v. Duplessis*" (2010) 55:3 *McGill LJ* 615.

1156 Rober Leckey, "Complexifying *Roncarelli*'s Rule of Law" (2010) 55:3 *McGill LJ* 721.

1157 Louise LeBel, "De *Dunsmuir À Khosa*" (2010) 55:2 *McGill LJ* 311.

1158 Marie-Claire Cordonier Segger, "Sustainability, Global Justice, and the Law: Contributions of the Hon. Justice Charles Doherty Gonthier" (2010) 55:2 *McGill LJ* 337.

1159 Emmanuel Gaillard, "Ordre Juridique Arbitral: Realite, Utilite et Specificite" (2010) 55:4 *McGill LJ* 891.

analyzed nearly 21,000 journals worldwide based on their overall quality.[1160]

This brings us to the Editorial Board of the volume—the heart of every MLJ project. While many interviews were offered to past members of the *Journal*, there is perhaps one unanswered interview that leaves the most glaring hole. In response to the initial email sent out to past *Journal* members, she replied, "I was only involved recently … but of course I would be happy to participate."[1161] But she never got the chance to provide her interview. At three o'clock in the morning of Saturday, 15 October, 2011, she was struck by a car going the wrong direction on a one-way street in Ottawa. That woman, Alexandra Dodger, former senior manager for volume fifty-five, was killed.

Grief flowed throughout the Faculty of Law, as Alexandra was one of the brightest shining lights wandering those halls during her time. Despite having grades near the top of her class, a position on the *Journal*, placing fourth globally for written submissions in the Philip C. Jessup International Law Moot with fellow *Journal* members Mary Race and volume fifty-five Case Comments Kabir Jamal, and a social skill-set that was second to none—she had decided to spend her articling year with Amnesty International. She was a rare combination of academic brilliance and smart, vocal activism. Of her deep belief in fighting for those who could only have-not, Alexandra once wrote that,

> I do think [we should] carefully consider how and when those of us privileged enough to get law degrees at an institution like McGill use our privilege. Some of us have other forms of privilege too – whether it is our skin colour, our gender, our income, our family connections, the passports we carry or a whole host of things arrived at by chance. The question of how people from dominant groups can work in solidarity with others should be something all participants in progressive movements for social change [to] consider…
>
> [W]e can start by shedding the myth that students from McGill give more to the organizations they intern with than they receive. [Human rights] internships aren't entirely altruistic – travel is exciting and the experience is certainly more interesting than writing memos in a cubicle all summer. Many hope to use the opportunity to launch their careers. Inevitably, 12 weeks of your work might not be worth as much as the experience of visiting a new continent, learning a new language, or slapping a UN related position on your CV. That's OK. Universities aim to educate, and for-credit internships are about learning. But the way in which we learn should be open to critique, scrutiny and mature forms of debate that aren't just mere parodies of legitimate concern.[1162]

Volume fifty-seven would dedicate its second issue to her memory and the Law Students Association of McGill soon announced the creation of an annual Alexandra Dodger Award for Social Justice in tribute to her life. In its preface, volume fifty-six senior manager Dina Awad wrote of Alexandra that, "She knew how to fight, but she could also startle you with her kindness."[1163] Dodger's commitment to society was so strong that shockwaves of her death went all the way to the Canadian Parliament, where Member of Parliament Dan Harris read the following aloud during a full session of the House of Commons on 17 October, 2011:

> Mr. Speaker, today I rise with a heavy heart to remember the life of a friend whose journey was tragically cut short this past Saturday at the age of 27. Alexandra Dodger was killed after being struck by a car near her home in Ottawa.
>
> Alex was an extraordinary woman who was passionate about life and was determined to improve the lives of those around her. She cared deeply about giving a voice to the voiceless. Alex had just graduated from law school at McGill earlier this year and started a promising career with Amnesty International. Alex dedicated so much of her time to many causes, one of which was the Ontario New Democratic Youth where I had the pleasure of working with her and where we became friends. There is no doubt in my mind that Alex was destined to do great things and was going to bring forth

1160 "ERA 2010 Ranked Journals List" Australian Research Council, online: < http://www.arc.gov.au/era/era_2010/archive/era_journal_list.htm >

1161 Email from Alexandra Dodger to James Cummins (17 November, 2010).

1162 Alexandra Dodger, "Snide Parodies Ignore Critical Questions and Human Rights Internships" *The Quid Novi* (3 November, 2009) 5 at 5.

1163 Dina Awad, "In Memory of Alexandra Dodger (1983-2011)" (2011) 57:2 *McGill LJ* vi at vi.

> positive change.
>
> I will cherish our time spent together and miss all the times that we will never have. On behalf of myself, Her Majesty's loyal opposition and all our staff, many who knew Alex well, I would like to extend our deep and sincere condolences to Alex's family, friends and colleagues, but especially to her mother and grandmother who must now endure what no parent or grandparent should have to.[1164]

Her memory would not go in vain—for, as Justice Abella put it in Alexandra's senior volume Annual Lecture, "It's not just what you stand for, it's what you stand up for."[1165]

The volume following Alexandra's was volume fifty-six. Volume fifty-six would be only the fourth volume to publish over 1200 pages, and the only one to ever do so and still complete its publication schedule on time. In fact, it would publish its volume earlier than any volume to come before it, in June of 2011. The volume's fourth issue was the longest non-special issue in MLJ history, and overall volume fifty-six was the third longest volume in the sixty years of the MLJ. It seems that the standard set by Patrick Healy and volume twenty-six was more than well established by this point.

The volume included the 2010 McGill Law convocation speech from Reinhard Zimmermann,[1166] Director of the Max Planck Institute for Comparative and International Private Law in Hamburg as well as Chair of Private Law, Roman Law and Comparative Legal History at the University of Regensburg; as well as articles from the Director of the Human Rights Centre at the University of Ottawa's Faculty of Law Karen Eltis;[1167] Gérard Bouchard,[1168] Governor General's Award winning author and co-Chair of the Bouchard-Taylor Commission, who wrote on the reasonable accommodation of minorities within Quebec; Daniel J. Moore Professor of Law at Seton Hall University, Stephen J. Lubben;[1169] Director of the National Programme at the University of Ottawa Faculty of Law, Aline Grenon;[1170] C.L. Lim,[1171] Chairman of the East Asian International Economic Law and Policy Program at the University of Hong Kong; Director of the Human Rights Center at Durham University Faculty of Law, Helen Fenwick;[1172] Chair of LLB Board of Examiners at Durham University Faculty of Law, Gavin Phillipson;[1173] Director of the Department of International Law and International Organisation of the University of Geneva, and Vice-Chair of the Board of the International Council of Human Rights Policy, Marco Sassòli;[1174] and former Executive Director of the Centre for Innovation Law and Policy at the University of Toronto Andrea Slane.[1175] A book review was contributed by Pedro J. Martinez Fraga,[1176] Coordinator of International Disputes for Latin America and Florida at DLA Piper LLP; and a book note was contributed by Noel Cox,[1177] Head of the Department of Law and Criminology at Aberystwyth University.

Editor-in-Chief of volume fifty-six related her experiences with two of the articles she was responsible for in an interview—in fact, they were the first article she worked on as EIC and the last. The first one was the Robert Danay article, which she had also worked on over the Reading Week following her election to Editor-in-Chief as her final assignment as an associate editor. She recalled that Danay,

> was going to be in the issue prior to

1164 Dan Harris, "Statements by Members: Alexandra Dodger" (17 October, 2011) 146:030, 1st Session, 41st Parliament. House of Commons Debates, online: < http://www.parl.gc.ca/HousePublications/Publication.aspx?Language=E&Mode=1&Parl=41&Ses=1&DocId=5172224. >

1165 Abella 2010, *supra* note 1149 at 886.

1166 Reinhard Zimmerman, "Graduation Address McGill University" (2010) 56:1 *McGill LJ* 231.

1167 Karen Eltis, "The Judicial System in the Digital Age: Revisiting the Relationship between Privacy and Accessibility in the Cyber Context" (2011) 56:2 *McGill LJ* 289.

1168 Gérard Bouchard, "Qu'est ce Que l'Interculturalisme" (2011) 56:2 *McGill LJ* 395.

1169 Stephanie Ben-Ishai & Stephen J Lubben, "Sales or Plans: A Comparative Account of the New Corporate Reorganization" (2011) 56:3 *McGill LJ* 591.

1170 Aline Grenon, "Le bijuridisme canadien à la croisée des chemins ? Réflecions sur l'Incidence de l'article 8.1 de la *loi d'Interprétation*" (2011) 56:3 *McGill LJ* 767.

1171 CL Lim, "East Asia's Engagement with Cosmopolitan Ideals under Its Trade Treaty Dispute Provisions" (2011) 56:4 *McGill LJ* 821.

1172 Helen Fenwick & Gavin Phillipson, "Covert Derogations and Judicial Deference: Redefining Liberty and Due Process Rights in Counterterrorism Law and Beyond" (2011) 56:4 *McGill LJ* 863.

1173 *Ibid.*

1174 Marco Sassòli & Marie-Louise Tougas, "International Law Issues Raised by the Transfer of Detainees by Canadian Forces in Afghanistan" (2011) 56:4 *McGill LJ* 959.

1175 Andrea Slane, "Guarding a Cultural Icon: Concurrent Intellectual Property Regimes and the Perpetual Protection of Anne of Green Gables in Canada" (2011) 56:4 *McGill LJ* 1011.

1176 Pedro J Martinez-Fraga, "The New Global Law by Rafael Domingo" Book Review (2011) 56:3 *McGill LJ* 767.

1177 Noel Cox, "The Queen's Other Realms: They Crown and Its Legacy in Australia, Canada and New Zealand by Peter Boyce" Book Note, (2011) 56:4 *McGill LJ* 1207.

mine, but logistically there wasn't enough time … so my volume was presented with the idea of taking on Danay and [Jennifer A.] Chandler,[1178] and I really liked Danay because it's IP related to defamation, and I liked the topic. The truth is that I'd also worked on it's footnotes as a junior and it had taken up so, so much of my time … it's a nightmare as an associate editor; it was probably the most difficult article I had to edit because the case law it refers to is old, old law from the UK. With the MLJ you have to find the original source and photocopy it, so you can imagine that that was quite the feat … not only for that, but also for really, really old case law from the circuit courts in the US; cases that weren't necessarily obscure, but they definitely weren't easy to find.

I remember spending time with the librarians down in the dungeons of Nahum [Gelber], back behind the locked door where they used to keep the original copies of the court reporters for the circuit courts and what have you. So they would have to unlock the door to take me back there to get one page photocopied from different cases, and then I had to go back if there was an error. It was really a test of: "Do you like this? Can you do this?" …

There were also the civil law cases from Quebec, the ones that were not even really reported, so also a nightmare to find—so even though we're in Quebec you have to find the paper copy, which were in the most obscure reporters and some of them weren't reported at all …

It was supposed to be done by Reading Week … and I had so much else to do over Reading Week; that was my one week off and I was trying to hire the team for the next year, but I spent the majority of Reading Week in the library until three in the morning—it was ridiculous; it just wouldn't end. I had visitors in town that week as well, and couldn't even see them because I was at the library until all hours of the night … And there it was back again at the end of May. That was the first one I worked on as EIC. But I really liked the article; it was the favourite article I worked on as an associate editor … And that's the one that was cited [by the SCC]—it was so cool that it was the article that I had worked so hard on in both my years.[1179]

It took less than a year before the first MLJ article from the volume was cited by the Supreme Court of Canada, and both volume fifty-five and volume fifty-four, the two preceding volumes, had also been cited very quickly by the SCC—creating a streak of three straight volumes that were cited in less than two years. As of January 2013, volume fifty-six actually had three different articles from its bounds cited by the Supreme court in less than two years, second in impressiveness to only volume fifty-four, which had received *five citations* by that same time, with volume fifty-five itself being cited twice by the high court since its completion. As a sign of the quality of the *Journal*'s most recent volumes, the five most recent volumes to be fully distributed by the end of August 2012, volumes fifty-two through fifty-six, had each been cited by the Supreme Court—and by September 2012, each had been cited at least twice. By January 2013, only two of the last twenty-five completed volumes had not been cited at least once.

Ross also recalled the final article she worked on as EIC, and how it related to the very start of her associate year. She recalled that,

> This was back when we used to do our *Journal* applications over the summer following 1L, and then you'd find out whether or not you'd received an interview at the end of August by email—as opposed to the new timeline where it all happens during the second semester [of 1L]. So I'd done the application, and finished it right before [performing] in a dance show … I also had swine flu while I was doing my application, and I remember lying on the floor of my apartment going through the footnotes and editing this article, and then I'd lie back down until I had a little more energy, and then I'd get up and do it again … Once you pick up the application you only have ten days, so the clock was ticking, and I knew I had my dance show at the end.
>
> So I wasn't entirely sure how the application had gone, I did my best but … I decided to take a little end-of-summer trip down to PEI, because as a child I'd read

1178 Jennifer A Chandler, "Technological Self-help and Equality in Cyberspace" (2010) 56:1 *McGill LJ* 39.

1179 Ross interview, *supra* note 1089.

> everything that Lucy Maud Montgomery had ever written, and I mean *everything*. I am not a fan of poetry, and I even read all of the poetry she wrote, and all of the diaries of hers that were published; here's the manically obsessed, detail-oriented EIC speaking—it had to be everything that was ever written on her, everything she'd ever written, even if it was the most *boring* letter. I read all her letters...
>
> So the actual day I was at the homestead re-creation of Anne of Green Gables, I was actually on [those] grounds when the email came in saying I got the interview ...[1180]

Ross then spoke of that final article she edited at the tail end of her tenure as EIC, recalling that,

> I remember getting the article in October... and when it came in I said "How perfect is this!"—IP, which I was really interested in, trademarks in particular, and then *Anne of Green Gables* as the case study? And that was the last article, I mean down to the bitter end in June—it was the last article that got done. I just stayed up all night, every night, getting it done. It was a really good article, so it went quite quickly thank goodness. It was one of the few things that kept me going at the very end—this article.[1181]

The article was she is speaking about, of course, *Guarding a Cultural Icon: Concurrent Intellectual Property Regimes and the Perpetual Protection of Anne of Green Gables in Canada* by Professor Andrea Slane.

The volume contained some firsts in terms of its roster of articles. The article by Bouchard was translated from French into English by the *Journal*, and both versions of the article appeared side by side in the third issue. This marked the very first time an article had been translated for publication in the MLJ. The volume also published the first partial Spanish article in MLJ history—with the publication of this volume's Annual Lecture, provided on March 30, 2011 by celebrated Mexican author, Chair-holder at Cambridge and Harvard University, as well as former Ambassador of Mexico to France, Carlos Fuentes.

The Lecture, however, was originally slated for January 12—as can be seen in the accompanying event poster, designed by volume fifty-six and fifty-seven Electronic Editor Waleed Bishouty—one of only two individuals to ever hold a senior position in both their associate and senior years. Nine days beforehand, on January 3, an email came in. Over the winter break the health of Fuentes' wife had taken a turn for the worse, and he had faxed a letter the day after Christmas to his literary agency to say he would need to be at her side during a surgery that was to take place over the exact date of the Lecture. Yet Fuentes promised to return later in the semester and did so at the end of March.

At a dinner the evening before the Lecture held at the University Club of Montreal, Fuentes dined with a small group of editors and managers, alongside a representative from the Faculty.[1182] Just recently there had been a vote of confidence held in the House of Commons, which the sitting party had not survived. An election was coming, but this was the farthest thing from most people's minds. After all, they were sitting at a table with one of history's greatest writers.

But as soon as there was a lull in the conversation, Fuentes turned to the table and said: "So ... your government has fallen."

The group of students were still laughing about it the next day—he wanted to know how the students felt about their country. He wanted to know what they felt about everything going on in the world at the time—the Arab Spring, American consumerism, and yes, even the domestic state of Canadian politics. For as Fuentes said to an audience member after his Lecture the following day, "You can't wait for inspiration, for the angel to come down, and flutter around you. You have to sit down, and do your work, and do your writing.... Many writers in Mexico and Latin America fail because they're waiting, really, for inspiration to arrive. So the inspiration isn't there; can't write? No, no, no!"[1183]

The speech was given in both French and English, as well as some Spanish. He discussed his days at law school in Geneva during the early 1950s, and how it impacted his vision of the world as an author and figure in Mexican society. During a lengthy question and answer period following the speech, Fuentes fielded questions on the state of the world both in his home of Mexico and abroad. A rousing wave of applause even came after one member of the audience asked Fuentes if he would consider running for President of

1180 *Ibid.*

1181 *Ibid.*

1182 The Faculty member was Professor Víctor Muñiz-Fraticelli, who was accompanied by his wife. Also at the table were Editor-in-Chief Sara Ross, Citations Editor Eva Warden, senior editors Youri Tessier-Stall and Andreea Vasiliu, and Electronic Editor Waleed Bishouty.

1183 Fuentes, *supra* note 120 at 1199 (footnotes).

their shared country. Just as he had at the dinner the evening before, Fuentes seemed as engaged with the McGill student body and local community as they were with him. It would be one of the final public lectures of Fuentes' career, as he would pass away just a little more than a year later. The article that appeared in the *McGill Law Journal* would be the last scholarly publication the great novelist would contribute to academia in his lifetime, published less than a year before his death.

Carlos Fuentes in foreground; Volume 56 Editor-in-Chief Sara Ross and McGill Professor of Law Víctor *Muñiz-Fraticelli in the background. (Courtesy of James Cummins)*

During volume fifty-six the MLJ finally moved its editorial processes completely onto the word processor, taking advantage of new changes in software—thus allowing the new editorial methodology. Now fully electronic, the speed of editing increased—though editors were still known to print out versions of the article after the fact in order to make sure they weren't missing anything. Another first this year came with the decision for the Dean to award the I. Ballon Medal to two different members of the Board, instead of just one, for the very first time: Executive Editor Amélie T. Gouin and Editor-in-Chief Sara Ross.

As at the point of writing most of the editors from this Board are only just graduating, there is nothing to say of their current professional attachments. However in addition to having two senior editors—Michael Bookman and Anja Kortenaar—along with an associate editor, Adela Gotz, selected for clerkships at the Supreme Court of Canada near the end of its tenure, volume fifty-six also saw two additional members selected as clerks for the Federal Court of Canada—senior editor Youri Tessier-Stall and Editor-in-Chief Sara Ross—as well as one as a clerk at the Federal Court of Appeal in senior manager Dina Awad.

They would pass the torch to volume fifty-seven, the board that would take the *Journal* into its sixtieth anniversary calendar year of 2012, en route to the sixtieth anniversary volume: volume fifty-eight. Contributors to volume fifty-seven included Deputy-President of the Supreme Court of Israel Justice Eliezer Rivlin;[1184] Justice Morris J. Fish[1185]—MLJ alumnus and the twenty-second Justice of the Supreme Court of Canada to provide either an article or live lecture to the *Journal*; and Francois Venter,[1186] Dean of Law at North-West University in New Zealand. Book reviews were contributed by authors including James McGill Professor of Law at McGill University and Director of the Quebec Research Center of Private and Comparative Law, Lionel Smith;[1187] and Hilmi M. Zawati,[1188] President of the International Legal Advocacy Forum.

The volume's Annual Lecture was provided by the Conflict of Interest and Ethics Commissioner of Canada Mary Dawson on February 29, 2012. Dawson was also the final drafter of both the Meech Lake and the Charlottetown Accord, Canada's two most significant attempts at constitutional reform of the past thirty years. In her speech she shared her personal experiences from behind the scenes during the drafting of the Accords, including stories about what had gone into the final and prior drafts, what did not, and the politics of how the

1184 Eliezer Rivlin, "Israel is a Mixed Jurisdiction" (2012) 57:4 *McGill LJ* 781.

1185 Morris J Fish, "The Effect of Alcohol on the Canadian Constitution ... Seriously" (2011) 57:1 *McGill LJ* 189.

1186 Francois Venter, "South Africa: A Diceyan *Rechtsstaat*?" (2012) 57:4 *McGill LJ* 721.

1187 Lionel Smith, "Restatement of the Law Third: Restitution and Unjust Enrichment, 2 vols by the American Law Institute" Book Review (2012) 57:3 *McGill LJ* 629.

1188 Hilmi A Zawati, "Protecting Civilians: The Obligations of Peacekeepers by the Siobhán Wills" Book Review (2011) 57:2 *McGill LJ* 383.

negotiations were handled. In addition to publishing the Lecture, the MLJ decided to offer the speech as a free audio file podcast to the public as a part of a new initiative to produce scholarly audio files for the legal community and public.

Original McGill Law Journal Annual Lecture poster, used to advertise at the McGill University Faculty of Law. Designed by Waleed Bishouty.

The podcast initiative of volume fifty-seven saw three podcasts recorded by the editorial staff and released for free on the online music provider iTunes U as well as on McGill web servers. The rest of the podcasts were not readings of articles, but original interviews between MLJ editors and highly esteemed members of the legal community. The interviews recorded were: Wainwright Emeritus Professor of Civil Law at McGill Pierre-Gabriel Jobin, interviewed by volume fifty-eight senior editor Nicola Langille; FR Scott Professor of Constitutional and Public Law at McGill and President of the Royal Society of Canada Roderick A. MacDonald, interviewed by volume fifty-eight senior editor Michael Shortt;[1189] and former Justice of the Supreme Court of Canada Ian Binnie, the twenty-third Supreme Court Justice to provide content to the *Journal* over the years, interviewed by volume fifty-seven senior editor Omar Soliman. The question and answer session following Mary Dawson's Annual Lecture was also provided in podcast form. The Chairperson of the committee responsible for the podcasts was senior editor Alexandra Masciuch, who said in an interview with the *McGill Reporter*, "The podcast series will be published in addition to, and not in place of, our traditional print scholarship."[1190]

Professor MacDonald, who was Dean of McGill Law during the 1980s and a member of the MLJ Board of Trustees during that time, was interviewed regarding his ideas of technology and the law. It is interesting to take MacDonald's words into consideration when noting the technological initiatives of the MLJ to bring legal ideas into closer contact with its audience. In his interview, he stated that,

> I think the biggest change that technology has had is that it's diminished and debased the human dimension of the practice of law; and that it has allowed people to do a lot of things that previously could only be done in conversation with other

1189 Both Michael Shortt and Nicola Langille were associate editors at the time of the interviews.

1190 Marie-Astrid Heyde, "McGill Physics Department and Law Journal Join the e-Culture" *McGill Reporter* (19 April, 2012), online: < http://publications.mcgill.ca/reporter/2012/04/mcgill-physics-department-and-law-journal-join-the-e-culture/ >

> people or in personal exchanges with other people, whether it be by telephone or by letter, or in person ... It has allowed the practice of law to flourish in the absence of intense interpersonal communication, and as a result I think that the practice of law has become more technocratic; less a human endeavour than it was.[1191]

As of 2012, the currently sitting Deans of Law at the University of Toronto (Mayo Moran), McGill University (Daniel Jutras), Queen's University (William F. Flanagan), Osgoode Hall (Lorne Sossia), Robson Hall (Lorna Turnbull), the University of Calgary (Ian Holloway), the University of Ottawa (Donna Greschner), Dalhousie University (Kim Brooks), and the Université Laval (Sylvio Normand), had all published in the MLJ or been on the *Journal* themselves at one point or another—comprising the Faculty heads of most of Canada's elite schools of law.

Most of the rest of Canada's elite Faculties all saw at least saw Deans do the same, including volume sixteen Notes and Case Comments Editor Lewis N. Klar (past Dean of Law at the University of Alberta), contributor Donna Greschner (past Dean of Law at the University of Victoria), contributor Kent Roach (past Dean of Law at the University of Saskatchewan and the University of Western Ontario), and contributor Edward Veitch (Past Dean of Law at the University of New Brunswick). At the University of British Columbia and Carleton, though no past Dean or Department of Law head had published in the MLJ, both institutions had past or present Presidents of their university do so in Michael Kelway Oliver (Carleton) and Stephen J. Toope (UBC). As for the Deans of McGill Law, every Dean since 1950 and one before that time—including Sydney A Bruneau,[1192] Peter Leuprecht, John E.C. Brierley, Maxwell Cohen, John W. Durnford, Gerard Fauteux, John P Humphrey, Yves-Marie Morrissette, Roderick A. MacDonald, WCJ Meredith, Daniel Jutras, Nicholas Kasirer, Stephen Toope, and FR Scott—each published in the MLJ. Over sixty years, whether it is in the realm of academic, the courts, or the legal profession, the *Journal* has established itself as an important part of both the legal community and Canadian history.

Bottom right Editor-in-Chief Sara Ross, beside associate editor Adela Gotz (bottom left); senior editor Youri Tessier-Stall talking to associate editor Priyanka Timblo in background; 2010 McGill Law Journal Christmas party at Ross's home. (Photo courtesy of James Cummins)

The *Journal* was published on time by volume fifty-six for the first time in a decade, and volume fifty-seven followed suit. Old traditions were being kept as new traditions were being created. The impact of these later volumes and editorial staffs on the legal and wider community has yet to truly be determined, but as volume fifty-two senior editor Héloïse Robinson wrote, "Twenty or thirty years from now, I think I will most remember [the] people that I met ... I would be very surprised if none of my colleagues from the *Journal* hold some of the most important positions in the legal profession ... as leading partners, academics, and judges."[1193]

And as for a perspective from the past, volume thirty Managing Editor Brian Pel—who has watched the *Journal* grow as a Trustee, then Advisor, for neary two decades—states that the main thing he's noticed over all those years is that, "I think there's just an extraordinary professionalism that you'd never expect from a student run publication—and it's just more and more apparent every year. The standard of the people who are working on the *Journal* just seems to go up and up."[1194]

1191 "Law and Technology: Interview with Professor MacDonald", *McGill Law Journal* podcasts, posted 3 April, 2012, online: < http://podcasts.mcgill.ca/tags/mcgill-law-journal/ >

1192 A Sydney Bruneau, "Shakespeare's Law" (1971) 17:4 *McGill LJ* 729.

1193 Robinson interview, *supra* note 1100.

1194 Pel interview, *supra* note 666.

Chapter Six:

Anatomy of a Journal

After reviewing the history of the MLJ volume by volume, a question still exists. We know how the *Journal* started, and we know what successes the *Journal* encountered along the way, but how exactly does the *Journal* work? Well, first off, you need editors—and to have editors, you need law students. So: why McGill Law? Executive Editor of volume eight Arnold Isaacson stated that he went to McGill because,

> Well, I thought it was the best law school; I didn't want to go out of the city. I didn't want to go to the Université de Montréal, my French wasn't that proficient. I did well in undergraduate school, and I was accepted to McGill. Actually, I applied to the Wharton School of Economics and I applied to Boston University as well, which I accepted, but I found that it was a bit of a strain on my Dad who would have to pay for a lot of stuff because I wasn't working. And so McGill was the best choice, and it was a good school, and I had a lot of friends here. And it's very important to have friends around you, especially when things happen.[1195]

Advertising Editor for volume four Yves Fortier gave a bit of a different answer, stating:

> All of my friends actually applied to go to law school on the other side of the mountain at the Université de Montreal, and my father was of the view that it would serve me in good stead if I did my law in English at McGill. And when I would answer to him that, "you know, I didn't think that I would be able to follow courses/lectures in English," then he said: "Native English speakers are in the same situation as you are – they've never done any law. Whether in French or in English, you'll all be on the same footing."[1196]

We also have the story of volume twenty-six Editor-in-Chief Patrick Healy, who returned to his family's native home of Quebec as a part of his journey into the law.

But we also know that not every McGill Law student comes from Montreal—in fact fewer and fewer have over the years. Of those, there are those who went to McGill Law because they were inspired by the events of the day, such as volume thirty-five senior editor Mayo Moran, who wrote that, "I was ultimately moved to study law by the tremendous debates around the *Charter*, and especially the equality guarantee, that were taking place when I was teaching in the early 80s. I had always been interested in law but with the advent of the *Charter*, law seemed to hold a greater transformative power."[1197] Then there are others, like volume one Editor-in-Chief Fred Kaufman, who used to spend a lot of time covering the courts as a reporter and saw a calling for himself in law; saw the law as something he could love doing.[1198] There are also those like John P Humphrey who, already enrolled at Osgoode Hall before coming to McGill Law, quickly realized that he could never live in Toronto.[1199]

There are those that come for the prestige of the school and those that come for its reputation in human rights; those that come to quickly get two degrees instead of one and those called by the siren-like beauty of the City of Montreal. There are those that come because the professors have good reputations, and some that come because the students have good reputations. There are some that come because they did not get in anywhere else, and some that come because they've dreamed of nothing else since high school.

Once you have law students, then you need to get them to apply to the *Journal*. Some apply on their own, as volume fifty-one Book Review Editor Aleksander Zivanovic described himself doing:

> I remember it was almost on a whim, I wasn't sure what the *Journal* was about but thought that even the process of applying would be a good practice of editing and interviewing skills … The weekend before

1195 Isaacson interview, *supra* note 213.

1196 Fortier interview, *supra* note 23.

1197 Moran interview, *supra* note 807.

1198 Kaufman interview, *supra* note 133.

1199 Hobbins, *supra* note 53 at 757.

> my application was due I was supposed to be out of town on a holiday break but I ended up taking the materials with me to the hotel and working on the "test" portion, trying to justify mock editorial decisions. I can't say the weekend was quite as leisurely as planned.[1200]

Volume forty-two Editor-in-Chief Martin Valasek recalled a similar experience, writing,

> I recall that the application process was painful, and a true test of one's commitment to work on the *Journal*. The application was due in the first weeks of September, just as everyone was enjoying the relatively light schedule of the beginning of the semester, and the many parties and pub crawls that ushered in the new academic year.[1201]

Others need no convincing at all, such as volume fifty-four senior editor Dorian Needham, who wrote that, "From a purely mercenary point of view, having the *Journal* on my resume gave me credibility in job interviews ... There is no particular story as to how I applied: I just had the application package mailed to my home in Victoria, completed it while sitting at a picnic table in the sun, and mailed it back in again."[1202] Still there are others, like volume fifty-three senior editor Stephanie Jones who "originally thought MLJ sounded rather boring. However, I knew 100% finals were even more boring";[1203] and her volume fifty-three fellow senior editor Héloïse Robinson, who wrote, "I wanted to join the *Journal* before I even began my legal studies at McGill."[1204]

But not everyone simply winds up on the MLJ doorstep. You have to get the word out, as volume thirty-two Editor-in-Chief Marc Lemieux recalled in the story of how he wound up on the *Journal*: "I remember an information session in the Common Room hosted by Vol. 31 Senior Board members. I attended out of curiosity, met among others Hélène Guay, and had a discussion with her that led to my applying to become part of the Junior Board of the *Law Journal*."[1205] Many simply join because their friends are on the *Journal*, and others apply by being harassed into doing so. While once upon a time Professors would encourage one to apply or recommend you do, today recruitment is a purely student-based enterprise. And it can be a tougher sell than most would imagine for, as author Scott Turow quoted a friend in his book *One L* as saying, "I figure people who make Law Review deserve it ... What a prize, huh? Fifty hours a week in hell."[1206]

Yet Turow also wrote that, "To me as a 1L, the [*Law Review*] was an object of deepening mystery ... By the end of September, the Law Review had begun to seem the centerpiece of that world of upper-year privilege in which 1Ls were not included."[1207] No doubt there are more than enough students each year willing to set aside summer days—or, more recently as the *Journal* has moved its recruitment process back to January, precious days of study—to eke out a completed application. Even if some executives would prefer their pick of the entire school.

It should be said that the *McGill Law Journal* is unique in the world of student law reviews as it does not consider grades when reviewing applications. Nearly every other review in the world does—some consider grades more important than any other aspect of the application. Even the mention of grades is, in fact, banned from an applicant's package at the MLJ. Instead, applicants are considered purely on their ability to do editorial work and their past experience. If you can do the footnotes and edit the text without making a complete mess of it, then you stand a good chance of making the MLJ. No need to carry a 4.0. It is a policy that has kicked the doors of elite privilege open for decades now, allowing anyone who can take the pressures and complete the work of the *Journal* to get their chance. The *Journal* also does not require candidates to enter an essay competition, as many American reviews do.

To understand just how different this is, J.C. Oleson once wrote that the number one universal characteristic of law reviews and journals is that,

> [T]hey are elitist. Whether based on grades, a write-on competition, or some combination of the two, law review membership is inherently selective. Some of the students who would give their eye teeth (or their eyes) to join the law review are not *invited* to join ... yet another blow to the ego for ambitious law students unaccustomed to failure.[1208]

1200 Zivanovic interview, *supra* note 1090.

1201 Valasek interview, *supra* note 934.

1202 Needham interview, *supra* note 1131.

1203 Jones interview, *supra* note 1116.

1204 Robinson interview, *supra* note 1100.

1205 Lemieux interview, *supra* note 725.

1206 Turow, *supra* note 986 at 270.

1207 Turow, *supra* note 986 at 83.

1208 Oleson, *supra* note 124 at 1337-38. Author's Emphasis.

Such a statement could not be further from the truth at the *McGill Law Journal*.

The contemporary application has been traditionally composed of an editing test upon an article intentionally littered with mistakes, both in the text and the footnotes; a request for the applicant to provide their own editorial decision about the test article, along with their reasons for the decision; and a cover letter and resume. The applicant has ten days to complete the test and submit their documents, during a week of their choosing over the span of a few months. There is no essay component—instead of seeing if you can write, they want to see if you can *edit*.

Once the deadline has passed, the applications are graded and compared by the incoming Executive Board, which has been just recently elected. Until 2010 the application process occurred over summer, but today the process has been changed to allow students to experience the application during the heat of law school—something closer to what they will experience if chosen to join the MLJ. The new executive itself also gets to feel what it is like to have a huge project—the hiring of their new board—in front of them as finals season comes bearing down. The outgoing Executive Board has no say in who gets picked.

To build their new team, the executive team selects a group of students to interview. Some executives choose to interview everybody, others only the top candidates who emerge from the editing tests. Some executive teams have very stringent mathematical grading systems to ensure there is no favouritism, while others hire more by feel. Either way, traditionally the new associate board is hired within forty-eight hours of the interview portion of the application. Tradition also entails that the Editor-in-Chief telephone each of the successful candidates personally to deliver the news—and that rejections not be made until each candidate has personally accepted. Some candidates pick the phone right up, others need to be tracked down—but all receive the news directly from the mouth of the EIC. It is a more complex system than the former method of posting a list of the names of the upcoming year's successful candidates for the junior or associate board that was used in years past.[1209]

Either first or second year students can apply, although you have to commit two full years to the *Journal* if you accept a position with them. All associate board members are automatically promoted to the senior board by the end of the year, so there is no further cutting down of the editorial staff. Most other law journals in the world do not accept many of their first year editors onto the senior board, but the MLJ is able to retain one hundred percent of the experience sown into the associate board. There are, however, elections to see who will hold the executive and special positions available on the senior board. Elections are held in the spring, with only associate board members allowed to run for positions—though all members can vote, except for the Editor-in-Chief, who serves as the tie-breaker. Some years almost all the positions are won by acclamation; in other years there are fierce campaigns.

Regardless of the result, the following afternoon requires everyone to go back to working side-by-side, and inevitably they do. After all, the selection process is a very small part of the work the Editorial and Managerial Boards do during the year. The bulk of it, is editing. But in order to edit you first need authors, and to have authors, you need referees. Some boards have no problem at all finding outside reviewers, while some have no luck at all. It takes a lot of patience to mine through lists of professors, reading about their recent scholarship and sub-interests, and then approach professors whose experience or interest matches the content of the article in a way that creates a connection between the need for the article to be reviewed and why the professor would want to do it. Very few professors and lawyers will simply say yes to anything; it is a sales job that requires research and careful letter drafting. If you get it right, then even if they do not have time they will often send you a list of their colleagues that could take their place. If you get it wrong, you will receive a letter asking why you just sent an article on air and space law to a tax specialist.

Even when the peer reviews are returned, nothing is as it seems. Simply skimming to see whether or not the reviewer recommends an acceptance or rejection will not do. The editor must carefully read the recommendation and think about how the article could or could not be improved. Some editors can remember the articles they rejected as well as they can remember those they worked to bring into shape for their volume. A good editor greets a peer review with the same eyes they meet the text of an accepted article with—unless of course the review trashes the article outright, which many do. At that point, as long as the review was well-conceived, less thought is typically required—unless the dreaded situation arrives of receiving one awful and one glowing review for the same article, at which point the hair starts to turn grey.

Soon enough, however, there is a pile of articles waiting to be revised. As Professor Lon Fuller called

1209 *McGill Law Journal*, "Junior Board of 1976-77". The document is undated but for the intended date of the first meeting of the new juniors with the rest of the board: 22 September, 1976. Therefore we can assume the date was in September 1976.

them, the authors' "babies" come into the inbox waiting to be raised appropriately. This is, of course, very sanitized language for what actually goes on when the paper is handed to its first editor. Volume twenty Editor-in-Chief F.H. Buckley wrote of other times in which the author and editor might not be so receptive of each other:

> Dealing with authors requires diplomacy. When I ripped apart a paper and rewrote it I was careful to praise the excellence of the author's prose. However I also sought, not always successfully, to preserve the author's voice, and to leave untouched the few papers that did not need an editor. The worst authors are those who think themselves stylists. They are loud and their style masks a want of clarity.[1210]

Buckley warned that at the end of the day "the editors will have to rewrite a fair bit of the articles, finding themes that lay hidden, even to the author, and killing the little babies of his precious little phrases."[1211] Sounds like Fuller's worst nightmare, though this kind of editing is rarely done in the contemporary era of the *Journal.*

Volume twelve Editor-in-Chief Stephen A. Scott recalled his own experiences as an author decades after his tenure as editor, to provide some perspective from the other side. He told the story of a time where,

> I did a light-hearted thing in the University of Ottawa review; a book review of *Jowitt's Dictionary of English Law.*[1212] It was light-hearted and fun, but then I got it back from an editor who had turned it into a *ponderous* piece, footnotes endlessly dragging the thing down *into the netherworlds*, and I lost my temper. And I said, "To hell with it, you publish it as it is, or return the copy of the dictionary." Fortunately a former colleague … was advisor to them and he told them that they had better just not try to rewrite my thing for me … especially as the thing was published and referred to in a library journal, and my old friend and mentor (and doctoral supervisor at Oxford) told me that was one of the best things I had ever written.[1213]

Scott also recalled a story about a symposium about Canadian constitutional reform he attended at Duke University, relating that,

> I did a piece on the amending formula and they published that in *Law and Contemporary Problems*, which is their law journal—a very good law journal—and then in a separate volume … The editors there were desperately serious; utterly without a sense of humour. I did this piece on the Canadian constitutional amendment formula, and its history, and unless you were particularly interested in constitutional amending formulas or Canadian history—and constitutional history in particular—you would probably be bored out of your mind by my piece. Why should you read it?
>
> But at the beginning there was a little humorous introduction, cause that's what you're supposed to do—when you give a paper, put a little humour into it—and I referred to a discussion in the *Federal Constitution Convention* in Philadelphia, 1787, where there was a proposal (kind of out of left field) by [George Mason] proposing that Congress be given the power to make sumptuary laws … laws where spending was controlled; luxury repressed, particularly any display of luxury unsuitable to your status … Where I refer to it, I express my relief that Congress cannot control the otherwise boundless limits of the hospitality which we were being shown by the Duke Law Faculty … that "Congress can't control this lavish display,"[1214] which was the only slightly amusing bit that anyone could find in there …
>
> *This these editors wanted to take out!*[1215]

As has been noted before, the author to have published the most pieces in the MLJ over its history is former Faculty Advisor H. Patrick Glenn. Recalling his experiences as an author, he said that the MLJ,

> [J]ust seemed to be the very

1210 Buckley interview, *supra* note 414.

1211 Buckley interview, *supra* note 414.

1212 Stephen A Scott, "Jowitt's Dictionary of English Law ed. by J. Burke" Book Review (1979) 11:3 *Ottawa L Rev* 811.

1213 Scott interview, *supra* note 278.

1214 Stephen A Scott, "The Canadian Constitutional Amendment Process" (1982) 45:4 *Law & Contemp Probs* 249 at 249.

1215 Scott interview, *supra* note 278.

appropriate place to publish what I was doing. I was writing on Quebec law in large measure, sometimes in French and sometimes in English, and the *McGill Law Journal* had an international audience that other journals in Quebec didn't have, but it was also well read in Quebec—so it just seemed to fit with the kind of things I was trying to do to immerse myself in local legal culture.[1216]

Glenn also spoke about the difference between the MLJ and other publications he has worked with in the past, stating that,

> I think that the *Journal* is more enlightened than other places. I have had some extremely frustrating experiences as per U.S. periodicals. The example that sticks in my mind is an article I published in a California journal written on the Guomintang regime in China—and they put a comma after Guomintang, indicating it was a place.[1217] It wasn't: it was a government ...
>
> I had a conversation with former Israeli Chief Justice [Aharon] Barak, who was *incensed* because they had massively rewritten an article for the *Harvard Law Review* for him.[1218] His staff discovered that what they had done is, basically, sent back to him all the suggestions made by Word Perfect under "style". He was almost livid.
>
> When I was at Harvard, Louis Sohn[1219] exploded in front of me too because they had rewritten an article that he had written for them. There are many people who will tell you many stories about the student-editing of journals...
>
> I found [the MLJ] more enlightened generally in terms of their willingness to let authors say it the way they want to say it. There have been particular editors that are more activist than others, and sometimes it takes you time to explain why you wrote it the way you did ... but I think generally it's a fairly happy style of editing they've done.[1220]

There were some authors, however, like volume four Case Comments Editor and future Justice Jean-Louis Baudouin, who did experience the dreaded fully red-marked return articles on two separate occasions during the 1970s and early 80s—articles marked-up so badly that he sent them to other journals for publication.[1221] However, as far as alumni submitting their pieces to the *Journal*, it has been a long time since the MLJ was seen as that presumptuous.

Most of what the editor does is invisible to the author or reader. As volume fifty-three senior editor Héloïse Robinson recalls,

> I remember spending countless hours trying to locate rare international sources in paper form ... we didn't take anything for granted, everything was carefully checked! ... I am not sure if [readers] always understand the extent to which each article is combed through with the utmost attention to detail. Every word, every sentence, every quotation is thoroughly reviewed, not only once, but many times by several different people within the *Journal*. Every citation is checked, not only to see if the commas conform to the McGill *Cite Guide*, but also to see if the substance of the quotation or argument is accurate. In addition, if at all possible, *Journal* members ensure that citations refer to official paper sources, and not to online sources.[1222]

As volume forty-five Editor-in-Chief Azim Hussain wrote, authors are "generally cooperative during this process because they [a]re simply happy to know that their submission w[ill] be published."[1223] As volume thirteen Managing Editor Richard Pound put it, for a student the experience "allows you the opportunity to punch above your weight by exposing you to judgmental challenges, material with which you are seldom familiar through normal classroom activity and to others in a wider academic circle than your

1216 Glenn interview, *supra* note 415.

1217 H Patrick Glenn, "The Grounding of Codification" (1998) 31:3 *UC Davis L Rev* 765 at 771—Ironically, grammar does dictate that *this time* a comma does actually have to come after the word.

1218 Aharon Barak, "A Judge on Judging: The Role of a Supreme Court in a Democracy" (1998) 116:1 *Harv L Rev* at 19.

1219 Future Professor Emeritus of Law at Harvard University and co-author of the controversial book *World Peace Through World Law* (Cambridge: Harvard University Press, 1958). H Patrick Glenn was pursuing his LLM at Harvard University at the time.

1220 Glenn interview, *supra* note 415.

1221 Baudouin interview, *supra* note 142.

1222 Robinson interview, *supra* note 1100.

1223 Hussain interview, *supra* note 988.

own surroundings at McGill."[1224] The typical editorial response is also one of pride to be working on the article. As volume forty-eight Case Comments Editor Hilary Stedwill put it,

> My best memory was finding an article I thought ought to be published and getting it in the *Journal*. In fairness, I've no idea now whether it was, in fact, a welcome addition to the volume of legal literature, but at the time I was convinced and was pleased when others in the academic community thought so too and consequently, the article was included among the *Journal*'s volumes.[1225]

Usually the editor and the author work in harmony, despite what the more extreme stories out there might convince one what is nearer the norm. What authors probably don't know, is that when an article is put out on peer review, the editors are really rooting for it; they attach themselves to the article and are excited to see if the academic community believes in the article too. If a recommendation to reject comes back, the editors that receive it are often even more upset than the author, who can simply resend it to another journal. And when a recommendation to accept rolls in, there is a general whipping up of excitement and positive energy that fills the Executive Board.

What is written in the article very likely matters to the editors working on it, and a healthy dose of respect is given to most authors who work with the *Journal* behind the scenes, even if all that is officially exchanged between the editor and author these days are brief emails. Gone are the days of the four hour meetings between authors and their editors. For an example of this kind of respect to the message of the author, volume forty-six Editor-in-Chief Robert Leckey shared a story that happened during his tenure:

> One of the worst memories was hearing from an author published in issue 1 that the version we had published did not incorporate his extensive changes submitted to us. And then I found, literally in a desk drawer, the mark-up that had never been dealt with. Stephen Toope advised me that the only thing to do was to republish the paper, in its revised version, in one of my remaining issues. At first that seemed excessive to me but I followed Stephen's advice and did it, and today it strikes me as unquestionably the right thing to have done.[1226]

The article in question was "From Sisyphus's Dilemma to Sisyphus's Duty" by Jean-François Gaudreault-DesBiens,[1227] and it is one of only three articles to have been published in the *Journal* twice—the others being the article and translation of the article "What is Interculturalism?" by Gerard Bouchard, and Claude-Armand Sheppard's volume six case comment "*Roncarelli v. Duplessis* Art. 1053 C.C. Revolutionized", which was republished in volume fifty-five's special issue on *Roncarelli*.

The editing of articles is an important function within the academic community. As Professor Roderick A. MacDonald once stated, "Authors are often the worst judges of their own work. Their preoccupations are with the specific points they want to make, and not with the assumptions underlying the arguments they are advancing."[1228] The editor is the reader that gets to talk back to the author, to let them know if what they are saying is clear or not. The editorial process is a dress rehearsal for the big show—the official debut of a new idea. Chief Justice Charles Evan Hughes of the Supreme Court of the United States once spoke on this subject matter, calling law reviews the fourth estate of the law.[1229]

But, in an analogy of something volume fifty-five senior editor Alexandra Dodger once said, it is folly to believe that these foreign lands of ideas that the editors are visiting are the only ones that benefit. It is the student that perhaps benefits most of all. For as Justice Antonio Lamer of the Supreme Court of Canada once wrote within the pages of the MLJ, "The lawyer's art ... is not only to know the law but also to know the code for concealing social and economic change in the interstices of jargon, precedent and legal fiction."[1230] Being on the *Journal* allows students a window into this higher level of dialogue and exchange that can be found in no other place. In this way, the editorial process is also a critical dress rehearsal for the student—for the grand performance that will become their legal careers.

There is also the educational aspect—that the *Journal* is a kind of a seminar in the self-teaching of discipline and lifelong learning. To that end, James

1224 Pound interview, *supra* note 341.

1225 Stedwill interview, *supra* note 1056.

1226 Leckey interview, *supra* note 1009.

1227 Jean-François Gaudreault-DesBiens, "From Sisyphus's Dilemma to Sisyphus's Duty? A Meditation on the Regulation of Hate Propaganda in Relation to Hate Crimes and Genocide" (2000) 46:1 *McGill LJ* 121; and (2001) 46:4 *McGill LJ* 1117.

1228 MacDonald, *supra* note 945 at 13.

1229 Newland, *supra* note 74 at 74.

1230 Lamer & Ryan, *supra* note 490 at 523.

Lindgren once wrote that a conference on the subject of law reviews "reminded me just how smart our best law students are. If these brilliant students are not succeeding as editors, I'm inclined to believe that the fault lies at our own door. We professors haven't given them the help they need. We have failed as educators."[1231]

Perhaps the staunchest modern critic of the student-run law review model is Justice Richard Posner of the United States Court of Appeals Seventh Circuit, the most-cited American legal scholar of the twentieth century,[1232] and former President of the *Harvard Law Review*, who—among other things—finds it appalling that a student-run body could ever be allowed to challenge the thinking of bodies like the US Supreme Court.[1233] The belief runs deep with irony, as upon the fiftieth anniversary of the *Review*, founding Editor-in-Chief John Jay McKelvey had written,

> It [must] be remembered that Harvard professors and students were at one time held up to scorn for venturing to question decisions of the Supreme Court of the United States, and daring to characterize the conclusions reached as "wrong in principle". The freedom and assurance with which the Harvard Law School student, and many times the professor, declared a decision of a high court to be wrong in principle, amazed both the lawyers and the judges of that day ... it was in these reviews that both the judges and practitioners found going on a continuous examination and criticism of the action of the courts by minds free from the restraint which precedent imposes upon the bench and the bar. The judge was being judged, and not in accordance with precedent, but in accordance with principle.
>
> There is no judge and no lawyer who is so sure that he is right that he can ignore the unprejudiced, serious discussion of his conclusions.[1234]

In this new paradigm, courts and lawyers are provided the ability to avoid Michel Foucault's "theatre of hell",[1235] whereby neutrality is threatened by proximity to a case and political want. Apparently this history lesson has escaped some. It is also hard to take Posner too seriously in his criticism of law journals, as within the same essay that he is criticizing them he simultaneously labels the surrounding era of his own Presidency at the *Harvard Law Review* as the "Golden Age ... for student-edited law reviews".[1236] This also calls to memory Jean-Louis Baudouin's early experience as Case Comments Editor in volume four.

For a 2012 perspective on the relationship between authors and editors, volume fifty-six Editor-in-Chief Sara Ross stated that she felt that student editors should look at their role as not "gate-keepers", but "facilitators", saying that,

> I think that this is the beauty of a student-run journal versus a faculty-run journal. As a faculty-run journal, it's hard not to be a gate-keeper, because you *are* an expert in certain fields, so you are ultimately, at base, poisoned from being a pure facilitator as you are so far away from being a blank slate. Now as a law student you can't really *truly* be a blank slate that just purely facilitates legitimate academic commentary, but you are closer to it than someone who has spent many, many years developing an expertise; developing a structure within legal academia. As students you have the unique opportunity to facilitate divergent views within a field, allowing views that are maybe controversial—that maybe you agree with or disagree with—to be heard, rather than just cutting things off where you disagree with them, which is hard to do when you've developed an utter expertise within a field. That's what I mean by facilitator.[1237]

So there we have it—our editors and our authors, the heart of any publication. There are, of course, logistical concerns outside of the content of the publication. One does have to keep up the business side of things—so we also have managers. Managers ensure the bills are paid, invoices are paid up, and revenue bases are continuously being tapped. As volume fifty-two Managing Editor Maegan Hough wrote, "Content may be king but someone still needs to be

1231 James Lindgren, "Reforming the American Law Review" (1995) 47:6 *Stan L Rev* 1123 at 1130.

1232 Shapiro, *supra* note 876.

1233 Richard A Posner, "The Future of the Student-Edited Law Review" (1995) 47:6 *Stan L Rev* 1131 at 1137.

1234 McKelvey, *supra* note 59 at 879-80.

1235 Michel Foucault, *The Spectacle of the Scaffold* (London: Penguin Great Ideas, 2008) at 59

1236 Posner, *supra* note 1233 at 1133.

1237 Ross interview, *supra* note 1089.

sure the electricity stays on."[1238] From annual alumni donations drives to harassing old advertisers to get back on board, there is plenty of hustle that needs to go into the infrastructure of the corporation. The role managers play is immeasurably important, as has been highlighted throughout this book.

Of the managerial concerns is always the effort to "harness technology in the service of the law rather than leave law at the mercy of technology,"[1239] as the Honourable John Turner wrote in his MLJ article. While making editing and communications faster, there are other concerns that come with technology. As volume twenty-eight Editor-in-Chief Stephen J. Toope explained,

> I think there's probably a positive and a negative as to how this evolved. Practically speaking it could make things easier but I think there are more venues available to authors now ... I mean that was always an issue. I remember having to really talk with authors about whether we were their first choice and whether they'd accepted elsewhere and now if you're submitting to twenty or thirty places as people do—that makes life pretty hard.[1240]

Having the management ensuring that all the pitfalls of modern technology do not engulf the overall project is essential. There is always the additional fear that the Internet has rung the death knell of the paper-based publication. In response to this, during volume fifty-four, Managing Editor Eytan Bensoussan remembers that "every time someone would cancel their subscription, I would call them up and I'd say 'well why are you [no longer] subscribing and what could we do differently'?"[1241]

Bensoussan stated that this kind of action "was probably what consumed most of my time, and for me was actually the most interesting by far."[1242] His words sum up one of the key ingredients that management brings to the table—while many publications simply sit back and ponder questions such as this, the management board of the MLJ goes out and finds the answers. There are perks, however, that come from this kind of work that are not experienced by the editorial side—as Advertising Editor for volume four Yves Fortier admits, "Cold calls ... [were] an easy way to become known before the recruitment started."[1243]

Hough added that,

> Being Managing Editor was definitely a crash course in management of both my peers on the executive and the management team working under me. I developed more practical skills from the mistakes made in that arena than I did in all my classes combined! I also was thrown into the management of an established business and had to get up to speed quickly ...
>
> I think being Managing Editor and being thrown in over my head definitely helped me overcome my fears and allowed me to be more open to different careers. Learning to be in charge of a team and having to present to the Advisory Board and work with the faculty and administration forced me to be more outgoing.[1244]

Another distinct component of the MLJ is the French editorial side. Over the years the French editorial board has evolved into an autonomous working machine, soliciting and reviewing its own articles and bringing articles from their initial stage right to the proofs stage. Yet the two editorial sides are still a cohesive unit. As volume forty-one senior editor Marie-Pierre Olivier explained:

> The *Journal* made me discover a new world, in a way, as it gave me the opportunity to interact with students I would have not met otherwise. Being part of the Francophone minority at McGill and coming straight from CEGEP, most of my friends had a similar background. Thanks to the *Journal*, I got to meet more Anglophone students, from various academic years and with different backgrounds. These encounters and friendships, as well as the feeling of belonging to a group ... made my years at McGill much more fulfilling.[1245]

1238 Interview of Maegen Hough by James Cummins (10 January, 2011).
1239 Turner, supra note 323 at 7.
1240 Toope interview, *supra* note 577.
1241 Bensoussan interview, *supra* note 1129.
1242 *Ibid.*

1243 Fortier interview, *supra* note 23.
1244 Hough interview, *supra* note 1238.
1245 Oliver interview, *supra* note 916.

Volume thirty-seven Book Review Editor Renée Thériault wrote further on the subject, stating that, "The *Journal* was the quintessential symbol of the unique character of McGill's Law Faculty – bilingual and bijuridical – which are the very same features that attracted me to the Faculty from the outset, and resonated throughout my involvement at the *Journal* in particular."[1246]

There has been a lot of self-criticism among editors and managers of the MLJ over the last few decades as to the accommodation of French scholarship into the *Journal*. However, consider the following table, which reviews eight of the main Canadian law journals that focus on publishing articles in both French and English. The table reveals, on average, how many contributions in the non-dominant language of the journal appeared in their tables of contents during their most recent volumes:

Name of Law Journal	# of Articles Published over Previous Five Volumes in non-Dominant Language
University of New Brunswick Law Journal	2 French Articles
Queen's Law Journal	2 French Articles
Thémis (Université de Montréal)	3 English Articles
Manitoba Law Journal	3 French Articles
Ottawa Law Review	11 French Articles (one a translation)
Cahiers des droit	13 English Articles
Canadian Bar Review	40 French Articles
McGill Law Journal	**42** French Articles

Figure 4: Data Selected from the last Five Volumes of Each Journal Starting with their Most Recent Completed Volume as of 2011—to that end, only one of the *Manitoba Law Journal*'s French articles was published within the last six years. Book reviews and book notes have been excluded.

As can plainly be seen, the MLJ is by far the most successful university-based journal in the country when it comes to accommodating both of Canada's official languages—printing substantially more contributions in French than the rest of the nation's university-based journals published in the non-dominant language of their journal combined. It should also be considered that fifteen of the total count for the *Canadian Bar Review* come from a single special issue[1247]—which skewed their number upwards over its historical average. Even still, the steadier total of the MLJ saw more French submissions published. As there are no other major jurisdictions in the world where scholarship is actively balanced between two languages within the jurisdiction's major law reviews, this makes the MLJ the most balanced bilingual legal journal in the world today.

This cannot come purely from the city the MLJ is in, because two other Montreal journals are on that list; and it cannot just be that both a B.C.L. and LL.B. are offered in both official languages as a part of the same program, as this also exists at the University of Ottawa—also on this list. The University of New Brunswick is, in fact, in the only officially bilingual province in Canada, and its university's journal is on the list. As was pointed out previously in the discussion about transsystemia, the bilingual nature of the *Journal* is a product of serious effort.

There are other balances that the MLJ takes seriously. A study of US law journals of the period between 2005 and 2008 showed that only about twenty-five percent of articles published in US law reviews had at least one woman author.[1248] During the period between 2005 and 2008, the *McGill Law Journal* saw about forty percent of its articles published with at least one female author attached to it—which is just about the same percentage of lawyers in Canada who are women.[1249]

> There is also a conscientious effort between junior and senior boards within the MLJ to not create a hierarchical environment socially. As volume fifty-one Book Review Editor Alexander Zivanovic stated, his "Best memories were undoubtedly working with senior members who took the time to teach you things, and then trying to do the same for the next generation. There's an art to doing it well that when one can achieve it leaves an indelible impression on both sides of the experience."[1250] Gary Nachshen, the man who filled Zivanovic's position twenty years before, during volume thirty-one, called it an "*esprit de corps* which developed among Board members."[1251]
>
> Senior editor for volume fifty-five Mary Race shared that the mentorship of senior members of the board often went far beyond the practice and processes of editing, as she wrote that,
>
> Getting to know the students in

1246 Theriault interview, *supra* note 854.

1247 (2010) 88:2 *Can Bar Rev*.

1248 Jonathan Gingerich, "A Call for Blind Review: Student Edited Law Reviews and Bias" (2009) 59:2 *J Legal Educ* 269 at 271.

1249 Michael Ornstein, "Racialization and Gender of Lawyers in Ontario" *Law Society of Upper Canada* (April 2010) at 18, online: < http://www.lsuc.on.ca/media/convapril10_ornstein.pdf >

1250 Zivanovic interview, *supra* note 1090.

1251 Nachshen interview, *supra* note 721.

> the upper years was one of the primary benefits of joining the MLJ. The senior editors, always patient and helpful, became great mentors not only within the MLJ setting, but beyond, helping me with the process of law firm interviews, clerkship applications, etc. In turn, I was able to mentor some junior editors when my turn as a senior came around.[1252]

Senior editor for volume fifty-two Héloïse Robinson wrote that getting to know others on the board also provided more than just a professional leg-up, writing,

> Some of my most pleasant memories from my time at the *Journal* were the social events, like the Christmas parties – it was great to get together and have a more relaxed time. It was also a good occasion to discover other talents of *Journal* members – for example David was revealed as a great cook! I also remember a more relaxed day at the *Journal* when Maegan brought her new kitten to the *Journal*'s offices, which provided a happy distraction for many of us![1253]

David and Maegan were the Editor-in-Chief and Managing Editor of her volume. Even if recollections of footnote after footnote are burned into the brains of many former editors, as volume twenty Editor-in-Chief F.H. Buckley wrote, "In the end, one remembers one's friends and little else."[1254]

Indeed, what was remembered far more than the specifics of how the printing got done or what authors had said to them about this removed sentence or that inserted comma, was a host of social anecdotes. Some, after they had come out of the editor or manager's mouth, were followed by something to the effect of "I trust that you will remove any part of this which is inappropriate." It was a lot of trust that judges, professors, and high ranking lawyers put in their contemporary cousins at the MLJ—a trust that was well placed. However, most anecdotes did pass the original "Should I really have said that?" and "Should you really have said that?" litmus tests.

To make everything work at the *Journal*, though, you need a leader. Perhaps the loneliest job on the *Journal* is that of Editor-in-Chief. As volume forty-six Editor-in-Chief Robert Leckey put it more succinctly than most,

> The editor in chief really has very little concrete leverage: it's very rare for the student's credits to be withheld, and so you're basically dealing with volunteers. And when they turn out to be less motivated or careful than you thought, it's hard to know how to handle that.
>
> It is a very unpleasant feeling to review a piece that has supposedly been checked and to see one or two things you know can't possibly be right (such as a pinpoint to p. 17 of an article that starts on p. 100), and to realize that you can't trust anything in it.
>
> I was finished my volume before I left in late September 2001 for my exchange in Paris. So what I am about to say is vicarious: it has always struck me as nightmarish to be slaving on as editor in chief finishing up the volume after the rest of the team has left.[1255]

No editor-in-chief wanted to discuss their having to stay months past their tenure to complete their volume, which is hardly surprising as they very likely did not want to complain. The problem is not a new one. It has been, over the past decade, more common than not for every other editor to largely disappear come April, and evaporate entirely come August. At that point there is, many times, only the editor-in-chief left with every task and every little detail that has to get done to put their volume's issues out. A quick look at the publication dates of some fourth issues over this period reveals that a final release five or six months into the following scholastic year is not unheard of. The team is gone and only one person is responsible to carry the burden of an institution typically populated and run by *thirty-six or more people*.

This is even more stunning considering that the MLJ is one of the only major student-run law journals in the country that has only one editor-in-chief. The *University of Toronto Faculty of Law Review*, *Alberta Law Review*, and *Queen's Law Journal*, all have two editors-in-chief, and the *Ottawa Law Review* has three. *Osgoode Hall Law Journal*, *Manitoba Law Journal*, and *Saskatchewan Law Review* all have Faculty editors-in-chief. There are no other law reviews in Canada that publish four issues per year that have only one editor-in-chief—the *University of British Columbia Law*

1252 Race interview, *supra* note 1142.

1253 Robinson interview, *supra* note 1100.

1254 Buckley interview, *supra* note 414.

1255 Leckey interview, *supra* note 1009.

Review, for example, has one but only publishes two issues per volume. It can very well be said given this context that Editor-in-Chief of the MLJ is the most difficult student editorial position in the country.

Today it doesn't matter where you are in the world, as EIC you are on call until your final issue is in the mail. Recent editors-in-chiefs and their hardest working executives have been stuck on email figuring out the solutions to various problems from all across the world—from New York City (volume fifty-five Editor-in-Chief Seo Yun Yang) to Italy (volume fifty-six Editor-in-Chief Sara Ross) to the Caribbean (volume fifty-six Executive Editor Amélie Gouin) to Israel (volume fifty-seven Editor-in-Chief Will Colish) to Madagascar (volume fifty Editor-in-Chief Fabien Fourmanoit, who after asking his executives to only use the phone sparingly due to long distance charges, wrote, "I'll tell the lemurs you said hello!").[1256]

If it wasn't enough for the Editor-in-Chief to see their grades marred by a year of rarely sleeping, never eating, and doing nothing but *Journal* work, to have to continue this at an even harder pace alone after more than a year of doing it with a team is the greatest untold story of the MLJ. Many times that EIC's past associate board, now the *Journal*'s senior board, has nothing but disdain for the situation—as they become very suddenly concerned with completing the massive workload represented by their own volume. In a sense, the system works. Instead of sliding further and further behind by allowing new boards to pick up the slack as occurred in the volumes before F.H. Buckley or Patrick Healy's tenures, the clock today is always reset. How the system works is a great mystery, however. Some of these editors-in-chief had to perform superhuman feats to get things done, without recognition, without credits, without pay. The oral history of the *Journal* reveals that only one editor-in-chief didn't stick it out, leaving the completion of the *Journal* to hired support staff. Being elected Editor-in-Chief can change your life, but for many it becomes just what Leckey labelled it, a nightmare, when everyone else is gone.

This is one place where the MLJ of today perhaps has failed. Volume thirty senior editor Nicholas Kasirer, whose story of travelling across the English Channel to stay up all night in the effort of getting the *Journal* out, was paraphrased in the minutes of the 2008 Board of Advisors meeting, which he followed up by explaining that,

> [I]t's a new philosophy that we work only during the school year – during the credited year. It is sad that we only work for credits. Students used to just "do it" for the pride of the *Journal*. Be careful of our rewards system because it makes students flee in the end ... [I] went to Harvard recently and visited the *Law Review*: [the] culture is very different – students did it for the sheer pride of it.[1257]

There could very well be more reasons for this shift towards placing the brunt of the work of an off-year at the *Journal* on the shoulders of the Editor-in-Chief. Editors face potential political costs in the future by penalizing each other in a peer-only environment, as those below you at the time could be your boss in a few short years. There are also the increased pressures of the transsystemic program, whereby students for the last decade have been required to do two degrees at once. Whatever it is, as has always happened in the past, the MLJ will likely figure things out. The last past-due volume saw both Executive Editors helping the Editor-in-Chief right until the end, along with substantial support from the following volume's Executive. That example, at the very least, gives future editorial teams cause for hope.

There have been other eras like this, where something amiss went on for nearly a decade, before it got solved—thus is the life of an organization run by a constant stream of new editors. In the end, though, it is the Editor-in-Chief that must guide the ship with no excuses. Thus volume twenty Editor-in-Chief F.H. Buckley gave the following advice for those looking to assume the position:

> You should have absorbed such an understanding of legal principles, in your first year and a half at law school, that you can safely skip virtually all of the rest of your classes. You should be a quick study, and be able to ace a course after fours days study. Doubtless it is easier as you now have an obligatory fourth year. Yet that is the model. You will do most of the work, but must make it seem as though you are only one amongst many. For editing purposes you must have a close ally who can assist in the other of our official languages. You will need a business manager who knows his way around a budget and a smooth-talking advertising manager. If you can, besides this, find two or three people on whom you can rely as editors, consider

1256 Fabien Fourmanoit, "Memorandum to the Executive Board" (19 July, 2004) 1 at 3.

1257 Minutes 08, *supra* note 1110.

> yourself lucky.
>
> And then you have the junior board, who will beg you to load work on them. They will very simply adore you, and you should on occasion condescend to speak to them, simply for the thrill it will give them. When I took the job I considered that I had left the law school. I had a new set of friends and colleagues, and they were the whole of my McGill experience thereafter. As most become good friends it was all I needed.[1258]

It is a huge role to fill. You are President of a corporation (in theory before, in law now) without the option of a strong-armed method of leadership—you can only rule by finesse. In hindsight, many editors-in-chief have some kind of apology they would like to make to their staff, for things that went on in their heads at the time that nobody else noticed. Volume thirty-two Editor-in-Chief himself wrote that, "I was an Editor-in-Chief who had more vision than people or political skills. I am pleased to report to those who may have found I was lacking in this latter respect that some of those important skills were acquired subsequently!"[1259]

The stress of the job leads only the foolish to believing they succeeded—though almost all of these young people did. To assume such a position of authority barely out of one's teen-hood is something that challenges all to the very edge of their abilities. Again, the most amazing story from the league of former editors-in-chief is that they not only survived the trauma, but that a smile creeps across many of their faces while remembering their tenure; and that they forgave those other members of the MLJ who came into the office to complain about the way the EIC was doing things, whilst that member was simultaneously late on their last assignment—or at the very least, that the EIC did not smack them upside the head.

The leadership at the MLJ is the responsibility of the other four executives as well. Today the English Executive Editor, French Executive Editor, Coordinating Editor, and Managing Editor might be mistaken as President of their own parts of the *Journal* at times, putting their own style and applying their own rules to their corner of the enterprise. The Citations Editor also has almost complete autonomy as well, since professors, courts, and lawyers from all over the world send in many dozens of questions per year as to how to properly cite different documents within their publications. Sometimes the answer is just hidden in the *Guide*, while other times the MLJ has to research the question, make a call, and then record it for future editions. The Citations Editor can spend up to several hours on one question, just to make sure they get it right, for as Arthur D. Austin wrote of legal citation back in the 1980s, "What started as incidental and functional, footnoting now is thought to be a Frankenstein monster, rambling uncontrolled at the bottom of the page."[1260]

Some Citations Editors also serve as Cite Guide Editors, though not always, as can be seen in a list of each edition of the *Guide*'s editors:

First Edition: Robert Metcalfe, *Associate Editor for Volume Twenty-Nine*, and Sonia Struthers, *Senior Editor for Volume Thirty-One*, whose official titles were "Project Co-ordinators"

Second Edition: Michael Waterston, *Citations Editor*, and Randall Hofley, *Senior Editor for Volume Thirty-Three*

Third Edition: Lisa Yarmoshuk, *Citations Editor for Volume Thirty-Seven*

Fourth Edition: Sebastien Beaulieu, *Editor-in-Chief*; Sarah Maywood, *Executive Editor*; and Paule Morisset, *Executive Editor for Volume Forty-Three*

Fifth Edition: Timothy Reibetanz, *Cite Guide Editor for Volume Forty-Seven*

Sixth Edition: Eliezer Rosenblatt, *Cite Guide Editor for Volume Fifty-One*

Seventh Edition: Svetlana Samochkine, *Cite Guide Editor for Volume Fifty-Five*

Some of these editors worked further past the end of their official senior year with the *Journal* than their Editor-in-Chief.

The Executive Editor position is likely the least appreciated of all the marquee positions. While the Citations Editor can often lay claim to the editorship of the *Guide*, or networking with future colleagues, and the Managing Editor and Editor-in-Chief have something that will still look stand-out on a resume forty years down the road, Executive Editors are faced with a similar workload but far less recognition. It is

1258 Buckley interview, *supra* note 414.

1259 Lemieux interview, *supra* note 725.

1260 Austin, *supra* note 650 at 1133.

not a bad gig—the position is still lauded by employers and you have far more contact with the associate board, which gains you a positive reputation around the Faculty—but it is far more important than just taking care of tasks the Editor-in-Chief doesn't have time to do.

The quality of the *Journal*'s Executive Editors is, by some measure, more important to the success of the *Journal* than the quality of the Editor-in-Chief. The length of time it takes to get a volume out is often directly related to the level of dedication and skill shown by the Executive Editors—how much they are willing to put in over the year. While the Editor-in-Chief and Managing Editor are the face of the *Journal* to the Faculty and the broader legal community, the Executive Editors are the face of the executive to the rest of the Editorial Board. They are the ones there to mentor the associates and maneuver through the everyday problems of editorial consistency—the number one goal and most cherished accomplishment of almost every volume.

Some Executive Editors ran for the position, some fell back on it after a failed bid for Editor-in-Chief, but nevertheless they put in the hours that many senior editors would simply refuse to even look at for only a few more credits. They are far closer to the heartbeat of the *Journal* than the EIC, which allows them the all-important ability to take the MLJ's pulse at any given point in time. The overnight maturing process this requires is quite stunning to watch. As Robert Weisberg put it, tongue-in-cheek, during an anthropological viewing of the contemporary law review:

> The law review is a well-tuned instrument of cultural transmission—it allows editors to go through a delayed, but intense, adolescent crisis. That is, it permits young members of the tribe to work out their inevitably conflicted attitudes toward their parent figures by simultaneously deferring to their awesome intellectual and moral authority while impudently attacking, degrading, and correcting the products of their genius. The result is the fully socialized new tribal leader.[1261]

Whatever the process is, its torrid pace between spring elections and the hiring of a new associate board less than two months later is—at the very least—intense. Though as volume forty-eight Editor-in-Chief Carole Chan stated upon the occasion of the *Journal*'s fiftieth anniversary: "It's exciting to be involved in this legacy ... to uphold that standard."[1262]

The broader team, the Editorial Board, is composed of senior and associate editors—all of whom still put in hours not fathomed by students outside the *Journal*'s walls. In many ways, here it is not how smart you are, but how hard you work. Stephen J. Toope mentioned that "reliability ... was just crucial because if you had people who might be very, very bright, but were always losing things then the whole thing just doesn't work very well."[1263] They are the individuals who first trek over to the library to hunt down every source in every article. Every single source from every single footnote is tracked down in its original form, checked for both content and the exactness of quote replication, publication information, and so forth, proof of which is then photocopied so that the information can be double-checked by the Executive Editors and Editor-in-Chief.

Today, huge binders are created for each article. If the source the footnote points to is quoting another source altogether, then that second source is tracked down. If that additional source again turns out not to be the original—and quotes another source—then the next source is tracked down, and so on. Books and periodicals are called in from all over the world to the McGill library so that each source can be verified. Nothing is taken for granted. During volume fifty-six, a team of associate editors spent over thirty hours trying to decipher a small portion of very old legislative documents in Hebrew—and did not stop until the job was done. Another article from that volume required the translation of a Japanese judicial decision not available in any other language. It was reminiscent of the Russian translation problems during the preparation volume forty-four's special issue of the Civil Code of Russia—only the volume fifty-six translations were done for just regular, run-of-the-mill articles, and without the support of an international team of experts.

It does not matter if only one copy of an old document from the American colonies circa 1750 exists—the team will track down a copy and photocopy it for the binder. And this is before the team begins to reformat every citation into the proper format according to the *Guide*. As volume forty-two Citations Editor Don McGowan put it, "I spent [hours] locked in a room with my computer ... trying to figure out how things should be cited. Seriously, that's something you can spend a lot of time on."[1264] Hundreds of hours of work go into every article to ensure that once it is published in the

1261 Weisberg, *supra* note 73 at 1149.

1262 Rhonda Mullins, "50 Years of Scholarly Excellence" *McGill Faculty of Law Newsletter 2002/2003* (2003) at 10.

1263 Toope interview, *supra* note 577.

1264 McGowan interview, *supra* note 938.

Journal, you may not agree with what it says, but you can trust that it is based on accurate research that has not been skewed in any way.

The workload of an MLJ editor can really only be seen in a comparison between it and other journals of its stature. The average length of the MLJ over volumes fifty-four through fifty-six, is 1003 pages, which was produced by a student staff of thirty-six people—for an average of 27.9 pages per staff member. This is one of the highest averages in the world, representing one of the toughest workloads in the world for a law journal member—with the only close competitor in Canada being the *Alberta Law Review*. The following chart provides an even broader context, including the top ranked student-run journals from Australia, Canada, and the US—the three nations in the world where the upper-echelons of legal publishing revolves around student-run law journals:

Journal	Average Length	Number of Staff	Avg. Pages per Editor
McGill LJ	1003 (4 issues)	36	27.9
Alta L Rev	1074 (4 issues)	39	27.5
Harv L Rev	2174 (8 issues)	88	24.7
Colum L Rev	2179 (8 issues)	93	23.4
NYUL Rev	2027 (6 issues)	98	20.7
Yale LJ	2102 (8 issues)	102	20.6
Sydney L Rev	695 (3 issues)	35	19.9
Melbourne UL Rev	1152 (3 issues)	64	18
Stan L Rev	1578 (6 issues)	91	17.3
Queen's LJ	801 (2 issues)	61	13.1
UBC L Rev	482 (2 issues)	39	12.4
Ottawa L Rev	445 (2-3 issues)	77	5.8

Figure 5: Article indexes and advertisements have been excluded from page counts. Statistics are taken from the last three fully published volumes of each journal as of November 12, 2011, and restricted to journals that are fully student-run—without any editorial support from Faculty (even if only one faculty member is involved), as Faculty editors are paid employees of the university.

Then there are the associate and senior managers who might not be involved in the accounting or collections, but fill in the gaps between what the *Journal* wants to do and what it can do. The little things around the office can be as important as the most complex problems. Making sure all the little pebbles are out of the way so that the team does not find themselves tripping unnecessarily is critical. As Beverley McLachlin of the Supreme Court of Canada once joked about her role on the Court upon the tenth anniversary of her tenure as Chief Justice,

> Not the least of the administrative accomplishments of the past ten years has been improving the quality of coffee in the Supreme Court of Canada. The first promise I made to my colleagues upon becoming Chief Justice was to improve the quality of Courthouse coffee ... Within a few weeks, we were all enjoying high-quality cappuccino. Whatever else they may say about my time as Chief Justice, I comfort myself with the knowledge that no one can dispute that the quality of the coffee has improved.[1265]

Of course the managers of the MLJ are too busy to be brewing coffee. Once the Executive Board decides to have an event, the Management Board arranges the space, the food, the liquor permits, the invitations, the advertising, the sponsors, get speakers and guests to commit to coming, design the posters, bring in the materials the day of the event, set up the event, run the event, and then strike the event—making sure everything they begged, borrowed, or stole is put back where it came from by the end of the night. Trying to find those last two rented wine glasses out of 250 that have been passed around throughout the Faculty for the last four hours can be a nightmare in and of itself. In their downtime, managers now join the editorial side in preparing the editing templates and reviewing some of the hundreds of articles submitted every year to the MLJ, in a recent effort to bring the roles of each board somewhat closer together.

And last, but not least, for any journal of this kind to exist, you need a Faculty of Law. The Faculty Advisor to the *Journal* can often remain in the background for years, but many times they are there right alongside the MLJ, giving support to whatever it decides to do next. Volume twelve Editor-in-Chief Stephen A. Scott himself served as Faculty Advisor for volumes fifteen and sixteen. As he described of his experience, "The *Law Journal* managed itself. I gave advice when needed and didn't meddle."[1266] Scott also recalled a moment with Dean Maxwell Cohen when he was Editor-in-Chief,

1265 Beverley McLachlin, "The First Decade of the 21st Century: The Supreme Court of Canada in Context" Remarks before the CBA Conference on the McLachlin Court's First Decade (19 June, 2009) at 7, online: < http://www.supremecourtlaw.ca/userfiles/file/english/speeches/S_C_C_in_Context.pdf >

1266 Scott interview, *supra* note 278.

where,

> Max sent me a manuscript—a speech given by the Speaker of the House of Commons, Mr. Speaker [Alan] Macnaughton—for publication. I wasn't going to publish it, it was kind of unsuitable; it was an after-dinner speech and there wasn't much substance to it. And actually, Max Cohen responded very meekly. He said, "Yes, you're quite right, there really isn't much substance in it", or something to that effect … I politely, I assume, declined it, and he agreed with me. It was an interesting demonstration of the relations between the Faculty and the *Journal*, in that he did not think it his role to push stuff on me—even if he might have wanted to please the Speaker.[1267]

Volume twenty-eight Associate Editor Marc Barbeau wrote of his Faculty Advisor Professor Yves-Marie Morissette, who was Advisor to volumes twenty-six through thirty-one, stating that, "He was a great guy; great professor; great mentor to me personally. I enjoyed every interaction I had with him … I spent a lot of time just going to his office and talking about things, law and whatever."[1268] Volume twenty-six Editor-in-Chief Patrick Healy also mentioned that Morissette "became a very dear and friend remains my closest friend in Montreal to this day."[1269]

Healy would himself go on to become a Faculty Advisor to the *Journal* from volume thirty-six through forty-one, the same length of tenure as Morissette, exactly ten years after Morissette had taken the position. Volume thirty-six Editor-in-Chief Julia Hanigsberg remembered that the "tremendous support provided by the faculty is something that sticks with me. The Dean, the Faculty Advisor Patrick Healy, and the entire faculty enabled those of us who were working on the *Journal* to be fully engaged in the intellectual life of the faculty."[1270] Still involved as a MLJ trustee, the Dean she spoke of was now-Dean Yves-Marie Morissette.

Things have changed over time. As Faculty Advisor of volumes one through five Jean-Gabriel Castel expressed of his days with the *Journal*,

> You had the Toronto law journal, you had the *McGill Law Journal*—you had at the most three or four. In the states, you had several hundred periodicals, so we had much more influence … The *McGill Law Journal* and the few other Canadian legal periodicals that existed at the time … If you wrote in there, you had much more influence than today, where you have a dozens of legal periodicals; in the States, scores of them … By starting the *McGill Law Journal* at a time when there were very few legal periodicals, at least people who were respected experts in their fields had a voice, which was listened to by the judiciary. Especially as the tradition that existed in England at the time was never to cite a living author—not the case in Canada, and that was another incentive for people to write in the … *McGill Law Journal*.[1271]

The anatomy of the *Journal*, as this chapter purports to describe, is of course only the dry bones of the matter. The flesh and blood upon those bones should hopefully have flowed from the previous chapters, but there is no guarantee of that. In the end, the *Journal* is a living institution that is often nothing like it was mere months before. What can be said, however, is that it is one of the great expressions of the brilliance of youth that exists in Canadian society—it is immediate, and maintains a substantial legacy year after year.

1267 *Ibid.*

1268 Barbeau interview, *supra* note 586.

1269 Healy interview, *supra* note 413.

1270 Hanigsberg interview, *supra* note 853.

1271 Castel interview, *supra* note 44.

Chapter Seven:

Roads Not Yet Travelled

"I should have seen to it, these young folk have no sense."

Anton Chekov's *The Cherry Orchard*[1272]

Gaylord Parkinson, Chairman of the Republican Party in California in 1965, uttered the phrase, "Thou shalt not speak ill of any fellow Republican,"[1273] which famously helped lead to the election of Ronald Reagan as Governor of the State. There is another general rule in American politics, which states that no past President should ever attack those that come into office after them. The gist of the rule is that no one can ever know what you are going through but those that came before, and to sever those ties is just foolish. Similarly, support from your current and past peers is sometimes all you can count on in life as a *Journal* member. There is perhaps no better way of describing why *Journal* editors stick together as tightly as they do over time as a group.

But what is the substance or root of this ethic; those within this brotherhood/sisterhood; those within this pure ground where scholarship is all that matters? Does it all revolve back to Albert Camus' antihero Jean-Baptiste Clamence and his claim that law is done "out of self-interest to begin with and later out of conviction?"[1274] Do people really start out at a law journal due to the resume-building prospect of joining the group and only later come to grips with that which they can provide to each other and the world? Or is it the opposite: does wisdom exist only at the beginning and—as Clamence claims—the shelters of Descartes are, over time, turned into nothing but an asylum?[1275] Perhaps, instead, the whole enterprise is entirely altruistic (a doubtful

1272 Anton Chekov, "The Cherry Orchard" in *Five Plays* (London: Oxford's World Classics, 1998) at 294

1273 Brian Williams, "the 11th commandment" (17 October, 2007), online: < http://dailynightly.msnbc.msn.com >.

1274 Albert Camus, "The Fall" (New York: Vintage International, 1991) at 41.

1275 *Ibid* at 116.

hypothesis).

Regardless of its origin, according to many today looking back on their time with the *Journal*, the experience provided them with skills they still use and memories they still cherish. The annual rigour of producing a volume of the MLJ, starting from scratch only to then hand the institution off to another set of young scholars, is indeed more than a purely Sisyphean task. It is true that many join the *Journal* to improve their job prospects, and the MLJ does, but the MLJ offices are more than a workplace. As volume twenty-eight Associate Editor Marc Barbeau put it,

> I think [the *Journal*] actually focused me on law beyond the fact … I'm going to explain this in a more accurate way. I was focused in my first year just on passing, passing my courses, passing my classes, not failing. Going from that mindset to another mindset, was a necessary rite of passage if you will …
>
> The *Law Journal* exposed me to people who were dedicated, committed, intelligent …we're all dedicated, intelligent, committed at a law faculty, but it was a group of people that were committed to doing something important. It seemed important to us at least. And that exercise of actually applying oneself, not just individually to pass your classes, but to producing something, doing it properly, thinking about it … actually producing something that is meaningful to the legal community—that process gave me a different perspective of what I was doing at the law faculty …
>
> I looked around me and I saw people suddenly who were already or on their way to being very accomplished… particularly in my position, as someone who was still shaping his young adulthood, having all of these people around me was hugely important—immeasurably important.[1276]

Volume twenty-six Editor-in-Chief Patrick Healy talked about the immediate impact the *Journal* had on his own early career.

> [I]t had a very decisive influence on my career path, because it was as a result of my work at the *Journal* that I was offered a job with the Law Reform Commission. I think that it was thought, rightly or wrongly – I hope rightly – that my work on the *Journal* showed a measure of self-discipline, and an ability to write, and an ability to deal with texts in a critical fashion … I was offered two jobs at the Law Reform Commission, one in administrative law and one in criminal law. And I have every reason to believe that it was directly linked to my work at the *Journal*.[1277]

Volume thirty-nine Editor-in-Chief Erica Stone also felt that her time on the *Journal* was integral to her career path, writing,

> What I do today has been profoundly affected by my experience on the *Journal*. During my tenure I learned about my preferences and my aptitudes. Today, I am a legal researcher and writer, working in the health policy and medical malpractice field. I have worked in government and in private practice in a major law firm. I am now happily practicing in my chosen field as an independent contractor for my former law firm, something I might not have chosen to do had I not had the previous experience of running an office, following budgets, and being my own boss.[1278]

The continual movement of individuals through the *Journal*, starting out as law students, leaving as future lawyers or scholars, clerks or judges, has produced a strong tradition of future success at the MLJ, as can be seen throughout this book. For as H. Patrick Glenn once wrote about the culture of McGill Law, "Tradition conceived as information has no borders."[1279]

After their time on the *Journal*, members go on to a great variety of pursuits. Some very lucky ones are able to transition directly into a clerkship with the Federal Court system. Stephen J. Toope was asked to compare his experiences as an SCC clerk and his experiences with the *Journal*, and replied that,

> I think being an editor at the *Journal* and being a law clerk, I felt that I really had to make sure that I was operating at the top of my game. You couldn't just wing it. I mean as a student your exam comes up, you study for it, you want to do well but if it doesn't go as well as you had hoped it's not really a disaster whereas if you don't

1276 Barbeau interview, *supra* note 586.

1277 Healy interview, *supra* note 413.

1278 Stone interview, *supra* note 885.

1279 H Patrick Glenn, "Doin the Transsystemic: Legal Systems and Legal Traditions" (2005) 50:4 *McGill LJ* 863 at 897.

turn in the *Journal* or if you don't actually get the memo done for your judge you've got a big problem. So I think that [a] sense of responsibility is very parallel … [as] was working as a team. Even though at the Supreme Court the teams are smaller, I worked really closely with some of my colleagues who were other law clerks and then I was working with the judge and another clerk in the chambers so I think [what is also similar is] working together and actually divvying up the work and making sure it gets done and then feeling responsible to other people.[1280]

Others, like volume twenty Editor-in-Chief F.H. Buckley, go directly into academia, as Buckley recalled,

> Being the editor-in-chief helped get me into Harvard. When I informed my principal at Blakes, Bob Donaldson, that I wished to postpone my articles, he sighed and said that the firm policy was to permit one to go off on frolics if one wished. I never regretted the decision. I played a great deal of squash (English ball) at Harvard, and subsequently my year in Cambridge helped when I had to decide whether to go into teaching. I approached my mentor at the firm, Brian Westlake, and asked for his advice. "There's a difference between being bored," he said, "and appearing bored." That was when I knew I should become a law teacher.[1281]

In discussion of what things an academic can take from the *Journal* throughout their career, volume forty-six Editor-in-Chief Robert Leckey wrote that now,

> I suppose I appreciate better the things that are important to faculty members—having confirmation of publication if you are submitting a renewal or tenure file, the year of publication on the spine of a journal for reporting purposes—than I did as a student. And I suppose too that the way I interact with journals as an external reviewer reflects my appreciation of the student editor's task.
>
> I think my time at the journal has affected the way I interact with other journals. Knowing how easily things can go wrong in the editing and publication process, I'm a very meticulous and hands-on author![1282]

Volume twelve Editor-in-Chief Stephen A. Scott also shared his path towards an academic career, remembering that:

> In June of 1957 if you had told me that in exactly ten years time, June of '67, I would be taking an appointment as a professor of law, I would have thought you were a raving lunatic … When I was in third year, Max Cohen invited me to join the teaching staff—now, you may be saying "oh, he's hot stuff this Scott, invited out of third year law to take an appointment"—but you have to look at the context of those years. The economy was booming. If you wanted to be an architect, you were an architect—you didn't ask if anything was being built and whether there were jobs for architects. You assumed there were jobs and you did what you wanted to do.
>
> So if you had a—maybe a bookish, if you want to call me that—an academically oriented law student who was bilingual and had good results academically, then in that sense it was a seller's market from the standpoint of the law student. Max Cohen was simply grabbing an available, bilingual, promising (if you want to call it that) law student in market conditions where he wouldn't necessarily find [another] …
>
> In that context I was taken on, and I was really scared of my bar exams, because in those days you had to memorize the *Civil Code*. It was really demanding … I walked on the mountain for three months, marching up and down the mountain with a *Civil Code* in my hand memorizing the articles … Once I had the job, to stand in front of a classroom of students, to teach law if I had failed the bar exam, how could I possibly do that? I would be feeling like the most consummate jerk around. The pressure was really on.[1283]

Volume four Case Comments Editor Jean-Louis Baudoin recalled his own path into academia as well, stating that,

1280 Toope interview, *supra* note 577.

1281 Buckley interview, *supra* note 414.

1282 Leckey interview, *supra* note 1009.

1283 Scott interview, *supra* note 278.

Volume 49 associate board recruitment poster, used to advertise at the McGill University Faculty of Law. Top row: Volume 37 Solicitations Editor Adelle Blackett, Volume 12 Case Comments and Book Review Editor Armand de Mestral, Volume 12 Editor-in-Chief Stephen A. Scott, and Volume 26 Editor-in-Chief Patrick Healy. Bottom row: Volume 34 Executive Editor David Lametti, Volume 30 senior editor Nicholas Kasirer, and Volume 36 senior editor Geneviève Saumier.

> When I graduated from McGill I think I was nineteen years old, and I couldn't practice at that time because the age of majority was 21. So I was articling with what is now Norton Rose … and they said "you know, we can use your services for at least one year, but what do you plan to do?" and I said "I'll try to get a scholarship and go abroad."
>
> So I did a PhD in Paris for three years… and at that time I think I had drank from the cup of theory. And practice really did not interest me at all … but during my years as a law professor I [still] always practiced, mostly pleading in the Supreme Court and the Court of Appeal.[1284]

Other editors and managers go off into the business world. Volume eleven Articles Editor David O'Brien discussed his own path in that direction:

> I always had a bend towards economic issues which I then of course combined with law and for a while when I practiced law I was actually a trial lawyer which was [unusual]. Usually when someone moves from law to business they've been doing business law for a long time and I had actually been a trial lawyer for the first five years or so and then gradually moved to more business law and the truth was I was recruited to the job as General Counsel of Petro Canada, which had just started up in Calgary …
>
> From what I know most lawyers who have gone into business … tend to have done it in an area where the law was a critical piece to the success of the business. What I mean by that is that they were usually heavily regulated businesses … So most of the lawyers that moved into executive positions moved into them in regulated industries, where the outcome was dependent on hearings and so forth. Mine was totally different. I went into an industry where you had to be entrepreneurial and it didn't depend on your legal training *per se*, although your legal training can be a wonderful background in terms of analysis, critical thinking, et cetera …
>
> As a matter of fact over the years I've been approached by a lot of lawyers who have gotten to a stage in their careers where they really wanted a change and they were inquiring of me as to whether I could give them advice as to how to do that. Unfortunately there's no cookie-cutter answer to it.[1285]

1284 Baudouin interview, *supra* note 142.
1285 O'Brien interview, *supra* note 262.

As was stated previously, O'Brien would go on to become the Chairman of the Royal Bank of Canada and Chancellor of Concordia University after his tenure at Petro Canada.

Volume fourteen Articles Editor Robert Leclerc also shared his path into business, writing,

> The firm had undertaken a governance review and established a fresh program for the structure and administration of Milner Fenerty. I had chaired the governance committee and perhaps as a result of my work in this area became the candidate of choice to lead the firm. My time as Chairman and CEO was most interesting and accompanied by all the customary challenges and some that were unexpected. The merger with and into what has become FMC occurred subsequent to my departure – which is not to say I would have been opposed to the notion of building the firm and having it evolve as events transpired.
>
> I was asked to become the non-executive Chairman of Echo Bay Mines Ltd. and wanted to combine this with a few other business activities I had been considering. After 28 years of practicing law, partly (three years) taken up with executive responsibilities, it seemed time for a change in direction. It is not that I found the law suddenly not to my liking. Simply stated, it was time to explore life from the client side of the desk. My foray into the business world turned out to involve more than had been anticipated, as conditions within Echo Bay and in the precious metals mining industry at the time (1997) led to my assuming the CEO role at Echo Bay. There was much work to do and the challenges increased in the then prevailing climate of low commodity prices. With no time for other opportunities, my entire focus became Echo Bay and the mandate to lead the company through difficult times. Ultimately we merged with others to create a new version of Kinross Gold Corp. Upon completion of the merger in early 2003, I retired as CEO of Echo Bay.[1286]

There is also the route of in-house counsel, which Citations Editor for volume forty-two Don McGowan followed. He explained that,

> I am basically Forrest Gump. I was working at Osler's in Montreal, had done a rather large policy study for the [American Bar Association] on open-source software licensing and why governments shouldn't dedicate tax dollars to supporting it. It turns out that if you write that study, there's a job waiting for you at Microsoft. (At least there was in 2004.) So I ended up in the Regulatory Affairs and Public Policy group at Microsoft working on policy analysis and also on providing the legal advice for the security technologies in most of Microsoft's software and hardware. One of those items was the Xbox 360, and that led to my getting the job as lead attorney for Microsoft Game Studios. And from there it was only one headhunter away from Pokémon …
>
> In-house you basically trade the annoyance of timesheets for the annoyance of meetings. It's the way the perceptions change when you're employed by the client. You can't any longer step back and say, "Well, that's a stupid decision, but if you lose the lawsuit it's not my problem." It really does become your problem, and so you have more skin in the game. The hours in the office might be fewer (and even that's not always the case), but you don't really leave it behind anymore.[1287]

Others still go into the public sector, such as volume twenty-three senior editor Elaine Feldman, who also wrote of her career path:

> [I]t was happenstance. After I graduated from McGill Law School, I joined the Dept of Foreign Affairs and International Trade (back then it was just External Affairs). I have spent most of my career in the Foreign Service, abroad and in Ottawa. Much of that was in the field of trade policy, including two postings to Geneva to Canada's Permanent Mission to the GATT and then to the WTO. I was most recently Assistant Deputy Minister, North America at DFAIT and was asked

1286 Leclerc interview, *supra* note 359.

1287 McGowan interview, *supra* note 938.

> to take on the position of President of CEAA last July …
>
> As President I provide leadership and direction to the approximately 250 staff to ensure that the Agency provides Canadians with high-quality environmental assessments that contribute to informed decision making in support of sustainable development.[1288]

Volume fifty-three senior editor Stephanie Jones, today early on her career with the public sector, spoke about working at the Legislative Services branch of the Department of Justices, writing,

> Statutes in general and legislative drafting in particular were not something that were given much attention in law school, but I would encourage anyone who liked MLJ to consider legislative drafting. There is a similar balance between law and language, the overall structure and the painstaking attention to detail and, at least at the federal level, you also get to work in English and French. If you thought it was fun to publish an article, imagine how much more fun it could be to publish a law![1289]

There is also the realm of international organizations. Volume thirteen Managing Editor Richard Pound described his path as leading from a combination of his life experiences, writing that his work with the International Olympic Committee and as Chancellor of McGill University,

> [R]eally started during what was then the "4th year" of law, which was the Bar admission process of the day. I was invited to become the Secretary of the Canadian Olympic Association, which led to becoming president following the 1976 Montreal Games and then to becoming a member of the International Olympic Committee. I expect that was the combined result of having been an Olympic athlete, being a Chartered Accountant and being a member of the Bar …
>
> I think I have always understood that one has a duty to give back to the organizations and institutions which have helped one to develop and to have opportunities which one might not otherwise have had. I believe very much in higher education and have tried to give such support for it, principally through McGill, as I can. I never refuse an invitation to address students, at whatever level they may be, university or pre-university.[1290]

Still others find a life outside the strain of the legal-industrial complex, like volume twenty-one Editor-in-Chief Laura Falk Scott, who wrote,

> In 1981 I joined Joseph E. Seagram and Sons, Limited, the Canadian subsidiary of The Seagram Company Ltd., at that time the world's largest distiller. I was the first in-house counsel for the operation, and created its legal department, eventually becoming General Counsel and Vice President, Legal Affairs. After fifteen years with the company, my position was eliminated as part of company-wide restructuring. After that I never again worked in law.
>
> Subsequently, I became involved with the arts, especially visual and performing arts, as well as writing. Upon moving to California in 1999, my husband and I opened an arts and craft boutique which we operated for three years, providing an outlet for his retail expertise and my interest in identifying and supporting the work of artists. I joined the board of the local professional theatre company and then for four years worked at an experimental audio based theatre company, Antenna Theatre, as Project Director for a collaborative site-specific project with local high school students.
>
> I continue to pursue my interest in the performing arts as part of an improv troupe and board member of Marin Theatre Company, and in the visual arts as a docent for school tours at the San Francisco Museum of Modern Art…
>
> I have always been interested in the arts. In Montreal I was on the board of the English-language professional theatre, Centaur Theatre … I especially recall curating a show for the Centaur lobby: the

1288 Feldman interview, *supra* note 504.

1289 Jones interview, *supra* note 1116.

1290 Pound interview, *supra* note 341.

play onstage had to do with crime, and we hung the lobby with amazing art works created by prisoners from local prisons with excellent art therapy programs.[1291]

Another example is that of volume thirteen Contributing Editor Lionel Chetwynd, who recalled about his path to becoming an award-winning screenwriter that,

> I left school at fourteen. My family had problems so I had to go to work. I did try to go back to school the following year but I got expelled, so I was out on the street. The thing that turned me around was the army, interestingly enough I joined the Black Watch—and eventually go to school with the sons of the officers who used to push me about. The Black Watch was the aristocracy, the officer corp. They were the barons … but I was a private soldier.
>
> In the army I entered a couple of playwrighting contests with the CBC and actually won one. So I had it in the back of my mind that, boy, if you could be a writer—I could jump everything, I could get there, somehow. I could rectify the lack of an education. But when I got out of the army it wasn't that easy. I tried writing, I wanted it, but it wasn't going to happen for me …
>
> I got into Sir George [Williams University], did very, very well there and was the valedictorian. I was a good debater, and we beat McGill: every year I debated McGill we beat them. And that had an enormous influence, I think, on getting me into the McGill law school with a scholarship—because I couldn't afford it. Now why I went to McGill? Look, I had … very narrow horizons—I mean four years earlier I had been in the army, and I had a CO. Now suddenly I've got a Bachelor of Arts degree and I have options that weren't imaginable to me …
>
> I remember having a conversation with [a friend] who I knew from high school, and he said "What are you going to do?" and I said, "I don't know, but you know if there's a God, I bet he began as a Jewish lawyer in Montreal." I could think of nothing greater; that was my horizon, if you will …
>
> What happened to me at the law school—which was extraordinary—was I learned how to write. I had this ambition to write, and I'd lucked in with this one play, but I had no understanding of things like elegance of style; precision in language. I remember someone, probably [Professor] Ron Cheffin,[1292] though maybe it was [Professor] Hamish Gow again, who said, "They asked Auden, 'what is poetry?' And he answered, 'Excellent speech'." So I learned in the McGill law school how to express myself—how to express my ideas—and [it] was a simple leap from there, in using the same skills to express the ideas of characters who were *not* me but whom I constructed. I succeeded in a very particular niche in what I did: it was the scholarly stuff. That's the surprise at the end of the day. I'm the guy who did *Kissinger and Nixon*;[1293] I did all these things that required deep research and understanding. Almost everyone I came up with has been out of the [film] business for years now—I'm still working. Just now I've started on adapting Mordecai Richler's *Solomon Gursky* for the CBC.
>
> The reason I still do it is because of the things I learned at McGill. I left Canada and went to work for Columbia Pictures, but at some point early on I realized that I had been given the tools—in the law school—to actually take this ambition to write creatively; use the toolbox they'd given me, and I could to it. And I did … What I got out of McGill law school was mental discipline and a rigour—and part of that, frankly, was Armand de Mestral looking me in the eye and telling me … "You're lazy", that's what he was saying, "You're walking in here, a big debater, *big guy*—well it's not about that here. This is really about intellectual discipline," and he made me do it! I owe a lot to Armand. It was those experiences that made it possible for me, later, to make a living the

1291 Falk Scott interview, *supra* note 442.

1292 Ronald Cheffin was the Faculty of Advisor of the *McGill Law Journal* for volume six.

1293 Lionel Chetwynd, *Kissinger and Nixon* television film, directed by Daniel Petrie (Atlanta: Turner Home Entertainment, 1996).

way I have …

McGill didn't build my vocabulary, but it did discipline my mind. It did force me to rigour, and the *McGill Law Journal* was a big part of that. Because they denied me what I was [always] getting. Whatever I wanted I could have, until I came up against these guys—the last line of defence of the old way of seeing things and doing things. Which by the way, in retrospect, was a better way… They were the last of their sort. So I would write these reports and people would be like "Oh man, you've got to read this: this guy's great!" I learned to use simple language; I learned to support what I had to say. And I realized, you know what, *I could write screenplays.* I know how to do that now! …

I realize too that I gained a lot of confidence. I was in school with people whom I had thought were so much better than me. Like many people, my bravado and leadership as a student leader derived from a sense of very low self-esteem … McGill was something else, it lifted me up to a whole other level; I felt I could run with the Arabian horses.[1294]

Solomon Gursky Was Here, Chetwynd's latest project, in an interesting turn of events, is said to be a thinly veiled recreation of the story of the Bronfman family[1295]—founders of the Seagram Company, which Laura Falk Scott worked for throughout the career she had in law.

The vast majority of *Journal* members, however, become lawyers. It is difficult to find a former *Journal* member that stayed within private practice without becoming partner in time, and those young enough to still be working as associates often have their position at the *McGill Law Journal* etched across their biography page on the firm website. If each editor that had achieved professional distinction and developed truly unique experiences in private practice had been mentioned in the book, the manuscript would no doubt have doubled in length! As volume thirty-one Managing Editor Raj Pande wrote,

To the law students out there – do not let anyone tell you that private law practice limits your mobility. As a second year associate at a large law firm, I had the chance to get assigned to the firm's Tokyo office for two years. That experience was the beginning of a long practice that has given me the chance to work and live in several international cities, and work with multi-national clients based in many countries. My practice today is truly global with daily involvement with clients, other participants, law firms and assets located in many jurisdictions around the world.[1296]

So what of the future of the *McGill Law Journal*? Kristen Konrad Robbins-Tiscione wrote recently that in the electronic age the teaching legal writing is becoming a more and more difficult task.[1297] With the ability for individuals to express themselves in short bursts via electronic communications, editorial tasks draw students back into the fullness and complexity language can offer. While the norm of acceptable misspelling within emails flourishes in certain corners of the world, at the *Journal* individuals are still expected to consult the *Canadian Oxford Dictionary* to ensure the word they are using is not just spelled correctly, but spelled correctly according to the right dictionary.

Whereas during Morin's time there was a lack of meeting places for legal scholars in the sense that they were isolated from one another in their offices at different institutions or on different floors, today there is a lack of meeting place due to the accommodation of the convenient. A true intellectual debate can definitely occur over social media or instant messaging, but the verification and permanent publication of a debate is what gives content authority. A clash of ideas is not necessarily the same thing as the clashing of formally structured and well-founded ideas. The MLJ, perhaps in the electronic age more than ever, is the premiere bastion of this kind of knowledge creation.

As Justice Antonio Lamer wrote in the MLJ back in 1977,

If the experience of the 20th century has shown anything, it is that parliamentary institutions have not been able to duplicate the great work of the legal profession in keeping the ordinary law responding to the dynamics of hundreds of thousands of individual cases.

1294 Chetwynd interview, *supra* note 346.

1295 Graham D Talyor, "Seagram Comes to Scotland: The Role of Local Players in the Overseas Expansion of a Canadian Multinational, 1949-1965" (2009) 7:1 *Business and Economic History* 1 at 4 online: < http://h-net.org/~business/bhcweb/publications/BEHonline/2009/taylor.pdf >

1296 Pande, *supra* note 723.

1297 Kristen Konrad Robbins-Tiscione, "From Snail Mail to E-mail: The Traditional Legal Memorandum in the Twenty-First Century" (2008) 58:1 *J Legal Educ* 32 at 38-40.

> The assumptions of the 19th century legal philosophers have not always coincided with the priorities of, and massive demands placed upon, a contemporary Parliament.[1298]

The *Journal* is also a vehicle for keeping our future legal profession on its heels; to force it to move forward, and to keep rethinking our imperfect civilization. Especially as Lamer also reminds us that, "Law is one of the few disciplines dealing with the public which makes little effort to discover if its consumers are satisfied."[1299]

John Ralston Saul stated in his Annual Lecture that "originality produces fascination and fascination produces respect."[1300] This is a lesson to remember for all future volumes. The role of the MLJ is not purely to publish the latest findings of elite professors, though this is a major part of the function of the *Journal*. It is also to create dissent; to get professors and lawyers talking; to produce things that make people disagree. If, as then-Minister of Justice John Turner claimed, the law must be a living thing if it is to serve its purpose,[1301] then the *Journal* also has a role in providing oxygen for the marathon in front of it. There are still many outstanding issues in our society. For example, Turner wrote in his article that,

> The poor do not use lawyers. They are often thought of as having no need of lawyers. Too many of us think of lawyers as counsellors to corporations, drafters of estate plans or wills, advisors on creditors' rights. But if the poor are rarely plaintiffs they are often defendants. They are bewildered and bemused by legalities they face daily as parents, consumers, tenants, recipients of public assistance and accused offenders. Too often the poor see the law not as a friend but as an enemy, not as an aid but as an adversary, not as a remedy but as an obstacle.[1302]

This is a problem that has by no means gone away. And the urgency behind solving such an issue is spurred on in a way it likely could never be through any other venue than the canon provided by the MLJ—and its reminder that over thirty years ago people were saying the same things as we are today, with the same urgency. Though the apocalyptic visions of some prior authors could no longer be published seriously today, it is important to note that there are other issues like this that were written of in the *Journal* decades ago that perhaps have gotten even worse.

In this sense, the *Journal* not only serves the purpose of pressing the world forward, but it also serves as a venue to remind the world, and Canada specifically, of its past. This function is only strengthened by the continued force of each new Editorial and Management Board, who maintain the health and prosperity of the institution, and ensure its annals are still heralded as one of the world's best. The most elegant part of the *Journal*'s history is, no doubt, the trust each passing board—and each passing generation—places in a suddenly selected group of young people, who have no experience to their name in many cases, to continue on one of the most substantial legacies that any institution of this kind can claim. There is a trust placed in the hands of each new associate editor, each new associate manager, each new executive member, and each new theory of how to get things done. Thus far it appears that this trust has been well-placed, and there is nothing in the *Journal*'s present that would indicate this will change.

1298 Lamer & Ryan, *supra* note 490 at 521.
1299 *Ibid* at 528.
1300 Saul, *supra* note 1126 at 694.
1301 Turner, *supra* note 323.
1302 *Ibid* at 6.

Annual photo of the McGill Law Journal, Volume 56 (above); Senior Board of the Journal in the newly traditional "funny" picture, Volume 56 (bottom).
Photo taken in the Faculty of Law Common Room in Old Chancellor Day Hall, McGill University.
(Courtesy of Filipe Estrela, long time photographer for the McGill Law Journal, 1997-present)

Appendix A

Complete bibliography of McGill Law Journal articles cited by the Supreme Court of Canada

David Angus, "Abuse of Rights in Contractual Matters in the Province of Quebec" (1962) 8:2 *McGill LJ* 150.
- ***Houle v Canadian National Bank*, 1990 SCC 3, [1990] 3 SCR 122.**

Russel Lawrence Barsh & James Youngblood Henderson, "The Supreme Court's *Van der Peet* Trilogy: Naive Imperialism and Ropes of Sand" (1997) 42:3 *McGill LJ* 993.
- ***R v Sappier*; *R v Gray*, 2006 SCC 54, [2006] 2 SCR 686.**
- ***Mitchell v Canada (Minister of National Revenue - MNR)*, 2001 SCC 49, [2001] 2 SCR 911.**

Jean-Louis Baudoin, « L'exécution spécifique des contrats en droit québécois » (1958-59) 5:2 *McGill LJ* 108.
- ***Nault v Canadian Consumer Co*, 1981 SCC 1, [1981] 1 SCR 553.**

Jean-Louis Baudoin, « Examen critique de la situation juridique de l'enfant naturel » (1966) 12:2 *McGill LJ* 157.
- ***Quebec (Attorney General) v A*, 2013 SCC 5.**

Gérald A Beaudoin, « La protection de l'environnement et ses implications en droit constitutionnel » (1977) 23:2 *McGill LJ* 207.
- ***R v Crown Zellerbach Canada Ltd*, 1988 SCC 1, [1988] 1 SCR 401.**

Stan Berger, "The Application of the Cruel and Unusual Punishment Clause Under the Canadian Bill of Rights" (1978) 24:2 *McGill LJ* 161.
- ***R v Smith*, 1987 SCC 1, [1987] 1 SCR 1045.**

Stéphane Bernatchez, « Les rapports entre le droit administratif et les droits et libertés : la révision judicaire ou le contrôle constitutionnel? » (2010) 55:3 *McGill LJ* 641
- ***Doré v Barreau du Québec*, 2012 SCC 12, [2012] 2 SCR 395.**

Alain-François Bisson, « La Disposition préliminaire du *Code civil du Québec* » (1999) 44:2 *McGill LJ* 539.
- ***Prud'homme v Prud'homme*, 2002 SCC 85, [2002] 4 SCR 663.**

André Braën, « L'arrêt *ITO-International Terminal Operators Ltd.* c. *Miida Electronics Inc.*, ou comment écarter l'application du droit civil dans un litige maritime au Québec » (1987) 32:2 *McGill LJ* 386.
- ***Monk Corp v Island Fertilizers Ltd*, 1991 SCC 1, [1991] 1 SCR 779.**

JEC Brierley, "The Trust in Quebec" (1980) 25:4 *McGill LJ* 421.
- ***Royal Trust Co v Tucker*, 1982 SCC 1, [1982] 1 SCR 250.**

John Borrows, "Creating an Indigenous Legal Community" (2005) 50:1 *McGill LJ* 153.
- ***R v Marshall*; *R v Bernard*, 2005 SCC 43 [2005] 2 SCR 220.**

Germain Brière, « Le mariage putatif » (1959-60) 6:4 *McGill LJ* 217
- ***Paré v Bonin*, 1977 SCC 2, [1977] 2 SCR 342.**

JG Castel, "Recognition and Enforcement of Foreign Judgments in Personam and in Rem in the Common Law Provinces of Canada" (1971) 17:1 *McGill LJ* 11.
- ***Morguard Investments Ltd v De Savoye*, 1990 SCC 3, [1990] 3 SCR 1077.**

JG Castel, "The Uncertainty Factor in Canadian Private International Law" (2007) 52:3 *McGill LJ* 555.
- ***Club Resorts Ltd v Van Breda*, 2012 SCC 17**

Timothy A Caulfield, "Underwhelmed: Hyperbole, Regulatory Policy, and the Genetic Revolution" (2000) 45:2 *McGill LJ* 437.
- ***Harvard College v Canada (Commissioner of Patents)*, 2002 SCC 76, [2002] SCR 45.**

Ronald I Cohen, "Nuisance: A Proprietary Delict" (1968) 14:1 *McGill LJ* 124.
- ***St Lawrence Cement Inc v Barrette*, 2008 SCC 64, [2008] 3 SCR 392.**

Loretta N Colton, "*R.* v. *Stinchcombe*: Defining Disclosure" (1995) 40:2 *McGill LJ* 525.
- ***A (LL) v B (A)*, 1995 SCC 4, [1995] 4 SCR 536.**

Eric Colvin, "Legal Theory and the Paramountcy Rule" (1979) 25:1 *McGill LJ* 82.
- ***M & D Farm Ltd v Manitoba Agricultural Credit Corp*, 1999 SCC 2, [1999] 2 SCR 961.**

Paul A Crépeau, « Réflexions sur le fondement juridique de la responsabilité civile du transporteur de personnes » (1960-61) 7:4 *McGill LJ* 225
- ***Comité régional des usagers des transports en commun de Québec v Québec (Urban Community Transit Commission)*, 1981 SCC 1, [1981] 1 SCR 424.**

Giuseppina D'Agostino, "Healing Fair Dealing? A Comparative Copyright Analysis of Canada's Fair Dealing to U.K. Fair Dealing and U.S. Fair Use" (2008) 53:2 *McGill LJ* 309.
- ***Alberta (Education) v Canadian Copyright Licensing Agency (Access Copyright)*, 2012 SCC 37, [2012] 2 SCR 345.**
- ***Society of Composers, Authors and Music Publishers of Canada v Bell Canada*, 2012 SCC 36, [2012] 2 SCR 326.**

Robert Daigneault, « La portée de la nouvelle loi dite 'du pollueur-payeur' » (1991) 36:3 *McGill LJ* 1027.
- ***Imperial Oil Ltd v Quebec (Minister of the Environment)*, 2003 SCC 58, [2003] 2 SCR 624.**

Robert Danay, "The Medium is not the Message: Reconciling Reputation and Free Expression in Cases of Internet Defamation" (2010) 56:1 *McGill LJ* 1.
- ***Crookes v Newton*, 2011 SCC 47, [2011] 3 SCR 269.**

Nathalie M Derzko, "Plant Breeders' Rights in Canada and Abroad: What are These Rights and How Much Must Society Pay for Them?" (1994) 39:1 *McGill LJ* 144.
- ***Harvard College v Canada (Commissioner of Patents)*, 2002 SCC 76, [2002] SCR 45.**

Marie Deschamps, « Vers une approche renouvelée de l'indivision » (1984) 29:2 *McGill LJ* 215.
- ***Coopérants, Mutual Life Insurance Society (Liquidator of) v Dubois*, 1996 SCC 1, [1996] 1 SCR 900.**

Bernard M Dickens, "Medically Assisted Death: *Nancy B.* v. *Hôtel-Dieu de Québec*" (1993) 38:4 *McGill LJ* 1053.
- ***AC v Manitoba (Director of Child and Family Services)*, 2009 SCC 30, [2009] 2 SCR 181.**

Nitya Duclos & Kent Roach, "Constitutional Remedies as 'Constitutional Hints': A Comment on *R.* v. *Schachter*" (1991) 36:1 *McGill LJ* 1.
- ***Schachter v Canada*, 1992 SCC 2, [1992] 2 SCR 679.**

Karen Eltis, "The Judicial System in the Digital Age: Revisiting the Relationship between Privacy and

Accessibility in the Cyber Context" (2011) 56:2 *McGill LJ* 289.
- ***AB v Bragg Communications Inc*, 2012 SCC 46.**

André Émond, « Existe-t-il un titre indien originaire dans les territoires cédés par la France en 1763? » (1995) 41:1 *McGill LJ* 59.
- ***R v Van der Peet*, 1996 SCC 2, [1996] 2 SCR 507.**

Brian Etherington, "The Enforcement of Harsh Termination Provisions in Personal Employment Contracts: The Rebirth of Freedom of Contract in Ontario" (1990) 35:2 *McGill LJ* 459.
- ***Machtinger v HOJ Industries Ltd*, 1992 SCC 1, [1992] 1 SCR 986.**

JM Evans, "Trial Division of the Federal Court: An Addendum" (1977) 22:1 *McGill LJ* 132.
- ***Martineau v Matsqui Institution*, 1980 SCC 1, [1980] 1 SCR 602.**

Guy Favreau, "Constitutional Amendment in a Canadian Canada" (1966-67) 12:4 *McGill LJ*: 384.
- ***Reference re: Amendment of Canadian Constitution*, 1982 SCC 2, [1982] 2 SCR 791.**

Colin Feasby, "*Libman v. Quebec (A.G.)* and the Administration of the Process of Democracy under the *Charter*: The Emerging Egalitarian Model" (1999) 44:1 *McGill LJ* 5.
- ***Harper v Canada (Attorney General)*, 2004 SCC 33, [2004] 1 SCR 827.**

Norman M Fera, "Certiorari in the Federal Court and Other Matters: A Reply to the Addendum" (1977) 23:3 *McGill LJ* 497
- ***Martineau v Matsqui Institution*, 1980 SCC 1, [1980] 1 SCR 602.**

Patrick S Florencio, "Genetics, Parenting, and Children's Rights in the Twenty-First Century" (2000) 45:2 *McGill LJ* 527.
- ***Harvard College v Canada (Commissioner of Patents)*, 2002 SCC 76, [2002] SCR 45.**

IH Fraser, "Some Comments on Subsection 92(10) of the *Constitution Act, 1867*" (1984) 29:4 *McGill LJ* 557.
- ***Consolidated Fastfrate Inc v Western Canada Council of Teamsters*, 2009 SCC 53, [2009] 3 SCR 407.**

GHL Fridman, "The Wrongdoing Plaintiff" (1972) 18:3 *McGill LJ* 275.
- ***Hall v Hebert*, 1993 SCC 2, [1993] 2 SCR 159**
- ***Canada Cement LaFarge Ltd v British Columbia Lightweight Aggregate Ltd*, 1983 SCC 1, [1983] 1 SCR 452.**

Patrice Garant, « La justice municipale au regard des chartes: quelques observations au lendemain de la grande réforme » (1991) 36:1 *McGill LJ* 39.
- ***R v Lippé*, 1991 SCC 2, [1991] 2 SCR 114.**

Dale Gibson, "Constitutional Amendment and the Implied Bill of Rights" (1966-67) 66:67 *McGill LJ* 497.
- ***Reference re Remuneration of Judges of the Provincial Court (PEI)*, 1997 SCC 3, [1997] 3 SCR 3.**

Daphne Gilbert, "Time to Regroup: Rethinking Section 15 of the *Charter*" (2003) 48:4 *McGill LJ* 627.
- ***Withler v Canada (Attorney General)*, 2011 SCC 12, [2011] 1 SCR 396.**
- ***R v Kapp*, 2008 SCC 41, [2008] 2 SCR 483.**

H Patrick Glenn, « La responsabilité des juges » (1983) 28:2 *McGill LJ* 228.
- ***Ruffo v Conseil de la magistrature*, 1995 SCC 4, [1995] 4 SCR 267.**
- ***Morier v Rivard*, 1985 SCC 2, [1985] 2 SCR 716.**

H Patrick Glenn, "Professional Structures and Professional Ethics" (1990) 35:2 *McGill LJ* 424.
- ***Ruffo v Conseil de la magistrature*, 1995 SCC 4, [1995] 4 SCR 267.**

Marc Gold, "Comment: *Andrews v. Law Society of British Columbia*" (1988-89) 34:4 *McGill LJ* 1063.
- ***McKinney v University of Guelph*, 1990 SCC 3, [1990] SCR 229.**

E Richard Gold, "Biomedical Patents and Ethics: A Canadian Solution" (2000) 45:2 *McGill LJ* 413.
- ***Harvard College v Canada (Commissioner of Patents)*, 2002 SCC 76, [2002] SCR 45.**

Sébastien Grammond, « Les effets juridiques de la *Convention de la Baie James* au regard du droit interne canadien et québécois » (1992) 37:3 *McGill LJ* 761.
- ***Quebec (Attorney General) v Moses*, 2010 SCC 17, [2010] 1 SCR 557.**
- ***R v Van der Peet*, 1996 SCC 2, [1996] 2 SCR 507.**

Sébastien Grammond, « La protection constitutionnelle des droits ancestraux des peuples autochtones et l'arrêt *Sparrow* » (1990-91) 36:4 *McGill LJ* 1382.
- ***R v Van der Peet*, 1996 SCC 2, [1996] 2 SCR 507.**

PPC Haanappel, « Faute et risque dans le système québécois de la responsabilité civile extra-contractuelle », (1978) 24:4 *McGill LJ* 635.
- ***Lapierre v Québec (Attorney General)*, 1985 SCC 1, [1985] 1 SCR 241.**

Patrick Healy, "Statutory Prohibitions and the Regulation of New Reproductive Technologies under Federal Law in Canada" (1995) 40:4 *McGill LJ* 905.
- ***Reference re Assisted Human Reproduction Act*, 2010 SCC 61, [2010] 3 SCR 457.**

Patrick Healy, "*R. v. Bernard*: Difficulties with Voluntary Intoxication" (1995) 40:2 *McGill LJ* (1990) 35:4 *McGill LJ* 610.
- ***R v Robinson*, 1996 SCC 1, [1996] 1 SCR 683.**
- ***R v Daviault*, 1994 SCC 3, [1994] 3 SCR 63.**

Celeste Hutchinson, "Case Comment on *R. v. Kapp*: An Analytical Framework for Section 25 of the *Charter*" (2007) 52:1 *McGill LJ* 173.
- ***R v Kapp*, 2008 SCC 41, [2008] 2 SCR 483.**

David Philip Jones, "*Howarth v. National Parole Board*: A Comment" (1975) 21:3 *McGill LJ* 434.
- ***Martineau v Matsqui Institution*, 1980 SCC 1, [1980] 1 SCR 602.**

Rosalie Jukier, "*Banque Nationale du Canada v. Houle* (S.C.C.): Implications of an Expanded Doctrine of Abuse of Rights in Civilian Contract Law" (1992) 37:1 *McGill LJ* 221.
- ***Garcia Transport Ltée v Royal Trust Co*, 1992 SCC 2, [1992] 2 SCR 499.**

Kenneth Jull, "*Clarkson v. R.*: Do We Need a Legal Emergency Department?" (1987) 32:2 *McGill LJ* 359.
- ***R v Smith*, 1989 SCC 2, [1989] 2 SCR 368.**

Daniel Jutras, « Culture et droit processuel: le cas du Québec » (2009) 54:2 *McGill LJ* 273.
- ***Globe and Mail v Canada (Attorney General)*, 2010 SCC 41, [2010] 2 SCR 592.**

Robert A Kasting, "Recent Developments in the Canadian Law of Solicitor-Client Privilege" (1978) 24:1 *McGill LJ* 115.

- ***Lavallee, Rackel & Heintz v Canada (Attorney General)*, 2002 SCC 61, [2002] 3 SCR 209.**
- ***Solosky v The Queen*, 1980 SCC 1, [1980] 1 SCR 821.**

Dennis R Klinck, "'The Rise of the 'Remedial' Fiduciary Relationship: A Comment on *International Corona Resources Ltd. v. Lac Minerals Ltd.*" (1988) 33:2 *McGill LJ* 600.

- ***Lac Minerals Ltd v International Corona Resources Ltd*, 1989 SCC 2, [1989] 2 SCR 574.**

Bartha Maria Knoppers, "Reflections: The Challenge of Biotechnology and Public Policy" (2000) 45:2 *McGill LJ* 559.

- ***Harvard College v Canada (Commissioner of Patents)*, 2002 SCC 76, [2002] SCR 45.**

Vern Krishna, "Characterization of Wrongful Dismissal Awards for Income Tax" (1977) 23:1 *McGill LJ* 43.

- ***Schwartz v Canada*, 1996 SCC 1, [1996] 1 SCR 254**

Gérard V La Forest, "Delegation of Legislative Power in Canada" (1975) 21:1 *McGill LJ* 131.

- ***British Columbia (Milk Board) v Grisnich (c.o.b. Mountainview Acres)*, 1995 SCC 2, [1995] 2 SCR 895.**

Andrée Lajoie, « De l'interventionnisme judiciaire comme apport à l'émergence des droits sociaux » (1991) 36:4 *McGill LJ* 1338.

- ***Little Sisters Book and Art Emporium v Canada (Minister of Justice)*, 2000 SCC 2, [2000] 2 SCR 1120.**

Louise Langevin, « Liberté de choix et protection juridique des conjoints de fait en cas de rupture: difficile exercice de jonglerie » (2009) 54:4 *McGill LJ* 697.

- ***Quebec (Attorney General) v A*, 2013 SCC 5.**

Brian Langille, "The Freedom of Association Mess: How We Got into It and How We Can Get out of It" (2009) 54:1 *McGill LJ* 177.

- ***Ontario (Attorney General) v Fraser*, 2011 SCC 2, [2011] 2 SCR 3.**

François Larocque, « La *Loi sur l'immunité des États* canadienne et la torture » (2010) 55:1 *McGill LJ* 81.

- ***Kuwait Airways Corp v Iraq*, 2010 SCC 40, [2010] 2 SCR 571.**

Gerald E Le Dain, "Security Upon Moveable Property in the Province of Quebec" (1956) 2:2 *McGill LJ* 77.

- ***Caisse populaire Desjardins de Val-Brillant v Blouin*, 2003 SCC 31, [2003] 1 SCR 666.**

WR Lederman, "The Process of Constitutional Amendment in Canada" (1966-67) 12:4 *McGill LJ* 371

- ***Re: Resolution to amend the Constitution*, 1981 SCC 1, [1981] 1 SCR 753.**

WR Lederman, "The Concurrent Operation of Federal and Provincial Laws in Canada" (1963) 9:3 *McGill LJ* 185.

- ***GMAC Commercial Credit Corporation – Canada v T.C.T. Logistics Inc*, 2006 SCC 35, [2006] 2 SCR 123.**
- ***Bank of Montreal v Hall*, 1990 SCC 1, [1990] 1 SCR 121.**
- ***Multiple Access Ltd v McCutcheon*, 1982 SCC 2, [1982] 2 SCR 161.**

Pierre Legrand Jr, « Pour une théorie de l'obligation de renseignement du fabricant en droit civil canadien » (1981) 26:2 *McGill LJ* 207.

- ***Bank of Montreal v Bail Ltée*, 1992 SCC 2, [1992] 2 SCR 554.**

Pierre Legrand Jr, « La dynamique de l'impunité : autour de la défense d'*ex turpi causa* en *common law* des délits civils » (1991) 36:2 *McGill LJ* 609.

- ***Hall v Hebert*, 1993 SCC 2, [1993] 2 SCR 159.**

Roderick A Macdonald, "Reconceiving the Symbols of Property: Universalities, Interests and Other Heresies" (1994) 39:2 *McGill LJ* 761.

- ***Caisse populaire Desjardins de l'Est de Drummond v Canada*, 2009 SCC 29, [2009] 2 SCR 94.**

Patrick Macklem, "First Nations Self-Government and the Borders of the Canadian Legal Imagination" (1991) 36:1 *McGill LJ* 382.

- ***Delgamuukw v British Columbia*, 1997 SCC 3, [1997] 3 SCR 1010.**
- ***R v Van der Peet*, 1996 SCC 2, [1996] 2 SCR 507.**

Timothy Macklem, "Faith as a Secular Value" (2000) 45:1 *McGill LJ* 1.

- ***Syndicat Northcrest v Amselem*, 2004 SCC 47, [2004] SCR 551.**

Louis Marquis, « La notion d'arbitrage commercial international en droit québécois » (1992) 37:2 *McGill LJ* 448.

- ***Dell Computer Corp v Union des consommateurs*, 2007 SCC 34, [2007] 2 SCR 801.**

Paul Martel, « L'arrêt *Banque Nationale du Canada c. Houle* : Lumières nouvelles sur l'abus de droit et le "voile corporatif" » (1987) 33:1 *McGill LJ* 213.

- ***Houle v Canadian National Bank*, 1990 SCC 3, [1990] 3 SCR 122.**

Daniel N Mettarlin, "The Quebec Trust and the Civil Law" (1975) 21:2 *McGill LJ* 175.

- ***Royal Trust Co v Tucker*, 1982 SCC 1, [1982] 1 SCR 250.**

Micheline McNicoll, « La réparation : une question de contrôle judiciaire » (1986) 32:1 *McGill LJ* 187.

- ***Laurentide Motels Ltd v Beauport (City)*, 1989 SCC 1, [1989] 1 SCR 705.**

Gérard Mémeteau, « Perte de chance en droit médical français » (1986) 32:1 *McGill LJ* 126.

- ***Laferrière v Lawson*, 1991 SCC 1, [1991] 1 SCR 541.**

Paul Michell, "Just Do It! Eskridge's Critical Pragmatic Theory of Statutory Interpretation: Book Review" (1996) 41:3 *McGill LJ* 713.

- ***2747-3174 Québec Inc v Quebec (Régie des permis d'alcool)*, 1996 SCC 3, [1996] 3 SCR 919**

Benioit Moore, « Culture et droit de la famille: de l'institution à l'autonomie individuelle » (2009) 54:2 *McGill LJ* 257.

- ***Quebec (Attorney General) v A*, 2013 SCC 5.**

Yves-Marie Morissette, "The Exclusion of Evidence under the Canadian Charter of Rights and Freedoms: What to Do and What Not to Do" (1984) 29:4 *McGill LJ* 521.

- ***R v Burlingham*, 1995 SCC 2, [1995] 2 SCR 206.**
- ***R v Collins*, 1987 SCC 1, [1987] 1 SCR 265.**

Norval Morris, "The Habitual Criminal" (1967) 13:4 *McGill LJ* 534.

- ***R v Lyons*, 1987 SCC 2, [1987] 2 SCR 309.**

Pierre-Emmanuel Moyse, « La nature du droit d'auteur : droit de propriété ou monopole? » (1998) 43:3 *McGill LJ* 507

- ***Théberge v Galerie d'Art du Petit Champlain Inc*, 2002 SCC 2, [2002] 2 SCR 336**

David J Mullan, "Natural Justice and Fairness -- Substantive as well as Procedural Standards for the Review of

Administrative Decision-Making?" (1982) 27:2 *McGill LJ* 250.
- ***Domtar Inc v Quebec (Commission d'appel en matière de lésions professionnelles)*, 1993 SCC 2, [1993] 2 SCR 756.**

André Nadeau, « L'autorité de la chose jugée » (1963) 9:2 *McGill LJ* 102.
- ***Roberge v Bolduc*, 1991 SCC 1, [1991] 1 SCR 374.**
- ***Rocois Construction Inc v Québec Ready Mix Inc*, 1990 SCC 2, [1990] 2 SCR 440.**

Jennifer Nedelsky. "Embodied Diversity and the Challenges to Law" (1997) 42 *McGill LJ* 91.
- **R *v* S (RD), [1997] 3 SCR 484.**

MH Ogilvie, "The Reception of *Photo Production Ltd. v. Securicor Transport Ltd.* In Canada: *Nec Tamen Consumebatur*" (1982) 27:3 *McGill LJ* 424.
- ***Hunter Engineering Co v Syncrude Canada Ltd*, 1989 SCC 1, [1989] 1 SCR 426.**

David M Paciocco, "Self-Incrimination: Removing the Coffin Nails" (1989) 35:1 *McGill LJ* 73
- ***R v Stillman*, 1997 SCC 1, [1997] 1 SCR 607.**

Hugues Parent, « Histoire de l'acte volontaire en droit pénal anglais et canadien » (2000) 45:1 *McGill LJ* 975.
- ***R v Ruzic*, 2001 SCC 1, [2001] 1 SCR 687.**

Steven Penney, "Taking Deterrence Seriously: Excluding Unconstitutionally Obtained Evidence Under Section 24(2) of the *Charter*" (2004) 49:1 *McGill LJ* 105.
- ***R v Grant*, 2009 SCC 32, [2009] 2 SCR 353.**

Jean Pineau, « La Législation maritime canadienne et le Code civil québécois » (1968) 14:1 *McGill LJ* 26.
- ***QNS Paper Co v Chartwell Shipping Ltd*, 1989 SCC 2, [1989] 2 SCR 683.**
- ***Zavarovalna Skupnost Triglav (Insurance Community Triglav Ltd) v Terrasses Jewellers Inc*, 1983 SCC 1, [1983] 1 SCR 283.**

Danielle Pinard, « Le principe d'interprétation issu de la présomption de constitutionnalité et la *Charte canadienne des droits et libertés* » (1990) 35:2 *McGill LJ* 305.
- ***Lavallee, Rackel & Heintz v Canada (Attorney General)*, 2002 SCC 61, [2002] 3 SCR 209.**
- ***Committee for the Commonwealth of Canada v Canada*, 1991 SCC 1, [1991] 1 SCR 139.**

Caroline Pratte, « Essai sur le rapport entre la société par actions et ses dirigeants dans le cadre du *Code civil du Québec* » (1994) 39:1 *McGill LJ* 1.
- ***Fédération des producteurs acéricoles du Québec v Regroupement pour la commercialisation des produits de l'érable inc*, 2006 SCC 50, [2006] 2 SCR 591.**

Tim Quigley, "Reform of the Intoxication Defence" (1987) 33:1 *McGill LJ* 1.
- ***R v Daviault*, 1994 SCC 3, [1994] 3 SCR 63.**
- ***R v Penno*, 1990 SCC 2, [1990] 2 SCR 865.**
- ***R v Bernard*, 1988 SCC 2, [1988] 2 SCR 833.**

Ed Ratushny, "Is There a Right Against Self-Incrimination in Canada?" (1973) 19:1 *McGill LJ* 1.
- ***R v S (RJ)*, 1995 SCC 1, [1995] 1 SCR 451.**
- ***R v Hebert*, 1990 SCC 2, [1990] 2 SCR 151.**
- ***Rothman v The Queen*, 1981 SCC 1, [1981] 1 SCR 640.**
- ***Marcoulx and Solomon v The Queen*, 1976 SCC 1, [1976] 1 SCR 763.**

Alain Roy, « Le contrat de mariage en droit québécois: un destin marqué du sceau du paradoxe » (2006) 5:4 *McGill LJ* 665.
- ***Quebec (Attorney General) v A*, 2013 SCC 5.**

Nathaniel H Salomon, "Labour and Material Payment Bonds" (1973) 19:3 *McGill LJ* 433
- ***Citadel General Assurance Co v Johns-Manville Canada Inc*, 1983 SCC 1, [1983] 1 SCR 513.**

FR Scott, "Federal Jurisdiction Over Labour Relations – A New Look" (1960) 6:3 *McGill LJ* 153.
- ***United Transportation Union v Central Western Railway Corp*, 1990 SCC 3, [1990] 3 SCR 1112.**

Stephen A Scott, "The Bank is Always Right: Section 165(3) of the Bills of Exchange Act and its Curious Parliamentary History" (1973) 19:1 *McGill LJ* 78.
- ***BMP Global Distribution Inc v Bank of Nova Scotia*, 2009 SCC 15, [2009] 1 SCR 504.**
- ***Boma Manufacturing Ltd v Canadian Imperial Bank of Commerce*, 1996 SCC 3, [1996] 3 SCR 727.**

Stephen A Scott, "Canadian Federal Courts and the Constitutional Limits of Their Jurisdiction" (1982) 27:1 *McGill LJ* 137.
- ***Monk Corp v Island Fertilizers Ltd*, 1991 SCC 1, [1991] 1 SCR 779.**

KR Simmonds, "The Limits of Sovereign Jurisdictional Immunity" (1965) 11:4 *McGill LJ* 291
- ***Congo (République démocratique) v Venne*, 1971 SCC, [1971] SCR 997.**

Ronald B Sklar, "Similar Fact Evidence – Catchwords and Cartwheels" (1977) 23:4 *McGill LJ* 60.
- ***R v B (CR) [CRB]*, 1990 SCC 1, [1990] 1 SCR 717.**
- ***R v Sweitzer*, 1982 SCC 1, [1982] 1 SCR 949.**

Brian Slattery, "The *Charter*'s Relevance to Private Litigation: Does *Dolphin* Deliver?" (1987) 32:4 *McGill LJ* 905.
- ***McKinney v University of Guelph*, 1990 SCC 3, [1990] 3 SCR 229.**

Jerome C Smyth, "Seizin in the Quebec Law of Successions" (1957) 3:2 *McGill LJ* 171.
- ***Hall v Quebec (Deputy Minister of Revenue)*, 1998 SCC 1, [1998] 1 SCR 220.**

Hamish Stewart, "The Confessions Rule and the *Charter*" (2009) 54:3 *McGill LJ* 517.
- ***R v Sinclair*, 2010 SCC 35, [2010] 2 SCR 310.**

GT Tamaki, "Lifting the Corporate Veil in Canadian Income Tax Law" (1962) 8:3 *McGill LJ* 159.
- ***Covert v Nova Scotia (Minister of Finance)*, 1980 SCC 2, [1980] 2 SCR 774.**

Sabine Thuilleaux & Dean M Proctor, « L'application des conventions d'arbitrage au Canada : une difficile coexistence entre les compétences judiciaire et arbitrale » (1992) 37:2 *McGill LJ* 470.
- ***Dell Computer Corp v Union des consommateurs*, 2007 SCC 34, [2007] 2 SCR 801.**

Stephen J Toope & Alison L Young, "The Confidentiality of Tax Returns Under Canadian Law" (1982) 27:3 *McGill LJ* 479.
- ***Slattery (Trustee of) v Slattery*, 1993 SCC 3, [1993] 3 SCR 430.**

Donovan WM Waters, "The Doctrine of Resulting Trusts" (1970) 16:2 *McGill LJ* 187.
- ***Goodfriend v Goodfriend*, 1972 SCC, [1972] SCR 640.**

Jeremy Webber, "The Limits to Judges' Free Speech: A Comment on the Report of the Committee of Investigation into the Conduct of the Hon. Mr. Justice Berger" (1984) 29:3 *McGill LJ* 369.

- ***Ruffo v Conseil de la magistrature*, 1995 SCC 4, [1995] 4 SCR 267.**

MS Weinberg, "The Judicial Discretion to Exclude Relevant Evidence" (1975)21:1 *McGill LJ* 1.
- ***R v Corbett*, 1988 SCC 1, [1988] 1 SCR 670.**

Ernest J Weinrib, "The Special Morality of Tort Law" (1989) 34:3 *McGill LJ* 403.
- ***Hall v Hebert*, 1993 SCC 2, [1993] 2 SCR 159.**

Ernest J Weinrib, "The Undisclosed Principle of Undisclosed Principals" (1975) 21:2 *McGill LJ* 298.
- ***Friedmann Equity Developments Inc v Final Note Ltd*, 2000 SCC 1, [2000] 1 SCR 842.**

Sara Weinrib, "An Exemption for Sincere Believers: The Challenge of *Alberta v. Hutterian Brethren of Wilson Colony*" (2010) 56:3 *McGill LJ* 719.
- ***R v NS*, 2012 SCC 72.**

José Woehrling, « L'obligation d'accommodement raisonnable et l'adaptation de la société à la diversité religieuse » (1998) 45:2 *McGill LJ* 325.
- ***Syndicat Northcrest v Amselem*, 2004 SCC 47, [2004] 2 SCR 551.**
- ***Congrégation des témoins de Jéhovah de St-Jérôme-Lafontaine v Lafontaine (Village)*, 2004 SCC 48, [2004] 2 SCR 650.**
- ***Multani v Commission scolaire Marguerite-Bourgeoys*, 2006 SCC 6, [2006] 1 SCR 256.**

M Kevin Woodall, "Private Law Liability of Public Authorities for Negligent Inspection and Regulation" (1992) 37:1 *McGill LJ* 83.
- ***Brown v British Columbia (Minister of Transportation and Highways)*, 1994 SCC 1, [1994] 1 SCR 420.**

Harvey Yarosky, "The Criminal Liability of Corporations" (1964) 10:2 *McGill LJ* 142.
- ***R v Canadian Dredge & Dock Co*, 1985 SCC 1, [1985] 1 SCR 662.**

Jacob S Ziegel, "Some Aspects of the Law of Contempt of Court in Canada, England and the United States" (1960) 6:4 *McGill LJ* 228.
- ***R v Vermette*, 1987 SCC 1, [1987] 1 SCR 577.**
- ***R v McKeown*, 1971 SCC, [1971] SCR 446.**

Margriet Zwarts, "The Duty of Fair Representation: Individual Rights in the Collective Bargaining Process, or Squaring the Circle" (1982) 28:1 *McGill LJ* 59.
- ***Canadian Merchant Service Guild v Gagnon*, 1984 SCC 1, [1984] 1 SCR 509.**

Appendix B

Original mastheads from McGill Law Journal, Volumes 1 to 58

Volume One: Issues One and Two

THE McGILL LAW JOURNAL

EDITORIAL BOARD

JACQUES-YVAN MORIN
Editor-in-Chief

JAMES A. ROBB
Comment Editor

FRED KAUFMAN
Article Editor

JOHN L. BISHOP
Case Editor

NATALIE FOCHS ISAACS
Book Review Editior

JOHN J. PEPPER
Managing Editor

RAYMOND LACHAPELLE
GERALD J. McCARTHY
MURRAY B. SPIEGEL
JEROME C. SMYTH

EDWIN J. COSFORD
MELVIN L. ROTHMAN
JOHN H. QUAIN
JACK SHAYNE
AL DOYLE

PERRY MEYER
DAVID J. DOHAN
NICHOLAS VLAHOS
JEAN D. ETHIER

THE McGILL LAW JOURNAL

EDITORIAL BOARD

FRED KAUFMAN
Editor-in-Chief

JEROME C. SMYTH
Managing Editor

DAVID KIRSHNBLATT
Executive Editor

NICHOLAS VLAHOS
Article Editor

MURRAY B. SPIEGEL
Book Review Editor

JOHN BISHOP
Case and Comment Editor

KATHRYN H. MASON
Editorial Associate

JEAN D. ETHIER
Circulation

JOHN J. PEPPER
Advertising

JACQUES-YVAN MORIN
Advisory Editor

Volume One: Issues Three and Four

THE McGILL LAW JOURNAL

THE McGILL LAW JOURNAL

Volume Two

EDITORIAL BOARD

JOHN E. M. LAWRENCE
Editor-in-chief

JOHN CIACCIA
Managing Editor

HARVEY CRESTOHL
Articles Editor

MICHAEL AWADA
Executive Editor

GODFROY MARIN
Case and Comment

LAURENCE CAPELOVITCH
Book Reviews

S. F. MACBRAYNE
International Air Law

DIANE E. HOLMES
Circulation

JOHN GOMERY
Advertising

Faculty Adviser: ASST. PROF. J. G. CASTEL

Volume Three

EDITORIAL BOARD

HAROLD W. ASHENMIL
Editor-in-chief

IRVING I. FINKELBERG
Managing Editor

BENJAMIN J. GREENBERG
Executive Editor

ROLLIN L. GALLAY
Co-Ordinate Editor

DEREK A. HANSON
Advertising Editor

D. A. B. STEEL
Articles Editor

J. ARCLEN BLAKELY
Advertising Editor

NICOLE B. VAILLANCOURT
Circulation Editor

MORTIMER M. TEITELBAUM
Comment Editor

WILLIAM N. GAGNON
Circulation Editor

Editorial Assistants

RAYMOND T. BARAKETT, JEAN-LOUIS BAUDOUIN, B. ROBERT BENSON, YOINE J. GOLDSTEIN, J. PHILIPPE GUAY, DONALD J. JOHNSON, PIERRE LAMONTAGNE, SYDNEY B. SEDEROFF, CLAUDE ARMAND SHEPPARD, MARY R. STAVERT.

Faculty Adviser: ASSOC. PROF. J. G. CASTEL

Volume Four

Volume Five

EDITORIAL BOARD

Volume Six

Editor-in-Chief
A. Derek Guthrie

Executive Editor
A. Polger

Managing Editor
Robert J. Cowling

Advertising Editors
Brahm Gelfand
Louis Drazin

Circulation Editors
W. C. McCallum
R. James Plant

Articles Editor
George A. Rosenberg

Case and Comment and Book Review Editor
Roy L. Heenan

Junior Editors
Brahm Campbell
Michael Dennis
Mary Herzberg
Norman May
Daniel Mettarlin
Alan M. Stein
Harvey Yarosky

Editorial Assistants
B. Lacombe
Joyce Blond
Hubert Senecal

Secretary
Lise Desnoyers

Faculty Advisor
Ronald I. Cheffins

EDITORIAL BOARD

Volume Seven

Editor-in-Chief
Norman M. May

Executive Editor
Alan M. Stein

Managing Editor
Hubert Senécal

Advertising Editors
Brahm Campbell
Michael Dennis

Circulation Editor
Joyce Blond

Articles Editor
Harvey Yarosky

Case and Comment and Book Review Editor
Daniel Mettarlin

Junior Editors
David Angus
Morris Fish
Carmen Galileo
Alan Golden
Arnold Isaacson
Arnold Sharp

Editorial Assistants
Joseph Blumer
Gerald Postelnik
Guy Bouthillier

Secretaries
Deonisia Zerbisias
Denise David

Faculty Advisor
Paul-A. Crépeau

EDITORIAL BOARD

Volume Eight

Volume Nine
(original not available: copy from 2007 website archival project—French not in original)

Volume Ten (original not available: copy from 2007 website archival project—French not in original)

Editor-in-Chief
Joseph J. Oliver
Rédacteur en chef

Managing Editor
Barry H. Shapiro
Administrateur

Executive Editor
Jack R. Miller
Secrétaire général

Circulation Editors
Allen Feldman
C. Ralph Lipper
Abonnements

Advertising Editors
Irwin Cotler
Avrum Rubinger
Publicité

Articles Editor
C.J. Michael Flavell

Case and Comment and Book Review Editor
John R. Garson
Chroniques de législation et de jurisprudence

Co-ordinating Editors
Jean Bélanger
Gordon L. Echenberg

Junior Editors
Joel I. Bell
Warren A. Black
L. Michael Blumenstein
Jack B. Boidman
Bruce Cleven
David P. O'Brien
Larry S. Sazant
Eric M. Smith
Samuel Wex
Judith S. Zeisler
Brian H.D. Danny

Editorial Assistants
Bernard K. Schneider

Secretaries
Ludmila Nemec
Manon Turbide
Secrétaires

Faculty Adviser
Paul-André Crépeau
Professeur conseil

Volume Eleven (Checkmarks not in original, were added to replicated copy)

Editor-in-Chief
Larry S. Sazant

Managing Editor
✓Bruce Cleven

Executive Editor
Warren Black

Circulation Editors
Jack B. Boidman
Brian H. D. Danny

Advertising Editors
L. Michael Blumenstein ✓
Samuel Wex

Articles Editor
✓David P. O'Brien

Co-ordinating Editors
Joel I. Bell ✓
P. Michel de Grandpré ✓
Jean Elie ✓
Stanley L. Selinger ✓

Case and Comment and Book Review Editor
✓ Eric M. Smith

Junior Editors
Arthur H. Campeau
Earl S. Cohen
Charles E. Flam
William Fraiberg
Jean-Paul Hubert
Norman S. Kessner
Steven Kleiner
A.L.C. de Mestral
Gerald Nemiroff
Allan Salomon
Arthur M. Sanft
Stephen A. Scott
H. Bernard Shaffer
Sharon Sholzberg

Faculty Advisers
John E. C. Brierley
Geoffrey N. Pratt

Volume Twelve

Editor-in-Chief

Stephen Allan Scott

Managing Editor

Charles E. Flam

Executive Editor

Jean-Paul Hubert, jr.

Advertising Editors

Harold Dizgun
George F. Lengvari, Jr.
Earl S. Cohen

Circulation Editors

Steven Kleiner
Gerald Nemiroff
Howard Bernie Shaffer

Articles Editor

Arthur H. Campeau

William Fraiberg
Norman S. Kessner
James E. Khazzam
Arthur M. Sanft

Case and Comment, Note, and Book Review Editor

A.L.C. de Mestral

Junior Editors

Richard A. Beaulieu
Ronald L. Berger
Jonathan Stephen Chait
Harold Lionel Chetwynd
David Mark Doubilet
Michael Lawrence Garonce
Allan Lufty
James Marunczak
Paul Nadler
Douglas Pascal
Richard Pound
Vincent Mark Prager
Irwin Rudick
Robert S. Vineberg

Faculty Advisers

John E. C. Brierley
Ivan Vlasic

Volume Thirteen

Editor-in-Chief

Douglas Pascal

Managing Editor

Richard Pound

Executive Editor

Michael Garonce

Circulation Editors

Vincent Prager
Leslie Morris

Advertising Editor

Robert Vineberg

Articles Editor

Allan Lutfy

Special Features Editor

Ronald Berger

Unreported Judgments Editors

Jonathan Chait
David Doubilet

Contributing Editors

Richard Beaulieu
Lionel Chetwynd
Irwin Rudick

Case and Comment, Note, and Book Review Editor

Paul Nadler

Junior Editors

Howard Buckman
David Cayne
Norman Caplan
Ronald Cohen
Donald Devine
Sean Harrington
Daniel Lack
Robert Leclerc
Normand Lepine
Philippe Lette
Sheldon Price
Simon Schwartz
Moey Segal
Abraham Slawner
Arthur Steckler
Lawrence Tanny
Douglas Tees
Richard Uditsky
Michael Vineberg

Faculty Advisors

John E. C. Brierley
Ivan Vlasic

Volume Sixteen

MANAGING BOARD

André T. Mécs
Editor-in-Chief

Rubin Strauber
Executive Editor

Josef J. Fridman
Managing Editor

SENIOR BOARD

Warren Baer
Advertising Editor

Lewis N. Klar
Notes and Recent Cases

Pierre Lamarche
Unreported Judgments and Book Reviews

Zavie Levine
Articles Editor

JUNIOR BOARD

Jean-Pierre Bélisle
Charles Boivin
Barry Feinstein
Robert Gould
Julius Grey
Joel King
Gilbert Holzer
Marc Leiter
Allan A. Mass
Marvin A. Segal

FACULTY ADVISORS

Martin Bradley
John P. Humphrey
Stephen A. Scott

Volume Seventeen

MANAGING BOARD

Joel King
Editor-in-Chief

Allan A. Mass
Executive Editor

Marc Leiter
Managing Editor

SENIOR BOARD

Charles Boivin
Marvin A. Segal
Advertising Editors

Barry Feinstein
Robert Gould
Julius Grey
Gilbert Holzer
Articles Editors

JUNIOR BOARD

Jean-Pierre Bessette
Stuart Cobbett
Tam Davis
Steve Feldman
Avram Fishman
David Flicker
Michael Kaylor
Murray Perelman
William Samis

FACULTY ADVISOR

Brian Slattery

Volume Eighteen

MANAGING BOARD

MICHAEL DAVID KAYLOR
Editor-in-Chief

STUART H. COBBETT
Executive Editor

AVRAM FISHMAN
Managing Editor

SENIOR BOARD

THOMAS R.M. DAVIS
STEPHEN B. FELDMAN
DAVID W. FLICKER
MURRAY J. PERELMAN
WILLIAM SAMIS

JUNIOR BOARD

CLAUDETTE BELLEMARE
RICHARD CÔTÉ
PATRICK M. CUMMINS
J. DAVID FINE
GRAHAM NEVIN
NORMAN S. RANKIN
GARY RUBY
JON H. SCOTT

FACULTY ADVISOR

H. PATRICK GLENN

SECRETARY

LOIS C. DUBIN

Volume Nineteen

SENIOR BOARD

GRAHAM NEVIN
Editor-in-Chief

CLAUDETTE BELLEMARE
Executive Editor

NORMAN S. RANKIN
Managing Editor

GARY RUBY
Advertising Editor

JON H. SCOTT
Index Editor

J. DAVID FINE
Jurisprudence Editor

PATRICK M. CUMMINS
Circulation Editor

RICHARD CÔTÉ
Book Review Editor

JUNIOR BOARD

FRANCIS BUCKLEY
BOB DOUMANI
ADELLE FRUMAN
LARRY MOROZ
BERL NADLER
CHARLES SCHMIDT
GEORGES DJANDJI
ISSIE FISHMAN
CATHIE HALPENNY
ERIC NADLER
FRAN NORYCH
JACK ZWICKER

FACULTY ADVISOR

H. PATRICK GLENN

SECRETARY

MARIA WEHM

Volume Twenty

Volume Twenty-one

Volume Twenty-six

Volume Twenty-seven

Volume Twenty-eight

SENIOR BOARD
COMITÉ DE RÉDACTION

Editor-in-Chief
Stephen J. Toope
Rédacteur en chef

Associate Editor
Marc Barbeau
Rédacteur en chef adjoint

Executive Editor
Barbara Ursel
Secrétaire général

Managing Editor
Vonnie Eng
Administratrice

Editors - Collaborateurs

Comments
Douglas Benedon
Chroniques de législation et de jurisprudence

Solicitations
Claire Apostoli
Sollicitations

Advertising
Mark Krajicek
Publicité

Book Reviews
Martine Turcotte
Chronique bibliographique

Circulation
Leslie A. Stratford
Abonnements

Neil L. Cobb
Oleh Ilnyckyj
Jean-François Léger
Ann Scholberg
Theresa M. Siok
Alison L. Young

JUNIOR BOARD/COMITÉ DE RÉDACTION ADJOINT

Alan S. Alexandroff
Nancy E. Brown
Brian Dillon
Allan Garber
Daniel Gogek
Akira Hara
Lise Hendlisz
Donna Kaufman
Patricia Lawson
Robert Metcalfe
Dominique Monet
Kim Rodgers
William R.C. Tresham
Demetrios G. Xistris
John Yatsko

Faculty Adviser
Yves-Marie Morissette
Professeur conseil

Typist
Maria Wehm
Dactylo

Volume Twenty-nine

SENIOR BOARD
COMITÉ DE RÉDACTION

Editor-in-Chief
Daniel Gogek
Rédacteur en chef

Associate Editor
Robert Metcalfe
Rédacteur en chef adjoint

Executive Editor
John K. Rodgers
Secrétaire général

Managing Editor
Demetrios G. Xistris
Administrateur

Editors – Collaborateurs

Comments
Patricia Lawson
Chroniques de législation et de jurisprudence

Book Reviews
Lise Hendlisz
Chronique bibliographique

Advertising
William R.C. Tresham
Publicité

Circulation
Nancy E. Brown
Abonnements

Alan S. Alexandroff
Brian Dillon
Allan Garber
Donna Kaufman
Brian Mitchell
Dominique Monet
John Yatsko

JUNIOR BOARD/COMITÉ DE RÉDACTION ADJOINT

Hélène Guay
Michael R.L. Hooton
Nicholas Kasirer
Paul A. Kettunen
Maryanne Kramer
Gary Lawrence
Véronique Marleau
Grant McCrea
Mary Mullens
Peter Oliver
Brian Pel
Alain Roberge
Paule Robitaille
Yves Sicard
Jane Weary

Faculty Adviser
Yves-Marie Morissette
Professeur conseil

Typist
Elizabeth Loggie
Dactylo

Volume Thirty

SENIOR BOARD
COMITÉ DE RÉDACTION

Editor-in-Chief
PETER OLIVER
Rédacteur en chef

Associate Editor
GRANT MCCREA
Rédacteur en chef adjoint

Executive Editor
HÉLÈNE GUAY
Secrétaire générale

Managing Editor
BRIAN PEL
Administrateur

Comments
YVES SICARD
Chroniques de législation et de jurisprudence

Alumni Coordinator
MICHAEL R.L. HOOTON
Coordinateur des anciens

Book Reviews
GARY M. LAWRENCE
Chronique bibliographique

Advertising
VÉRONIQUE MARLEAU
Publicité

Circulation
PAUL A. KETTUNEN
Abonnements

Editors – Collaborateurs

ANN CRAWFORD
MARY MULLENS
NICHOLAS KASIRER
ALAIN ROBERGE
MARYANNE KRAMER
JANE WEARY

JUNIOR BOARD/COMITÉ DE RÉDACTION ADJOINT

DANIEL A. BILAK
JILL FRANK
DALE LYSAK
RAJ PANDE
ANNE SPAFFORD
SHAUN CATHCART
JANE GRAHAM
DONALD L. MUNN
HENRY K. SCHULTZ
SONIA J. STRUTHERS
GAD COHEN
MARK G. HANCHET
GARY NACHSHEN
MICHAEL SHUSTER
PAUL WICKENS

Faculty Adviser
YVES-MARIE MORISSETTE
Professeur conseil

Typist
SUSAN ALLAN
Dactylo

Volume Thirty-one

SENIOR BOARD
COMITÉ DE RÉDACTION

Editor-in-Chief
HENRY K. SCHULTZ
Rédacteur en chef

Associate Editor
JILL FRANK
Rédacteur en chef adjoint

Executive Editor
JANE GRAHAM
Secrétaire générale

Managing Editor
RAJ PANDE
Administrateur

Comments
DONALD L. MUNN
Chroniques de législation et de jurisprudence

Alumni Coordinator
DANIEL A. BILAK
Coordinateur des anciens

Book Reviews
GARY NACHSHEN
Chronique bibliographique

Advertising
DALE LYSAK
Publicité

Circulation
ANNE SPAFFORD
Abonnements

Editors – Collaborateurs

SHAUN CATHCART
MICHAEL SHUSTER
GAD COHEN
SONIA J. STRUTHERS
MARK G. HANCHET
PAUL WICKENS

JUNIOR BOARD/COMITÉ DE RÉDACTION ADJOINT

CHRISTIAN ALLARD
FRED ENNS
MARIE HUDSON
NIS MOLLER
CHANTAL ROY
MARCEL R. BANASINSKI
ROBERT J. GRENIER
MARC LEMIEUX
HOLLY NICKEL
KATHRYN SABO
ROBERTO CUCCI
JANET HENCHEY
FARREL G. MILLER
DAVID OLIVER
ROBERT SPIEGEL

Faculty Adviser
YVES-MARIE MORISSETTE
Professeur conseil

Typists
SUSAN ALLAN
NICOLE LEGER
Dactylos

Volume Thirty-two

Editor-in-Chief
MARC LEMIEUX
Rédacteur en chef

Associate Editor
ROBERTO CUCCI
Rédacteur en chef adjoint

Executive Editor
FRED ENNS
Secrétaire général

Managing Editor
HOLLY NICKEL
Directrice administrative

Advertising/Publicité
ROBERT J. GRENIER

Alumni
CHRISTIAN ALLARD

Circulation/Abonnements
FARREL G. MILLER

Comments
NIS MOLLER
Chronique de jurisprudence

Book Reviews
JANET HENCHEY
Chronique bibliographique

MARCEL R. BANASINSKI
CHANTAL ROY
MARIE HUDSON
KATHRYN SABO
DAVID W. OLIVER
ROBERT SPIEGEL

Junior Board/Comité adjoint

STEPHEN DOUGLAS
RANDALL HOFLEY
MARILYN PREUS
ROBERT SNOWDON
NATHALIE VÉZINA
VINCENT GALLO
DEREK LINFIELD
MARK ROPPEL
JOE STARNINO
MICHAEL WATERSTON
HOWARD GREENSPOON
DANIEL O'CONNOR
RON SCHLUMPF
LIESBETH VANDENBOSCH
M. KEVIN WOODALL

Faculty Adviser
G. BLAINE BAKER
Professeur conseil

Typist
NICOLE LÉGER
Dactylo

Volume Thirty-three

Editor-in-Chief
M. KEVIN WOODALL
Rédacteur en chef

Associate Editor
NATHALIE VÉZINA
Rédactrice en chef adjointe

Executive Editor
RON SCHLUMPF
Secrétaire général

Managing Editor
DEREK LINFIELD
Directeur administratif

Comments and Book Reviews
STEPHEN DOUGLAS
JOE STARNINO
Chroniques bibliographique et de jurisprudence

Citations Editor
MICHAEL WATERSTON
Rédacteur des références

Editors / Rédacteurs
VINCENT GALLO
MARILYN PREUS
RANDALL HOFLEY
MARK ROPPEL
LIESBETH VANDEN BOSCH

Advertising/Publicité
ROBERT SNOWDON

Alumni/Anciens
DANIEL O'CONNOR

Circulation/Abonnements
HOWARD GREENSPOON

Associate Board / Comité adjoint

KENNETH S. ABOUD
ROBERT D. CAMPBELL
DOUG CUNNINGHAM
KEVIN KYTE
BARBARA LEITER
LINDA ADAMS
JONATHAN COLOMBO
G. SCOT DIAMOND
DAVID LAMETTI
R. WADE LITCHFIELD
GARY F. BELL
SUSAN CORISTINE
SHAHIR GUINDI
PIERRE LAROUCHE
SUZANNE MERCURE

Faculty Adviser
STEPHEN J. TOOPE
Professeur conseil

Typist
NICOLE LÉGER
Dactylo

Volume Thirty-six

Rédactrice en chef
Julia E. Hanigsberg
Editor-in-chief

Rédacteur en chef adjoint
Neil M. Berlad
Associate Editor

Secrétaire générale
Evelyn Jerassy
Executive Editor

Directrice administrative
Marla J. Weinstein
Managing Editor

Chronique de jurisprudence
Michelle Marsellus
Comments

Chronique bibliographique
Daniel Urbas
Book Reviews

Rédactrice des références
Elizabeth Massey
Citations Editor

Sollicitations
Joanna Rainbow
Solicitation

Rédacteurs/Editors
Marc Darmo Andrea P. Morrison Geneviève Saumier Michael Wilhelmson

Publicité/Advertising
Grant Vipond

Anciens/Alumni
T. Viresh Fernando

Abonnements/Circulation
Nathan Schipper

Comité adjoint/Associate Board
Helen Antoniou
Karen Capen
Kirsten Hillman
Scott Levitan
Jean-Paul Poitras
Adelle Blackett
David Chemla
Hanson R. Hosein
Kelly Mulcair
Renée Thériault
Eric Buzzetti
Michelle Cumyn
Mahmud Jamal
Kim Neufeld
Lisa Yarmoshuk

Professeur conseil
Patrick Healy
Faculty Advisor

Dactylo
Nicole Léger
Typist

Volume Thirty-seven

Rédacteur en chef
David A. Chemla
Editor-in-chief

Rédactrice en chef adjointe
(textes français)
Michelle Cumyn
Associate Editor
(French submissions)

Secrétaire général
(textes anglais)
Jean-Paul Poitras
Executive Editor
(English submissions)

Directeur administratif
Hanson R. Hosein
Managing Editor

Chroniques de jurisprudence
Mahmud Jamal
Comments

Chroniques bibliographiques
Renée Thériault
Book Reviews

Références
Lisa Yarmoshuk
Citations

Sollicitations
Adelle Blackett
Solicitation

Rédacteurs/Editors
Helen Antoniou Eric Buzzetti Karen Capen Kirsten Hillman Kelly Mulcair

Publicité/Advertising
Kim Neufeld

Anciens/Alumni
Scott Levitan

Comité adjoint/Associate Board
Heather Andersen
Sivan Fox
Ron Labossière
Mark Phillips
Matt Taylor
Randal Barker
Michel Généreux
Chris Naudie
Lise Rochette
Nan Wang
Julie Beauchemin
Chris Kent
Alain Olivier
Egya Sangmuah
Moray Welch

Ordinateurs
Daniel Shap
Computers

Professeur conseil
Patrick Healy
Faculty Adviser

Dactylo
Nicole Léger
Typist

Volume Thirty-eight

Rédacteur en chef
MARK PHILLIPS
Editor-in-chief

Rédactrice en chef adjointe (textes français)
JULIE BEAUCHEMIN
Associate Editor (French submissions)

Secrétaire général (textes anglais)
CHRISTOPHER P. NAUDIE
Executive Editor (English submissions)

Directeur administratif
RANDAL J.C. BARKER
Managing Editor

Chroniques de jurisprudence
HEATHER ANDERSEN
Comments

Chroniques bibliographiques
LISE ROCHETTE
Book Reviews

Références
NAN WANG
Citations

Rédacteurs de la note
SIVAN FOX, MATT TAYLOR
Note editors

Rédacteurs/Editors
MICHEL GÉNÉREUX
ALAIN OLIVIER
MORAY WELCH

Publicité/Advertising
CHRIS KENT

Anciens/Alumni
RON LABOSSIÈRE

Comité adjoint/Associate Board
RICHARD AFTANAS
MICHEL ARÈS
MARK CHAPMAN
LOUIS CHARETTE
LARISSA EASSON
CAROLINE FERLAND
CLAIR FITZGERALD
SARAH GAGAN
FRANCIS HARVEY
PATRICIA MAUFFETTE
GREG MOORE
CHANTAL PLAMONDON
ERICA STONE
CAROLINE THOMASSIN
ED VANDENBERG
LANDON YOUNG

Conseiller financier
DEREK GALBRAITH
Financial Adviser

Réseau informatique
DANIEL SHAP
Network supervisor

Communications interréseaux
ANDREW BLEAU
Inter-Network Communications

Professeur conseil
PATRICK HEALY
Faculty Adviser

Dactylo
NICOLE LÉGER
Typist

Président d'honneur Campagne de financement
BRAHM GELFAND
Honourary President Fundraising Campaign

Volume Thirty-nine

Rédactrice en chef
ERICA STONE
Editor-in-chief

Rédactrice en chef adjointe (textes français)
CHANTAL PLAMONDON
Associate Editor (French submissions)

Secrétaire général (textes anglais)
ED VANDENBERG
Executive Editor (English submissions)

Directrice administrative
CAROLINE THOMASSIN
Managing Editor

Chroniques de jurisprudence
CLAIR FITZGERALD
Case Comments

Chroniques bibliographiques
CAROLINE FERLAND
Book Reviews

Références
MARK CHAPMAN
Citations

Sollicitations
LOUIS CHARETTE
Solicitations

Rédactrices de la note
LARISSA EASSON, SARAH GAGAN
Note Editors

Rédacteurs/Editors
MICHEL ARÈS
PATRICIA MAUFFETTE
GREG MOORE
LANDON YOUNG

Marketing
RICHARD AFTANAS

Anciens/Alumni
FRANCIS HARVEY

Comité adjoint/Associate Board
MARTIN-PIERRE BOULIANNE
SYLVIE DROUIN
PAUL GOLDING
JAY HOWARD
ALEXANDRA KAU
HEIDI KESSNER
JODI LACKMAN
MI NGUYÊN
MICHAEL PADFIELD
FRED PURKEY
KIM SCHENCK
CHRISTOPH SICKING
LÉNA TAYLOR
FRÉDÉRICK TÊTU
SUSAN WELLS

Conseiller financier
DEREK GALBRAITH
Financial Adviser

Réseau informatique
JONATHAN CUTLER
DONNA BLOIS
ANDREW BLEAU
Computer Network

Professeur conseil
PATRICK HEALY
Faculty Adviser

Dactylo
NICOLE LEGER
Typist

Volume Forty

Rédactrice en chef
JODI LACKMAN
Editor-in-chief

Rédacteur en chef adjoint (textes français)
MARTIN-PIERRE BOULIANNE
Associate Editor (French submissions)

Directeur administratif
FRED PURKEY
Managing Editor

Secrétaire générale (textes anglais)
SUSAN WELLS
Executive Editor (English submissions)

Chroniques de jurisprudence
LÉNA TAYLOR
Case Comments

Chroniques bibliographiques
KIM SCHENCK
Book Reviews

Références
JAY HOWARD
Citations

Sollicitations
MICHAEL PADFIELD
Solicitations

Rédacteur de la note
CHRISTOPH SICKING
Note Editor

Administration / Management
HEIDI KESSNER
ALEXANDRA KAU

Rédacteurs / Editors
SYLVIE DROUIN
PAUL GOLDING
MI NGUYÊN

Comité adjoint / Associate Board
MICHAEL F.E. AKKAWI
FRÉDÉRIQUE AMROUNI
CELINE BASTIN
CAROLINE BOUTIN
NICOLAS CLOUTIER
DAVID COHEN
MARY-PAT CORMIER
PHILIPP DUFFY
MARIE-CHRISTINE HIVON
ELIZABETH LAI-FOOK
CHARLES MORGAN
MARIE-PIERRE OLIVIER
HIROKO SAWAI
CRAIG SHEPHERD
DANIEL STEINER
HILARY WILLIAMS

Conseiller financier
DEREK GALBRAITH
Financial Adviser

Professeur conseil
PATRICK HEALY
Faculty Adviser

Éditique
NICOLE LEGER
Desktop Publishing

Volume Forty-one

Rédactrice en chef
MARY-PAT CORMIER
Editor-in-chief

Rédactrice en chef adjointe
MARIE-CHRISTINE HIVON
Associate Editor-in-chief

Directeur administratif
MICHAEL F. E. AKKAWI
Managing Editor

Rédactrice en chef adjointe
FRÉDÉRIQUE AMROUNI
Associate Editor-in-chief

Chroniques de jurisprudence
HILARY WILLIAMS
Case Comments

Chroniques bibliographiques
DANIEL STEINER
Book Reviews

Sollicitations
M. CRAIG SHEPHERD
Solicitations

Rédacteur de la note
CHARLES MORGAN
Note Editor

Administration
PHILIPP DUFFY
Management

Rédacteurs / Editors
CÉLINE BASTIN
CAROLINE BOUTIN
DAVID COHEN
ELIZABETH LAI-FOOK
MARIE-PIERRE OLIVIER
HIROKO SAWAI

Comité adjoint / Associate Board
STEPHEN BECKER
CARL CHASTENAY
KAREN CHEONG
MARC ROBERT COTIE
NANCY HOI
LISA HORVATH
MARGOT KANE
EMILY McCARTHY
DON McGOWAN
RIVA RICHARD
LAURIE SARGENT
SHIRLEY SENOFF
NADINE L.C. THWAITES
MARTIN J. VALASEK
MEREDITH D. YOUNGER

Conseiller financier
DEREK GALBRAITH
Financial Adviser

Professeur conseil
PATRICK HEALY
Faculty Adviser

Éditique
FRED PURKEY
Desktop Publishing

Assistante à la production
NICOLE LEGER
Production Assistant

Appendix C

Complete list of the *McGill Law Journal* Boards of Trustees:
(excluding Faculty Advisors, Editors-in-Chief, and Managing Editors)

Volume 48: (2003)

Justice Charles D. Gonthier
Justice Michel Proulx
Justice A. Derek Guthrie
Brian C. Pel
Dean Peter Leuprecht
Professor John Swan

Volume 47: (2002)

Justice Charles D. Gonthier
Justice Michel Proulx
Justice A. Derek Guthrie
Brian C. Pel
Dean Peter Leuprecht
Professor John Swan

Volume 46: (2001)

Justice Charles D. Gonthier
Justice A. Derek Guthrie
Justice Michel Proulx
Brian C. Pel
Dean Peter Leuprecht
Professor John Swan

Volume 45: (2000)

Justice Charles D. Gonthier
Justice Michel Proulx
Mr. Brian C. Pel
Ms. Sonia Struthers
Dean Peter Leuprecht
Professor John Swan

Volume 44: (1999)

Justice Charles D. Gonthier
Justice Michel Proulx
Mr. Brian C. Pel
Ms. Sonia Struthers
Dean Peter Leuprecht
Professor John Swan

Volume 43: (1998)

Justice Charles D. Gonthier
Justice Michel Proulx
Mr. Brian C. Pel
Ms. Sonia Struthers
Dean Stephen Toope
Professor John E.C. Brierley

Volume 42: (1997)

Justice Charles D. Gonthier
Justice Michel Proulx
Mr. Brian C. Pel
Ms. Sonia Struthers
Dean Stephen Toope
Professor John E.C. Brierley

Volume 41: (1996)

Justice Charles D. Gonthier
Justice Michel Proulx
Mr. Brian C. Pel
Me. Louise Pelly
Dean Stephen Toope
Professor John E.C. Brierley

Volume 40: (1995)

Justice Charles D. Gonthier
Justice Michel Proulx
Mr. Brian C. Pel
Me. Louise Pelly
Dean Stephen Toope
Professor John E.C. Brierley

Volume 39: (1994)

Justice Charles D. Gonthier
Justice Michel Proulx
The Honorable Fred Kaufmann
Me. Louise Pelly
Professor John E.C. Brierley
Dean Stephen Toope

Volume 38: (1993)

Justice Charles D. Gonthier
Justice Michel Proulx
The Honorable Fred Kaufmann
Me. Louise Pelly
Professor John E.C. Brierley
Dean Y.-M. Morissette

Volume 37: (1992)

Mr. Justice Fred Kaufman
Me Louise Pelly
Professor John E.C. Brierley
Mr. Justice Michel Proulx
Justice Charles D. Gonthier
Dean Yves-Marie Morissette

Volume 36: (1991)

Madame Justice Claire L'Heureux-Dubé
Mr. Justice Fred Kaufman
Me Louise Pelly
Dean Yves-Marie Morissette
Professor John E.C. Brierley
[The process of replacing Yves Fortier with Michel Proulx was underway]

Volume 35: (1990)

Madame Justice Claire L'Heureux-Dubé
Mr. Justice Fred Kaufman
Me. L. Yves Fortier
Me Louise Pelly
Dean Yves-Marie Morissette
Professor John E.C. Brierley

Volume 34: (1989)

Madame Justice Claire L'Heureux-Dubé
Mr. Justice Fred Kaufman
Me. L. Yves Fortier
Me Louise Pelly
Dean Roderick A. Macdonald
Professor John E.C. Brierley

Volume 33: (1988)

Madame Justice Claire L'Heureux-Dubé
Mr. Justice Fred Kaufman
Me. L. Yves Fortier
Me Louise Pelly
Dean Roderick A. Macdonald
Professor John E.C. Brierley

Volume 32: (1987)

Madame Justice Claire L'Heureux-Dubé
Mr. Justice Fred Kaufman
Me. L. Yves Fortier
Me Louise Pelly
Dean Roderick A. Macdonald
Professor John E.C. Brierley

Volume 31: (1986)

Professor J.E.C. Brierley
Mr. Justice Fred Kaufman
Madame Justice Claire L'Heureux-Dubé
Dean R.A. Macdonald
Yves Fortier
Me Louise Pelly

Volume 30: (1985)

Professor John Brierley
Me Yves Fortier
Hon. Claire L'Heureux-Dubé
Hon. Fred Kaufman
Dean Roderick MacDonald
Me Louise Pelly

Appendix D

List of former McGill Law Journal members who received clerkships with the Supreme Court of Canada

<u>1970-71</u>
Volume fifteen Editor-in-Chief Léonard Serafini
(Douglas Charles Abbott)

<u>1979-80</u>
Volume twenty-five junior editor Philip Girard
(Willard Zebedee Estey)

<u>1981-82</u>
Volume twenty-three Editor-in-Chief Cally Jordan
(Robert George Brian Dickson)

<u>1986-87</u>
Volume twenty-eight Editor-in-Chief Stephen J. Toope
(Robert George Brian Dickson)

<u>1987-88</u>
Volume thirty Associate Editor Grant McCrea
(Gérald La Forest)
Volume thirty senior editor Nicholas Kasirer
(Jean Beetz)

<u>1988-89</u>
Volume thirty-two Editor-in-Chief Marc Lemieux
(Claire L'Heureux-Dubé)

<u>1989-90</u>
Volume thirty-two Editor-in-Chief Marc Lemieux[1303*]
(Claire L'Heureux-Dubé)
Volume thirty-four Executive Editor David Lametti
(Peter Cory)

<u>1990-91</u>
Volume thirty-four Editor-in-Chief Gary F. Bell
(William Stevenson)
Volume thirty-three Citations Editor Michael Waterson
(Antonio Lamer)

<u>1991-92</u>
Volume thirty-three senior editor Randall Hofley

1303 * Only until December 1989, in order to bridge the gap between himelf and the clerk who would replace him, who arrived in January of 1990. See email from Marc Lemieux to James Cummins, November 25, 2011. From the first clerks through the 2006-07 clerkship session, only eighteen other clerks had their terms extended beyond the initial year long term. See http://www.thecourt.ca/clerks-of-the-supreme-court/.

(Beverley M. McLauchlin)
Volume thirty-four senior editor Pierre Larouche
(Charles D. Gonthier)
Volume thirty-five Associate Editor Sally Gomery
(Frank Iacobucci and Claire L'Heureux-Dubé)
Volume thirty-five Book Review Editor David Platts
(Peter Cory)

<u>1992-93</u>
Volume thirty-six Editor-in-Chief Julia E. Hanigsberg
(Peter Cory)
Volume thirty-six Executive Editor Evelyn Jerassy
(John C. Major)

<u>1993-94</u>
Volume thirty-seven Executive Editor Jean-Paul Poitras
(Charles D. Gonthier)
Volume thirty-seven Comments Editor Mahmud Jamal
(Charles D. Gonthier)

<u>1994-95</u>
Volume thirty-seven Book Review Editor Renée Thériault
(Claire L'Heureux-Dubé)
Volume thirty-eight Associate Editor Julie Beauchemin
(Peter Cory)

<u>1995-95</u>
Volume thirty-six senior editor Geneviève Saumier
(John Sopinka)

<u>1996-97</u>
Volume thirty-nine Citations Editor Mark Chapman
(John C. Major)

<u>1998-99</u>
Volume forty-two Editor-in-Chief Martin J. Valasek
(Charles D. Gonthier)

<u>1999-2000</u>
Volume forty-two Book Reviews Editor Laurie Sargent
(Claire L'Heureux-Dubé)

<u>2001-02</u>
Volume forty-five Editor-in-Chief Azim Hussain
(Charles D. Gonthier)

<u>2002-03</u>
Volume forty-six Editor-in-Chief Robert Leckey
(Michel Bastarache)
Volume forty-six Executive Editor Pierre-Hughes Verdier
(Charles D. Gonthier)

2003-04
Volume forty-seven Book Review Editor Grégoire Webber
(Ian Binnie)
Volume forty-eight senior editor Manachem M. Luftglass
(Frank Iacobucci)

2006-07
Volume forty-nine Managing Editor Reuben Kobulnik
(Morris J. Fish)
Volume fifty senior editor Derek McKee
(Beverley M. McLauchlin)

2008-09
Volume fifty-two Editor-in-Chief David Sandomiersky
(Beverley M. McLauchlin)
Volume fifty-two senior editor Ivo Entchev
(Marshall Rothstein)
Volume fifty-two senior editor Katie Gibson
(Louise Charron)
Volume fifty-three senior editor Sean Kelly
(Louis LeBel)

2010-11
Volume fifty-four Editor-in-Chief Erin Morgan
(Ian Binnie)
Volume fifty-four senior editor Palma Paciocco
(Louise Charron)

2011-12
Volume fifty-five Editor-in-Chief Seo Yun Yang
(Louise Charron)

2012-13
Volume fifty-five senior editor Mary Race
(Louis LeBel)
Volume fifty-six senior editor Michael Bookman
(Louise Charron)
Volume fifty-six senior editor Anja Kortenaar
(Ian Binnie)
Volume fifty-seven senior editor Adela Gotz
(Thomas Cromwell)

2013-14
Volume fifty-seven Executive Editor Katie Webber
(Morris J. Fish)
Volume fifty-seven Citations Editor Ilana Ludwin
(Marshall Rothstein)

Appendix E

The McGill Law Journal's Original Constitution (1952)

McGILL LAW JOURNAL

EDITORIAL BOARD

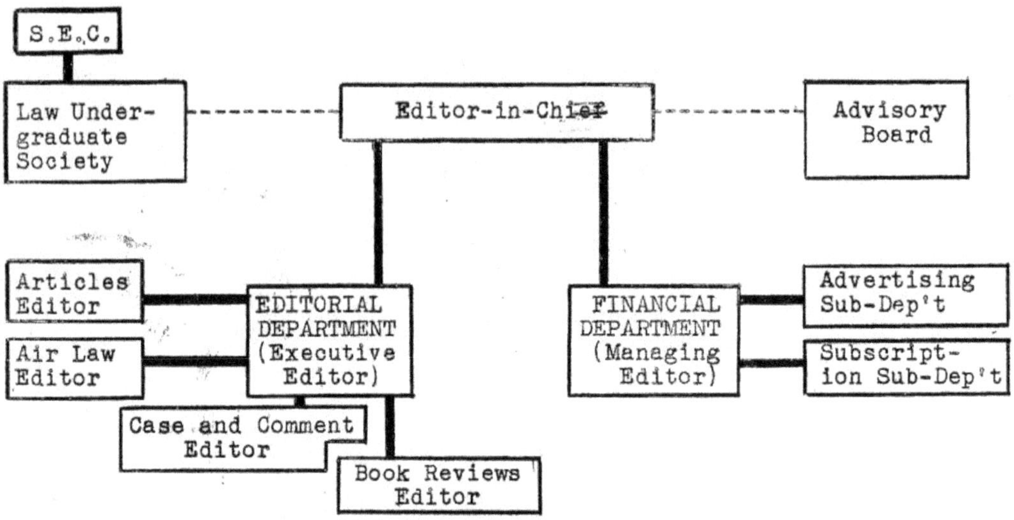

CONSTITUTION

OF THE McGILL LAW JOURNAL

Article 1. There shall be a publication to be known as " The McGill Law Journal ".

Article 2. Purpose.
The purpose of this publication is to give as wide a distribution as possible to the Articles, Comments and opinions therein contained.

Article 3. Contents.
This publication shall contain material relevant to legal studies and research and more particularly shall treat of the law of the Province of Quebec and International Air Law.

Article 4. Editorial Board.
There shall be a body known as the Editorial Board, the officers of which shall be appointed according to the provisions below.

Article 5. Quorum.
The quorum of the Editorial Board of the McGill ~~Law Journal shall be two thirds of its member-~~ ship.

Article 6. Status of the Editorial Board.
The Editorial Board shall be a standing committee of the Students' Society, as provided for in Article VIII (3) of the Constitution of the Students' Society of McGill University.

Article 7. Advisory Board.
There shall be an Advisory Board composed of members of the Faculty of Law.

Article 8. Chairmanship.
The Chairman of the Editorial Board shall be the Editor-in-Chief of the Journal.

Article 9. Duties and Responsibilities of the Editor-in-Chief.
The duties and responsibilities of the Editor-in-Chief shall be as follows :-

(1) To coordinate the various Departments of the Journal;

(2) To make all major policy decisions in conjunction with the various Editors and Departments;

(3) To act as liaison with the Advisory Board, the Faculty, the Bar, the Law Undergraduate Society and with the public in general;

(4) To call and chair meetings of the Editorial Board;

(5) To be an ex-officio member of the various Departments of the Editorial Board;

(6) To read all galleys and page proofs and to evaluate the articles, comments and book reviews submitted for publication and to edit the Journal according to such decisions;

(7) To plan coming issues in conjunction with the various Editors and Departments; and

(8) To have the authority to make final decisions on all matters, subject to the counseling of the Advisory Board.

Article 10. Powers of the Editorial Board.
The Editorial Board shall have the power to appoint by resolution such Committees and Officers to perform specific tasks as it deems advisable.

Article 11. Departments.
The Editorial Board shall comprise two Departments, namely (1) the Editorial Department and (2) the Financial Departments to perform the functions associated with such bodies.

Article 12. Structure of the Editorial Board.

The Editorial Board shall be composed of students and shall comprise :

(1) An Editor-in-Chief, to be appointed by a majority vote of the Editorial Board, with the subsequent approval of the Executive of the Law Undergraduate Society and of the Advisory Board;

(2) An Executive Editor, to be Chairman of the Editorial Department and to be appointed by the Editor-in-Chief after prior consultation with the Advisory Board;

(3) A Managing Editor, to be Chairman of the Financial Department and coordinate the various Sub-Departments thereof and to be appointed by the Editor-in-Chief after prior consultation with the Editorial Board;

(4) Editors to be in charge of the various Sub-Departments and to be appointed* by the Editor-in-Chief, the Executive Editor and the Managing Editor;

*jointly

(5) Other members to be appointed jointly by the Editor-in-Chief, the Executive Editor, the Managing Editor and the various Editors mentioned in the above paragraph.

Article 13. Criteria of Appointment to the Board.

The capacity for critical thought, hard work, clear writing and academic standing shall be the criteria by which candidates to the Editorial Board shall be selected and appointed.

The Editorial Board shall have the power to establish whatever competition it deems necessary for appointment.

Article 14. Amendments.

Subject to the following paragraph, this Constitution may be amendmed by a two-thirds vote of the Editorial Board.

All such amendments are subject to ratification by the Students'Executive Council. Such ratification shall make the amendment effective from the day it was passed by the Editorial Board.

Prepared by the Editor-in-Chief
Approved by special Committee,
November 24, 1952.
Approved by ....
....
Approved by ....
....

EDITOR'S MEMORANDUM

Re : Correspondence with the Yale Law Journal and the Harvard Law Review.

The Editor-in-Chief,
The Harvard Law Review,
Gannett House,
Cambridge 38, Mass.

(COPY)

Dear Sir :-

At the request of the Advisory Board of the McGill Law Journal, I am writing to you in order to find out certain details about the selection and appointment of students to the Editorial Board of your Law Journal.

You have had several years of experience in this field and we would like, basing ourselves on your answers to the questions below, to formulate a clear policy on those problems. The following are the specific questions that have come to our mind :

1. From what year are the Editors and members of your Editorial Board appointed ?
2. How long do they serve on the Board ?
3. What are the criteria of appointment ?
4. Are they selected by the Faculty, by the Board, by the students themselves or by some other means ?
5. How are the various responsibilities assigned between the members of the Board ?
6. What are the exact task and responsibilities of the Editor-in-Chief ?

Your answers and any other information you might care to furnish will greatly help us in our undertaking to publish the McGill Law Journal. They will contribute to the betterment of our standards and that of legal writing in general.

Thanking you in advance, I remain, dear Sir,

Yours very truly,

Jacques-Yvan Morin,
Editor.

A similar letter was sent to the Yale Law Journal, the Kentucky Law Journal, the Georgetown Law Journal, the Tulane Law Review and Professor T.A. Smedley ~~(Washington and Lee University School~~ of Law).

ANSWERS

As of November 25, 1952, only The Yale Law Journal and the Harvard Law Review have answered our letter. However, it is submitted that both series of answers give an accurate picture of what the Editor wanted to find out about the selection and appointment of students to the Editorial Board and other questions stated in the letter above.

----

1. From what year are the Editors and members of your Editorial Board appointed ?

YALE : Students are elected to the Board and Officerships at the end of their second year in Law School. This follows a year of competing for membership on the Board. At the end of the Fall semester, the top thirty or so students of the First Year class are invited to compete. Fifteen or twenty more are invited at the end of the Spring semester. Each group has one academic year in which to earn 2½ credits -- the requirement for election to the Board. A completed Note equals one credit; a completed Comment two credits. Officers are chosen from those who have already been selected to the Board or, in the case of the second group of competitors, from those who are reasonably assured of meeting their competition deadline. It is important to point out that the student is not competing against his fellow classmates. He is competing only against the Journal standard of acceptable material. Each competitor, if his work meets this standard, will be elected. There is competition among the group only in the sense that the best people will get the Officerships.

HARVARD : Each year we invite to join the Editorial Board approximately 25 men who have just completed their first year of law school and 10 men who have completed their second year.

----

2. How long do they serve on the Board ?

YALE : Except for a few short weeks at the end of their second year, Officers and Board Members serve during their Third Year in Law School.

HARVARD : The men serve on the Board from their appointment until their graduation from law school, except in the event that a man appointed at the end of his first year does not maintain a B average during his second year, in which case he is asked to resign.

----

3. What are the criteria of appointment ?

YALE : The capacity for critical thought, hard work and clear writing are the criteria by which all people are judged - particularly for Officerships. Moreover, only these qualities in the performance of Journal work are considered. Outside experience, grades, popularity etc. are totally irrelevant.

HARVARD : Appointment is based entirely on academic standing. In selecting men who have finished their second year of work the grades of the first and second years are given equal weight.

----

4. Are they selected by the Faculty, by the Board, by the students themselves or by some other means ?

YALE : The Journal is student controlled. The Faculty will never interfere in our acceptance or rejection of articles, the views expressed in the Journal, or the selection of Board members or Officers. There is a strong tradition in the Law School against any meddling with the Journal. This is best illustrated by the action of last year's Officers in rejecting two articles written by members of the Journal's Board of Directors (composed of five faculty members). There were neither protests nor ill feelings. The action was among the unquestioned prerogatives of the Officers.

HARVARD : The new members are selected by the Editor-in-Chief, but since as a matter of practice the selection is based entirely on academic rank, there is no discretion involved except in determining how many men from each class will be selected. As a matter of custom these numbers do not fluctuate very much from year to year, however, so there is little room for arbitrary action.

----

5. How are the various responsibilities assigned between the members of your Board ?

YALE : Most of the work is done by competitors and Officers. Competitors write the student section and the Officers edit their work. Each Officer has a different set of duties. The Case Editor is in charge of finding suitable topics for student treatment. There are five Note and Comment Editors who do initial edit work. When a student piece is turned in, they discuss it at length with the competitor, and then with the Executive Editor decide whether or not they accept it. If accepted, the Note and Comment Editor will continue to work on it until the text is satisfactory and footnotes are done. The piece then goes to a final Editor (Editor-in-Chief or Executive Editor). The Article Editor is in charge of soliciting, evaluating and editing contributions from non-students for our Article section. He also solicits and edits book reviews; he does not edit student work. The Executive Editor , aside from his evaluation and final editing duties, is in charge of the student competition. He will activate the lazy and advise the incompetent to resign. The Execubive Editor, Article Editor and Editor-in-Chief make most of the major policy decicions. The Managing Editors have the tedious task of checking all copy to ensure its conformance with Journal form, collating all corrections on galleys and page proofs (each is checked by competitors as well as by the writer and the editor who worked on it), and supervising the assignment of competitors to source checks of all student material, as well as assignment of the same belabored competitors to read galley and page proofs. In short, the Managing Editors are the Journal's liaison with the printer. Non-Officer Board Members are supposed to assist the Case Editor in topic selection; advise competitors when they are working on first drafts, write one publishable piece in their Third Year. The last function has not been performed in many years, and the first two are often done ineptly. While some give willingly of their time and ability, enthusiasm is generally not too high among Board members.

HARVARD : At the end of each year elections are held to select officers for the succeeding year. All members of the Board who are at that time finishing their second year of law school work are candidates. After comprehensive discussion of the preceding year's work of each candidate, the third year men on the Board by a preferential ballot eliminate a part of them. Those eliminated then join the third year men in discussing the qualifications of the remaining candidates. Several more eliminations result in the selection of the President (Editor-in-Chief). The President then appoints nine other officers from among those who were last eliminated in the election. These officers head up the various departments of the Review for the next year. The two Note Editors manage the preparation of the student Notes; the two Case Editors handle the preparation of our Recent Case section, etc. The Treasurer handles business activities, press relations, and supervises the allocation of the working time of the members of the Board among the various departments.

----

6. What are the exact task and responsibilities of the Editor-in-Chief ?

YALE : The listing is as follows : final edit student work; evaluate articles in conjunction with Article Editor; plan student sections of coming issues in conjunction with Executive Editor; read all galleys and page proofs; make all major policy decisions in conjunction with Executive Editor and Article Editor; conduct meetings of Officers, competitors, etc.; act as liaison with Faculty Committee and non-law school persons.

HARVARD : The President coordinates the various departments of the Review and approves all material before it is sent to press. He serves as a sounding board for the finished product and often detects inadequacies in reasoning, style, or form which did not appear to those who were more deeply involved in the preparation of the work. He also joins with the Article Editor in dealing with authors and prospective authors of articles and in determining which articles will be published. On all matters he has authority to make the final decision.

(signed) YALE : Ernest Rubenstein,
Editor-in-Chief.

HARVARD : Raymond L. Falls Jr.,
President.

Courtesy of McGill Archives, see McGill Archives file 574, RG37 c.17 *McGill Law Journal.* As an aside, Raymond L. Falls went on to become a Partner and Senior Counsel with Cahill, Gordon & Reindel in New York City; and Ernest Rubenstein went on to become a partner with Paul Weiss in New York City, and then Managing Director of the Board of Carl Marks & Co. L.P. (a financial services firm). Neither achieved the national prestige in their lives that Fred Kaufman or Jacques-Yvan Morin, the man who sent them the letters, did.

www.ingramcontent.com/pod-product-compliance
Lightning Source LLC
LaVergne TN
LVHW081948200926
848484LV00009B/2529